A History of Women in America

by
Carol Hymowitz
and
Michaele Weissman

in cooperation with the
Anti-Defamation League of
B'nai B'rith

BANTAM BOOKS
TORONTO • NEW YORK • LONDON • SYDNEY • AUCKLAND

A HISTORY OF WOMEN IN AMERICA
A Bantam Book / December 1978
2nd printing . . . . . February 1980
3rd printing . . . . November 1981

ISBN 0-553-20762-8

Published simultaneously in the United States and Canada

Bantam Books are published by Bantam Books, Inc. Its trademark, consisting of the words "Bantam Books" and the portrayal of a rooster, is Registered in U.S. Patent and Trademark
Office and in other countries. Marca Registrada. Bantam
Books, Inc., 666 Fifth Avenue, New York, New York 10103.

PRINTED IN THE UNITED STATES OF AMERICA

11 10 9 8 7 6 5

To Allen Levi,
who understood women and words,
and shared with love in
the making of this book

And to Hannah Jackins Berson
who has lived through it all
and is undefeated.

Acknowledgments

This book would not have been possible without the help of many people who offered advice and caring along the way. We are especially grateful to Cecilia Hunt, our editor at Bantam Books, whose skill and commitment sustained us and this project; to Martin Baron who believed in this book before we did and offered essential editing help early on; to Alice Kessler Harris who generously shared her knowledge of women's history, providing trenchant criticism; to Stan Wexler, Director of Publications, and Oscar Cohen, Program Director, of the Anti-Defamation League who gave us the chance and patiently awaited the results.

The vast and diversified materials at the New York Public Library were essential to our work. The Library also provided us with a home—the Frederick Lewis Allen Room—in which we could keep our books and papers, share the agonies and triumphs of other writers, and complete this book. We are also grateful to Radcliffe College for making the extensive resources of its Schlesinger Collection so readily available.

Gloria Jacobs provided invaluable research assistance and analysis of the contemporary women's movement. Kay Day shared her deep understanding of black women under slavery. Copyeditor Ruth Hein's lucid style and deep historical knowledge helped make this manuscript readable. Ann Novotny and Rosemary Eakins dug deep in the archives for pictures to highlight the way women have lived.

Family and more friends than we have space to name listened to our rantings and ravings, helped us laugh at ourselves, left us alone when we were working and believed we really would finish.

Our special thanks to Laura, who understood the process, to Fannie and Dmitris, who helped us find our way. . . .

And to Leonard Shecter who asked the question, "So what are you going to do with your life, kid?"

Contents

Introduction

When we began writing this book some years ago, little material concerning the history of women in America was available. Now many excellent books, particularly narrowly focused scholarly works, exist. Nevertheless, many women and men are still unaware of the rich and diverse history of American women. We hope this book will serve as an introduction and broaden our readers understanding of women, their role in the American past, and American history in general.

We are convinced of the importance of women's history. For women to have a clear idea of where they are going, they must know where they have been. We believe, for example, that if the twentieth-century women's movement is to flourish, women need to understand the successes and the failures of the nineteenth-century women's movement.

In presenting a general history of women in the United States, we tried to strike a balance between describing the lives of average women and the lives of extraordinary women. We hope that the individual women and the social movements (abolition, suffrage, labor and so on) which we emphasize will highlight for our readers the issues, conflicts, and historical times of the mass of women.

Space and time and our lack of specialized knowledge prevented us from covering all that we would have liked. Perhaps the most glaring omission is native American women. The diversity of native American cultures makes meaningful generalizations on the part of nonspecialists virtually worthless. In our discussion of black women, a particularly noticeable omission is the period from 1880 to 1920 when black women individually and as a group struggled against nearly insuperable odds to maintain and lead their communities and to sustain their families.

Noticeable too is the omission of women in the arts,

and to a lesser extent professional women. Often the conditions out of which these women emerged and the obstacles they had to overcome were similar to those of women in the various reform movements, including the nineteenth-century women's rights movement. We hope that our discussion of the lives of the pioneer feminists will provide some insight into the lives of these other pioneering women.

In writing this book we struggled between two poles. On one hand, women's experience can be seen as a document of oppression. There is no doubt that women have been and continue to be oppressed—that they have been systematically excluded from institutional and economic life and this exclusion is still going on. On the other hand, women as human beings are far greater than the sum total of their oppression. The historical limitations placed on women have more often than not been the starting point rather than the final statement about women's lives. Women living under all manner of conditions and in all times have created meaning, purpose, beauty and dignity in their lives despite the limitations placed upon them by the larger society.

To get close to the reality of how women have lived these two polar views must be merged. This is what we have attempted to do. If we have succeeded it is because women have succeeded. If we have failed, the failure is ours and not that of our subject.

Carol Hymowitz
Michaele Weissman
New York, December 1977

Early America and the
Revolutionary War

1

Founding Mothers

The fate of the European women who came to the New World in the early days of colonial settlement was a life of nearly ceaseless hard work. Many who came were already accustomed to physical labor. Those who were not quickly adapted. In a totally undeveloped and sparsely populated land, the labor of every able-bodied settler was desperately needed, and women's traditional work—providing food, clothing, shelter, and the rudiments of hygiene—was essential to survival.

The demands of the New World allowed colonial women more freedom "to do" than was often available to women of later generations. This latitude was the product not of ideology, but of necessity. Colonial society did not support the idea of equality between men and women. European men brought with them to America the tenet that woman was man's inferior. This belief in female inferiority, however, was minimized by the conditions of the New World. So long as the colonies remained relatively undeveloped, women enjoyed a limited kind of independence.

Women were an integral part of all permanent settlements in the New World. When men traveled alone to America, they came as fortune hunters, adventurers looking for a pot of gold; such single men had no compelling reason to establish communities. Women acted as civilizers for men living alone in the wilderness. Where there were women, there were children who had to be taught. There was a future—a reason to establish laws, towns, churches, schools. The organizers of Virginia understood as much when they sought to attract women to their colony so that the men who came "might be faster tied to Virginia."[1] The labor provided by a wife and children also helped transform the forest into farmland. In the early days of the Georgia settlement the proprietors advertised for male recruits with "industrious wives."

In many cases women emigrated together with men.

Such was the case throughout New England and the middle colonies, where whole families often came in search of religious freedom. Elsewhere, particularly in the South, women had to be lured to America. Some colonies offered women the right to own their own land. Lord Baltimore of Maryland offered 100 acres for a planter, 100 acres for a wife, and 50 for a child. Women heads of families were treated in the same way as men.

Other less conventional methods were used to encourage female emigration. The British crown, which chartered the majority of settlements, allowed women convicts the option of emigrating to the colonies rather than serving out jail sentences at home. Many female prostitutes and thieves settled in the New World rather than submit to the notorious severity of English criminal "justice." (Daniel Defoe's novel *Moll Flanders* is about such a woman—a London prostitute transported to America—who makes good.) Many of these women convicts were brought as indentured servants; they were obligated to serve a master for a number of years, without wages, before they were allowed their freedom.

Marriage was another inducement that encouraged women to come to the New World. Throughout colonial times men outnumbered women by three to one, or more. Women could be assured of finding husbands in America. One eager publicist for Carolina wrote, "If any maid or single woman have desire to go over, they will think themselves in the Golden Age, when men paid a Dowry for their wives; for if they be but civil, and under 50 years of age, some honest man or other will purchase them for their wives."[2]

In 1619 an enterprising sea captain who had advertised for single women looking to marry transported 144 of them to Virginia. The captain paid for the women's passage and, on arrival, he sold them as "wives" for 120 pounds of fine Virginia tobacco apiece. There are reports of other captains who kidnaped young women off the streets of London rather than going to the trouble of advertising.

Of the 144 women who emigrated to Virginia in 1619 looking for husbands, only 35 were still alive six years later. Conditions in the New World, particularly for the first settlers, did not encourage long life. The months-long sail across the Atlantic was perilous—epidemics often carried off half or more of the passengers. At the end of the journey, there were new dangers to be faced.

What is surprising is not the number of women who died early, but the number who survived. The bravery and stamina of the women in colonial times were renowned. William Byrd described one such woman living in a back settlement of Virginia in 1710, saying she was "a very civil" woman who showed "nothing of ruggedness, or immodesty in her carriage, yet she will carry a gun in the woods and kill deer, turkeys, etc., shoot down wild cattle, catch and tye hogs, knock down beeves with an ax and perform the most manful exercises as well as most men in these parts."[3]

The lives of colonial women and men tended to center around farm and family. For the most part a traditional division of labor was observed, whereby men did the outside work—planting and harvesting crops—while women worked inside, transforming the raw products into usable commodities.

All of woman's work on the farm came under the general heading of "housewifery." What it included varied somewhat from region to region. The wives of southern planters rarely did their own weaving and spinning, while in the northern colonies these tasks took up many hours of a woman's day. In the South women tended their own herbal gardens and were expected to be expert at doctoring. White southern women of means were often responsible for the health needs of their slaves as well as those of their own families.[4]

New England houses were small—one or two rooms and a loft. The houses of southern planters were larger and more lavish. The roughest living was on the frontier, where a house was often a one-room shack, sometimes even a lean-to or wigwam. William Byrd, commenting on one of these back-country homes, noted that it contained a dozen adults and children plus the household animals all "pigged lovingly together."[5] Life on the frontier was long on mud, disease, and loneliness, short on the amenities. One historian has called the American frontier a slum with trees.[6]

Despite local variations, women's activities were much the same throughout the colonies. First came supervision of the house. Women swept, scrubbed, laundered, polished. They made their own brooms, soap, polish. They carried water and did the laundry. They made starch. They ironed. They built fires and carried firewood. They made candles. They sewed everything—sheets, clothing, table linen, diapers. Women were usually in charge of the family bookkeeping. They ordered provisions, paid bills, and made sure the books were balanced.

It is virtually impossible for twentieth-century people to imagine the enormous job of food preparation in colonial times. Cooking was done on an open hearth that had to be tended constantly. Kettles, made of iron, often weighed forty pounds. Without refrigeration, meats had to be preserved by salting or pickling. Rich and spicy sauces were the style, since they were needed to preserve food or to cover the taste of food that had been badly preserved. Women kept their own gardens, every fall putting up vast amounts of home-grown vegetables and fruit. They ran home bakeries and dairies, did the milking, made butter, and kept the hen yard.

Spinning and weaving cloth was another arduous job, involving more than a dozen operations from start to finish. Colonial women were also expected to be expert at knitting, quilting, and all sorts of sewing and embroidery. The following account, taken from the diary of a young colonial woman in 1775, indicates the emphasis placed on spinning, weaving, and needlecrafts. It also highlights the heavy work load colonial women took for granted.

> Fixed gown for Prude . . . mended mothers riding hood, spun short thread . . . fix'd two gowns for Welsh girls . . . carded, spun linen . . . worked on cheese basket . . . hatched flax with Hannah, we did 51 pounds a piece . . . pleated and ironed, . . . milked cows . . . spun linen . . . did 50 knots . . . made a broom of guineau wheat straw, spun thread to whiten . . . set a red dye, spun harness twine, scoured the pewter.[7]

Colonial women also worked outside the home. In the villages, towns, and small cities of the eighteenth century they performed virtually every kind of job held by men. Women ran taverns, inns, and boarding houses. They were blacksmiths, silversmiths, wheelwrights, sailmakers, tailors, teachers, printers, newspaper publishers, and shopkeepers of every sort.

Many women learned their trades from their husbands.

A blacksmith, for example, would teach his wife the skill. If a tradeswoman was widowed, she frequently assumed the full responsibility for the business she had built with her husband. Many women acted as their husbands' business agents. Given the power of attorney by their mates, they were involved in all aspects of finance, including bringing debtors to court.

That colonial women often participated in various sorts of legal proceedings is indicative of the colonial society's pragmatic approach toward women. Pre-Revolutionary Americans often bent the Common Law system (which in England largely excluded women) to suit their needs. Daniel Boorstin has explained this anomaly by noting that colonial America had no learned monopolies. Or, as William Byrd put it in a letter discussing the attractions of the New World, America was free from "Those three scourges of mankind—priests, lawyers and physicians."[8] In the early days there were no bar associations or medical associations establishing proficiency requirements. In consequence, a woman with aptitude could learn a skill informally and practice a profession.

One of the most interesting women to lead a public life in colonial times was Margaret Brent, often referred to in seventeenth-century records as Mistress Margaret Brent, Spinster. Margaret, her sister Mary, and two brothers emigrated to Maryland from Great Britain in 1638. Lord Baltimore, the proprietor of Maryland, attracted the Brents—who were wealthy Catholics—to his colony with promises of large land grants and the chance to live free of anti-Catholic discrimination.

The Brent sisters established their own plantations, which they ran without their brothers' help. In fact, Margaret Brent often acted as her brothers' representative and business adviser. Collecting payment in those days often involved suing in court. Records show Mistress Brent participating in 134 separate court actions during the eight years between 1642 and 1650. She usually won her case.

Brent's close personal friendship with Lord Calvert, Maryland's governor, eventually pushed her into the all-male world of politics. When Calvert lay dying in 1647, he called Brent to his bedside. In the presence of witnesses he made what has been called "perhaps the briefest will in the history of law": "I make you my sole executrix.

Take all and pay all."[9] As executrix, Brent assumed responsibility for Calvert's estates. Since Calvert had been granted the power of attorney for his brother, Lord Baltimore, the proprietor of Maryland, at Calvert's death the power of attorney for Lord Baltimore, then in London, fell to Mistress Brent.

At the time Maryland was not a peaceful colony. Calvert's enemies hoped to take advantage of the confusion following his death to seize control, and it seemed for a time that they might succeed. The man Calvert named to the governorship, Thomas Greene, was not equal to the job. After Calvert's death the army was close to revolt; Brent appeased the military by paying the soldiers their long-overdue wages, raising the necessary funds by selling some of Lord Baltimore's cattle. She took other steps as well to stabilize the situation in Maryland. Members of the Assembly later told Lord Baltimore that "all would have gone to ruin" were it not for her actions.

Brent had so far established herself as a major political figure that many in the colony believed that she, not Thomas Greene, ought to be governor. Brent, however, did not seek to unseat Greene. In January 1648 she appeared before the Maryland Assembly and asked for two votes: one as Calvert's executrix, the other as Lord Baltimore's "attorney." It was the first time in parliamentary history that a woman had sought political recognition in a governing body. Governor Greene refused to have Brent seated, and the Assembly acceded to his wishes.

Subsequently Brent left Maryland and moved to Virginia, where she established a new plantation, which she called Peace. She continued throughout her life to be active in business, but she avoided politics.[10]

It seems probable that throughout most of the colonial period more women practiced medicine than did men. Women were nurses, apothecaries, unlicensed physicians, and midwives. Only surgery—which at that time meant performing amputations—was dominated by men. The kind of doctoring women did was often an extension of their work at home. A woman charged with the well-being of a family learned to care for the sick, to treat common illnesses, and to make the aged and the dying comfortable. A woman with particular skill in this area could earn money by caring not only for the members of her family but for others as well.

In the same way a woman who kept an herb garden and had an interest in botany could earn a living making medicines, tonics, and syrups. These women apothecaries varied in their level of sophistication. Though some lacked knowledge beyond folklore, many others were serious scientists who devoted much time to studying the healing properties of plants. Such skill was attested to by a French visitor to Virginia who wrote of Mary Byrd, "She takes great care of her Negroes . . . and serves them herself as a doctor in times of sickness. She had made some interesting discoveries of the disorders incident to them and discovered a very salutary method of treating a sort of putrid fever which carries them off."[11]

There is evidence to indicate that the women who practiced medicine in the 1700s often did a better job than the male professionals of the 1800s. Medicine in the 1700s was very practical and down to earth. Doctoring women focused on relieving the patient's symptoms, while male doctors of the next century were far more concerned with expounding learned—though usually inaccurate—theories concerning the origin of the disease.

The efficacy of the eighteenth-century brand of care was seen in the practice of midwifery, which was the only form of medicine women participated in that was often licensed. Midwives had to serve lengthy apprenticeships before being certified. As apprentices they observed hundreds of deliveries and, for the most part, learned how to let nature take its course. Midwives seem to have taken good care of their female patients and most certainly did less harm than male doctors in the 1800s, many of whom routinely infected their patients with "puerperal sepsis" (childbed fever) by failing to wash their hands.

The women workers described so far were part of colonial America's pool of "free labor." As "free" workers, women had some control over their earnings and over the products of their work. Another sizable class of women workers in colonial America were not "free," however. These were the indentured servants and the slaves.

It is estimated that half the migrants to the colonies came under indenture, and that a third of these were women. Most of the women who came to the New World in this situation were convicts from Great Britain. Women thieves, prostitutes, and vagrants were given the choice of emigrating or of serving lengthy prison terms. Sometimes the choice was Virginia or the noose. Depending on the crime, the period of bonded labor generally ran from four to seven years.

Indentured servants were transported to the colonies by sea captains who usually landed them in the middle colonies or the South; New England had relatively few indentured servants. The ship's captain assumed the expense of the passage. In the New World the captain "sold" his cargo of female servants for somewhere between ten and thirty pounds apiece, depending on the woman's age, health, and skills.

The relationship between indentured servant and master was a contractual one. Each side had legal responsibilities to the other—though, needless to say, the master usually had the upper hand. Servants had rights to food, clothing, and shelter. While masters had the right to work the indentured servant from sunup to sundown, they were prohibited from working a servant to death. In some cases masters were taken to court by their servants for failure to live up to their responsibilities. More often, however, it was the servant who was prosecuted, and indentured women tended to be punished more harshly for offenses than were men. Punishment was usually in the form of additional years of servitude.

The master was legally bound to provide certain necessities for starting a new life when the indentured servant's term of labor expired. The outfit usually included a new set of clothes, bushels of corn, perhaps tools for farming, and sometimes a parcel of land in an unsettled part of the colony. Male and female indentured servants were entitled to the same "freedom dues."

Indentured women were not allowed to marry during their term of service. Sexual transgression—becoming pregnant out of wedlock—was punished severely. An indentured servant woman who bore a child was usually made to add a year onto her service as repayment for the time she could not work during and after her pregnancy.[12]

The choice of a marriage partner was probably the most important decision in the life of a colonial woman. Colonial society put great pressure on people to wed. A woman who did not marry was pitied and treated as less than an adult and, in several colonies, men who did not marry paid higher taxes than did family men. Rarely did single people run their own homes; instead, they were expected to align themselves with the family of a close relative.

Throughout the colonies young people were more or less free to choose their own mates—within certain boundaries. No person, male or female, was supposed to marry without parental consent. Young people were expected to marry persons of similar background. Parents were not supposed to push young people into marriages against their will, but among wealthy colonialists, particularly in the South, parents sometimes threatened to withhold an inheritance or a dowry to coerce children into marriages based on mercenary considerations.

In general, courtship customs were fairly relaxed. Young people spent much time together in group activities—skating, berrying, picnicking, riding, dancing. There were few chaperones, and courting couples usually had enough privacy to get to know one another.

Marriage was treated as an important social institution rather than a purely private affair. A man or woman who broke an engagement, for example, was often called to church or court and charged with breach of promise. If no satisfactory explanation could be produced, a stiff fine was levied against the jilter, to be paid to the injured party. Legal solutions to romantic difficulties were often sought. In New England, if a man "of good character" was refused permission to court by a young woman's parents, he could sue. Often he won his case. This custom was unique to Puritan New England, however; in no other area were there legal procedures for circumventing parental wishes. (Nevertheless, throughout the colonies young people could and did elope.)

Courtship customs among the Puritans were particularly interesting. Bundling was one of the most famous. Young couples who were serious in their courting spent the night in bed bundled in heavy bedclothes—with a "bundling board" between them. Apparently intercourse was not supposed to occur. What did take place, however, was considered a matter among the young woman and man and their consciences.

The origin and even the point of this custom is not entirely clear. There is no doubt, however, that bundling enjoyed popular approval. New Englanders persisted in the custom for 150 years or more. It faded during the French and Indian War, in the mid-1700s, when French soldiers misused the privilege, bundling with women whom they had no intention of marrying. As late as 1770, however, John Adams, future President of the United States, wrote, "I cannot entirely disapprove of bundling."[13] (John Adams and his future wife Abigail Smith are not known to have indulged in bundling.) The custom continued among the Pennsylvania Dutch well into the 1800s.

The Puritan view of engagement as a legally binding state led to the practice of the "pre-contract." Young people who were planning to marry went to church and swore their troth. Once this ceremony was completed, they were married for all practical purposes. The commitment was considered a very serious one. If the young woman became pregnant after she was pre-contracted but before she married, no one was scandalized; the wedding date was simply pushed forward. One historian has discovered that of 200 persons admitted to the Congregationalist church in Groton, Massachusetts, between 1761 and 1775, about one-third confessed to having engaged in premarital sex. The confession was made by an equal number of men and women.[14]

Throughout the colonies sexual transgressions committed by people not planning to marry, or already married, were considered far more serious than such acts by engaged couples. Women who bore children outside of marriage could be taken into court and sentenced to public whipping, branding, or fines. If a woman could not support her child, the court might demand that she reveal the father's name to force him to support his offspring. If she refused, there would be further punishment. If the woman did not know who the father was, or if she refused to say, the child was often taken from her and apprenticed to a tradesperson until the age of twenty-one.

In the view of most colonists, adultery was the worst crime a woman could commit. This attitude prevailed especially among families with property. Since men controlled nearly all property, it followed that no husband wanted a child fathered by another man to inherit his worldly goods. In strongly religious communities there was an attempt to treat male and female adulterers alike. Both were forced to go to church and confess in public. In New England confession was the only punishment demanded from those of high rank, while those of less social distinction often were branded, whipped, or dunked in a river.

Though divorce existed, for the most part social pressures against it were so extreme, and grounds so difficult to obtain, that in practice it was not a real option. An unhappy couple could be granted a legal separation, but it was a precarious situation for the woman. In many areas there were no laws forcing a man to support a wife with whom he was not living. Unless she had family money or skills by which she could support herself, or unless she was separating from a generous spouse, she would find it virtually impossible to leave her husband. In a separation the woman usually lost everything; even the children stayed with the father.

Rather than endure the legal formality of separation, many women simply ran away. Women on the run usually went west, where they could get a piece of land and often a new "husband." In fact such women were bigamists, but outside the more populated centers no one really cared. Even in cities such legalities were sometimes shrugged off. There is some doubt, for instance, whether Benjamin Franklin's wife's first husband was dead when she married Franklin.

Men often put items in newspapers to announce that their wives had "eloped from my bed and board." Sometimes these notices were printed to let merchants know the husband was no longer responsible for the wife's debts. Sometimes the ads were taken out in an attempt to recover the wife's belongings. Legally all property in a marriage, including a woman's clothing, belonged to her husband.[15]

Women sometimes made off with large amounts of cash, silver, and jewelry. Often these goods were part of the woman's dowry, over which she lost legal control at marriage. Usually, however, women took the bare essentials when they ran away, as the following item from the Maryland Journal indicates. The advertisement charged one Anne Campbell with "robbing" her husband "of all her wearing apparel, a fine pair of English cotton curtains . . . two pillow cases . . . and a sidesaddle."[16] This was not a great deal with which to start a new life.

For women marriage meant bearing children, lots of

them. A popular colonial toast celebrated "Our land free, our men honest, and our women fruitful."[17] Families with a dozen children were common. Martha Jefferson Randolph, daughter of Thomas Jefferson, was the mother of twelve. Another wealthy Virginia lady, Martha Laurens Ramsey, bore eleven children in sixteen years. The sister of George Washington, Betty Washington Lewis, added eleven children to the three her husband had by his first wife. Mary Heathy of South Carolina bore seven children to her first husband, seven to her second and three to her third—seventeen in all! (Many of the very largest families, with sixteen, eighteen, or more children, came from widowed men who married a second and sometimes a third or fourth wife.)

Maternal and infant death rates were appallingly high. Giving birth every year was a terrible physical hardship. Infants born to mothers in weakened physical condition often did not survive their first year. A mortuary poem engraved on the tombstone of a Massachusetts woman told the all too familiar story:

> She'd fourteen children with her
> At the table of the Lord[18]

The story of Mrs. Henry Laurens is not uncommon. Born in 1731, she married Henry Laurens, a southern planter, when she was nineteen years old. During the next twenty years she gave birth to twelve children. Seven of them were buried before her. In 1764 her husband wrote that it had been a year of sorrows. His eldest daughter had died; his wife was extremely ill. During the next four years Mrs. Laurens' health continued to deteriorate. Her husband wrote that she "suffered extremely"; nevertheless, she continued to bear children. Finally, in 1768, Mrs. Laurens, emotionally and physically exhausted by the birth and death of her last infant, gave birth to one more baby girl. Then, at the age of thirty-eight, Mrs. Laurens died. Her husband called her death a "stroke of providence." The last child she bore lived to be twenty-one years old before dying in childbirth.[19]

Colonial people lived closely with death. Women gave birth at home, and they died at home. Most families experienced the death of at least one or two children. Sometimes living so close to death added a gray pallor to daily life. The little books children read at the time seem morbid by twentieth-century standards, including such verses as the following.

> At night lie down, prepared to have thy sleep,
> Thy death thy bed—thy grave.

Often, however, their familiarity with death and so many of the painful aspects of living strengthened colonial women. Whether they were bolstered by religious convictions, as so many colonials were, or a belief in what they called providence, colonial women often exhibited great fortitude and courage.

For the most part colonial women were fully equal to the realities of their lives. No doubt there were frightened women unable to endure the hardships, but these were a minority. Taken as a whole, the image of themselves that colonial women left behind is extraordinary for its spirit, energy, and stamina. It is a picture later generations of women shut off from the world looked back on with great respect and not a little nostalgia.

2

Suffer Not a Woman to Speak

No body of ideas had a greater influence on American colonials than did Protestant theology. Some Catholics and Jews lived in early America, but most colonials identified with one or another Protestant sect. While religious practices and the degree of religious intensity varied from region to region, it is safe to say that religious beliefs were a mainstay of most colonials' lives.

RELIGION

The most numerous denominations in colonial America were the Congregationalists in New England; the Baptists in Rhode Island and elsewhere; the Anglicans in the South, who were replaced by Methodists after 1760; and the Quakers in Pennsylvania. Most of the Protestant groups in the colonies, except the Quakers, were strongly influenced by Calvinist thought and held many beliefs in common. Most of them emphasized original sin and preached the salvation of the few. They believed the majority of mankind to be damned. The devil was portrayed as constantly seeking to undermine the faith of a God-fearing person. All believed that the Old and New Testaments were written by the hand of God and contained a literal description of how the deity wanted human beings to live.

Scripture told woman that she, like man, was created in God's image, and to this degree scripture recognized a spiritual equality between the sexes. Yet throughout Old and New Testament literature woman was also told that it was her duty and responsibility to be subservient to men. In Genesis, God spoke directly to Eve, assigning her the unique punishment of being ruled by her husband.

> I will greatly multiply thy sorrow and thy conception;
> In sorrow thou shalt bring forth children;
> and thy desire shall be to thy husband,
> And he shall rule over thee. [Genesis 3:16]

15

For Christians in general, and Calvinists in particular, the story of Adam and Eve was of extreme importance. By being the first to fall under the serpent's spell, Eve was believed to have unloosed the devil in the world. In the Calvinist view few could escape this taint of original sin and achieve salvation. Eve's fall was taken as proof that women were more susceptible to the devil than men and interpreted as a warning to men to beware the seductive power of woman. Adam, after all, ate the apple at Eve's behest.

The conservative "scriptural" attitude toward women can be seen in the treatment of Anne Hutchinson by the Puritans of Massachusetts Bay Colony. Hutchinson, her husband, and her family were among the first settlers to emigrate from Great Britain to the Bay Colony. The daughter of a famous Puritan preacher, she was particularly well educated in religious subjects.

During 1635 and 1636 Hutchinson held Sunday evening prayer meetings in her Cambridge home at which the day's sermons were discussed. Hutchinson later claimed in court that only women attended these meetings, though some historians think both men and women were in attendance. Either way, Hutchinson soon became a lay preacher of great influence.

Hutchinson's meetings were tolerated by the men who ran the community as long as she adhered to orthodox religious views. Very quickly, however, she veered from accepted Calvinist theology. Hutchinson did not agree that it was within the clergy's power to declare who were the elect. She did not recognize the fierce Puritan God who saved only a few church-going souls. All could be saved, she said, by discovering the light within them.

Hutchinson's "heresy" put her on a collision course with the leaders of the colony. In Massachusetts, a theocracy, the ministers ran the government. To disagree with orthodox religious ideas, as she did, was political treason.

Most historians agree that the uproar caused by Hutchinson's preaching was fundamentally political; her beliefs posed a threat to the established order. The fact, however, that Hutchinson was a woman added fuel to the fire. Her belief in herself, her "masculine" sureness of mind, was highly offensive to those in power.

To the male leaders of the colony Hutchinson was a

criminal three times over—a religious heretic, a political traitor, and a woman who did not conform to her role. Calvinist theologian John Knox had written that "woman in her greatest perfection was made to serve and obey man."[1] Hutchinson was imprisoned and tried twice, by both civil and ecclesiastic courts. It is clear from the transcripts of these proceedings that the crime of not conforming to her sexual role was the felony most despised by her judges.

Hutchinson was accused of provoking other women "to be rather a husband than a wife . . . a preacher than a hearer . . . a magistrate than a subject." Minister John Cotton, once Hutchinson's mentor, reported in court that her doctrine of individualism was so depraved that though he did not think "you had been unfaithful to your husband, yet, that will follow upon it."[2] Cotton's statement highlights the state of mind of the colony's leaders. Though sexuality had nothing whatever to do with Hutchinson's rebellion, the very fact that she was a woman made them view her crime in sexual terms.

Hutchinson was found guilty and ordered "as a leper to withdraw" from Massachusetts. She and her family moved first to Rhode Island and later to Long Island, where they were massacred by Indians. The Puritans believed the slaughter an appropriate punishment. "God's hand is seen herein," wrote one about the death of Mistress Hutchinson and her children.[3]

Arthur Schlesinger, Sr., has called the witchcraft frenzy which swept through Salem, Massachusetts, "a case in community hysteria."[4] No doubt Schlesinger was correct in believing that witch hunts were aberrations within colonial society, but the fear of witchcraft which led to the execution of many women (and some men) during the 1600s must be looked at more closely. A morbid preoccupation with the devilish powers of women often lay dormant in the minds of colonial people. A single event which appeared to be caused by supernatural powers could unleash that morbid fear.

The most famous witch hunt occurred in Salem in 1692. During that summertime outbreak, two hundred persons were accused. One hundred and fifty, mostly women, were imprisoned. Fifty confessed to committing witchcraft and trafficking with the devil. Twenty-eight were condemned to die. Fourteen women and six men, one of them an ordained minister, were actually executed, some in the most gruesome ways. Many proclaimed their innocence to the end.

The Salem ordeal began in child's play. The family of a Salem minister had as its servant a slave woman from Barbados named Tituba. The favorite stories of the minister's two young daughters were those told by Tituba concerning voodoo in the Caribbean. It became a game for the children to act as if they were possessed by devils. For a while they kept their activity secret, but as their games grew into an obsession, the girls' behavior became more bizarre. Eventually they came to believe their own play-acting. As their conviction grew, so did a kind of hysteria. At odd moments the girls' bodies jerked; convulsions overtook them; horrible words came from their mouths; they howled like dogs.

It seemed obvious to their terrified parents that some horrible demon had possessed the children. They demanded to know who was responsible for bewitching them. For the girls to confess that it had been a game would have meant a serious punishment; instead, they began naming names.

The girls' accusations kindled a hysteria that raged through the small community. Somebody's cow ran away; a witch must have been responsible. A child was sick and died; a witch must have cursed him. Soon the entire community was in an uproar. Accusations and counteraccusations were made. As the hysteria spread, it consumed all other interests. No crops were planted throughout that spring and summer.

Cotton Mather accused a Salem beggarwoman of riding on a pole with the devil to a witches' meeting. A five-year-old child was accused of biting two adults and leaving the mark of the devil on their arms. It was said that witches tormented a family—making beds fly out windows while stones and bricks flew in. A woman claimed to have been carried by the devil to a high mountain, where he showed her his kingdom and promised that if she would sign her name in his book she would reign as queen.[5]

Perhaps the most startling aspect of the witchcraft frenzy is the number of women who confessed. No doubt some of those who admitted practicing sorcery were mentally deranged. For many women in colonial New England, day-to-day life was full of monotonous drudgery. Believing oneself invested with magical powers must have been a very strong and not unappealing fantasy.

Other women may have confessed out of a kind of neurotic guilt. As noted, some of the religiously inspired assumptions about women in early times were not very flattering. Most women had the spirit to accept and transcend the idea of their own sinfulness, but some were overwhelmed by a sense of their own evil. When accused of witchcraft, such women confessed because they felt themselves guilty of grave crimes, though perhaps not the ones with which they were charged.

The kind of morbid personality just described also occurred in women who were not driven to confessing to witchcraft. The daughter of the diary-keeping Judge Samuel Sewall was one of these pitiable types. The judge recorded in his diary the following incident from young Betty's childhood.

> When I came home my wife met me in the entry and told me Betty had surprised them. It seems Betty Sewall had given some signs of dejection and sorrow; but a little while after dinner she burst into an amazing cry. . . . Her mother asked the Reason . . . at last she [Betty] said she was afraid she could go to Hell, her Sins not pardoned. . . . She read out of Mr. Cotton Mather—why had Satan filled thy Heart? which increased her Fear. Her Mother asked her whether she had pray'd. She answered Yes, but fear'd her prayers were not heard, because her sins were not pardoned.[6]

One historian described Betty Sewall as, "A frightened child, a retiring girl, a vacillating sweetheart, an unwilling bride, she became the mother of eight children; but always suffered from morbid introspection, and overwhelming fear of death and the future life, until at the age of thirty-five her father sadly wrote, 'God has delivered her now from all her fears.' "[7]

Such excessive sensitivity to the morbid aspect of Protestantism recurred among many nineteenth-century women, particularly those taken with the evangelical spirit. For the majority of colonial women, however, religious beliefs were comforting and sustaining, helping to give meaning to human life—its pleasures as well as its times of suffering and loss.

Not to be overlooked are the aspects of Protestantism that added to women's sense of worth and equality. The recognition among Protestants that woman's soul needed "saving" as much as man's helped promote female literacy. Arthur Schlesinger, Sr., has surmised that on the eve of the American Revolution the colonial population had the highest literacy rate in the world. If that indeed was the case, the reason for it lay in the Protestant attitude toward basic education for children of both sexes.

So important to salvation was reading scripture that most Protestant churches ran some sort of informal day school for at least a few months of the year. Boys and girls were taught the rudiments of reading and writing. The Puritans in New England passed laws requiring every village of one hundred or more families to establish a publicly funded day school for girls and boys. It was the Quakers, however, who most thoroughly educated their children. Wherever they settled, the Quakers established schools notable for their high standards. Quaker girls were the only females in the colonies consistently exposed to a curriculum more demanding than "reading, writing and 'rithmetic."

At least in theory, all Protestant denominations advocated a single standard of ethical and moral behavior for women and men. When in the 1830s the abolitionist Sarah Grimké claimed that "what is morally right for a man is morally right for woman," she was expressing a concept inherent in all Protestant thought. During colonial times the Quakers placed the greatest emphasis on the primacy of individual conscience.

Quaker women were encouraged to speak out on spiritual and moral issues. Quaker meetings were divided along sexual lines, and women ran their own meetings. The Friends (Quakers) were the only colonial group to sanction women preachers.

Quaker ministers were not appointed but acknowledged. Any person could be recognized as a preacher. Mary Fisher, the most famous seventeenth-century preaching woman, who traveled alone as a Quaker missionary to Turkey and eventually settled in South Carolina, began life as an English servant girl. Women who wished to do missionary work carried with them documents certifying that they belonged to a Quaker meeting, were of good faith, and had permission from their husbands to travel. It appears that men, too, needed the permission of their wives before undertaking a mission abroad.[8]

The dozens of preaching Quaker women who came to the colonies in the 1600s did not have an easy time. Most of the colonies had established religions during the first century of settlement, and all agreed that the Friends preached heresy. Quaker women who attempted to preach in the 1600s were fined, whipped, jailed, pilloried, and in some few instances hanged.

In the 1700s religious feelings were less feverish, and for the most part Quaker preachers could travel and speak where they chose. Among the best-known female Friends of this era was Sophia Hume, granddaughter of Mary Fisher. There are some few instances of colonial preaching women who were not Quakers. Most were members of new sects. Barbara Heck established the first Methodist church in America in the mid-1700s, and women were among the most active converts. About the same time the New Light Baptists allowed women to speak out in church; for this practice, however, they were disowned by traditional Baptists.

When these new Protestant sects became more established, however, they invariably shoved women out of the pulpit. Women who had had the courage and stamina to express unpopular opinions and embrace new beliefs were then excluded from the clergy because the new clerical power structures were patterned on traditional models and contained a world view that could not encompass women in leadership and decision-making roles.

LAW

Some legal scholars have noted a similarity between women and slaves under Common Law. In many instances married women under the law were treated, not as persons, but as property belonging to their husbands. The similarity ends there. Married white women in Britain and colonial America did not usually live as slaves did. The potential for the oppression of women was present in the legal system, however. The husband who chose to abuse his wife encountered few legal obstacles to prevent him from doing so.

English Common Law was imported to the American colonies during the 1600s. Most—though not all—of the colonies based their legal codes on the Common Law system. Connecticut was an exception, deriving its system from the Old Testament, and Louisiana, on joining the Union in the early 1800s, maintained its French Napoleonic code. These exceptions aside, throughout the colonies Common Law was the predominant legal influence, and after the Revolution the British system became the basis for federal law.

In some important respects Common Law was an enlightened system. The Common Law criminal code granted rights to accused persons that were unknown elsewhere in the world. The idea of a suspect's being considered innocent until proven guilty, for example, was unique to English Common Law. In the 1800s, when feminists assailed the Common Law system, it was not the criminal code to which they objected. The basis of women's complaint with Common Law rested on its civil code.

The fundamental principle in civil law was the right of the individual (male) to own property. Common Law protected property owners from the incursions of other private citizens and from the state. A magistrate, for example, could not enter a home without a search warrant. Unfortunately the Common Law emphasis on property rights created a huge disparity between the rights of single women and those of married women.

With the exception of the right to vote and the right to sit on a jury, single women were treated more or less as men. Because the single woman had no man to "protect" her property, she needed legal rights to protect herself. Married women, on the other hand, had the same legal rights as idiots and children—virtually none. In Common Law a married woman was known as a *femme coverte*, meaning that her legal rights were covered by her husband. The basis for the *coverture* was the Common Law belief that husband and wife are one flesh, one unit, one person. It was clearly understood, however, that the "one person" was the husband. William Blackstone, author of the much read *Commentaries on The Laws of England*, wrote of the *coverture*, "By marriage the husband and wife are one person in law; that is, the very being or legal existence of the woman is suspended during the marriage, or at least incorporated and consolidated into that of the husband; under whose wing, protection and cover, she performs everything."[9]

Under *coverture* married women had no property and no money of their own. Even a married woman's clothing and household goods belonged to her husband. A married woman's dowry and any inheritance she might receive also belonged to him. In most instances he could sell her property without her consent. Nor did a married woman control her own wages. She could work all day as a servant, and her husband was legally free to take her earnings and allow her to starve. A married woman could not buy or sell anything without her husband's permission. She could not make contracts, sue in court, or be sued.

Even if a woman outlived her husband, she continued to feel the discriminatory effects of the Common Law. In Great Britain property passed from father to eldest son or, in the absence of a son, from eldest male to closest male blood relation. If a husband died without leaving a will, his wife usually inherited one third of his estate, but only to use so long as she lived; after her death her inheritance reverted to the male heir. Because the inheritance was not hers outright, the widow could not sell any property connected with the estates. At the time of the American Revolution most of the colonies changed their inheritance laws, allowing male and female children to inherit equal portions of the father's wealth and property. It was not until the 1850s, however, that the law was changed to give widows absolute ownership of one-third of their husband's estate.

Most of the American colonies made alterations in the Common Law code granting women three important rights married women in Britain did not possess. In general, colonial courts recognized a wife's right to share her husband's home and bed; a wife's right to be supported by her husband, even if he abandoned her; and a wife's right to be protected from violence at her husband's hand.[10]

The negative factor in these colonial additions to Common Law was the fact that women were denied the right to sue in court. If a husband refused to feed or lodge his wife, it could hardly be expected that he would go to court and, in his wife's name, sue himself for lack of support. Similarly, if a husband beat his wife, there was no way she could approach the court and use the force of law to make him stop. So long as women were denied direct access to the courts, the few legal rights they possessed in theory remained essentially meaningless.

Taken by themselves, Common Law statutes concerning property often led to inconsistent legal rulings. A perfect example of property law's potential for illogic is contained in the following. At twenty-one years of age a single woman could go into business. She had the right to make contracts, sue for payment, and the like. If she were capable, she could make a fortune and accumulate vast land holdings. If she married at twenty-two, and her husband turned out to be a gambler, in many colonies he had the right to gamble away her property and every cent she possessed.

To counteract this sort of illogic in property relationships, Great Britain set up the so-called Courts of Equity, which existed outside the system of Common Law. In equity courts judges were called upon to make rulings based on common sense and logic. Equity provided a way for a married woman to own property exclusive of her husband. Legally binding agreements could be drawn up allowing women total control over real estate, cash, stocks, bonds, jewelry, and so forth. Just as Common Law was imported to America, so was the law of equity, and after the American Revolution equity principles were incorporated into state and federal law.

Equitable agreements functioned chiefly in two forms. A couple that was soon to be married could write a *marriage contract* specifying that certain property or cash belonged solely to the wife. Rich fathers often insisted upon such contracts to protect their daughters' dowries and inheritances from husbands who might turn out to be greedy, stupid, or debt-ridden. A married woman could also own property through an *equitable trust*, given as a gift or an inheritance. A relative or friend or even a husband could establish a trust for a married woman. Equitable trusts were available to children and the mentally disabled as well as to married women.

The issue of equity law is a controversial one in American women's history. Some historians have accused nineteenth-century feminists of covering up the existence of equity law in order to build a stronger case for their campaigns to win legal reform. These accusers, however, ignore a crucial truth—equitable solutions to women's legal difficulties were available only to a small minority of women.

Leo Kanowitz, a legal scholar, discusses the shortcomings of equity in his book *Women and the Law*. He lists four major drawbacks to equity practices. First, during the early days of American law some states had no equity courts. Second, equity agreements had to be made before the damage was done; once a husband managed to get hold of a woman's estate, it was too late to resort to equity. Third, equity was designed to protect the daughters of the rich, who had inherited wealth; it did nothing for women of lesser means. Finally, equity law pertained only to property; concepts of equity did not touch upon other major areas in which women were denied legal rights, including family law, divorce law, and politics.[11]

Blackstone's *Commentaries,* published in 1765, is the fifth reason why equity was only occasionally invoked to right the wrongs to which married women in America were subject. Blackstone almost entirely overlooked the changes equity had wrought in the legal position of married women. Moreover, he overstated the liabilities imposed on married women within Common Law.

Blackstone's work, especially his treatment of equity practices, was quickly discredited in England. In the colonies, however, legal scholarship was not very sophisticated. Because Blackstone was easy to read, his book was enormously influential for a hundred years. Such legal scholars as Thomas Jefferson criticized Blackstone and condemned those lawyers who relied on his work, but vast numbers of American lawyers knew little law besides the *Commentaries.* Not until the emergence of the women's rights movement in the 1800s was a serious challenge to Blackstone's ideas concerning woman's legal status put forward in the United States.

3

Remember the Ladies

It has been estimated that at the time of the American Revolution no more than 40 percent of the nation favored it. Samuel Eliot Morison has written that the Revolution was fought not to win freedoms from the British Crown but to protect freedoms Americans already possessed. Prior to 1763 colonial legislatures had the power to raise taxes to pay for defense and to pay the salaries of local officials. Between 1763 to 1774 King George III instigated a number of acts of parliament that attempted to take from the colonies the power of self-taxation. Revolutionary groups, the so-called Sons of Liberty, were organized to resist these "despotic" laws.[1]

The Daughters of Liberty, unlike their male counterparts, were formed not to engage in sabotage or violence but to participate in boycotts of British products. The Revenue Acts, the Townshend Acts, and other parliamentary edicts heavily taxed imported products including paper, sugar, glass, silk, linen, madeira wine, and tea. Women patriots refused to buy these products; many eventually refused to buy all British goods, even those not taxed.

The boycotts created new styles. Homespun cloth, made by women patriots, was worn on all occasions by all social classes. Spinning bees became patriotic events. A Massachusetts leader of the Daughters of Liberty wrote of the new style in clothing, "I hope there are none of us but would sooner wrap ourselves in sheep and goatskin than buy English goods of a people who have insulted us in such a scandalous way."[2]

One upper-class lady in Philadelphia wrote to a family member describing her efforts to aid the Patriot cause and her deep feelings about the cause.

I will tell you what I have done. . . . I have retrenched every superfluous expense in my table and family; tea I have not drunk since last Christmas, nor bought a new

gown. . . . I have learned to knit and am now making
stockings of American wool for my servants, and this way
do I throw in the mite to the public good. I know this,
that as free I can die but once, but as a slave I shall not be
worthy of life.[3]

For a variety of reasons tea became a symbol of American resistance to the Crown. Women organized Anti-
Tea Leagues and refused to buy or drink "the pestillent
British herb." Colonials were passionate tea drinkers, as
the English are to this day, and giving up tea was a major
sacrifice. Women brewed native concoctions of dried herbs
and leaves. Because these pseudo-teas were not very
tasty, Americans eventually switched their allegiance to
coffee.

In Edenton, North Carolina, a group of fifty-one wom-
en announced its intention to boycott British tea and
cloth. In a document that came to be known as the
Edenton Proclamation, the women stated that they had a
right and a duty to participate in the political events of
their time and region. There was little in English political
history to give eighteenth-century women the idea that
they had political rights of any sort. The Edenton women
did without precedents; they simply stated that they had
political rights and intended to exercise them.

No women attended the Continental Congress or the
state congresses convened to consider the deteriorating
relationship with Great Britain. Male patriots recognized
the importance of the agitation carried out by the Daughters of Liberty, but they made no effort to share political
power with women. There were very few women or men
who understood the irony of the Patriot attitude toward
women. Few women asked to share in the rights of political liberty that American men were demanding from
the Crown. Most women simply accepted the political
division of labor that asked women to take part in the
struggle for freedom but did not offer them the rewards.

One woman who did not bow to the exclusion of wom-
en from the inner circle was Mercy Otis Warren. The
most important woman intellectual of the Revolution,
Mrs. Warren was the sister of patriot James Otis, the
wife of patriot Joseph Warren, and the friend of leaders
of the American Revolution. She was a loving wife, referring to her husband as "the best friend of my heart,"

and the mother of five sons. But politics rather than her family was at the center of Mercy Otis Warren's life.

Using an assumed masculine name, Mrs. Warren published many political tracts; these were widely read and debated. She tended to favor the position of the most radical American leaders, and she spoke out in favor of independence before the Continental Congress was ready to take such a stand.

During the long war Mrs. Warren corresponded with almost every major American leader—among them Jefferson, Washington, John Adams, Dickinson, Gerry, and Knox. Her letters discussed the form the projected government would take when it was organized. Mrs. Warren, an antifederalist who favored states' rights over the rights of the national government, feared the effect of power on those who governed. She believed that the only way to protect against the misuse of power was to put tight restriction on those who ruled.

Despite the admiration heaped on her by the male leaders of the Revolution, Mrs. Warren worried that politics was not a proper occupation for a woman. John Adams addressed himself to this concern when he wrote, "Tell [Mrs. Warren] that God Almighty has entrusted her with powers for the good of the world which instead of being a fault to use, it would be criminal to neglect."[4]

No doubt the future president's encouragement pleased Mrs. Warren, but Adams failed to address himself to the heart of the matter. If Mrs. Warren had so chosen, she could have asked her friend why it was necessary for a woman with talent entrusted by "God Almighty" to publish her books under a man's name in order for them to be seriously considered by the public. The time for most women to ask such probing questions about their own lot in America had not yet come. One woman, however, who was close to both John Adams and Mercy Warren, was willing to question the sexual status quo. She was Adams' own wife, Abigail. We shall return to her below.

When the fighting began, any questions about women's work as distinct from men's work lost much of their importance. On the day after the Patriot defeats at Lexington and Concord, the women of Groton, Massachusetts, dressed in men's clothing, armed themselves with muskets and pitchforks and set out to defend the local bridge from the retreating British. The women captured a small group of British soldiers, including a courier carrying valuable intelligence, and handed their prisoners over to the local militia.

This type of incident occurred over and over again during the war. With less than half the American population committed to the Patriot cause in 1776, the efforts of rebel women were desperately needed. The line between soldier and civilian was never very distinct.

As many as 20,000 women marched with the British and American armies.[5] These women acted as paid and unpaid cooks, nurses, doctors, laundresses, guides, seamstresses, and porters. Many traveled with their husbands because they had nowhere else to go. Others were single women able to earn a living caring for male soldiers. It appears that more women served with the British than with the American army. The reason is, quite simply, that wherever they marched or fought, Americans could rely on local patriots to take care of their needs. The British, fighting on alien soil, were compelled to travel with a paid staff.

Marching with an army took its toll. One matron described the appearance of the British force as it entered Cambridge, Massachusetts. "I never had the least idea that the Creation produced such a sordid set of creatures in human figure—poor, dirty, emaciated men, great numbers of women, who seemed to be the beasts of burden, having a bushel basket on their back, by which they were bent double, the contents seemed to be pots and kettles, various sorts of furniture, children peeping through gridirons and other utensils, some very young infants who were born on the road, the women bare feet, clothed in dirty rags."[6]

A description of the attempted American assault on Montreal, organized by General Benedict Arnold, shows the difficulties women who traveled with the armies often faced. Hundreds of women participated in this ill-conceived campaign. A series of delays prevented the marchers from leaving during the summer. They finally began their march in the late fall, when game was unavailable in the forest to provide food. Few were equipped with the proper clothing for the long and cold northern winter. Guides were ill-informed; women and men lost their way and froze to death. Much of the armies' food supplies sank when a flotilla of barges overturned. Men and women died of starvation. Pneumonia and typhoid decimated the rag-tag and hungry army.

James and Jemina Warner were practically newly-weds when they set out on the march to Canada. One chronicler noted that the young couple "appeared to be much interested in each others welfare and unwilling to be separated." James Warner—less able than his wife to withstand the exhaustion, cold, and hunger—straggled be-hind. At one point he became separated from the group of Pennsylvania militia with whom he and his wife were traveling. Jemina asked her fellow marchers to wait while she ran back through the woods to find her husband. The troops waited for an hour. When the young couple did not appear, they went on.

A Connecticut man, marching behind the Philadelphia troops, wrote about what happened next. When Jemina found her husband several miles back, he was dying. She stayed with him until he finally "fell victim to the King of Terrors." Then, "having no implements with which she could bury him she covered him with leaves, and then took his gun and other implements and left him with a heavy heart. After traveling twenty miles she came up with us."[7]

The most dramatic stories from the Revolution concern the women who fought. Some actually donned men's clothes and joined the army; others replaced their fallen husbands on the battlefield; and still others, frontier wom-en, protected their homes and settlements. It is impossible to give a precise number of women who were fighters; in terms of the army proper the percentage must have been very small. What is interesting, however, is the treat-ment accorded these women in their own time. Not only were they celebrated as heroines, but in many cases they were rewarded in the same manner as male fighters with an army pension after the war was won.

Because of the following famous bit of doggerel, genera-tions of American schoolchildren have known of the ex-ploits of Molly Hays, known as Molly Pitcher.

> Moll Pitcher she stood by her gun
> And rammed the charges home sir
> And thus on Monmouth's bloody field
> A sergeant did become sir.

There are conflicting stories about this heroine. Most scholars agree that she was the wife of John Casper Hays, an American artillery soldier from Pennsylvania. Apparently Molly traveled with the army, and during the bloody battle of Monmouth Courthouse, fought during a heat wave, she carried "pitchers" of water to her husband and other American soldiers. When Hays fell, either because of a wound or from heat exhaustion, his wife took his place at the heavy overheated gun. It has been claimed that she single-handedly "sponged, loaded, aimed and fired" the cannon in addition to nursing her husband.

It is not clear whether Molly Pitcher was actually made a sergeant on the battlefield in recognition of her brave deeds or whether the anonymous poet who told her story merely employed some poetic license. It is known from existing archives, however, that the state of Pennsylvania granted Mrs. Hays a pension for "services rendered in the Revolutionary War."

Deborah Sampson Gannett, also known as Timothy Thayer and Robert Shurtleff, twice joined the American army. The first time, when she joined as Timothy Thayer, Sampson used the bounty she was paid to go on a drinking spree. Her sex was discovered, and she was forced to resign. The second time, in 1781, using the name Robert Shurtleff, Sampson successfully joined a Massachusetts outfit. She was sent to West Point, and during her eighteen months of service she participated in many raids against the British and their Indian allies.

During a skirmish with Indians outside Philadelphia, Deborah suffered a serious thigh wound. Shortly after recovering she moved with her regiment south to Virginia. From Virginia, Sampson returned to West Point, where she was mustered out of the army with an honorable discharge on October 23, 1783. She notes that it was sad to give up her uniform in which she was "safe from insult and annoyance" as she roamed the world.[8]

In 1784 she married Benjamin Gannett, a farmer from Sharon, Massachusetts, and they had three children. Benjamin was not a very good provider. Deborah supplemented the family income by going on the lecture circuit, traveling the country to tell her story. With the help of Paul Revere she was able to receive an army pension from both the federal and the Massachusetts governments.

Deborah died in 1827 at the age of sixty-seven. Ten years later her husband applied for and received a widower's pension based on his wife's military service. It took another 130 years before the American government would again grant husbands pensions based upon their wives' service. Not until the mid-1970s did the Social Security Administration reestablish the precedent begun with Benjamin Gannett by a ruling that the spouse of a working woman deserved the same benefits as the spouse of a working man.

Many tall tales have been told about the Patriot activities of Nancy Hart Morgan, who lived with her husband and eight children in a backwoods section of Georgia known as the Hornet's Nest. The most famous of these incidents concerns a raid on the family farm by five Tories, at a time when Nancy and one daughter were home alone. Mrs. Morgan allowed herself to be "captured" and set about cooking dinner for her enemies. While her daughter was sent to get help by pretending to fetch water, Mrs. Morgan lulled the Loyalists with a jug of homemade whiskey. When they were sufficiently mellow with drink, she grabbed their weapons, and before help arrived, she had shot one Tory dead, mortally wounded another, and captured the remaining three. When reinforcements appeared, Nancy insisted on celebrating the rout by hanging her captives.

Nancy Morgan's thirst for blood was not unusual in the South. Samuel Eliot Morison has said that the "looting, vandalism, and savagery" carried out by Cherokee Indians and Tories in North and South Carolina "makes Sherman's march through Georgia in 1864 seem a picnic in comparison."[9]

The renowned South Carolina planter Eliza Lucas Pinckney was one of those hardest hit by British plundering in the South. Thirty-five years before the Revolution, the sixteen-year-old Eliza had settled with her invalid mother in the steamy country outside Charleston. Eliza's father, a career officer in the British army, was stationed in the Caribbean. Since the Lucas family was close to bankruptcy, it was left to Eliza to turn the family's land into a profitable investment.

At the time rice was South Carolina's only substantial cash crop. Eliza decided to diversify. For ten years she experimented with processing indigo into a blue dye. In the course of her work she became a natural scientist and an expert in modern agricultural methods. Eventually indigo made her a wealthy woman and helped to strengthen the economy of South Carolina.

Later Eliza married a neighbor and friend, Colonel Pinckney, who was considerably older than she. When the Revolution broke out, Eliza had been a widow with two sons for a number of years. Had she followed her economic interests, Eliza would have supported the Tories. By siding with the Patriots, she cut herself off from trade with Great Britain, South Carolina's major market.

A reader of Enlightenment thinkers, Eliza believed in the principles of political liberty that were the basis of Revolution. Her ideals cost her a great deal. Her mansion in Charleston was commandeered by the British; her jewelry, silver, china, and other household furnishings were stolen. Other goods were destroyed. Her plantations were seized, her crops looted, her animals slaughtered, and her fields burned. By 1782 Eliza and her sons were economically ruined.

A major factor in the defeat of the British was the Englishmen's inability to understand the motivation of the American population, male and female. Late in the war a young officer wrote to General Burgoyne to note that even if the British were to defeat all the men in America, they would still have to contend with all the women. The British never really understood the significance of this remark. Because the English discounted the political passion of American women, they fell easy victims to the stratagems of female rebels.

These stratagems took a variety of forms. In occupied Charleston it took British officers quite a while to understand why the fat women who left town every day were coming back thin: rebel women were carrying food on their persons to rebel soldiers stationed outside of town. Early on in the war a young woman from Connecticut, twenty-two-year-old Deborah Champion, was able to carry vitally needed intelligence dispatches to General Washington in Cambridge, Massachusetts, because it never occurred to the British that a sweet-faced woman might be a spy. Champion, cool and easy, rode for two days through enemy territory and past enemy sentries to safely complete her mission. Champion, who has been called the female Paul Revere, was unlike the famous silversmith in that she was not captured by the British—her "night ride" was a success.

The British did remarkably little to protect themselves against spies. Wherever they were stationed, British officers seized the largest and most fashionable houses for themselves. Often they shared these homes with allegedly neutral inhabitants. Such was the case in Philadelphia, where General Howe was billeted in the home of a wealthy mortician, Lydia Darragh.

Howe chose to hold his staff meetings in the dining room, while Mrs. Darragh eavesdropped from an upstairs bedroom. On many occasions she sewed messages for General Washington behind the buttons of her young son's coat and then sent him out on errands, during which he would sneak through British lines and into the American general's camp. Mrs. Darragh is credited with delivering to Washington the important information that General Howe was planning to leave Philadelphia and carry out a surprise attack on the American army. This intelligence is believed to have saved the American troops from a rout.

Of all the actions American women took to help win the Revolution, it was perhaps the plainest and least dramatic activities that were most effective. American women kept the economy of the new nation alive during seven long years of war. They planted and harvested, and they traded and manufactured the goods needed to sustain the army and the civilian population. When inflation made American money nearly worthless, women reverted to a system of barter.

When Abigail Adams, then the mother of four young children, was left alone to manage the family farm in Braintree, Massachusetts she was overwhelmed by the responsibility. She wrote to her husband in Philadelphia attending a session of the Continental Congress, asking him to return home. "I cannot consent," she wrote, "to your tarrying much longer." But Abigail, like tens of thousands of Patriot women, learned to manage, and to manage well, without the help of men.[10]

In later life Abigail's son, John Quincy Adams, recalled an incident typical of his mother's bravery and resourcefulness. In 1775 British troops from Boston were advancing on Braintree, searching for Patriot arsenals. All day neighbors traveled the road in front of the Adams' farmhouse, retreating from the expected attack. Abigail was alone in her home with her children. When rebel troops arrived, they advised Abigail to flee. Instead she stayed, handing over all her precious pewter to the Minutemen, helping them melt down the metal for bullets. The rebel soldiers departed, and Abigail remained, expecting the worst but refusing to give in to the panic that possessed some of her neighbors. "Do you wonder," wrote her son, "that a boy of seven who witnessed this scene is a patriot?"[11]

For ten years prior to, during, and following the war Abigail Adams was alone while her husband conducted the affairs of state in New York and Philadelphia, and later in Paris and Amsterdam. As a farmer, businesswoman, and financial manager she was far more gifted than her husband. By wise investment and frugal living she was able to stretch the family's limited means. The Revolution bankrupted many of its leaders; many, like Jefferson, died in debt. Adams, however, was on sound financial ground, thanks to Abigail.

Mrs. Adams, the model of housewifely virtues, was also devoted to her family. She supervised the education of her four children, teaching them to love learning and instilling them with her own very strict moral and religious code. Her marriage was a lifelong love match. She was married to John Adams for nearly fifty years, sharing the sometimes violent vicissitudes of his career. The ten years they were apart during and after the American Revolution cost her a great deal. Describing her life without her husband, Abigail once lamented, "How empty are my days . . . how lonely my nights."[12] But she sacrificed her own happiness to what she considered her duty.

The fulfillment Mrs. Adams experienced in her roles not only as wife and mother, but also as daughter and sister did not blind her to the injustices to which women were subjected. In the hundreds of letters Mrs. Adams wrote to her husband it was often her habit to refer to herself as "Portia." Borrowing a name from literature was an eighteenth-century convention, but the character Mrs. Adams chose tells a great deal about her. Shakespeare's Portia was a lawyer, an educated woman who loved justice and took her place as an equal in the world of men and public events.

Perhaps the greatest source of personal dissatisfaction for Abigail Adams was her lack of formal education. The shortcomings in her learning were apparent in her spelling and grammar. Mrs. Adams felt shame at the limitations in her knowledge and fervently hoped for the day when girls would have the chance to share an equal education with boys. This hope was one she expressed to her husband and others on every possible occasion.

John Adams, well aware of his wife's gifts, commented more than once that Abigail had the quality of mind to make a superior statesman. Abigail Adams was not content to bask in private in her husband's praise. She would have preferred to take her place in public as a political leader. Mrs. Adams spelled out her grievances with the male power structure in a letter she wrote to John in March 1776.

By the way, in the new code of laws which I suppose it will be necessary for you to make, I desire you would remember the ladies and be more generous and favorable to them than your ancestors! Do not put such unlimited power in the hands of husbands. Remember all men would be tyrants if they could. If particular care and attention is not paid to the ladies, we are determined to foment a rebellion, and will not hold ourselves bound by any laws in which we have no voice or representation.[13]

John Adams was not pleased by his wife's letter. He answered, with the following.

As to your extraordinary code of laws, I cannot but laugh! We have been told that our struggle has loosened the bonds of government everywhere—children and apprentices . . . schools and colleges. . . . Indians and Negroes grow insolent. But your letter was the first intimation that another tribe more numerous and powerful than all the rest, were grown discontented. . . . Depend on it, we know better than to repeal our masculine systems. Although they are in full force, you know they are little more than theory. We are obliged to go fair and softly, and you know in practice we are the subjects. We have only the name of masters, and rather than give up this which would completely subject us to the despotism of the petticoat, I hope General Washington and all our brave heroes would fight![14]

Mrs. Adams was disappointed with her husband's response to her demand that the new republic recognize the political rights of women. After receiving his mocking letter, she wrote to Mercy Warren complaining about her husband's attitude. Warren took the more conventional view that the disabilities women faced were the result of shortcomings in the female character. Abigail Adams was nearly alone in her outspoken insistence that men misused their political power when they denied women equal rights as citizens.

The Nineteenth Century:
Slaves, "Ladies," Reformers,
and Working Women

4

Black Bondage/White Pedestal

BLACK BONDAGE

Slavery in the American South was an economic system based upon falsehood. The lie proclaimed that black slaves were not human. As subhuman beings, blacks could be denied all the legal, civil, and political rights bestowed, in fact or in theory, on other Americans. White Southerners accepted the lie as truth. Black slaves did not.

Blacks responded to slavery with a constant assertion of their own humanity. By surviving, by defying white stereotypes, by cherishing their family relations, by overt and covert acts of sabotage, blacks resisted their enslavement. Despite the cruel system under which they lived, blacks created for themselves a culture rich in love for one another, in community, and in human meaning.

Slavery as an economic and social system was far more varied than is usually supposed. The region in which slaves lived, the kind of work they did, the special skills they possessed, the sort of white person who owned them —all affected the quality of their lives.

The lives of slaves in towns and cities differed from those of farm and plantation slaves. Urban slaves were often hired out by their masters for a year at a time as skilled or unskilled laborers. A female slave in town might work as a maid, nanny, cook, baker, dressmaker, milliner, or seamstress.

Urban slaves had greater freedom of movement and association than did their sisters and brothers on the plantation. They had frequent contact with the South's one quarter of a million free blacks, most of whom lived in towns. Free blacks secretly taught many town- and city-dwelling slaves how to read and write. The contact between free blacks and slaves was feared by the slave-owning class, who rightly believed that this interchange fed the discontent in the hearts of slaves.

Close to half the slaves in the South lived on small

farms worked by twenty slaves or even fewer. Relatively little is known about life on these establishments, since small planters did not usually leave detailed records. It is commonly assumed that those living on smaller farms were better off than were slaves on large plantations. It is known that members of slave families on small farms were less frequently sold away from each other than were those on large plantations.

In general, slaves in the Old South (Virginia, Maryland, the coastal regions of Georgia, and the Carolinas) lived and worked under far better conditions than did slaves in the deep South (Alabama, Mississippi, Arkansas, Louisiana, and Texas). In the Old South traditional ideas about the duties of "superior" beings to their "inferiors" tended to soften some of the worst features of slavery. Virginia planters, for example, saw themselves as dutybound to protect their own slaves and perhaps even intervene on behalf of slaves treated brutally by a neighbor. Though the impact of "chivalry" must not be overestimated, it did in fact exert some social pressure on the side of kindness to slaves.

Speculators developed the deep South into a cotton-producing region. Sugar was also a very important crop there. In this area chivalry was no match for the profit motive. Fanny Kemble, the English actress who lived in Georgia for a short while in the early 1840s, was told that in the cotton belt slaveholders viewed their slaves as "livestock." One former slave spoke of the terror blacks felt at the prospect of being sold down the river. "It is an awful thing to a Virginia slave to be sold for the Alabama and Mississippi country. I have known some of them to die of grief and others to commit suicide on account of it."[1]

Throughout the South, "house slaves"—those who worked in the "big house" as the personal servants of the white owners—generally had an easier life than did so-called field hands. House servants often ate better food, wore better clothes, and were more likely to have the chance to learn to read and write than those who worked in the fields.

House servants on large plantations were exposed to every secret of the white family. An English commentator on life in America noted with disgust that a young white woman, who sat at dinner with her arms clutched to her body rather than touch elbows with the men next to her, thought nothing of lacing her corset in front of her family's black butler. The personal slaves of the mistress and master slept in the same bedroom with those they served, in case the white couple needed some service during the night.

Because these slaves were treated as nonexistent by oblivious whites, they were often able to use the information gathered in the big house to their own advantage and to the advantage of their fellow slaves. Sometimes a house servant, treated as a nonperson, was pushed beyond endurance. The historian Eugene Genovese notes that every now and then a house slave would slash the throats of his "white family."[2]

Slave owners organized the lives of their slaves so as to extract from them the highest possible rate of productivity. Coercion was at the heart of the system. All slave owners relied on violence or the threat of violence to control slaves. When slaves failed to perform at a pace whites considered adequate, they were beaten.

Designed to "teach them a lesson," the punishment was also supposed to serve as a warning to other potentially recalcitrant blacks. The slave narratives contain hundreds of descriptions of such chastisements. The details of a beating inflicted on one slave woman from Georgia are typical.

> When dey ready to beat you dey'd strip you stark mother naked and dey'd say, "Come here to me, God damn you. Come to me clean! Walk up to dat tree and damn you, hug dat tree!" Den dey'd tie your hands round de tree, den tie you feets, den dey'd lay de rawhide on and cut your buttocks open. Sometimes they'd rub turpentine and salt in de raw places, and den beat you some more.[3]

The work demanded from slave women was particularly arduous, since they were asked to perform in three areas. Most did as much or almost as much field work as men. Further, they were expected to do "woman's work" in the slave quarters. Their third job was to reproduce. Fanny Kemble, whose hatred of slavery eventually shattered her marriage to slave owner Pierce Butler, observed the work situation of male and female slaves. "The middle-aged men do not appear to me overworked. . . . The principal hardships fall to the lot of the women—that is, the principal physical hardships."[4]

Kemble's belief that female slaves were overworked was echoed by many slave women. One former slave from North Carolina recalled her life in bondage as toil without cease.

> I never knowed what it was to rest. I just work all de time from mornin' till late at night. I had to do everythin' dey was to do on de outside. Work in de field, chop wood, hoe corn, till sometimes I feels like my back surely break. . . .
>
> Ole Marse strop us good if we did anythin' he didn't like. Sometimes he get his dander up and den we dassent look around at him, else he tie you hands afore your body and whip you, just like a mule. . . .
>
> In de summer we had to work outdoors, in de winter in de house. I had to card and spin till ten o'clock. Never get much rest, had to get up at four de next mornin' and start again.[5]

On large farms, work was usually organized in one of two ways—either by tasks or by gangs. Under the task system a slave or group of slaves was given a set amount of work to accomplish for the day. When the task was finished, the slaves had met their obligation for the day. If tasks were assigned reasonably, slave women might have a little time for themselves at the end of the day, perhaps to work on their own small vegetable gardens.

Tasks were usually though not always allotted according to age, sex, and the strength of the laborer. On plantations female slaves were often in charge of groups of slaves assigned to complete particular tasks—spinning so much cotton, cutting so much hay, curing so much tobacco, and the like.

The task system, though often abused, is generally considered to have been fairer than the gang system, under which large groups of slaves worked in the fields, with the strongest setting the pace and others expected to keep up. Strong young male slaves, called "drivers," made sure the pace did not slacken.

During the winter months, when there was less field work, and in the evenings slave women spent many hours spinning, weaving, quilting, candle and soap making, basket and mat weaving. In addition they had to cook, clean, wash, and mend for their own families. Black men's domestic responsibilities involved obtaining extra food for their families by hunting, fishing, and trapping. Slave men and women generally shared responsibility for cultivating the private garden plots some whites allowed their slaves.

To some extent the traditional division of labor in the slave quarters was used as a means of social control by whites. Life ran more efficiently when each gender was assigned specific roles. But the needs of the slaveholders were only part of the picture.

Slaves preferred organizing their lives so as to emphasize the importance of family units. Even when it meant additional work, slave women preferred cooking for their own families to taking their meals in a communal kitchen. In some cases where masters tried to replace family meals with communal ones, slaves used all their power and influence to successfully resist such a change.

Most slave owners lightened the work load of pregnant slave women. The cumulative effects of many pregnancies and chronic overwork could nevertheless be devastating. Slave women grew old and sick before their time. In addition, physically spent women often had sickly babies, and the infant mortality rate in the slave quarters was substantially higher than among whites.

Fanny Kemble recorded the gynecological complaints of her husband's female slaves. Slave women of childbearing age suffered from dropped wombs, ruptured uteruses, temporary insanity, chronic rheumatism, back trouble, abscesses, ulcers, and epilepsy—all attributed to too-frequent childbearing and overwork. In her journal Kemble described the condition of individual women slaves owned by her husband's family.

Sally . . . has had two miscarriages and three children born, one of whom is dead. She came complaining of incessant pain and weakness in her back. Sarah . . . had had four miscarriages, had brought seven children into the world, five of whom were dead, and was again with child. She complained of dreadful pains in the back, and an internal tumor which swells with the exertion of working in the fields; probably, I think, she is ruptured. . . . Molly's . . . was the best account I have yet received; she had had nine children, and six of them were still alive. . . . There was hardly one of these women . . . who might not have

been a candidate for a bed in a hospital, and they had
come to me after working all day in the fields.[6]

Slave infants and their mothers were valuable property
and many slave owners did a better job of protecting their
investment than did the Butler family. Nevertheless, the
scene described by Kemble was far from the worst. In
Alabama and Mississippi it was often the practice to treat
pregnant and post-partum women exactly as all other
workers. Those who could not keep up with the work pace
were beaten. One former slave told the story of a woman
in an advanced state of pregnancy who was stripped, tied,
and beaten for three days in a row by an overseer because
she failed to complete her assigned tasks. Finally the overseer succeeded in beating the poor woman to death.

Slavery was a spiritual and emotional assault on blacks
as well as a physical one. In response slaves developed a
prodigious solidarity, protecting each other when possible
and comforting each other when necessary. The pressures
on slaves did create occasional traitors, but acts of treach-
ery were minor compared to the spirit of cohesion and
support which usually marked life in the slave quarters.

Underlying the solidarity of blacks as a group was the
solidarity of the slave family. In law there was no such en-
tity as slave marriage; in practice the formal alliance was
universal throughout the South. Most owners supported
slave marriage because of its stabilizing effect upon life
in the quarters. Whites knew that a married slave with
children was less likely to run away or cause other kinds
of "trouble" than was an unattached slave.

Most slaves were allowed to choose their own mates.
Slaves who lived on small farms usually chose mates
from nearby farms. Slaves on larger establishments often
chose mates from their own plantations. In some cases
slave owners made the decision. The more humane owners respected slave marriages and were willing to sell or
buy a slave in order to bring together a man and woman
who wished to marry.

Some slaves preferred to marry outside their plantations. Women who did not live on the same farm as their
husbands were called "broadwives." The man of the couple was generally given a pass to visit his wife on Wednes-
day and Saturday nights and all day Sunday.

Men with "broadwives" exposed themselves to the slave

patrols. The patrollers, called "patterollers" by the slaves, were poor whites pressed into duty in rural areas to see that no slaves traveled about at night without the proper credentials. Though the patrollers were notorious for their brutality, male slaves often preferred to take their chances with the patrols in order to marry the woman of their choice and gain the freedom of movement that went with having a "broadwife."

Marriage ceremonies for slaves presented a problem for whites. Since throughout the South slave owners had the power to sell slave husbands and wives away from one another, the official wedding service could never be read because no slave could be married "until death do us part." One slave preacher's solution was to declare those he wed married until "Death or Buckra part you"— "Buckra" being the slave term for white planter.[7]

When marriages did not work out, they were dissolved, often with permission from the white owner. In such cases it was considered acceptable to marry again. Sometimes masters solved the problem of a bad slave marriage by selling one of the partners. As long as the marriage was not a good one in the eyes of the couple, the sale was accepted, and the remaining slave chose another mate.

Slaves took their marriage vows seriously. The vast majority of blacks were monogamous, and adultery was considered a major offense. Even in the face of attacks on black women by white men, which black men were powerless to prevent, blacks sustained their marriages. Genovese believes that the white male perception of the strength of the marital bond between Blacks probably acted as a deterrent to rape, at least in some instances. Though this thesis is impossible to prove, we do know that black husbands often attempted to protect their wives in any way possible. Many offered to take beatings in place of their wives.

Many children who grew up in slavery remembered the loving relationship between their parents. A former slave whose father was a driver on a neighboring plantation belonging to a sadistic white and run by a sadistic black, recalled how her mother used to care for her father.

So often he came home all bloody from beatings his old nigger overseer would give him. My mother would take those bloody clothes off of him, bathe de sore places and grease them good and wash and iron his clothes so he could go back clean.[8]

The following is a tale of lifelong love recited by a ninety-year-old former slave, remembering her many years with her husband.

We lived together fifty-five years and we always loved each other. He ain't never whip nor cuss me and though we had our fusses and our troubles we trusted in de Lord and we got through. I loved him durin' life and I love him now, though he's been dead for twelve years. We had eight chillens, but only four of dem are livin'. [She lists the children one of whom was named after Florence Nightingale.]

I can't be here so much longer now cause I'se getting too old and feeble and I want to go to Jim anyhow. I thinks of him all de time, but seems like we're young again when I smell honeysuckles or see a yellow moon.[9]

As a general rule women were allowed between four and six weeks of rest after delivery. During this time they cared for their infants and did no field work. Slave mothers almost always nursed their own infants. On some plantations women were considered half-hands so long as they continued to nurse small children. As such they did half the work expected of other adult slaves. Elsewhere new mothers returned to the fields for a full day after their few weeks of rest. Babies were carried out to them for feeding at midday and perhaps in the early evening. With their parents most often at work in the fields, slave children became communal property to be mothered and fathered by anyone who happened to be near.

In some cases small children remained at home in the care of a grandmother. But most often infants and toddlers spent the day in a children's house, where an elderly slave was in charge. She was helped by slightly older children who actually did most of the baby tending. The children's houses were not remembered with affection. One former slave recalled sleeping in the one-room house as well as spending his days there. The house was so crowded, he said, that "you couldn't stir us with a stick."

My mammie was named Jennie and I don't think I had any brothers or sisters, but they was a whole lot of children at the quarters that I played with and lived with. I didn't live with Mammy because she worked all the time, and us children stayed in one house.

This same slave recalled that all the children ate out of the same dish. "When we eat we had a big pan and all ate out of it. One what ate the faster got the most." He also reported that until they were twelve years old girl and boy slaves wore the same clothing—a long shirt with nothing on underneath.[10] Feeding slave children out of a common pot as though they were animals and ignoring their desire for modesty were common practices throughout the South. This treatment was part of the attempt to condition slave children to view themselves as less human than whites and perhaps not human at all.

The relationship between white and black children was a complex one. Often they played together, and many slave children did not realize how different from their white playmates they were until the latter went off to school—something the blacks were forbidden to do. White children often attempted to subvert this arrangement by teaching their black friends how to read and write.

Affection between black and white children or white adult and black child, no matter how sincere, served the interest of whites. Kind feelings for the white family would further tie blacks to their slavery and increase their dependence on whites. In some cases it drove a wedge into the relationship between slave child and parent. Young slaves realized early that their own parents lacked the resources to shower them with the gifts, sweets, and indulgences which whites could afford to hand out freely.

The affection of slave children for slave owners was a very bitter pill for slave parents to swallow. The depths of this feeling can be seen in the recollection of a former slave who was taken at a young age to live with her mistress. The slave girl's mother had cried when her child was taken from her, but Sarah, the child, preferred the good food and comforts that went along with living with whites. After the Civil War Sarah's mother came to claim her daughter. As an old woman Sarah recalled what happened next.

I didn't want to go; I wanted to stay with Mis Polly. I begun to cry and Mammy caught hold of me. I grabbed

Mis' Polly and held so tight dat I tore her skirt bindin'
loose and her skirt fell down about her feets.

"Let her stay with me," Mis' Polly said to Mammy. But
Mammy shook her head. *"You took her away from me
and didn't pay no mind to my cryin', so now I'se takin'
her home. We'se free now, Mis' Polly, we ain't gwine be
slave no more to nobody."*[11]

Though an uncommon occurrence (it was mostly teenagers who were sold), one of the most heartrending
aspects of slavery was the sale of small children away
from their mothers. Such sales took place throughout
the South, but particularly in Virginia and other areas
undergoing economic decline after the 1830s. Young
slaves were expensive to support, and while they brought
a far higher price on the market when full-grown, many
slave owners simply could not afford to keep them.

One of the most trenchant comments on this subject
came from Delia Garlic, a former slave born in Virginia.
Twelve of her thirteen brothers and sisters were sold
"down river" to the cotton belt before Delia was born.
Eventually she and her mother were separated and sold.

Slavery days was hell. I was growed up when de War
come, and I was a mother before it closed. Babies snatched
from deir mother's breast and sold to speculators. Chillens
was separated from sisters and brothers and never saw
each other again. 'Course dey cry. You think they not cry
when dey was sold like cattle? I could tell you about it
all day, but even den you couldn't guess the awfulness of
it.[12]

The speculators referred to by Delia Garlic were
slave traders (soul drivers, the slaves called them) who
bought groups of slaves and transported them down river
for sale. The speculators were universally feared by
blacks, who would try to hide their children if they had
been alerted in advance that one was to appear. Usually
the slaves had no warning. When they returned to their
cabins after a day's work, they simply found one of their
children missing. The speculator had come and gone.

Mothers who lost their children often suffered intolerable grief. One slave woman purchased away from her
husband and child by a speculator threw herself over the

side of the ship taking her to Natchez for sale and was drowned. A former slave who eventually escaped to the North recalled meeting a woman whose seven children had all just been sold on the auction block. "I met that mother in the street and her wild haggard face lives today in my mind. She wrung her hands in anguish and exclaimed, 'Gone! All gone! Why don't God kill me?' "[13] It was God alone, however—or more specifically, faith in Jesus' promise of a better life to come—which often comforted these women and helped them endure their suffering.

The very whites who controlled the system accused black women of lacking maternal feeling. Anthropologist Sidney Mintz, commenting on this aspect of slavery, notes, "Surely it must be one of history's deftest ironies that oppressors have always sought to rationalize their oppression by *blaming the oppressed* for the state to which it has reduced them."[14] It was much easier for whites to believe that black women had little love for their children than to admit to themselves that they were guilty of the inhumane act of tearing those children from the arms of their mothers and fathers.

The following story, told by a proslavery Southerner, is interesting because it belies many of the white South's own shibboleths concerning blacks. The author was clearly a racist, as some of his descriptive details reveal; yet he understood the depth of family feeling common to slaves. The incident he described took place on the auction block where a crippled man, his wife, and his children were about to be sold away from each other. Israel, the male slave, spoke to the crowd of whites about to place their bids.

> "Yes, sir, I kin do as much ez ennybody; and marsters, ef you'll only buy me and de chillum with Martha Ann, Gord knows I'll wuk myself to deth for you." The poor little darkeys, Cephas and Melinda, sat there frightened and silent, their white eyes dancing like monkey-eyes, and gleaming in the shadows. As her husband's voice broke on her ear, Martha Ann, who had been looking sadly out of the window in a pose of quiet dignity, turned her face with an expression of exquisite love and gratitude towards Israel. She gazed for a moment at her husband and at her children, and then looked away once more, her eyes brimming with tears.[15]

Israel, Martha Ann, and their children were in fact bought by one master; had the story not had a "happy ending," it probably would never have been told, for when it came to slavery most southern whites, particularly the men, had selective memories.

No aspect of slavery was as destructive to blacks as the sexual attack on black women. The threat of sexual abuse, which usually began when female slaves entered puberty, continued all their lives. Not all whites condoned or encouraged this situation. One South Carolina planter advertised for an overseer who was "capable, sober and not passionate."[16] Condoned or not, however, sexual abuse existed, and few planters objected publicly. To oppose the rape of black women in effect meant opposing slavery. The sexual abuse of female slaves was the result of a system that made white men the owners of black women and then placed them in intimate contact with each other.

When a slave woman was sold, she might be told to open her mouth so a prospective buyer could look at her teeth. She might just as easily be told to drop her dress so her body could be inspected. If she was eighteen or nineteen and had not borne a child, she could be taken into a room where her sexual organs were examined to guarantee she was without defect. She had no right to refuse any of this treatment. Her body was not considered her own. Control over her body was passed from white person to white person, along with a bill of sale.

The system in the South robbed black women of the most primary sexual right—choice. It also left them almost totally without protection. The law was the law of white males, and it did not even recognize the idea of rape against black females. Rape is a violation of a woman's will, and the slave laws did not permit a black woman to have a will of her own.

Because black women did not have any right of refusal, it is possible to say that all sexual contact between black women and white men in the South was a form of rape. Even if individual white men did not force individual black women, coercion was built into the system. Often black women acquiesced to the desires of white men because they understood the realities of power in the situation and were attempting to win a protector for themselves and their children.

This was true of the relationship between a quadroon slave named Cynthia and a slave trader named Walker. Her story was told by a slave belonging to Walker who later escaped to the North. Walker purchased Cynthia in St. Louis along with a load of other slaves, and he took them all down the Mississippi for sale in Natchez. He prepared a room for Cynthia and went to her at night, telling her that if she would become his mistress he would set her up as the housekeeper on his farm in St. Louis. Otherwise he threatened to "sell her as a field hand on the worst plantation on the river." Eventually Cynthia agreed to his proposition. She went to live on the farm and bore Walker four children. The escaped slave who narrated her story received information about her ultimate fate. "I have been credibly informed," he wrote, "that Walker has been married, and, as a previous measure, sold poor Cynthia and her four children into hopeless bondage."[17]

Even better-intentioned men than Walker were often unable to do much to protect their slave mistresses. The former slave Archibald Grimké recorded the story of his mother, Nancy Weston. Nancy was taken as the mistress of a white widower, a lawyer named Henry Grimké who in fact was a moderate opponent of slavery. She had two children by him, and a third was on the way when Grimké died. In his will Grimké wrote, "I leave Nancy and her two children to be treated as members of the family." Henry Grimké's white son threw Nancy out, leaving her to support herself and her children. Later, when the son married, he decided he needed Nancy's children as servants and seized them back into slavery.[18]

A former slave, who took the name of Linda Brent when she wrote her memoirs, lived with a master who did not actually beat her. Instead, he hounded her psychologically with constant threats of violence and obscene accusations from the time she was sixteen. Linda wrote about his inexorable assault.

> My master met me at every turn, reminding me that I belonged to him and swearing by heaven and earth that I would submit to him. If I went out for a breath of fresh air, after a day of unwearied toil, his footsteps dogged me. If I knelt before my mother's grave, his dark shadow fell on me there.[19]

Brent continued to refuse her master for a dozen years, during all of which time he continued to torment her. In her mid-twenties Brent attempted to run away. Her passage was booked on a boat, but the attempt to escape failed. Instead, for seven years Linda Brent lived secretly in a hole in the ground under a shed in her grandmother's back yard, occasionally coming out at night. After seven years of being buried alive, she carried out a successful escape. When she arrived in the North, she became an active abolitionist.

Brent noted that the sexual attack on black women by white men corrupted white women as well as their men. Her metaphor for the sexually perverse environment fostered by slavery was peculiarly apt. "I lived," she wrote, in a "cage of obscene birds."[20] Brent recorded the story of the daughter of a brutal white who took a slave lover and bore him a child. Her act was one of retaliation against her father. Brent commented that the daughter chose as her lover the cruelest and most degraded slave on the plantation. Her goal appears to have been to dishonor her father in the same manner that white women were dishonored by their fathers and husbands. Similar stories are scattered through slave literature.

More typical was the attack of white women against black women and their children. Brent documents this process as well.

> Southern women often marry a man knowing that he is the father of many little slaves. They do not trouble themselves about it. They regard such children as property, as marketable as the pigs on the plantation; and it is seldom that they do not make them aware of this by passing them into slavetrader's hands as soon as possible and thus getting them out of their sight.[21]

Some white women were as sadistic as the worst white men. One slave mistress forced a slave girl to walk across a bed of hot coals; another beat a nine-month-old slave baby to death.

Often the violence of white women was triggered by the sexual triangle of slavery. A white woman who knew of or suspected a sexual relationship between her husband and a slave woman often chose to attack the black

woman rather than her husband. This was true in the
case of Patsey, whose story was told in detail by a former
slave and edited by Gerda Lerner.

> Patsey was slim and straight. . . . There was an air of lofti-
> ness in her movement, that neither labor, nor weariness,
> nor punishment could destroy. . . . She was a skilled team-
> ster. She could turn a farrow as the best, and at splitting
> rails there was none that could excell her. . . . Such light-
> ning like motion was in her fingers . . . that in cotton
> picking time, Patsey was queen of the field.
>   Her back bore the scars of a thousand stripes . . . be-
> cause it had fallen her lot to be the slave of a licentious
> master and a jealous mistress. . . . In the Great House,
> for days together, there were high and angry words . . .
> whereoff she was the innocent cause. Nothing delighted
> the mistress so much as to see her suffer . . . Patsey walked
> under a cloud. If she uttered a word in opposition to her
> master's will, the lash was resorted to at once, to bring
> her to subjection; if she was not watchful, while about her
> cabin, or when walking in the yard, a billet of wood, or a
> broken bottle, perhaps, hurled from her mistress' hand
> would smite her unexpectedly. . . . Patsey had no comfort
> of her life. . . .
>   To be rid of Patsey—to place her beyond sight or reach,
> by sale or death, or in any other manner, of late years,
> seemed to be the ruling thought and passion of my mis-
> tress.[22]

In 1920 the black historian, poet, and civil-rights activist W. E. B. DuBois wrote of his feelings concerning
the white South and its treatment of blacks. Much in
the South, including slavery itself, DuBois could find it in
his heart to forgive. "But one thing I shall never forgive,"
he wrote, "neither in this world nor the world to come:
its wanton and continued and persistent insulting of the
black womanhood which it sought and seeks to prostitute
in its lust."[23]

Southern white men abused black women and then
proclaimed that black women were wanton, immoral, and
sexually degraded. This racist view permeated northern
as well as southern minds; perhaps most damaging, it
sometimes distorted black women's perception of themselves. The abuse of black women was also destructive of
the relationship between black men and black women.

Black slave women could not depend on the protection of their men as women have usually been able to do. Slavery deprived black men of the sense of dignity and self-worth which traditionally has gone along with a man's ability to protect his wife, daughters, and sisters from attack. Slave men who went to the defense of their women, as some did, often faced death at the hands of whites. White men controlled the system; there was no question of a "fair fight" between white assailants and black protectors. Not surprisingly, many slave men did not interfere.

RESISTANCE

In every aspect of their lives—in work, with each other, in relation to their children—slaves never accepted their status as property. They strove to sustain their sense of self-worth and self-expression. This day-to-day struggle was perhaps the most profound aspect of slave resistance.[24]

Slaves also practiced overt forms of resistance. Though they had little opportunity to engage in organized acts of mass resistance or armed insurrection—though such did occur—they did find many other ways to overtly challenge white control over their lives.

Slaves understood very well that their labor enriched their owners. They often defied masters and the slave system by not working. Female slaves feigned pregnancy; all slaves feigned illness, and some feigned chronic disabilities. Numerous reports in slave literature tell of slaves, allegedly too old or lame to do heavy work, who after the Civil War obtained their own farms on which they labored vigorously for many years.

Slaves also participated in deliberate slow-downs. If they worked as fast as they were able, slaves realized, they would constantly be driven at that pace; instead, they chose a slower one. Slave owners fretted constantly about this costly form of resistance, but they were virtually powerless before it. One southern doctor, so taken in by the slaves' slow way of moving, theorized that they were all stricken by a disease which, he said, prevented them from moving more quickly.

When they were driven at a pace they considered unreasonable, slaves often walked off the job. Individual slaves ran away for weeks at a time, hiding in nearby swamps or woods. Eventually the missing slave would contact the master, usually through an intermediary, and negotiate the terms of his or her return. In this way slaves were able up to a point to set their own work conditions and to some extent avoid punishment. Sometimes whole groups of slaves would take to the swamp together and refuse to return until a less brutal overseer was hired. In such cases slave owners usually agreed; overseers were expendable, compared to a valuable slave work force.

Slaves destroyed vast amounts of white-owned property through arson and sabotage. Fanny Kemble remarked that slaves on her husband's plantations often "forgot" to put out the fires they set to cook their lunches and consequently burned down large portions of woods. One critic, discussing slave work habits, noted that "they break, waste and destroy everything they handle—abuse horses and cattle—tear, burn or rend their own clothing, and steal others to replace what they have destroyed. . . . They slight their work—cut up corn, cotton and tobacco, when hoeing it . . . and seem to be insensible to pain when subjected to punishment."[25]

Such blatant destruction of property was not accidental. As a rule slaves were far more astute psychologically than their masters. In unhappy situations they used their insights about the make-up of whites to harass their masters and diminish their profits while themselves suffering as little punishment as possible.

When pressed by particularly brutal whites, slaves sometimes responded with violence. In one remarkable instance a ten-year-old slave girl threw a large rock at a white woman who had beaten her small sister to death. The white woman was blinded in one eye. The slave girl's mistress reacted to the blinding of her own mother by saying, "I guess Mama has learned her lesson."[26]

Some slaves seem to have had a gift for resistance. These independent spirits defied the system whether they were themselves actively brutalized or not. A former slave woman with the deceivingly gentle name of Delicia Patterson was this kind of servant. Patterson does not seem to have minded taking a beating so long as she got her licks in first.

I got whipped only once in the whole fifteen years I was there, and that was because I was working in the garden with one of my owners daughters and I pulled up something that she did not want pulled up, so she up and slapped me for it. I got so mad at her. I taken up a hoe and run her all the way in the Big House, and of course I got whipped for that.[37]

When she was about to be sold, Delicia Patterson's behavior was even more extraordinary.

When I was fifteen years old, I was brought to the courthouse, put on the auction block to be sold. Old Judge Miller from my county was there. I knew him well because he was one of the wealthiest slave owners in the county, and the meanest one. He was so cruel all the slaves and many owners hated him because of it. He saw me on the block for sale, and he knew I was a good worker. So, when he bid for me, I spoke right up on the auction block and told him: "Old Judge Miller don't you bid for me, 'cause if you do I would not live on your plantation. I will take a knife and cut my throat from ear to ear before I would be owned by you." So he stepped back and let somebody else bid for me.[38]

Patterson was sold for a high price to an Englishman named Steele and his southern wife. When Mrs. Steele encouraged her husband to mildly rebuke Delicia, the slave ran away for two weeks and refused to return until her owner promised she would never be bothered again. After the war she worked for the Steeles for wages until she heard Mrs. Steele refer to her as "our nigger." Then Patterson quit.

Patterson's threat to slit her own throat was not the sort of remark slaveholders took lightly. Slaves who mutilated or killed themselves took a kind of horrible revenge on their masters; damaged slaves were worth little money, and dead slaves none at all.

In extreme situations slaves actually committed suicide rather than continue to live in bondage. This course was especially common among slaves newly imported from Africa. Women driven to these extraordinary measures sometimes also killed their children. One slave woman was said to have murdered all thirteen of her infants rather than see them grow up to be slaves. Another woman, whose escape attempt failed, murdered one of her children, then tried to kill herself and her remaining child.

In general slaves were more likely to escape, or attempt to escape, than to take their own lives. Slaves ran to freedom through the woods in the dead of night; they swam to freedom when they had no boats; light-skinned slaves passed themselves off as whites and rode horses to freedom. They did without food and traveled on foot. They invented every imaginable kind of ruse. They used their intelligence and cunning, and then they relied on faith.

The woman who was the guiding light to all slaves who dreamed of freedom in the years before the Civil War came to be known as Moses. Like the biblical Moses, Harriet Tubman heard her people cry out in bondage, and she led them to freedom. Between 1850 and 1860 she "stole" some three hundred slaves from the South, including babies drugged with paregoric to keep them quiet, and led them to new lives in New York and Canada. She made nineteen separate trips South and back to the North. Slave owners offered a $40,000 reward to anyone who could take the woman called Moses dead or alive. But she was never captured, nor were any of the people she piloted.

Tubman was born in Maryland around 1820 and lived to be ninety-three years old. Both her parents were slaves, as were her ten or eleven brothers and sisters; eventually she was able to rescue most of her family, including her elderly parents. Tubman's owner was both cruel and impecunious. When she was thirteen years old, he struck her with a heavy weight in what was called "an ungovernable fit of rage," inflicting what must have been a very serious skull fracture. Throughout her life she suffered from periodic blackouts, which resembled a deep sleep. This ailment did not interfere with her work of freeing slaves or acting as nurse, scout, spy, and military officer during the Civil War, when she was known as General Tubman.

Her life in slavery was one of constant misery; she was hired out to the most brutal whites. It was the expectation of being sold away from her family into the deep South that triggered her decision to flee. She made her first trip North alone, and when she arrived in "Canaan," she felt a great loneliness. She described what happened next.

So it was wid me, I had crossed de line of which I had so long been dreaming. I was free; but dere was no one to welcome me to de land of freedom, I was a stranger in a strange land, and my home after all was down in de old cabin quarter, wid de ole folks, and my brudders and sisters. But to dis solemn resolution I came: I was free, and dey should be free also; I would make a home for dem in de North, and de Lord helping me, I would bring dem all dere.[29]

During her many trips South and North ferrying slaves, Tubman was helped in two ways—by the institution known as the underground railroad and by her deep, very personal faith in God. The underground railroad was a loose, secret network of free blacks and whites in the border states and in the North who helped runaway slaves in disregard of the laws of the South and the federal fugitive slave act passed in 1850. Members of the underground railroad, many of whom were Quakers, fed and hid fugitives and provided them with horses, wagons, and stratagems of escape.

There is no doubt that Tubman's religious faith was the spark that made her brave actions possible. She saw herself as a vehicle through which her redeemer was assisting her people. Because she never doubted, she was able to act quickly and to follow her instincts. Her remarkable faith did not lesson her pragmatism. On one occasion, when a male slave in one of her parties grew weary of the hundreds of miles covered on foot and wanted to turn back, Harriet pulled out the pistol she always carried and turned to him, saying, "Dead niggers tell no tales; you go on or die."[30]

On another trip she discovered that pursuers were on her trail. She sent her charges North while she boarded a train going South. She figured, accurately, that those following her would never imagine that she would go deeper into slave territory. On another occasion she made a foray into the very town where a former master lived. Before walking the streets, she purchased two chickens. She hunched herself over like an old woman, a sunbonnet covering her face. When she turned a corner and spotted the white man, she yanked at the string holding the chickens. As the birds began to scream and flutter, she bent down to quiet them. Her former master passed by, brushing the skirts of the woman with a $40,000 bounty on her head. He never noticed her.

Tubman was always guided by a principle. It is a testament not only to slaves hungering to escape bondage, but to all people who have sought to end their enslavement.

> I had reasoned dis out in my mind; there was one of two things I had a right to, liberty or death. If I co'l' 've one, I would have de oder; for no man should take me alive. I should fight for my liberty as long as my strength lasted, and when de time came for me to go, de Lord would let dem take me.[31]

White Pedestal

The white upper-class woman married to wealthy plantation owners in the South played an important role in the slave system. The mistresses supervised the details of slaves' lives and often provided them with whatever comforts were allowed. Plantation mistresses frequently nursed their slaves, made their clothes, adjudicated disputes, taught religion, and trained young slaves to be house servants. In addition, white women usually supervised the work of slaves in the kitchen, barnyard, smokehouse, and creamery.

Plantation mistresses often worked very hard. One South Carolina woman married to a wealthy planter kept a diary recording her daily activities.

> A plantation life is a very active one. This morning I got up late having been disturbed in the night, hurried down to have something arranged for breakfast, Ham and Eggs . . . wrote a letter to Charles . . . had prayers, got the boys off to town. Had work to cut out, gave orders about dinner, had the horse feed fixed in hot water, had the box filled with cork; went to see about the carpenters working at the Negro houses . . . and now I have cut out the flannel jackets.[32]

Implicit in the slave system was the idea of the master as patriarch, the stern father of his family. The plantation mistress was expected to temper her husband's "justice" with mercy. Some white women experienced their responsibilities as a burden. One wrote, "It is the slaves who own me. Morning, noon, and night, I'm obliged to look after them, to doctor them, and attend to them in every way."[33]

For white women as well as black, the most destructive aspect of slavery stemmed from the sexual exploitation of female slaves by white men. In such sophisticated cities as Charleston and Natchez the sexual connection between black women and white men occurred far more frequently than in most rural areas. But wherever a white wife knew or sensed that her husband had sexual contact with black women, she was likely to feel humiliated. Often the white wife lived in close proximity to her husband's mistress and the mulatto half sisters and brothers of her own children.

Mary Boykin Chestnut, an astute upper-class woman from Charleston, South Carolina, married to a United States senator who later became a leader of the Confederacy, wrote angrily about the sexual promiscuity of white men.

> Like the patriarchs of old, our men live all in one house with their wives and their concubines; and the mulattoes one sees in every family partly resemble the white children. Any lady is ready to tell you who is the father of the mulatto children in everybody's household but her own. Those, she seems to think, drop from clouds. My disgust is sometimes boiling over. Thank God for my country women, alas for the men.[34]

Mrs. Chestnut was a fervid supporter of the Confederacy; yet she prayed that the end of the Civil War would mean the end of slavery. Southern women, she wrote, hate slavery worse than Harriet Beecher Stowe (author of *Uncle Tom's Cabin*). Another plantation wife wrote, "I saw slavery in its bearing on my sex. . . . I saw that it teemed with injustice and shame to all womankind and I hated it."[35]

Particularly galling to Chestnut and others was the silence demanded of women. Men might ignore their marriage vows and trample on Christian morality; but women were not allowed to criticize them for their behavior. "The ostrich game," Chestnut wrote, "is thought a Christian act."[36]

Underlying the moral outrage of white women was a profound sense of rejection. It was not easy for the mistress of a plantation to live surrounded by mulatto children and believe that her husband preferred their black mother to herself. While some white women responded to this unpleasant situation with anger and violence, expressed not toward their men, but toward black women, a few white women developed at least a partial sense of solidarity with slave women. As Mrs. Chestnut mused, it was not only slave women who were sold at auction. "You know," she wrote, "how women sell themselves and are sold in marriage from Queens downward, eh? You know what the Bible says about slavery and marriage. Poor women, poor slaves."[37]

Why did upper-class southern white women ignore the infidelities of their husbands? Many historians feel that they were bought off. W. J. Cash, author of *The Mind of the South,* suggests that in exchange for their silence, upper-class southern women were compensated with chivalrous veneration which not only satisfied the women's need to feel valued, but also assuaged men's guilt about their promiscuity. Wrote Cash, "The revolting suspicion in the male that he might be slipping into bestiality was got rid of by glorifying her."[38]

The women's silence, of course, allowed men to pretend that their sexual alliances with slave women did not exist. The more guilt white men felt at impregnating black women and seeing their own daughters and sons born into slavery, the more they praised the upper-class white women and proclaimed them the most morally superior females ever to walk the earth. As Cash has written, "the upshot . . . was downright gyneolatry,"—that is, the worship of upper-class white women.

She was the South's Palladium, this Southern woman—the shield-bearing Athena gleaming whitely in the clouds, the standard for its rallying, the mystic symbol of its nationality in face of the foe. . . . Merely to mention her was to send men into tears—or shouts. There was hardly a sermon that did not begin with tributes to her honor, hardly a brave speech that did not open and close with the clashing of shields and the flourishing of swords for her glory. At the last . . . the ranks of the confederacy went rolling into battle in the misty conviction that it was wholly for her that they fought. Woman!!!![39]

This attitude was pure myth. Most southern white women were not plantation women and did not own slaves. They were members of the poor white rural and urban class. The pedestal of white womanhood was reserved for a small minority of white plantation wives and daughters. But the legend served its purpose as a rallying point, and long after slavery was abolished, the myth was sustained in the minds of southern whites.

5

The Making of a Middle-Class Lady

Following the Revolutionary War and in the first decades of the 1800s a new middle class emerged in the Northeast. While the majority of Americans continued to live on farms, members of this middle class lived in towns and cities and derived their wealth from commerce.

Commercial development had been fostered by a small group of men who controlled the nation's shipping and importing businesses. Their ships carried overseas such agricultural products as cotton and wheat and returned with English and French manufactured goods. In time shippers and importers invested the money they earned through trade in America's first factories.

The business of business took middle-class men away from their homes, leaving women alone in them. Women of the middle class were isolated from the world of men and commerce.[1]

Family membership had always been women's most important affiliation. In the past it had been an affiliation women shared with men. On colonial farms, where the labor of both sexes was equally necessary, men and women were partners. The significance of the family as a primary economic unit was maintained throughout the 1800s for the majority of Americans who continued to live on farms. Among the emerging middle class, however, such was not the case.

Among the new middle class, home and family came to be seen as separate from the world of work and money. Women were affected by this change in very significant ways. In their homes, middle-class women continued to perform their traditional work—to cook and clean, make clothing and other household goods, care for children. What they did, however, was no longer considered "real work," because, unlike men, they earned no money thereby.

Cut off from the money economy, a woman might labor all day, producing all sorts of goods and services vital to the well-being of her family, and yet in the eyes of the world she did not work. For the first time in America a class of women emerged who were seen as being "supported" by their husbands. No longer partners, they had become dependents.

Industrialization further devalued women's work. With industrialization the factory gradually replaced the home as the major producer of goods to be consumed by the family. The development of an industrial economy capable of generating enormous wealth did not emerge fully until after the Civil War. As the factory system grew, however, women who lived in towns and cities came to be dependent on their husbands' earnings to buy factory-made goods.

The devaluation of women's work in the home went hand in hand with a closing off of other economic opportunities. Women who left the home and sought work outside were limited in the ways they could earn money. Many of the trades women had practiced in colonial times now required formal training, from which women were excluded. Only a few kinds of low-paid work were available to women: domestic service, teaching, sewing, factory operative.

Taking much of its economic importance from the middle-class home did not diminish the significance of home and family in the minds of nineteenth-century Americans. In fact, ideas about home and the women and children who resided there, safe from the "cruelties of the marketplace," came to assume new levels of emotional importance.

Home and family became the emotional receptacle for all the sentimental values and feelings middle-class men increasingly felt inhibited from exhibiting. In symbolic terms a wife came to be seen as her husband's "better half"; she embodied the purity, spirituality, and goodness which his life in business lacked. Men struggling in the world of commerce felt cut off from the tender side of their own natures. They tried to regain this aspect of themselves through women.

While few people living at that time saw the connection between the new sexual definitions and economic practices, many perceived the changing relationship between the sexes. Male and female authors wrote at length on what they called "man's sphere" and "woman's sphere."

An entire theory of human personality evolved, based on the belief that men and women were polar opposites, two separate branches of humankind with opposing characteristics. The idea that men and women were very different— that women, for example, were dependent and soft while men were independent and tough—had existed in the 1700s also. But in that epoch ideas about the qualities that men and women *shared* had been balanced against the perceived differences. In the 1800s the attributes shared by both sexes were more or less forgotten. Qualities of mind and character were seen as applying to one sex or the other—almost never to both.

In the 1700s it was possible to think of a woman as strong, brave, daring, hardy, adventurous. By the mid-1800s these qualities were thought to apply only to men. (An exception to this generalization occurred in the West, where definitions concerning the sexes were more fluid. See chapter 11, "The Maverick West.") Women who were obviously strong or brave were seen as deviant and maladjusted to their "natural sphere."

The concern with man's sphere and woman's sphere can be seen in the writing of the well-known Southern intellectual Thomas Dew.[2] He described the hardships faced by men in the marketplace and the almost brutal strength needed to survive in such a competitive atmosphere.

> He leaves the domestic scenes; he plunges into the turmoil and bustle of an active, selfish world; in his journey through life, he has to encounter innumerable difficulties, hardships and labors which constantly beset him. His mind must be nerved against them. Hence courage and boldness are his attributes.[3]

Dew described woman's sphere in terms strikingly different from those he used for that of men.

> Her attributes are rather of a passive than active character. Her power is more emblematic of divinity. . . . Woman we behold dependent and weak . . . but out of that very weakness and dependence springs an irresistible power.[4]

In literature geared for women no topic was discussed more exhaustively than woman's sphere and the attributes of a true woman. Sarah Hale, the publisher of the influential magazine *Godey's Lady's Book,* for decades made her living by offering month after month a dissection of the inner workings of a woman's world. Mrs. Hale had very definite ideas about woman's place and characteristics. A true woman, she wrote, was "delicate and timid"; "required protection"; "possessed a sweet dependency"; "was above all things modest"; and had "charming and insinuating manners."[5] Hale counseled women to devote themselves to their housekeeping as if it were a fine art. Women with servants, she advised, should be just as busy supervising domestic operations as women without such help.

Women's responsibility to adhere without question to their sphere was often seen as a moral issue. This attitude can be seen in the writing of Mrs. A. J. Graves. Of women Mrs. Graves wrote, "That *home* is her appropriate and appointed sphere of action there cannot be a shadow of doubt; for the dictates of nature are plain and imperative on this subject, and the injunctions given in Scripture no less explicit."[6]

In exchange for women's sacrifice of worldly interests, the sphere theory bestowed upon them an inflated regard approaching reverence. As Professor Dew wrote, "Her power is emblematical of divinity." Implicit in the sphere theory was a kind of bargain—so long as a woman acted the part of piety, purity, submission, and domesticity,[7] she was guaranteed the respect of her society. The bargain, however, contained a threat. If she stepped out of her sphere and sought a place for herself in the world, she was despised as an "unsexed" woman.

Nineteenth-century Americans referred to women who observed the proprieties demanded by woman's sphere as "ladies." In the 1800s this term applied to middle-class women whose husbands "supported" them, but it did not necessarily mean they were rich. In this sense the definition differed from usage in Europe, where a lady was an upper-class or aristocratic woman, and even from the eighteenth-century American use of the term, which also referred more to wealth and family standing than to behavior.

To some extent nineteenth-century Americans democratized the concept of the lady. To be a lady was no longer a social position to which a woman was born. Instead, women *became* ladies by staying at home, by behaving in what was considered a proper way, by devoting themselves to their husband and children, and by developing "feminine" traits.

Harriet Beecher Stowe, author of the famous anti-slavery novel, *Uncle Tom's Cabin,* was one of the growing class of nineteenth-century middle-class American ladies. In an essay called "The Lady Who Does Her Own Work," Mrs. Stowe noted that in no other country in the world could a woman without much money, forced to do her own housework, be considered a lady. While Mrs. Stowe thought it a very fine thing that middle-class women in America were honored as ladies, she also understood that the role was often a burden. To be always good and kind and gentle and concerned for others sometimes felt, in her words, "like a daily death."[8] Further, a certain style was expected of middle-class ladies; they did not have to be rich, but they were not supposed to look poor or overworked. For the lady who did her own work, this requirement sometimes created problems, as Mrs. Stowe, whose husband had no great gift for earning money, well understood.

> But when we have company! There's the rub! To get out all our best things and put them back, to cook all the meals and wash the dishes ingloriously—and make it all appear as if we didn't do it, and had servants like other people.[9]

To be a lady was largely a matter of economic class. Those women whose husbands did not support them were for the most part denied the status of ladies. Immigrant women, poor farm women, black women, and poor native-born women who worked in factories were never "ladies" in the nineteenth century.

WOMEN WITH MEN

The separation of the sexes into distinct spheres altered the relationship between men and women. By midcentury even quite young girls and boys did not spend a great deal of time together. Because men and women spent most of their time with persons of their own sex, they had little opportunity to learn about each other. Those occasions when the sexes did intermingle were often marked by a formality which all but precluded spontaneity, ease, and a sense of intimacy. Nineteenth-century patterns of court-ship added to the distance between men and women.

As noted, in the 1700s courting couples spent great amounts of time together, often in informal pursuits. The young John Adams, for example, visited the equally young Abigail Smith over a period of several years before they decided to wed. They were allowed the privilege of long walks and long talks on many subjects, alone as of-ten as with friends. Between visits they engaged in a very free correspondence, even before they became engaged.

Such liberties were not available to middle-class young people after 1840 or 1850. Instead they were given end-less amounts of advice concerning the proper way to be-have when in each other's company. Young women were warned not to get too close to young men. "Sit not with another in a place that is too narrow," wrote Mrs. Eliza Farrar. "Read not out of the same book, nor let your eagerness to see anything induce you to place your head close to another person's."[10]

Dr. William Alcott, who noted with great relief that the free courtship manners of earlier times had passed out of fashion, warned young people against dozens of dangers. Among them "conversation which is too excit-ing"; "the presence of exciting books"; "unnecessary heat"; "impure air"; "exciting drinks" (by that he meant tea or coffee); and "rich delicacies." "Any of these," wrote the doctor, "are made much worse, in their effect, by being taken at unseasonable hours."[11] He considered any time after 9 P.M. "unseasonable." Dr. Alcott also warned against the dangers of dancing, attending large parties, and keeping company unchaperoned.

By the time Dr. Alcott's *The Physiology of Marriage* was published in 1856, many of the practices he deplored were going out of fashion. The chaperone became insti-tutionalized in middle-class American social life in the 1850s. Courting couples, often even engaged couples, were not left alone for a moment. The rigid new manners regarding courtship led to what Dr. Alcott considered a most desirable end. "Fornication I do not believe to be as common now as 100 years ago," he wrote, and added, "at least not in New England."[12] While it is impossible to prove the correctness of Dr. Alcott's claim, it is very probable that at least among couples from the middle and upper classes, there was less premarital sex in 1856 than there had been in 1756, if for no other reason than lack of opportunity.

The clothing women wore emphasized the rigid restraints they were expected to exercise in the company of men. Nothing could have been more inhibiting than the corsets which came into fashion during the first decades of the 1800s and remained in fashion until the 1920s. These garments were made of silk or cotton and ribbed with several dozen whalebone or steel stays. The corset girded the female body from the chest to the hips and fastened in the front with hooks, buttons, or laces. When the hourglass figure became the style, corsets were constructed more and more narrowly through the middle.

Freedom of movement was inhibited by the corset; when laced tightly even breathing became a chore. The fainting and swooning attributed to many nineteenth-century ladies was often caused not by an innate delicacy, but by their constrictive underwear. The corset caused more than discomfort, when laced too tightly it could actually dislocate a woman's kidneys, liver, and other organs.

The hoop skirt fit on top of the corset. Made of steel or whalebone, the hoop was like a bird cage suspended from a woman's waist. Four or five feet wide at the base, it did a remarkably fine job of protecting a lady's virtue; dressed in one, a woman resembled a small, unapproachable fortress.

Just as the clothing they wore restrained women's bodies, so did prudish ideas about language restrain conversation. Nineteenth-century Americans had a mania for avoiding even the most oblique references to sex and sexuality. Words referring to parts of the body or even clothing, such as trousers, were removed from polite usage. Genteel people ate the bosom of chicken, not the breast, and sat on chairs with limbs, not legs.[13] This blushing in the face of nature led to damaging excesses. One medical professor expressed his pride in American women, who preferred to "suffer the extremity of danger and pain" rather than allow themselves to be examined by doctors. "I say it is evidence of a fine morality in our society," he concluded.[14]

Nineteenth-century men and women were extremely ambivalent toward sexuality in general and female sexuality in particular. It is ironic that in a time when women were defined almost exclusively by their sexual roles as wives and mothers they were also being told that they lacked desire for sex. Dr. Alcott wrote, "Woman, as is well known, in a natural state . . . seldom if ever makes any of those advances, which clearly indicate sexual desire and for this very plain reason, that she does not feel them."[15]

In the name of "modern science" nineteenth-century men and women were offered a truly awe-inspiring bundle of sexual misinformation. They were told, for example, that overly frequent intercourse would not only make them feeble, but would also prevent conception. Sex approximately once a month was considered an adequate amount by many physicians; by the end of the century couples were being told to abstain altogether except when they wanted to have a child. Men and women were also warned in the most dire terms by their doctors that sex during pregnancy would cause miscarriage or, worse yet, physical, emotional, or moral defects in their unborn children. Masturbation was believed to damage future offspring as well as causing "mania" and "idiocy" in the guilty party. Sex during the two years women were told to breastfeed their infants was condemned as damaging to mother's milk. These totally erroneous and totally illogical sexual ideas, it must be emphasized, were not spread by whispering old wives but by the most reputable and "up-to-date" nineteenth-century physicians.

It is impossible to know, of course, how much influence such sexual ideas had on the men and women of the nineteenth century. No doubt many married couples ignored the public wisdom about sex and privately enjoyed each other. It seems clear, however, that as the century progressed and as ideas about sexuality became more extreme, it was more and more difficult for women to feel comfortable with their own sexuality.

The declining birth rate in the late 1800s may be related to the antisexual beliefs of the era. Between 1860 and 1890 the birth rate among native-born, white women dropped by approximately 20 percent. Since the quality of information concerning birth control did not improve significantly during this time, it is permissible to speculate that the frequency of intercourse decreased for many couples. It may be that, women—told they were not sexual creatures, reared to feel disgust for their bodies, and flattered into believing they were the more moral sex —controlled the birth rate by insisting upon long periods of sexual abstinence.[16] (See also Chapters 10 and 13.)

One method of controlling the frequency of intercourse was for women to take to their beds, alone, suffering from ailments which may or may not have been imaginary. Chronic invalidism was a way of life for a small, but not inconsiderable, percentage of nineteenth-century women. Those most likely to suffer in this way were generally the wealthiest, who had the least demands made on their time. With so many constraints upon them and so few sources of stimulation, these women seem to have simply shriveled up, destroyed by the social and sexual atmosphere in which they lived.

Affluent women suffered from nervous headaches, palpitations, fits of swooning, anemia, weakness, and hysteria.[17] They also suffered from such very real diseases as tuberculosis, but even their susceptibility to that dread disease might have been considerably lessened had they lived more active lives. Much of their illness appears to have originated in emotional causes.

In some ways middle-class culture idealized female debility. The wan and sickly woman with white skin and an air of fragility, who lay on her bed and smiled a vague smile, was in a sense a nineteenth-century sex symbol. This woman, sapped of energy, was perceived as almost pure spirit and no body—a combination in females much to the liking of the nineteenth century.

In the late 1800s medical men actually came close to defining femaleness itself as an illness, as proof citing Darwin (incorrectly) and his theory of evolution. Evolution, they claimed, had played a dirty trick on women of the middle and upper classes: through excessively high development, their uteruses had become diseased. While these male "thinkers" found it unfortunate that so many uteruses were in so much trouble, they also found beauty in the thought of their women as overbred evolutionary anachronisms. For it was evolution, too, they claimed, which had done away with ladies' sexual appetites. Only "low" women, the story went, suffered from the indignity of sexual desire.

WOMEN WITH WOMEN

In the nineteenth century women spent less time with men than they had in the past and more time with other women.[18] For many women the most sustaining relationships were ones with female friends and relatives. Such connections tended to be at the heart of a woman's life. Both married and single women often preferred to be with other women. In female company the restraints and constraints and formality that marked women's behavior in the presence of men fell away.

Women's desire to spend time with each other was considered normal. Frequent and even daily visits between female friends and relations were a standard feature of nineteenth-century social life. Women who did not live near each other arranged lengthy visits as often as possible. Sometimes women friends summered together with their children. Between visits women who lived far from one another wrote long and intimate letters.

Women valued one another. As historian Carol Smith Rosenberg, who has studied and written about the relationships among these groups, noted, "Women, who had little status or power in the larger world of male concerns, possessed status and power in the lives of other women."[19]

Women were able to share the concerns of their sphere. They were with each other on all the important occasions of their lives. Elaborate female rituals accompanied marriage, birth and death. In difficult times they comforted one another. "Suppose I come down . . . and spend Sunday with you quietly," wrote one woman to her friend; "That means talking all the time until you are relieved of all your latest troubles and I of mine."[20]

Friendships between women often lasted a lifetime. Such was the case of the feminist leader Elizabeth Cady Stanton and her cousin Elizabeth Smith Miller. The closeness between these women, begun in childhood, continued through young womanhood, marriage, the middle years, and old age. The two visited often and wrote long informal letters in which they addressed each other with the nicknames of their childhood.

Often such friendships began in boarding school. Most middle-class girls in the 1800s went away to school in their mid-teens, even if it was only for a few months. Usually this was a young woman's first experience away from her mother and the whole community of female relatives and friends which made up her mother's circle. According to Carol Smith Rosenberg, the school experience was a kind of weaning, in preparation for the separation from mother and home that would occur when the young woman married. The friendships girls made at school filled the void created by this first experience of leaving home.

When girls left school, they returned to their homes to help their mothers with domestic chores and master the skills required of homemakers. School acquaintances were not forgotten. Visits with friends were a staple of young unmarried women's lives. Such visits provided not only companionship, but also an opportunity for meeting eligible young men. Friends tended to have brothers and cousins, and marriages frequently resulted.

Nineteenth-century mothers and daughters were often extremely close. An example of the warmth that existed between them even after daughters were grown with families of their own can be seen in a letter written by one elderly woman. "You do not know how much I miss you," she wrote to her daughter, "not only when I struggle in and out of my mortal envelop and pump my nightly potation and no longer pour into your sympathising ear my senile gossip, but all the day I muse away, since the sound of your voice no longer rouses me to sympathy with your joys and sorrows."[21]

Rarely did the tension which is often considered normal in the twentieth century exist between nineteenth-century mothers and daughters. A reason for the lack of conflict between the female generations may have been the shortage of alternatives for women. Daughters were very much like their mothers—they rarely had any choice but to marry, bear children, and stay at home, exactly as their mothers had.

Motherhood was considered a middle-class woman's most important job, and it was one many women enjoyed. Victorian women devoted themselves to their offspring with an emotional intensity that was quite new. For the first time the work of nurturing children came to be seen as a full-time occupation, belonging almost exclusively to women.[22]

In colonial times children had been viewed more or less

as miniature adults, with a tendency toward wickedness. It was in the 1800s that childhood was defined as a separate time in people's lives, a time of development, when children needed special kinds of care and attention and possessed a special capacity to enjoy life.

Victorians more or less discarded the earlier view that children had free will to do good or bad, replacing that idea with the notion that children had to be taught right from wrong. They believed that a mother's influence had a very great deal to do with the sort of person a child would become. Mothers were encouraged to teach their children all the rules of "nice" behavior, all the restraints and self-denial necessary to get along in nineteenth-century America. There was, of course, a great irony in the fact that women, so controlled and restricted by the social patterns of nineteenth-century America, became themselves the instruments of social control in the lives of their children.

Another even more important irony colored the lives of nineteenth-century women. Ideas about women's place in the nineteenth century forced women into very close relationships with one another. When women were together, they talked about their lives. Even as they comforted one another, they also complained, and eventually they grew angry. It was no accident that the nineteenth-century woman's movement was conceived at a ladies' tea party.

The solidarity that developed among women as a result of their shared exclusion from the world of men was eventually used to forge a revolution. When women began talking about their discontent—their desire for education, their desire for work outside the home, their desire to control their own money—they found that their feelings were shared. In time female friendships were transformed into political partnerships through which women would challenge the assumptions that kept them at home, in the company of other women and children, cut off from the world of men and power.

6

Origins of Feminism

The same ideas by which the Founding Fathers justified the American Revolution were used in the following century by the nation's first feminists to legitimize their sexual revolution. It was a British woman who first saw the logical connection between American libertarian values and women's rights. Living at the time of the American Revolution, Mary Wollstonecraft believed the much-discussed rights of man should be extended to include women. She was the first person to discuss woman's place in society in explicitly political terms. Her pioneering essay, *A Vindication of the Rights of Woman* (1792), was known throughout the 1800s as the "feminist bible."

Wollstonecraft's first political tract, *A Vindication of the Rights of Man* (1790), had been written to refute Edmund Burke's recently published essay, *Reflections on the Revolution in France*, which denied the legitimacy of revolution. The success of her *Vindication* encouraged her to continue political writing. Shortly after completing it, she followed it with the essay on women.

Wollstonecraft began *The Rights of Woman* by asserting that God had given "natural rights" to both sexes. Just as it was not God's intention for men to be enslaved by tyrants, so too, she claimed, it was not God's intention for women to be enslaved by men. Furthermore, she concluded, just as French and American men were justified in rising up against unjust monarchs, so women were justified in revolting against the tyranny of husbands, fathers, and brothers.

Having asserted that women were heir to the same rights in society as men and having justified some form of sexual revolution, Wollstonecraft turned her attention to the current condition of women in society. She believed that most women were more like oversized children than equal partners of men, and she blamed society for this situation. Women, she said, were subject to a "false system of education," which taught them "manners before morals." They were praised for behavior that would be punished in male children and punished when they exhibited what for Wollstonecraft were the "real virtues" —curiosity, independence, high spirits. In short, she contended, most girls were reared as though any form of rigorous exercise, mental or physical, would be fatal.

Wollstonecraft was also a trenchant critic of the institution of marriage as it existed in her day. As she acutely remarked, "Women were made to be loved, and must not aim at respect, lest they should be hunted out of society as masculine." She felt that the situation would not change so long as women were economically dependent on men. She characterized marriage as a form of legalized prostitution, women trading their bodies for economic security. Most marriages, in her view, were based on little more than lust, and when the lust was satisfied, both partners were left bored, disillusioned, and saddled with one another for life. She wanted to reform the relationship between the sexes and replace dependency with equality. "I do not wish [women] to have power over men, but over themselves," she said. Women capable of supporting themselves would have no need to "entrap" a man; such women could enter into "true marriages," based on friendship, respect, and love that went deeper than infatuation.[1]

A Vindication of the Rights of Woman was widely read in America by the women who helped spearhead the antislavery movement and, later, the women's rights movement. Many of the first American feminists wrote about Wollstonecraft's essay in their letters and diaries. The *Vindication* was important to them for three specific reasons.

Wollstonecraft's work was the first serious political and social manifesto to address itself to the condition of women. As a product of the same school of political thought which had given birth to the American republic, Wollstonecraft's *Vindication* helped legitimate feminist demands by linking feminism to the fundamental principles of American democracy; this political and philosophical consistency helped to position the women's rights movement within the mainstream of American reform. And finally, Wollstonecraft's sociological approach to the concepts of masculine and feminine helped to undermine popular, quasi-religious beliefs about what a woman was and what a woman could be and could do. Wollstone-craft's message, which was echoed by feminists throughout the second half of the nineteenth century, asserted that women who were given equal rights and equal opportunities could change, develop, and grow to become people whose contribution to society was as great and as varied as the contribution of men.

Like Mary Wollstonecraft, the early antislavery forces in America based their politics on the "natural rights" thesis. In the eyes of these foes of the South's "peculiar institution," the enslavement of black men and women was a horrendous denial of the fundamental principles of American government, which had been founded to protect, not abridge, political liberty. From the very first days of the union, ardent antislavery forces asserted the incompatibility of human bondage and democracy. Though the slavery issue was debated in the United States Congress for years, no solution emerged. Southern and northern moderates both wanted the gradual emancipation of slaves, but no one knew how or when to accomplish it. Using wily parliamentary tactics, the southern proslavery congressional bloc managed to cut short all debate within both houses of Congress.

Cut off from legitimate sources of political power, abolitionist sentiment boiled over into new areas. By 1830 the abolitionists had taken the "natural rights" argument far beyond its original political base. If liberty was man's right, given to him by God Almighty, the newly militant abolitionists claimed, then those who interfered with his liberty were much more than politically unenlightened—they were guilty of defying God's law. In other words, anyone who kept slaves or profited from an economy based on slavery was a sinner.

The meshing of politics and religion, typical of nearly all nineteenth-century reform movements, had profound effects upon the abolitionists and on the country at large. So long as the abolition of slavery in the United States was a question for the political arena, women were entirely excluded from the debate; at that time no American woman who had any pretensions to respectability dared to speak out on political issues. Religion, however, was something else. Because it dealt with matters of the heart, not the head, religion was considered part of woman's proper sphere. When the antislavery dialogue moved from Congress to the pulpit, women were drawn into the debate.

Ultimately the effect of women's participation in the antislavery cause was revolutionary. So carefully guarded for so long from the "vulgar" theater of politics and government, women were radicalized by their abolitionist experience. Furthermore, as Mary Wollstonecraft had understood in 1791, the "natural rights" argument was a ready-made feminist ideology.

Women's participation in the antislavery movement prepared them to fight for their own rights. As abolitionists, women learned to defy public opinion, to organize, petition, raise funds, and persevere. By fusing politics and religion, the antislavery movement opened the first narrow crack in the rigid separation of the masculine and feminine "spheres."

During the 1830s scores of women, many of them relatives of male abolitionists, organized female antislavery societies throughout the Northeast. Lucretia Mott—later revered as the "Mother" of the feminist movement—led the Philadelphia Female Anti-Slavery Society, ignoring the violently antiabolitionist feeling that prevailed among Orthodox Quakers and in Philadelphia society generally. Mott and her husband James organized "free stores" in Philadelphia which sold only those products grown, produced, or manufactured by free (nonslave) labor. Like many of the Quakers who participated in the antislavery crusade, Lucretia and James Mott rejected Quaker orthodoxy, which they considered rigid and unprogressive, in favor of a more socially activist splinter group of Friends called Hicksite Quakers.

In New York the Ladies' Anti-Slavery Society was guided by Julia and Susan Tappan, wives of the wealthy, crusading Tappan brothers, Lewis and Arthur. Massachusetts, under the influence of William Lloyd Garrison, was the hub of antislavery activity in the nation. Numerous women's antislavery groups were organized in the towns and villages surrounding Boston, producing dozens of women, such as Maria Weston Chapman and Lydia Maria Child, trained to lead. Throughout the state many iconoclastic clergymen supported the abolitionist cause and helped promote local women's antislavery societies.

Despite the best efforts of many talented female abolitionists, women were excluded from the center of antislavery activity throughout the 1820s and early 1830s. Female leaders had no formal power within the movement; while many, such as Lucretia Mott, exerted enormous influence, none could vote at leadership conventions. Women were expected to preach the antislavery message to other women, while male abolitionists assailed the power structure of the nation. In 1838, however, two sisters from Charleston, South Carolina, Sarah and Angelina Grimké, singlehandedly thrust woman's role in the antislavery movement onto center stage and forced unwilling men and women to recognize the parallel between the oppression of slaves and the oppression of women.

Sarah and Angelina Grimké were daughters of one of the South's most aristocratic families; their father was an assistant chief justice of South Carolina, their brother, a United States congressman. They were brought up on a large plantation, intimately in touch with slavery. Almost from childhood Sarah and Angelina were troubled by the South's "peculiar institution"; neither could forget the sight of slaves, beaten and bruised, just returned from the workhouse (where "bad" slaves were punished), nor could they overlook the inconsistency between human bondage and the Christian morality they were taught.

As young women, the sisters' moral objection to slavery was expressed in a series of religious crises. Each joined, then renounced, this church and that, looking for a spiritual answer to their dissatisfaction. Eventually Sarah joined Charleston's tiny Congregation of Friends. The Quakers were the only group in the South who publicly condemned slavery, and they were hated by nearly all Southerners. Sarah's conversion so mortified her family that when she decided to leave the South in 1822, they offered little resistance.

Sarah Grimké was twenty-nine years old when she settled in Philadelphia. Angelina, thirteen years Sarah's junior, joined her seven years later. Throughout the 1820s and early 1830s the sisters struggled unsuccessfully to adapt to the rigid Quaker orthodoxy. Try as they might, they could find no peace in or out of Quaker meeting.

The abolitionist movement was the answer the sisters eventually discovered for themselves. In the mid-1830s the newly established American Anti-Slavery Society—the national organization of radical abolitionists—demanded the immediate emancipation of all slaves. Defying the Quaker establishment, which was committed to gradual emancipation, Angelina sent a letter to William Lloyd Garrison, editor of *The Liberator*, in support of immediate abolition. In the opinion of the orthodox Quakers, Garrison was a dangerous extremist; nevertheless, Angelina wrote to him, "The ground upon which you stand is holy ground: never—never surrender it."

Angelina's letter was written in support of Boston abolitionists who had recently been subjected to mob violence. Of such persecution, Angelina noted, "If persecution is the means which God has ordained for the accomplishment of this great end, EMANCIPATION, then . . . I feel as if I could say, LET IT COME; for it is my deep, solemn deliberate conviction, that this is a cause worth dying for."[2]

Though Angelina had not given Garrison specific permission, her letter was immediately printed in *The Liberator*. Public response to this document, written by a Southerner, daughter of a slave owner, was overwhelming. Angelina's letter was reissued as a hugely successful pamphlet, and it was followed by several others, including one addressed to the Women of the South, which was burned in Charleston, the sisters' home town. Recognizing the sisters' potential propaganda value to the movement, in 1836 the American Anti-Slavery Society invited the sisters to New York, to meet with women of the city and discuss slavery.

The Grimkés spent the last months of 1836 and part of 1837 in New York, working as the first formally appointed female antislavery agents in the United States. Their "parlor talks" helped them to sharpen their critique of slavery. Listening to the women who attended their meetings, the Grimkés soon recognized the pervasiveness of race prejudice in the North. Eventually they came to understand that the enslavement of blacks in the South could not exist without the collusion—in the form of racial bias—of the North.

By the time the Grimké sisters left New York and traveled northward to continue their antislavery agitation, they were celebrities, and their reception in the freer air of Massachusetts was tumultuous. Within weeks of their arrival, the sisters were addressing huge public audiences of men and women.

Driven by moral necessity to testify against slavery, the Grimké sisters became the first respectable American women to speak in public. No doubt many people came just to gape at the two "unnatural" women on the podium, but the sisters' style had a way of winning the most skeptical audiences. Dressed with Quaker simplicity, their manner refined and "lady-like," the sisters hardly looked like "brazen" women. It has been estimated by Gerda Lerner, their biographer, that their sincerity won 25,000 converts to the abolitionist crusade in a single year.

The sisters had not intended to thrust the "woman question" into their antislavery tour. They did not invite men to their lectures, nor did they intend to speak in public. But when men arrived, and when their talks became too large to be held in private homes, they did not demur. Once the subject—"the woman question," as it was called—was engaged, the sisters would not back off. As Angelina had said in one of her pamphlets, "The denial of our duty to act, is a denial of our right to act; and if we have no right to act, then may we well be termed 'the white slaves of the North,' for like our brethren in bonds, we must seal our lips in silence and despair."[3]

When Catherine Beecher, the educational reformer, rebuked the Grimké sisters for speaking in public and forsaking "woman's sphere," the home, Angelina replied as follows.

> Now I believe it is woman's right to have a voice in all the laws and regulations by which she is to be governed, whether in Church or State: and that the present arrangements of society, on these points, are a violation of human rights, a rank usurpation of power, a violent seizure and confiscation of what is sacredly and inalienably hers. . . . If Ecclesiastical and Civil governments are ordained of God, then I contend that woman has just as much right to sit in solemn counsel in conventions, conferences, associations and general assemblies, as man—*just as much right to sit upon the throne of England or in the Presidential chair of the United States.*[4]

While conceding that women did, indeed, have a grievance, some abolitionists begged the sisters not to associate one cause with the other. These antislavery men believed that woman should wait her turn, that slavery was the issue of the hour, and that the radical feminism of the Grimkés would delay abolition. The Grimkés' rejection of this point of view caused a great stir within the Anti-

Slavery Society. The most dour abolitionists predicted that the Misses Grimké would end their public careers as ignominiously as had Fanny Wright, a utopian reformer and an outspoken foe of slavery who scandalized America in the early 1830s by publicly advocating free love.

Increasingly the antislavery cause and the cause of women's rights were fused in the sisters' minds. Both slaves and women, they perceived, were denied the rights guaranteed to all citizens by the Constitution and the Bill of Rights. The First Amendment, for example, guaranteed freedom of speech; yet on every side people were trying to deny the Grimkés this right. But for Sarah and Angelina there was no "slave problem," no "woman question"; there was only one issue—restoring to all human beings, regardless of race or sex, the rights which were bestowed on them by God and guaranteed by the law of the Republic.

As their New England tour progressed, newspaper men in particular were offended by the sisters' audacity. Some journalists referred to Angelina as "Devileena." Inevitably the sisters' unwed state encouraged speculation that the Misses Grimké, having failed to find white husbands, were willing and eager to take Negro mates. "Why are all the old hens abolitionists? Because not being able to obtain husbands they think they may stand some chance for a Negro, if they can only make amalgamation fashionable."[5]

The virulence of the press, however, did not match the outrage of the churches. To the majority of the clergy, Sarah and Angelina's public lobbying against slavery represented an un-Christian assault upon the social order and the sanctity of home and family. During the summer of 1837, the Congregationalist churches, heirs of the defunct Puritan theocracy, publicly condemned the behavior of the Grimké sisters in a Pastoral Letter. The document delineated in dire terms what would happen to such "unnatural" women as Sarah and Angelina. "If the vine, whose strength and beauty it is to lean upon the trelliswork, and help conceal its clusters, thinks to assume the independence and the overshadowing nature of the elm, it will not only cease to bear fruit, but fall in shame and dishonor into the dust."[6]

For several reasons the Pastoral Letter was a highly effective piece of antifeminist literature. First, the clergy was viewed as woman's ally, the natural protector of home and hearth, and its opinions were taken seriously by both men and women. Second, the letter took the New Testament as its authority, putting anyone who disagreed with it into the uncomfortable position of dissenting from Scripture. Third, the letter threatened women who assumed "the place and tone of man as a public reformer" with two very specific and frightening punishments: such women would lose the ability to have children, and even worse, they would end up in "shame and dishonor," in "degeneracy and ruin."[7]

The Pastoral Letter set the tone for most nineteenth-century antifeminist literature, but it did not deter the Grimkés. In a series of *Letters on the Equality of the Sexes,* Sarah met and matched the gusto of the Pastoral Letter. First, she absolutely denied that God had intended woman to be man's dependent; scriptural reference to woman's inferiority, she claimed, reflected the prejudices of men in biblical times, not the will of God. She claimed that woman had been created by God as man's equal, his companion and friend. "I ask no favors for my sex. . . . All I ask our brethren is, that they will take their feet from off our necks and permit us to stand upright on that ground which God designed us to occupy."[8]

Sarah continued by surveying the whole course of human history, recounting the wrongs done her sex. In a chapter on the United States she catalogued woman's grievances—inferior education, inequity in law, economic exploitation. In this chapter Sarah demanded equal pay for equal work and discussed the previously unheeded exploitation of working women. Elsewhere Sarah discussed the need for women to change themselves. While she placed most of the blame for the subjugation of women on men, she argued that women who devoted themselves to fashion, acted frivolously, affected ignorance, and leaned on men for protection were abetting their own oppression. It was her passionate conviction that women and men had the same rights and the same duties. "Whatsoever is morally right for a man to do," she noted, "it is morally right for a woman to do."[9]

After the publication of the Pastoral Letter resistance to the sisters' public appearances intensified. Some churches closed their doors to them. It proved difficult to hire halls, and some speaking engagements were canceled. Free speech and the right to free assembly became the sisters' mission as they completed the last lap of their New England tour.

In February 1838 Angelina addressed the legislature of the State of Massachusetts twice in one week. The ostensible reason for her appearance was the presentation of antislavery petitions signed by twenty thousand women, which the Grimké's had gathered during their tour. The symbolic significance of Angelina's appearance, however, far overshadowed the petitions she carried with her. She was the first women ever to speak before a legislative body in the United States; her addresses dramatically marked the beginning of the end of women's public silence.

In a letter to Theodore Weld, the man she subsequently married, Angelina recalled her terror as she approached the assembly hall, filled with fifteen hundred people, on the first day of her "command performance."

> I never was so near fainting under the tremendous pressure of feeling. My heart almost died within me. The novelty of the scene, the weight of responsibility, the ceaseless exercise of mind thro' which I had passed for more than a week—all together sunk me to the earth. I well nigh despaired.[10]

Despite her fear, she did not moderate her views. She spoke freely before the legislative body on both issues— abolition of slavery and the "woman question."

> These petitions relate to the great and solemn subject of slavery. . . . And because it is a political subject, it has often tauntingly been said, that women had nothing to do with it. Are we aliens, because we are women? Are we bereft of citizenship because we are mothers, wives and daughters of a mighty people? Have women no country— no interests staked in public weal—no liabilities in common peril—no partnership in a nation's guilt and shame . . . ?
> I hold, Mr. Chairman, that the American women have to do with this subject, not only because it is moral and religious, but because it is political, inasmuch as we are citizens of this republic and as such our honor, happiness and well-being are bound up in its politics, government and laws.[11]

Angelina's appearances before the Massachusetts legislature were the triumph and the swan song of the sisters' reforming careers. Angelina was already engaged to the high-minded abolitionist leader Theodore Weld. Soon after the couple was married, ideological differences with the sisters' old ally, William Lloyd Garrison, prompted Weld and the Grimkés to leave the abolitionist movement. While none of the three lost the passion for reform, the difficulties of eking out a living overwhelmed all of them. Weld attempted a number of careers—farming, teaching, administering a utopian commune—but with little financial success. Angelina bore two sons and a daughter; her difficult pregnancies resulted in a chronic gynecological problem which sporadically incapacitated her for the rest of her life. Sarah lived with Weld and Angelina, and because of her sister's recurrent illnesses, she became largely responsible for raising her nephews and niece.

The Grimké sisters' careers as women's-rights crusaders were short-lived, but their tradition-shattering work had an indisputably powerful effect upon other women. Nevertheless, it was not they who precipitated the formation of an organized women's rights movement in America. The nineteenth-century women's movement came into being as a result of the World Anti-Slavery Convention, which met in London in 1840 and voted to exclude women from participating in its proceedings. The many female antislavery leaders who had crossed the Atlantic to attend the convention were segregated in the gallery of the assembly hall, cut off from the male delegates by a low curtain. They were joined by the Grimkés' radical ally, William Lloyd Garrison, who chose not to participate in a convention that shunted women aside.

Attending the convention were Lucretia Mott and the twenty-five-year-old bride of abolitionist Henry Stanton, Elizabeth Cady Stanton (who was destined to lead the women's rights movement for half a century). In her memoirs Stanton recalled the World Anti-Slavery meeting and the resolve she made to start a society to "advocate the rights of women."

The acquaintance of Lucretia Mott, who was a broad, liberal thinker on politics, religion, and all questions of reform, opened to me a new world of thought. As we walked about to see the sights of London, I embraced every opportunity to talk with her. It was intensely gratifying to hear all that, through years of doubt, I had dimly thought, so freely discussed. . . . As Mrs. Mott and I walked home, arm in arm, commenting on the incidents of the day, we resolved to hold a convention as soon as we returned home, and form a society to advance the rights of women.[12]

Eight years were to pass before it was created.

7

The First Feminist Revolt

There had always been women rebels in the United States, but never before had women rebelled as a group. When Elizabeth Cady Stanton and Lucretia Mott decided to hold a women's rights convention, they helped set in motion a collective effort by women to achieve sexual equality.

There were thousands of participants in the movement and many leaders. Three women—Elizabeth Cady Stanton, Lucy Stone, and Susan B. Anthony—stood out. Their ideas and their actions strongly influenced the kinds of changes women were to make together.

These three "famous" women, prototypes of the kinds of women who became feminists, reveal a great deal about the nineteenth-century women's rights movement. The difficulties they experienced in their own lives were shared by many women of their time, both within and without the movement.

Elizabeth Cady Stanton (1815–1902) became disturbed about the lack of women's rights when she was a child. In her father's law office, she often listened to female clients who came to ask for legal help. Her father always told them that there were no laws protecting women's rights. Once, after a neighbor lost her farm to her husband's creditors, young Elizabeth became so angry that she threatened to cut all the bad laws from the books. Her father explained that old laws would have to be amended and new ones written before women could claim ownership of property and earnings. Years later Elizabeth petitioned the New York state legislature for those very rights.

Elizabeth grew up in a large, well-to-do family in Johnston, New York, just north of Albany. Both her parents came from prominent families. Margaret Livingston Cady, Elizabeth's mother, was the daughter of a Revolutionary War hero. Her father, Judge Daniel Cady, was a distinguished jurist and conservative politician who served several terms in the state legislature. Elizabeth was strongly influenced by him.

When Elizabeth was eleven, her brother died just after he had graduated from college. This event, Elizabeth later noted, "changed the course of my life." Judge Cady was overcome with grief. He had other children—five daughters—but not all five combined could make up for the loss of his only son. When Elizabeth tried to comfort him, he lamented, "Ah my daughter, I wish you were a boy."[1]

Elizabeth thought she could comfort her father by being "learned and courageous" like her brother. She became a scholar of Greek and an excellent horsewoman. No matter what she accomplished, however, her father's answer was always the same. When she presented him with the prize she had won in Greek, he told her: "My daughter, you should have been a boy."

Judge Cady's position was difficult for Elizabeth to understand. Throughout her life she continued to seek the approval that Judge Cady had so freely given to his son. As a grown woman, married with children of her own and well known as the founder of the women's rights movement, Elizabeth still felt "stung" when she could not win her father's praise. "I passed through a terrible scourging when last at my father's," she wrote after Judge Cady criticized her plan to lecture on the lyceum circuit.

> I cannot tell you how deep the iron entered my soul. I never felt more keenly the degradation of my sex. To think that all in me of which my father would have felt proper pride had I been a man is deeply mortifying because I am a woman! That thought has stung me to a fierce decision—to speak as soon as I can do myself credit.[2]

Judge Cady's attitude did not sour Elizabeth's girlhood. She grew up in a time when girls were still allowed to play as boys did. At an age when girls of a later generation were being laced into corsets, the Cady sisters were exploring the woods and learning to skate and sled.

Elizabeth, exuberant and fun-loving, excelled at climbing trees and running races. "All the boys and girls" of her town, she wrote, played "freely together . . . we made no distinction of sex . . . equality was the general basis of our relations."

The same equality applied in the classroom. Elizabeth attended Johnston Academy, a private coeducational school. When she was admitted to an advanced class to study classics and mathematics, she did not think it strange that she was the only girl among a dozen boys. Not until Elizabeth became a teenager did she realize how much her own horizons were to be limited by her sex. The boys of her class went on to Union College; Elizabeth, anxious for more schooling, could not attend. No college in the United States yet admitted women.

Elizabeth grew to womanhood in a time of transition. By 1830, when she was sixteen, ideas about woman's place were changing. As noted, women were being cut off from the world outside the home. Rigid ideas concerning the proper behavior of a lady were replacing the free manners of Colonial and early American times. Elizabeth, reared in relative freedom, disliked the new style.

The years between school and marriage were the most pleasurable of Elizabeth's early life. Following two years at Emma Willard's Troy Female Seminary (the present Emma Willard School), Elizabeth returned home. The Cady household was always filled with young friends and relatives, among whom Elizabeth felt very happy. Together they read and discussed political and economic theory, law, philosophy, and poetry. There were dances, too, as well as sports and visits. Elizabeth was extremely gregarious, she thrived in groups. Her need for companions had a great deal to do with when and how she conceived the women's rights movement.

Elizabeth was very close to Edward Bayard, the husband of her older sister Tryphena. From him she learned to "take nothing for granted," not to let "popular superstition" get in the way of "the pursuit of truth." Bayard, in turn, sought in Elizabeth the understanding and affection he lacked in his own marriage. As Elizabeth grew older, he found her more and more attractive. One day he confessed his love for her, but though Elizabeth shared his feelings, she would not act on them. Nothing, she felt, could come of their love but scandal and regret. At the same time, she began to wonder whether unhappy couples might not be better off separating than being miserably married.

Though divorce was a legal possibility, it was still dif-

ficult to obtain. Most states limited grounds for divorce
to bigamy, adultery, impotence, desertion, and extreme
cruelty. New York remained the most conservative, accepting only adultery. Only Indiana in 1824 made it legal
to accept any "just and reasonable grounds." Most courts
granted the custody of children to husbands, and where
alimony was awarded to a wife, she could not legally
bring suit for payment. Divorced women were dependent
on their husbands' "good will" for financial support and
rights to their children.

Along with the legal difficulties was the social stigma
attached to divorce. Divorced women were social pariahs,
disgraced in the eyes of their families and often shunned
by "polite" society. They were branded as "bad" and
"loose." Men who divorced suffered less, but they too
might find their careers and social standing ruined.

Elizabeth was to become one of the strongest nineteenth-century advocates for the right of every person to
dissolve an unhappy marriage. She considered the right
to divorce a choice every adult woman and man should
have. Her biographer, Alma Lutz, dates her concern with
divorce to her feelings about Edward Bayard.[3]

At the home of her reformer cousin, Gerrit Smith,
Elizabeth met Henry B. Stanton, an orator just becoming
known in the antislavery movement. The two were drawn
to each other, and when Henry asked her to marry him,
Elizabeth accepted.

Her father opposed the match. Henry was too radical
for Judge Cady's tastes. Eventually Elizabeth was to find
him not radical enough. At the World Anti-Slavery Convention, where they spent their honeymoon, Henry protested the exclusion of women delegates, but he did not
—as did William Lloyd Garrison—refuse to participate
in the convention himself. And a decade later, when
Elizabeth launched the women's rights movement, Henry
objected to a number of her goals. At the time, however,
there were only her father's doubts to contend with. Momentarily she gave in to Judge Cady and broke off her
engagement. But when Henry wrote to express his love for
her and to insist that she come with him to London, she re-
lented. She was twenty-five—old enough, she felt, to
know her own mind. She would marry Henry and work
with him for abolition.

What she saw and heard at the London convention

shattered those hopes. How could she work alongside Henry when all around her men were telling women already active in the movement to stay away and keep silent? She became convinced that her essential task was to work for her own rights and the rights of all women. "To me there is no question so important as the emancipation of women from the dogmas of the past, political, religious, and social," she subsequently wrote.

She was not ready to act, however. Elizabeth had had more opportunities than other women of her generation—more education, more leisure, more exposure to critical thinking. But she was not yet prepared to challenge the nineteenth-century assumption that women existed solely to fulfill their roles as wives and mothers.

When the Stantons returned to the United States, Henry pursued his career, leaving his wife at home. "Mr. Stanton announced to me in starting that his business would occupy all his time and that I must take entire charge of the housekeeping." Mrs. Stanton was also busy having babies; eventually there would be seven.

Elizabeth threw her whole self—her "soul," she called it—into her new "job." "I studied up on everything pertaining to housekeeping. I felt the same ambition to excel in all departments of the culinary art that I did at school in different branches of learning."

Elizabeth was equally ambitious as a mother. She rejected most of the current child-care methods. Doctors, she noted, rarely had any sustained contact with children and knew nothing about their real needs. She thought the practice of swaddling infants, binding their bodies to prevent their supposedly soft bones from breaking, cruel and harmful. A bandaged infant, she observed, had no room to move. She also thought it ridiculous for babies to be kept in dark, hot rooms and fed on rigid schedules. When her children were born, Elizabeth ignored all medical advice and followed her own "mother's instinct," if, as she told one doctor, "reason is too dignified a term to apply to a woman's thoughts."

She made attempts, too, not to become a shadow of her husband. At her wedding ceremony she had refused "to obey" Henry. Soon afterward she wrote to a friend that "though my great love for Henry may warp my judgments in favor of some of his opinions . . . I claim the right to look at his action and opinions with the same freedom and impartiality that I do at those of any other man." Though she took her husband's last name, she wanted to be known, not as Mrs. Henry, but as Elizabeth Cady Stanton.

> There is a great deal in a name. It often signifies much and may involve a great principle. Ask our colored brethren if there is nothing in a name. Why are slaves nameless unless they take that of their master? Simply because they have no independent existence. . . . Even so with women. . . . The custom of calling women Mrs. John This or Mrs. Tom That is founded on the principle that white men are lords of us all.[4]

In Boston, where the Stantons first settled, Elizabeth had many diversions. The city was the center of the reform spirit as well as home to such intellectuals and political activists as Ralph Waldo Emerson, John Greenleaf Whittier, and William Lloyd Garrison. There were concerts, lectures, and theaters, as well as conferences on temperance, prison reform, and peace. During her frequent visits to her parents' home she had the chance to lobby on behalf of the married woman's property act, then being considered by the New York state legislature.

All these enjoyments came to an end in 1847, when Henry Stanton decided to move his law practice to a small manufacturing town in western New York. Seneca Falls was good for Henry, but for Elizabeth it was a disaster. Henry was away on business much of the time. Elizabeth, burdened with a large family and little household help, was lonely and overworked. She began to understand the way most women lived their lives. In her memoirs she wrote of these realizations.

> I now fully understood the practical difficulties women had to contend with in the isolated household and the impossibility of woman's best development if in contact the chief part of her life with servants and children. The general discontent I felt with woman's portion, the chaotic conditions under which everything fell without constant supervision, and the wearied, anxious look of the majority of women impressed me with the strong feeling that some active measures should be taken to remedy the wrongs of society in general, and of women in particular.[5]

Eight years had passed since Elizabeth had first thought of organizing a convention to discuss the rights of women. She began to consider that plan once more. When she received an invitation to spend a day with Lucretia Mott, who was visiting women friends near Seneca Falls, Elizabeth found herself "pouring out the torrent" of her "long-accumulating discontent." The women sent a notice to the local newspaper, announcing a Women's Rights Convention, to be held five days later—on July 19 and 20, 1848.

Some sort of manifesto was needed to present the case for women's rights. Stanton suggested modeling it on the Declaration of Independence and thereby linking women's rights with the founding principles of the American republic. Her co-planners agreed, and together they drafted the Declaration of Rights and Sentiments.

Most of the more than three hundred people who attended the convention were women active in the antislavery and temperance movements. In addition there were several Irish immigrants who worked in the factories of Seneca Falls, as well as native-born women who did piecework at home for the glove-making industry.

One of the glovemakers was nineteen-year-old Charlotte Woodward, who applauded the goals set forth in the Declaration. She was tired of doing piecework for pennies—pennies that went not to her, but her father. Of the hundred women who signed the Declaration of Rights and Sentiments, Charlotte was the only one who lived to see all women in the United States win the vote—seventy-two years later.

Stanton had wanted to exclude men from the convention. As she put it, "woman alone can understand the height, the depth, the length, and the breadth of her degradation." But when several men arrived they were invited in, and when none of the women present felt confident enough to lead the meeting, James Mott, Lucretia Mott's husband, was appointed chairman.

There were several speeches before Stanton read the Declaration of Sentiments. In familiar language, it declared:

> We hold these truths to be self-evident: that all men and women are created equal; that they are endowed by

their Creator with certain inalienable rights; that among these are life, liberty, and the pursuit of happiness. . . .

Then the Declaration of Sentiments listed women's grievances.

The history of mankind is a history of repeated injuries and usurpations on the part of man toward woman, having in direct object the establishment of an absolute tyranny over her. To prove this, let facts be submitted to a candid world:

He has never permitted her to exercise her inalienable right to the elective franchise.

He has compelled her to submit to laws, in the formation of which she had no voice. . . .

He has made her, if married, in the eye of the law, civilly dead. . . .

He has so framed the laws of divorce, as to what shall be the proper causes, and in case of separation, to whom the guardianship of the children shall be given, as to be wholly regardless of the happiness of women. . . .

He has monopolized nearly all the profitable employments. . . .

He has denied her the facilities for obtaining a thorough education, all colleges being closed against her.

He allows her in Church, as well as State, but a subordinate position. . . .

He has created a false public sentiment by giving to the world a different code of morals for men and women. . . .

He has usurped the prerogative of Jehovah himself, claiming it as his right to assign for her a sphere of action, when that belongs to her conscience and to her God.

He has endeavored, in every way that he could, to destroy her confidence in her own powers, to lessen her self-respect, and to make her willing to lead a dependent and abject life.[6]

After the Declaration of Sentiments came twelve resolutions. The audience agreed quickly to the first eleven—including demands that women gain rights to own property and control wages; to exercise free speech; to obtain divorce; and to achieve equal opportunities in commerce, trade, the professions, and education. Then Stanton surprised the audience with one further resolution—that women be given the right to vote.

This demand was more shocking than all the others combined. Even Lucretia Mott was nervous about the twelfth resolution. Henry Stanton had left town rather than witness "the farce" he thought would occur when his wife proposed woman suffrage. There was no "farce"; by a small margin the resolution was approved by the convention.

The Seneca Falls Convention changed women's rights from an idea into an active goal, which many women hoped to achieve by working together. Such pioneer feminists as Mary Wollstonecraft and the Grimkés had protested woman's lot, but not until Seneca Falls did women join in their protest. It was only when women organized, when they came together as a movement, that they began to make headway against the oppression they faced.

Certainly not all or even most women in the United States became part of the movement. Many did not want change. They were not unequal to men, they claimed, only different; and being different, they did not "need" rights. Other women, especially poor women and black women, felt far more restricted by class or race than by sex.

Most of the women who joined the new women's rights movement, such as Stanton, were native born and middle class. They came from influential Yankee families whose roots dated back to the original Puritans. Like Stanton, they experienced and reacted to the changes taking place in woman's condition. They lived in small towns in the North and Midwest, where reform movements were strongest. And like Stanton, they were activists in those movements.

Women reformers were easy converts to women's rights. Reform gave women the chance to move from their homes into the world. Yet whether they became abolitionists, temperance advocates, or moral reformers, women were never treated as equals by their male counterparts. Fifteen years before the Seneca Falls Convention Sarah and Angelina Grimké had seen the contradiction in women fighting for the rights of others before their own rights were achieved. By the late 1840s many reforming women were ready to put their fight first.

Lucy Stone (1819–1893) was one of these women. In 1848 thirty-year-old Lucy Stone was already well known as a speaker for the Anti-Slavery Society. She began her speaking career with a firm resolve. "I mean to plead not for the slave alone but for suffering humanity everywhere. Especially do I mean to labor for the elevation of my sex."[7]

Like Elizabeth Cady Stanton, Lucy Stone's discovery of women's inequality came early. She grew up on a poor farm in western Massachusetts, the eighth of nine children born to Francis and Hannah Stone. The night before she was born, her mother milked eight cows and did her usual farm chores. When told that her new baby was a girl, she reportedly said, "Oh dear, I am sorry. A woman's life is so hard." She later told her daughter that women had been cursed from the time of Adam and Eve, and there was nothing they could do about it.

Lucy believed that her mother's life was difficult not because of Eve's curse but because she had too much work, too many children, and a tyrannical husband. "There was only one will in our home," Lucy later wrote, "and that was my father's." She remembered him as a harsh, stingy man who hardly ever expressed affection.

The Stones were orthodox Congregationalists who filled their children with fears of hell and damnation. They forbade even the smallest pleasures, such as reading novels. Lucy, a sensitive child, brooded about the state of her soul. Scriptural ideas about women depressed her. Her parents interpreted the Bible literally, but Lucy could not accept the biblical portrayal of women as subservient to men. When she read God's injunction to Eve in Genesis, she was so full of despair that, as she told her mother, she wanted to kill herself.

Lucy was determined not to end up a meek, overworked wife. She begged her father to let her stay in school until she could become a teacher and support herself. He consented to loan her the money and made her sign an IOU promising to repay him. All through her teens and early twenties Lucy taught school and continued her own education. She saved what she could from her teaching salary until she had enough money to pay for a term at a high school that admitted women. Then she went back to teaching until she had saved more money.

When she was twenty-five years old—nine years after she had started teaching—Lucy finally had saved enough money to pay for one term at Oberlin College. Founded in 1834, Oberlin was the first and still the only college in the nation that admitted women and blacks. Working as a housekeeper, a laundress, and a teacher, Lucy stayed for four years to complete her degree.

Oberlin was a station on the Underground Railroad and a school famous for its reform spirit. But to Lucy most of the faculty and students at Oberlin were not sufficiently reform-minded. "They hate Garrison and women's rights," she wrote her parents. "I love both and often find myself at swords' points with them." William Lloyd Garrison's anticlericalism was despised by the religious founders of Oberlin. And though the school allowed women an equal education, true sexual equality at Oberlin did not exist. Men were the "leading sex," Oberlin literature proclaimed. The male faculty, student body, and neighboring community opposed women's fight for full equality. When Abby Kelley Foster, a feminist abolitionist, spoke at Oberlin, one professor denounced her as "the specimen of what a woman becomes when she steps out of her place."

Lucy, too, was often under fire. With Antoinette Brown, her closest friend—later to become her sister-in-law, as well as the first formally educated woman minister—Lucy protested the rule that mandated debating classes for women but barred them from debating. When she and Antoinette won the right to debate each other, so many people came to hear them that Oberlin authorities quickly reverted to the old rule. Lucy then organized women students into debating teams. They met secretly in the woods and in the home of a sympathetic black woman.

By the time Lucy graduated from Oberlin, she had decided to become a public speaker and win public support for abolitionism and women's rights. Until the twentieth century the lecture platform was the most important means of mass communication. People in all parts of the country attended lectures regularly—for entertainment, for enlightenment, for information. Lectures were popular, but it was men, not women, who did the lecturing. Lucy's parents warned her that if she made a career of speaking, she would demean herself and disgrace the entire family. "You would not object or think it wrong for a man to plead the cause of the suffering and the outcast," Lucy told her parents, "and surely the moral character of the act is not changed because it is done by a woman."

She became a salaried speaker for the Anti-Slavery Society of Massachusetts. Whenever she spoke, she addressed the problems of women as well as of blacks. Agents of the Anti-Slavery Society objected; Lucy had been hired to talk about the evils of slavery, not the plight of women. "I was a woman before I was an abolitionist," was Lucy's response. "I must speak for the women."

In time women's rights became Lucy's first priority. On weekends she spoke in favor of abolition, but during the week Lucy spoke for "the elevation of my sex" wherever she could find an audience. Her lectures covered three topics—Woman's Social and Industrial Difficulties; Legal and Political Inequalities; and Moral and Religious Disabilities.

On the speaking platform Lucy faced the hoots, jeers, and physical violence of hostile audiences. Angry listeners tried to shout her down and threw spitballs at her. Sometimes mobs tried to attack her. Stone handled the heckling well. Once, when a man in the audience threw a prayer book at her, hitting her in the head, Lucy simply observed that only a man without a good argument would stoop to such a low one. On another occasion, in midwinter, icy water was sprayed on her from a hose; Lucy reached for her shawl, put it around her shoulders, and went on talking.

At first Lucy was alone, carrying on a "solitary battle for woman's rights." "Outside the little circle of abolitionists," she wrote, "I knew nobody who sympathized with my views." Her isolation changed after the Seneca Falls Convention of 1848. Almost as soon as the convention adjourned, women reformers "gave call" for new meetings to discuss their rights. In Ohio, Indiana, Pennsylvania, Massachusetts and New York women drew up resolutions, organized committees, and kept in touch with feminist activities elsewhere.

By 1850 Lucy was working in association with many feminists. Among them were Paulina Wright Davis, founder of the first feminist newspaper, *The Una*, and the first woman to lecture on female physiology and anatomy; Ernestine Rose, the foremost lobbyist for the pioneer New York State Married Woman's Property Act of 1848;

Lucretia Mott and her sister-in-law Lydia Mott; Harriet
Hunt, one of the first nineteenth-century women to practice medicine; and Elizabeth Cady Stanton. Such old
friends as Antoinette Brown and Abby Kelley Foster also
joined the women's rights movement.

Along with local meetings, feminists spoke on the lyceum circuit and held national conventions every year but
one between 1850 and 1860. The conventions were
the nineteenth-century version of consciousness raising.
The women who attended were inspired by a sense of
women's solidarity. Everyone was free to participate
and exchange views.

Various feminists emphasized different reforms for wom-
en. Elizabeth Cady Stanton argued for rights within marriage and easy divorce. Lucretia Mott, with her knowledge of scripture, denounced clergymen who preached
that God had made woman inferior to man. Ernestine
Rose spoke for legal rights. And Harriet Hunt, with her
knowedge of medicine, denounced doctors who proclaimed the physical inferiority of women. Women would
be strong, she said, when they took charge of their
own health care.

The "star" speaker during the first years of women's
rights was Stone. According to Stanton, she was "the
first who really stirred the nation's heart on the subject of
women's wrongs." Stone's power as a speaker is evident
from her address to the 1855 national women's rights
convention. She followed a male speaker who characterized the women's rights movement as being composed
of "a few disappointed women." Stone responded.

The last speaker alluded to this movement as being that
of a few disappointed women. From the first years to
which my memory stretches I have been a disappointed
woman. When, with my brother, I reached forth after
sources of knowledge, I was reproved with "It isn't fit for
you; it doesn't belong to women." Then there was but one
college in the world where women were admitted and that
was in Brazil. I would have found my way there, but by
the time I was prepared to go one was opened in the young
state of Ohio—the first in the United States where negroes
and women could enjoy opportunities with white men. I
was disappointed when I came to seek a profession . . . every employment was closed to me, except those of the
teacher, the seamstress, and the housekeeper.

In education, in marriage, in religion, in everything, disappointment is the lot of woman. It shall be the business of my life to deepen this disappointment in every woman's heart until she bows down to it no longer. I wish that women, instead of begging of their fathers and brothers the latest and gayest new bonnet, would ask of them their rights.[8]

Other feminists spoke with equally spontaneous passion. At the Akron, Ohio, women's rights convention of 1851, Sojourner Truth—a former slave and domestic worker, an evangelist active in both the abolitionist and women's movements—moved the audience to tears. The convention was on the verge of total disruption, with clergymen shouting down feminist speakers, when Sojourner Truth made her way to the platform. Not all the women present were entirely glad to see her. Many feared that if she spoke "every newspaper in the land will have our cause mixed with abolition." But Francis Gage, chairing the convention, recognized the black woman. "Sojourner Truth will speak," announced Gage. And when she spoke, everyone listened.

That man over there says that women need to be helped into carriages and lifted over ditches, and to have the best place everywhere. Nobody ever helps me into carriages or over mud puddles, or gives me any best place. And ain't I a woman? Look at me! I have ploughed and planted and gathered into barns and no man could head me. And ain't I a woman? I could work as much and eat as much as a man—when I could get it—and hear the lash as well. And ain't I a woman? I have borne thirteen children and seen most all sold off to slavery, and when I cried out with my mother's grief, none but Jesus heard me. And ain't I a woman?

Then they talk about this thing in the head; What's that they call it? [Intellect, whispers someone.] That's it honey. What's that got to do with women's rights or negro's rights? If my cup won't hold but a pint and yours holds a quart, wouldn't you be mean not to let my little half-measure full.

Then that little man in back there, he says women can't have as much rights as men 'cause Christ wasn't a woman. Where did your Christ come from? From God and a woman! Man had nothing to do with Him.

If the first woman God ever made was strong enough to turn the world upside down all alone, these women together ought to be able to turn it back, and get it right side up again! And now they is asking to do it, the men better let them.[9]

While Sojourner Truth and Lucy Stone could turn an angry audience into a receptive one, Americans in general remained hostile to feminism. Other reform movements could be embraced abstractly; they called on people to change the world. The women's rights movement made people angry and frightened because it asked them to change themselves.

Feminism threatened the most personal relationships in people's lives. Feminists asked men and women to think of themselves in new ways and to relate differently to each other. If wives, mothers, daughters changed, husbands, fathers, and sons would be called upon to change as well. Home and family would be altered.

One antifeminist wrote, "These garrulous women would upheave all existing institutions and overturn all relations between the sexes."[10] Interestingly, the antifeminists often understood the end result of the feminist platform more acutely than did feminists themselves. Many women in the movement thought of themselves as reformers, lobbying for a number of concrete, specific rights. Antifeminists saw through to the concepts behind those reforms; taken to their logical conclusion, feminist ideas were revolutionary.

Public resistance was strong when feminists merely took the speaking platforms and asked for change. When they actually changed themselves, openly and visibly, public reaction went wild. Such was the case when feminists shed their hoop skirts and corsets in favor of a costume including pants.

These trousers were first worn by Elizabeth Smith Miller, Stanton's cousin. Miller designed the first trouser outfit herself in 1850, but inspiration seems to have come from her father, Gerrit Smith, an active abolitionist and supporter of women's rights. He took a special interest in reforming women's fashion. The current style, he felt, made women weak, helpless, and passive. How could a woman "find her own way in the world," he asked, when she was weighed down by yards and yards of skirts? Smith urged feminists to "throw off" their "clothes' prisons"; until they did, he warned, "women will be dependent and poor."[11]

Elizabeth Smith Miller took her father's advice. She sewed herself a pair of ballooning trousers and wore them underneath a knee-length skirt. Stanton soon followed her cousin's lead, and she in turn was followed by her friend Amelia Bloomer. Soon Bloomer began advocating the style in the columns of her temperance newspaper. When hundreds of women wrote to her for sewing instructions, she published pictures and patterns. Because of this publicity, people began calling the new style "bloomerettes" and the "bloomer costume." The term "bloomers" stuck.

Many women tried bloomers—farm wives, pioneer women heading West on wagon trains, gymnasts, and skaters, but for the most part it was such feminists as Lucy Stone, the Grimké sisters, Paulina Wright Davis, and Elizabeth Cady Stanton who actually wore them.

By modern standards bloomers were hardly revealing. When they first appeared, however, many people thought them indecent. Women who wore bloomers revealed their legs; granted that these were covered with trousers, they were nevertheless legs, from the knees to the ankles. In 1851 most ladies would not admit that they had legs, much less display them.

Bloomers caused a greater public outcry than anything feminists had said or done up to that time. People reacted hysterically, as they might today if a group of men suddenly started wearing skirts. In the streets men stared, jibed, ridiculed, and attacked women who wore bloomers. Cartoonists and newspaper columnists had a heyday, ridiculing "Those women . . . dressed like men." Clergymen claimed that bloomers were "devilish."

Countering the attacks, Elizabeth Cady Stanton defended the bloomer costume.

> For us commonplace, everyday, working characters, who wash and iron, bake and brew, carry water and fat babies upstairs and down, bring potatoes, apples, and pans of milk from the cellar, run our own errands, through mud or snow; shovel paths and work in the garden, why "the drapery" [long skirts and petticoats] is too much—one might as well work with a ball and chain.[12]

But Elizabeth could not win over her own relatives, much less the public. Her husband was "amused." From Albany, where he was attending a session of the legislature, he wrote to his wife. "The worst thing about [bloomers] would be, I should think, sitting down. Then ladies will expose their legs somewhat above the knee to the delight of those gentlemen who are curious to know whether their lady friends have round and plump legs or lean and scrawny ones."[13] The rest of her family was mortified. Judge Cady wrote that "no woman of good sense and delicacy" would "make such a guy of herself," and he hoped that when Elizabeth came to visit she would not be in bloomers. Her sister Tryphena wept when she heard the news, and Harriet would not write. Even her sons, Daniel and Henry, attending Theodore Weld's progressive school, let their mother know that they did not want her to visit them in the "short dress."

When Henry Stanton ran for a second term in the state senate, Elizabeth's bloomers became a campaign issue. "Some good Democrats," she wrote to her cousin, "said they would not vote for a man whose wife wore bloomers. . . . This seemed to increase the activity of the street urchins who hissed and screamed 'breeches' . . . throughout the campaign."

Henry was reelected to the state senate despite his wife's costume. It was Elizabeth who suffered the campaign ridicule. "Had I counted the cost of the new dress," she wrote, "I would never have put it on; however, I'll never take it off, for now it involves a principle of freedom."[14]

She lasted in bloomers another three years. By then, not even the "principle of freedom" could keep her in them. "We put it on for greater freedom," she wrote, "but what is physical freedom compared with mental bondage?"[15] After 1854 Elizabeth had her new dresses made long and encouraged other feminists to do the same. One by one, Lucy Stone, the Grimké sisters, Ernestine Rose, all lowered their hems.

Gerrit Smith still insisted that if women abandoned their corsets, hoops, and long skirts, men would stop treating them like "playthings, idols, or dolls." Stanton no longer agreed. Bloomers, she said, would not produce political or social equality for women; more comfortable clothing for women would follow, not precede, such changes.

In the long run Stanton was right. For the time being, however, feminists failed to change fashion for themselves or for other women. It was easier for them to dress conventionally than to dress differently, even when they knew that their unconventional dress was more comfortable. Though Stanton told her children not to care what people thought, not to worry about being different,[16] she and other feminists did care and worry.

Feminists never questioned some aspects of conventional morality. Even at their most radical, they thought of themselves as ladies, and they assumed that being a "lady" was better than being simply a woman. Such attitudes made nineteenth-century feminists blind to some of women's most serious problems.

Most of the feminists did not question the nineteenth-century belief that women were asexual. They refused to talk about anything related to sex—such as pregnancy, abortion, and contraception—and they were even reluctant to discuss how women's sexual roles as housewives and mothers affected their lives. They chose to focus only on the public rights denied to women.

A few women—Paulina Wright Davis, Stanton, and Stone—recognized the importance of sexual issues. Davis' lectures provided some women with the only accurate information about their bodies available at the time. Stanton and Stone understood that for women to be equal they would have to change the way they lived with men. Their effort to redefine what it meant to be a woman, a wife, a mother was a lonely process. Few women in the movement joined them in the search, and they themselves were often unable to overcome the prejudices of their time.

Lucy Stone was the first of the early feminists to publicly propose a new model for marriage. In 1855 Stone married Henry Blackwell. At their wedding ceremony the couple protested the "present laws of marriage," refusing to obey them. Theirs would be an "equal and permanent partnership." If they had "domestic difficulties," they would not "appeal to the law" since the "present laws . . . confer upon the husband an . . . unnatural superiority and legal powers which no man should possess."[17]

Throughout her girlhood Stone had vowed she would never marry. She had been frightened by the example of her mother, worn and prematurely aged from bearing too many children. Like many women of her generation, she thought of sex as an unpleasant activity, desired only by men. Women could expect nothing from their couplings except children. Few people knew how to prevent conception except by abstaining from sexual intercourse, and many married women became pregnant every year.

Stone believed that most women would happily abstain from sex and that men should learn from women's "moral" example. In letters she urged her married brothers to space their children, as Angelina and Theodore Weld did, through abstinence. "Moral reform in marriage" was her phrase.

Her brothers scoffed. "This waiting three years as you intimate, Sis, is all nonsense," replied one. "You spoke of cohabitating only for the sake of children. . . . I suppose individuals do not cohabit for the sake of children only, but because they want to." A second brother wrote, "Lucy I think It As Great A Sin to not Suffer These Organs To Be Used At All As To Use Them Too Much."[18] But Stone continued to preach abstinence as the only solution. For herself, she thought it better to avoid sex altogether by never marrying.

Given her fears, Lucy Stone was not an easy woman to win, but Henry Blackwell was determined. Henry was the oldest son of an English immigrant family that settled in Ohio in 1832 and became active abolitionists and temperance reformers. The Blackwell family contained several independent, strong-minded women. Henry's mother and four maiden aunts dominated the family. All five of his sisters had careers and never married. Two sisters became doctors, Elizabeth being the first American woman to earn a medical degree. Lucy's feminism did not frighten Henry. He also shared her moralistic streak. He, too, had been raised on piety and purity and believed in the "moral improveability of man and society." In a courtship that lasted two years, most of it conducted through letters, Henry gradually wore down Lucy's objections to marriage. He promised her absolute freedom, support in her work, and total equality. "Equality with me," he wrote, "is a passion. I dislike equally to assume or endure authority."

At first Lucy welcomed Henry as a friend and nothing more. Women's rights was her life, and it would take a lifetime and longer to accomplish her goals. Besides, Lucy wrote Henry, she was too old for him (by seven years), and she was not suited for marriage—she was "not made to be a wife."

Henry was not discouraged. He persisted and eventually found the winning argument. By not marrying, he wrote, by not claiming her *right* to a good marriage, Lucy was making herself a slave to law and prejudice.

> Would it not be a slavish doctrine to preach that we ought to sentence ourselves to celibacy because men have enacted injustice into a statute—Lucy, dear, I want to make a protest, distinct and emphatic against the laws. I wish as a husband to renounce all the privileges which the law confers upon me which are not strictly mutual.

Lucy now began to consider the possibility of marriage.

> If there can be a true marriage between us, it is as much for my happiness and interest to assume it as for yours. . . . Do you suppose dear Henry that now when I believe I have a *right* to the marriage relationship, after having spent half my days on the barren desert of an unshared life, that I would voluntarily shut myself up to its utter loneliness still longer? Oh no.

All the while Henry was becoming more active in both the abolitionist cause and the women's rights movements. When he helped a slave girl to escape from the South, Lucy's mind was made up. "I read your deliverance from that railroad disaster—never until then had I known how dear, or how necessary you are to me. . . . My heart yearns toward you all the time . . . and only pray this . . . love may last forever."[19]

Lucy insisted on keeping her maiden name. She wanted to be known as Lucy Stone and not as Mrs. Blackwell. Well into the twentieth century women who followed her example were called Lucy Stoners.

The Stone-Blackwell marriage became a model for other reforming couples and for women who wanted to marry without relinquishing their careers. Together, Lucy and Henry developed a cooperative work partnership. Women's rights became a family activity. Lucy converted her husband to the movement and raised her only child, Alice Stone Blackwell, by its precepts. Henry stayed in business long enough to accumulate savings for their future; then he joined Lucy in her work. Together the couple spent close to forty years campaigning for women's rights. Eventually Alice took over their work.

The personal side of marriage was more difficult for Lucy. Shortly after her wedding she wrote that she wanted a child as soon as possible and would not leave her husband or home until she became pregnant. She worried about her ability to bear children, and after she was pregnant, she feared that she would die in childbirth.

After the birth of her daughter, Lucy retired from the lecture platform for several years to care for her child and home. Henry, still in business, traveled a great deal. Lucy, who had vowed that marriage would not interfere with her freedom, felt suddenly trapped in domesticity. During these years she suffered severe headaches followed by days of extreme depression. "I *am* trying to be a good wife and mother," she wrote to Henry, "but I have tried before and my miserable failures make me silent now."

Lucy did not relate her own difficulties to those of other women. Once married, in fact, she became less willing to discuss the problems of wives and mothers than she had been earlier. Privately she agreed with such feminists as Elizabeth Cady Stanton and Paulina Wright Davis that "the marriage question" was central to the women's movement. She was still concerned about "moral reform" in marriage. "It is very little to me," she wrote in 1856, "to have the right to vote, to own property, etc., if I may not keep my body and its uses in my absolute right." But, she concluded, "we are not ready for that question."[20]

Lucy resolved her personal difficulties with the help of her husband. Henry Blackwell was a man who put his wife's interests and career above his own. He realized that Lucy would never be content as a housewife. She needed a "public career," he wrote, and "personal independence." With Henry's help, Lucy eventually did more work for the women's movement than she had been able to do before her marriage. Henry financed many of her projects and accompanied her on lecture and campaign tours.

Elizabeth Cady Stanton had a very different kind of marriage. During the early years she wrote to and of her husband with affection; but the distance between them deepened as Elizabeth grew more committed to women's rights.

Henry Stanton was not like Henry Blackwell—nor, for that matter, like James Mott and many other husbands who joined their wives in the reform arena. Henry

Stanton liked going his own way, apart from his wife. He did not include her in his abolitionist activities, and his work as a lawyer, politician, and journalist kept him away from his home for long periods of time. As for the women's movement, Henry wanted as little to do with it as possible. In the 1880s, when Henry published his memoirs, he credited his wife once—for her work as an abolitionist. Absent altogether is any mention of women's rights. There are no personal references to Elizabeth.

Henry was as absent from Elizabeth's memoirs as she from his. Almost her only mention of him is the remark that she "lived with Mr. Stanton for almost fifty years, without more than the usual matrimonial friction." She has warm and loving words for her children and friends but only a few formal references to her husband.

In the 1850s Henry returned home frequently enough for Elizabeth to become pregnant every other year. Between 1851 and 1859 she bore four more children—two sons and two long-awaited daughters. It is difficult to assess the amount of anger Elizabeth felt about her husband's frequent absences from home or her frequent pregnancies. At least some of it is expressed in a letter dated 1853.

> The right idea of marriage is at the foundation of all reforms. . . . A child conceived in the midst of hate, sin, discord, nurtured on abuse and injustice cannot too much bless the world or himself. Man in his lust has relegated long enough the whole question of sexual intercourse. Now let the mother of mankind, whose prerogative it is to set the bounds to his indulgence, rouse up and give this matter a fearless thorough examination.[21]

Stanton sounds very much like Stone, advocating abstinence, and yet she did not believe that women were asexual. At the same time that she criticized "man's lust," she also thought it foolish for women to equate chastity with moral worth. She worried that too many women were "suffering from repression." They would be healthier, less prone to illness and hysteria, if they expressed their natural passions. Later in life she wrote in her diary, "A healthy woman has as much passion as a man and needs nothing stronger than the law of attraction to draw her to the male." She had "come to the conclusion that the first great work to be accomplished for woman is to revolutionize the dogma that sex is a crime, marriage a defilement, and maternity a bane."[22]

It was not sexuality to which Stanton objected. She sought control, not over "man's lust," but over her own body. Abstinence as a way to limit conception did not appeal to her.

Stanton seems to have found at least a partial answer. If she could not control whether and when she would have children, she could at least control how she had them. She believed that pregnancy was a natural state rather than an illness and that childbirth could be painless. She practiced this very modern view herself and preached it for other women.

Throughout each of her pregnancies Stanton did her usual work, right up to the last minute. She seems to have delivered each of her seven children easily, with only the help of a nurse and housekeeper. Within a day or two, sometimes a few hours, she would be up and about again.

This was a time when pregnant women of the middle class were advised to stay in bed from their seventh or eighth month of pregnancy until a month after they had delivered. Stanton saw this confinement as the cause of women's difficult labors and numerous postpartum ailments. She was convinced that her way was far healthier, and she loved to describe it to her friends and relatives. When her fourth son, Theodore, was born, she wrote to her husband, "I am regarded as a perfect wonder . . . many people are impatiently waiting for me to die in order to make their theories good, but I am getting better and stronger every day."[23] After the birth of her fifth child, her first daughter, she wrote to Lucretia Mott.

I never felt such sacredness in carrying a child as I have in the case of this one. She is the largest and most vigorous baby I have ever had, weighing twelve pounds. And yet my labor was short and easy. I laid down about fifteen minutes and brought forth this big girl. I sat up immediately, changed my own clothes, put on a wet bandage, and after a few hours' repose sat up again. Am I not almost a savage? For what refined, delicate, genteel, civilized woman would get well in so indecently short a time? Dear me, how much cruel bondage of mind and suffering of body poor woman will escape when she takes the liberty of being her own physician of both body and mind?[24]

Stanton was a loving mother. Instead of punishing her children, she tried to reason with them, often in playful ways. When her sons cursed, she cursed back until they asked her to stop. She made a contract with them that she would stop cursing if they did. Children, she felt, needed understanding more than discipline. "When your child cries," she told parents, "remember that it is telling you as well as it can that something hurts it, either inside or out, and do not rest until you find out. Neither spanking, shaking, or scolding can relieve pain."

Much as she loved her children, Stanton complained about the "too numerous and varied duties" that went with being a mother and housewife. "To keep a house and grounds in good order, purchase every article for daily use, keep the wardrobes of half a dozen human beings in trim order, take the children to dentists, shoemakers, and different schools, or find teachers at home" was too much for one woman to handle alone. "Woman's work," she concluded, "can never be properly organized in the isolated household." She mused about some "future time" when "cooperative housekeeping . . . might promise a more harmonious life."[25]

More than any other feminist of her time, Stanton recognized that so long as woman carried full responsibility for home and children, she would be defined solely by her sexual roles as wife and mother. As long as she was tied to the isolated household, she would have no chance to exert her own talents and ambitions.

As a feminist, Stanton fought long and hard for the right of women to function outside their homes. But the underlying dilemma remained—how could women find a place for themselves in the world when they were still tied to childrearing and housekeeping? Cooperative households remained a vague dream for the future, and Stanton never thought to insist that men should share the work of home and family with women, just as women should share public life with men.

All through the 1850s Stanton felt torn between her home duties and devotion to her children on the one hand and her wish to be out in the world fighting for women's rights on the other. She described herself as a "caged lioness," "longing to bring to a close housekeeping and children so as to have the time to read, think and

write." Only her "own strong self will" and two devoted
female friends, she later wrote, allowed her to persevere
through "some of the most despairing years of my life."[26]

To stay active in the women's rights movement, she
turned to writing. If she could not attend a convention or
a legislative hearing, she sent a resolution, a letter, some
document to show her support. During the 1850s she produced a vast body of written material on women's rights—
petitions, testimony, speeches, letters to editors of every
newspaper that criticized women's rights, and articles for
such reformist journals as Davis' *The Una* and Garrison's
The Liberator. Her ideas were novel and controversial. In
one column she suggested that boys learn to sew; in another
she advised girls to pay their own way at social engagements.

There was also the help of women. A capable and devoted housekeeper, Amelia Willard, freed Stanton to leave
home periodically for conventions and lecture tours. Amelia
was "a treasure, a friend, a comforter, a second mother to
my children. . . . But for this noble self-sacrificing woman,
much of my public work would have been quite impossible."

The most important person to enter Stanton's life
during the 1850s was Susan B. Anthony. With Stone
and Stanton, Anthony led the women's rights movement
for more than half a century. All three women worked
closely together during the early years of the movement.
But it was Elizabeth and Susan who became a perfect
team, separate from Lucy Stone.

During the years when Stanton was still bearing and
raising her children, Anthony kept her friend up to date
on all that was happening in the movement and all that
needed to be done. She made sure that Stanton stayed
active. If not for Susan, Elizabeth wrote some thirty years
later, she might have become "like too many women,
wholly absorbed in family selfishness."

Susan B. Anthony (1820–1906) built women's rights
into a national organization. A woman with extraordinary
executive abilities, she was called the Napoleon of the
movement.

Unlike Stanton and Stone, Anthony was not drawn instinctively to women's rights. Far from growing up feeling
unequal as a girl, she felt both loved and respected by her
father.[27] She was raised in a small town just east of Albany,

New York, almost midway between Lucy's and Elizabeth's hometowns. Like them, she was exposed early to the reform fervor that swept through upstate New York and western Massachusetts in the 1830s and 1840s.

The Anthony family, however, was very different from the Stones' and the Stantons.' Susan's parents applied reformist values to their own lives. Daniel Anthony was a free-thinking Quaker who defied the church elders to marry Susan's non-Quaker mother, Lucy Reed. Later Daniel became a temperance reformer and outspoken abolitionist.

A Quaker upbringing and her father's belief in equality between the sexes gave Susan more freedom than was enjoyed by most girls of her generation. Wanting all his children liberally educated, Mr. Anthony hired private Quaker teachers and later sent his daughters as well as his sons to private boarding schools. He encouraged his daughters to be independent. When Susan and her sister asked to do some work in his textile mill, he agreed, believing that women should acquire skills so that they could be self-supporting.

When Susan was fifteen, her father went bankrupt and lost his mill. The Anthonys moved from their large brick home to a farm outside Rochester, New York. Susan left school and took a teaching job to earn money.

For thirteen years she taught in one or another of the district schools. The years in Canjoharie, New York, the hometown of her mother's non-Quaker relatives, were especially pleasurable. Susan shed her Quaker black and gray dress for bright, stylish clothes, and she learned to dance. She socialized a great deal and had many suitors, several of whom proposed marriage. But Susan was not interested; she enjoyed being single and felt that her life was full without the encumbrances of a husband and children. Her parents and her brothers and sisters provided her with love and a home. Eventually she found a second family in the women's rights movement.

While Susan B. Anthony did not wish to marry, she did not want to teach school all her life either. She was promoted to "headmistress" of the female department at Canjoharie Academy, the highest position available to a woman; yet her salary was a fraction of the headmaster's. Frustrated by the inequities and hoping to find more satisfying work, she returned to her family's farm.

At home Susan discovered that her father had joined with the Garrisonian abolitionists who preached "immediate emancipation." Both her parents and her sister had attended the second 1848 women's rights convention in Rochester, New York, and had signed the Declaration of Sentiments. At first Susan was amused when her family spoke about women's rights. But they talked with such excitement about Elizabeth Cady Stanton, with her "black curls and ruddy cheeks," and Lucretia Mott, "who spoke so grandly," that she grew increasingly curious.

In 1851 Susan went to Seneca Falls to visit her friend Amelia Bloomer and to attend an antislavery meeting led by Garrison. It was on this visit that Susan and Elizabeth first met. They liked each other at once. Susan was drawn to Elizabeth's vitality and fervor about women's rights and Elizabeth to Susan's "good, earnest face" and to what she sensed was her "underlying strong character."

Meeting Stanton did not immediately convert Anthony to feminism. Her first reform venture was the temperance movement, for which she organized societies of women called the Daughters of Temperance. Stanton recognized that the goals of the temperance movement were essentially conservative, but she also saw that temperance work could lead women to feminism just as abolitionism had. When Anthony was reprimanded at the State Temperance Convention in 1852 for trying to speak—"the sisters were not invited here to speak but to listen and to learn," said the chairman—Stanton helped her to organize a separate Woman's State Temperance Society. Men were allowed to attend meetings and to speak but not to hold office.

At the society's first convention Stanton proposed that drunkenness be made grounds for divorce. Her idea was entirely too radical for the temperance workers who, along with most Americans, believed that marriage vows were forever no matter how bad the marriage. Steps were taken to silence Stanton and Anthony. At the next annual Woman's State Temperance Convention the by-laws of the society were rewritten to exclude women from office. As soon as men gained power, they changed the society's name to the People's League and ruled out all mention of women's rights.

Hurt and disappointed, Susan wrote long letters to Elizabeth. Her friend replied, "I do beg of you to let the past be past, and to waste no more powder on the Woman's State Temperance Society. *We have other and bigger fish to fry.*"[28]

A few months later, Anthony launched a new campaign. At the state teachers' convention in Rochester she sat silently with other women teachers in the back of the hall. The women listened to men teachers talk about the low status of their profession. Why, they asked, were teachers not treated with the same respect accorded to doctors and lawyers? Anthony rose from her seat and asked to be recognized. A half-hour debate followed in which male teachers tried to decide if a woman should be allowed to speak. After a close vote, Anthony was given the floor.

> It seems to me, gentlemen, that none of you quite comprehend the cause of the disrespect of which you complain. Do you not see that so long as society says a woman is incompetent to be a lawyer, minister, or doctor, but has ample ability to be a teacher, that every man of you who chooses this profession tacitly acknowledges that he has no more brains than a woman. And this too is the reason that teaching is less a lucrative profession, as here men must compete with the cheap labor of women. Would you exalt your profession, exalt those who labor with you. Would you make it more lucrative, increase the salaries of the women engaged in the novel work of educating our future Presidents, Senators, and Congressmen.[29]

Anthony believed that as long as women were viewed as inferior they would be exploited as cheap labor; and as long as they were exploited as cheap labor, they would be concentrated in low-paying, low-status jobs. Her point was that some occupations have low wages and status *because* women are the chief employees. Anthony said that male and female workers should receive the same wages. She also understood that for women to be truly equal economically, they had to have access to all the jobs that were considered the sole prerogative of men.

As a single woman supporting herself, Anthony took a special interest in woman's economic status. Before a woman could be free, she observed, she had to have "a purse of her own." She reached this conclusion when she returned to the towns where she had organized women's temperance groups. Most of these had collapsed for lack of funds. She commented on the situation in her diary.

> As I passed from town to town I was made to feel the great evil of woman's entire dependency upon man for the necessary means to aid on any and every reform movement. . . . Woman must have a purse of her own and how can this be so long as the Wife is denied the right to her individual and joint earnings. Reflections like these caused me to see and really feel that there was no true freedom for Woman without the possession of all her property rights, and that these rights could be obtained through legislation only, and so, the sooner the demand was made of the Legislature, the sooner would we be likely to obtain them.[30]

The passage reveals a great deal about Anthony's personality and what motivated her. She was quick to get to the problem at hand and to think of the most immediate way to solve it. She approached women's rights from the perspective of specific issues where change could be effected. One issue led to the next. The male prejudice she found in the temperance movement led her to confront the prejudice against women teachers and women workers in general. Immediately she turned her attention to what she could do then and there. Transforming women's working conditions would take a lifetime. The law could be changed more quickly. If women won property rights, they would be one step closer to "having purses of their own." "The sooner the demand was made . . . the sooner it would be accomplished." Beginning with a rather tentative interest in the ideas of feminism, therefore, Anthony became more and more absorbed in achieving rights for women.

Anthony's friendship with Stanton cemented her total commitment to the movement. It was Stanton who persuaded Anthony that her best energies were needed on behalf of women. Again and again Stanton pointed her friend in the direction of women's issues. Anthony's need "to do," to effect and influence change, gave Stanton exactly what she needed—a collaborator who could translate her ideas into action.

Both as friends and coworkers Susan and Elizabeth made a remarkably complementary team. Susan was shy yet driven, easily hurt and quick to criticize. She relied on

Elizabeth's steadying hand. When Susan needed humoring, Elizabeth teased; when her spirits were down, Elizabeth buoyed her up; when she had driven herself too hard, Elizabeth told her to rest. And Elizabeth, energetic but disorganized, found Susan's clarity a blessing. She gave Elizabeth direction and goaded her to work. In addition, Elizabeth felt that Susan understood her better than anyone, certainly more than her husband and neighbors.

> Henry sides with my friends, who oppose me in all that is dearest to my heart. They are not willing that I should write even on the woman question. But I will both write and speak. I wish you to consider this letter strictly confidential. Sometimes, Susan, I struggle in deep waters. . . . However, a good time is coming and my future is always bright and beautiful.[31]

In another letter, Elizabeth begged Susan to come for a visit.

> Men and angels give me patience. I am at the boiling point. If I do not find some day the use of my tongue on this question, I shall die of an intellectual repression, a women's rights convulsion. Oh Susan, Susan, Susan. You must manage to spend a week with me before the Rochester [1852] convention, for I am afraid I cannot attend. But I will write a letter.[32]

Stanton was the writer, the thinker, the philosopher. At home in Seneca Falls she "forged the thunderbolts" that Anthony then "fired" into the world. Whenever Anthony felt that her ideas needed to be crystallized, she called on Stanton. She would arrive at the Stanton household with her "little portmanteau . . . stuffed with facts and statistics—false interpretations of the Bible, statistics of women robbed of their property, shut out of some college, half paid for their work."[33] Then, while Anthony took charge of the children and housework, Santon would shut herself in the attic and transform her friend's facts into strong prose. When the document was complete, Anthony, the master strategist, would take off—to launch another large-scale campaign, to organize and preside at another convention.

Anthony's campaign to win "full and total" property rights for women in New York was undertaken in partnership with Stanton. The two women wrote a petition that asked for three legal reforms: control by women of their own earnings, guardianship of their children in case of divorce, and the vote. Stanton supplied Anthony with the details on women's long campaign in New York to win passage of the Married Woman's Property Act of 1848.

The New York law, the first of its kind, gave women control over the property they owned at the time of their marriage. The law also exempted a married woman's property from her husband's debts. At first Ernestine Rose, a Polish-born Jew who had worked with socialist Robert Owen in England, lobbied alone for the bill. She trekked up and down the state collecting signatures on petitions asking the New York legislature for its passage. Eventually Paulina Wright Davis and Elizabeth Cady Stanton joined her. It took twelve years, from 1836 to 1848, for the bill to pass, and the law by no means redressed all of the legal wrongs women faced. "At best," noted Ernestine Rose, "the Married Woman's Property Act was only for the favored few and not for the suffering many."[34] While it protected women who had inherited property, it did not give women control of their wages. Money earned by married women still legally belonged to their husbands.

It was these wage-earning wives Susan had in mind when she set out on her first petition campaign for total property rights. She planned to pressure the legislature into giving wives control of their wages, and she intended to gain her ends in less than twelve years.

Anthony was an organizational genius. She devised a canvassing plan that is used by political organizers to this day. She was determined to reach every person in the state, urging them to sign a petition in favor of the revised property law. To guarantee that no areas were overlooked, she named sixty women, one from each New York State county, to serve as captains. The canvassers began collecting signatures in the winter of 1854. Within six weeks, six thousand people had signed.

Stanton remained at home working on a speech in favor of legal rights for women. Anthony planned a women's rights convention in Albany while the legislature was still in session. She used her petitions to gain a hearing for the bills feminists supported, and Stanton spoke before the legislature's Joint Judiciary Committee.

No new laws for women were passed in 1854. Legislators considered women's rights a joke. More signatures were needed, and Anthony went out to get them. On Christmas Day 1855 she started out alone, with a bag of literature and fifty dollars loaned to her by abolitionist Wendell Phillips. For five months she traveled throughout the state, circulating petitions in fifty-four of the sixty counties.

Once again, when feminists presented the petitions, they were laughed out of the legislature. The report of the Assembly's Judiciary Committee commented on the situation.

> The ladies always have the best place and the choicest tidbits at the table. They always have the best seat in the cars and carriages, and sleighs; the warmest place in winter and the coolest place in summer. A lady's dress costs three times as much as that of a gentleman.[35]

Given these "advantages," women did not need legal rights.

Fatigued and disappointed, Anthony worried. It took so long to win rights for women, it required so much work, and she was carrying the load alone. She felt deserted by her closest allies. Stanton was pregnant at the time with her sixth child; Stone had momentarily retired from the lecture platform to care for her infant daughter; Antoinette Brown was also married and raising children. Anthony wished them to stop having babies and join her on the petition trail, as she wrote to Stanton.

> Those of you who have the talent to do honor to poor womanhood have all given yourself over to baby-making; and left poor, brainless me to do battle alone. It is a shame. Such a body as I might be spared to rock cradles. But it is a crime for you and Lucy Stone and Antoinette Brown to be doing it.[36]

Stanton, a wife and mother herself, understood Lucy Stone and Antoinette Brown in a way Susan did not. At the same time she did not take Anthony's criticisms as seriously as Stone did. She simply accepted Anthony's single-minded devotion to the movement and in turn tried to make her friend understand how matters stood for her and for other married feminists.

Let Lucy and Antoinette rest awhile in peace and quiet-
ness and think great thoughts for the future. It is not well
to be in the excitement of public life all the time; do not
keep stirring them up or mourning over their repose. You
need to rest too Susan. Let the world alone awhile. We
cannot bring about a moral revolution in a day or a year.
. . . It is not in vain that I myself have experienced all the
wearisome cares to which woman in her best estate is subject.[37]

Not even Stanton could change Anthony's feelings about
Lucy Stone, however. Anthony remained angry at Stone
for marrying and having a child, and Stone, sensitive to her
criticism, rebuked Anthony in turn. It was the beginning of
a breach that was to split apart the women's movement
following the Civil War.

In 1860 the New York state legislature finally passed a
bill granting married women rights to property and
wages. A wife could make contracts with her husband's
consent, and she could enter into contracts on her own
authority if he were an alcoholic, a convict, or insane. A
wife became joint guardian of her children. For the first
time a wife's inheritance became hers in every legal sense
on the death of her husband. Other states in the Northeast
and Midwest ultimately passed similar laws. Women were
still not equal to men under the law and they still could
not vote, but they had won some basic legal rights.

In the same year Stanton decided to discuss marriage
and divorce at the national women's rights convention.
She offered ten resolutions proposing liberal grounds for
divorce. According to Stanton, couples who were unhap-
pily married had "not only a right, but a *duty* to abolish"
their marriages. "There is one kind of marriage that has
not been tried," she went on, "and that is a contract made
by equal parties to lead an equal life with equal restraints and privileges on either side. Thus far, we have
had the man marriage, and nothing more."[38]

Stanton's proposals were not well received. Divorce was
unthinkable, unnatural, and "morally impossible," Antoinette Brown stated. Used as she was to that argument,
Stanton was unprepared for the attack by Wendell Phillips, who claimed that marriage was not a proper topic to
discuss at a women's rights convention. Since both men
and women married, marriage "applied equally to both

sexes." Feminists, argued Phillips, should limit themselves
to discussing the laws that rested unequally on women.

Anthony defended Stanton's resolutions.

> As to the point that this question does not belong to this
> platform, from that I totally dissent. Marriage has ever
> been a one-sided matter, resting most unequally on the
> sexes. By it, man gains all; woman loses all. . . . By law,
> public sentiment, and religion—woman has never been
> thought of other than a piece of property to be disposed of
> at the will and pleasure of man. . . . She must accept mar-
> riage as man proffers it, or not at all.[39]

Ernestine Rose, Lucretia Mott, and Lydia Mott also stood
by Stanton. But the majority of those attending the convention, including Lucy Stone, sided with Phillips. They
saw no connection between marriage and women's inequality.

Stanton was stunned. Phillips had been her teacher
and her mentor. She had learned about abolitionism from
him, and she had always been able to count on him to
understand and support her feminism. Suddenly that support was removed, and she felt betrayed. She expressed
herself in a letter to Anthony.

> With all his excellence and nobility, Wendell Phillips is a
> man. His words and tone and manner came down on me
> like a clap of thunder. We are right, however. My reason,
> my experience, my soul proclaim it. Woman's degradation
> is in man's idea of his sexual rights. Our religion, laws,
> customs are all founded on the belief that woman was made
> for man. . . . My own life, observations, thought, feeling,
> reason brought me to the conclusion. So fear not, I shall
> not falter. I shall not grow conservative with age.[40]

8

On the Loom: The First Factory Women

The development of an industrial economy in the 1800s changed the definition of women's work. All women continued to work in their homes, but only those who earned money for their labor were called working women.

Working women in the 1800s were usually schoolteachers, seamstresses, domestics, and factory operatives. None of these jobs provided women with status or a decent wage. Teaching was the most respectable job available to an unmarried woman who needed to earn a living. Most female schoolteachers began working while still in their teens. Those who did not marry and remained schoolteachers were doomed to a life of genteel poverty because of extremely low wages.

Throughout the 1800s household service provided employment for more women than any other occupation. Because few native-born white women were willing to do domestic work outside their own homes, it was generally new arrivals and free black women who worked as household servants. Domestics worked long hours, their pay was meager, and privacy and leisure time were practically nonexistent.

The emergence of an industrial economy created new conditions for working women. From the start of the Industrial Revolution women were needed to mass-produce the goods they had once produced for their families. Manufacturing was done both in the home and in factories. In general, married women who needed to earn wages worked at home while single women were hired to work in factories.

The most common home-manufacturing trade for women was sewing for the emerging ready-made clothing industry. In Troy, New York, the "collar and cuff capital" of the nation, hundreds of women worked at home making these items. Troy manufacturers delivered the raw materials to women at home and later picked up the finished products.

In the early 1800s home sewing for the ready-made clothing industry was considered "respectable" work for native-born white women. The work was considered an extension of women's traditional roles, since they had always sewn for their families. Now, doing the same kind of work on a larger scale, they could earn wages.

By the mid-1800s the nature of the home sewing industry had changed drastically; the work was done only by the poorest of native-born and immigrant women. In large cities such as New York and Chicago clothing manufacturers bought whole blocks of tenements and leased them to workers. Within these tenement sweatshops women and children labored for starvation wages.

This same pattern can be seen in the employment of single women in the textile mills of New England. In the 1820s and 1830s, after the invention of the spinning jenny and the power loom, textile mills sprang up in towns throughout New England, wherever there was a river to supply water power. Work in the mills was considered an excellent opportunity for unmarried women. There seemed to be little difference between a woman working a spinning wheel at home and a woman working a loom in a mill. The added attraction was that now women could earn money for their work. It was said that the mills would save young women from "idleness and its inseparable attendants, vice and guilt."[1] The "golden opportunity" that the mills seemed to promise, however, proved to be illusory.

Francis Cabot Lowell, scion of an illustrious American family and a pioneer in the American textile industry, promoted the idea of female factory workers when he founded what was to become the most famous mill town in the nation. Young single women were in many ways the most likely candidates for employment by Lowell. Most of the New England men were needed on farms, and married women had families to care for. Single women who had finished school but were not yet absorbed in households of their own were available and already skilled in the work of making cloth. They could be recruited at one-third to one-half the wages demanded by men.

During the 1820s and 1830s single women from Massachusetts, New Hampshire, Vermont, and Maine traveled to the mill towns to sign up for work. The mill owners demanded twelve to thirteen hours of labor a day, six days a week, and each worker had to agree to work for at least one year. There was no shortage of workers. Most of the women were between the ages of sixteen and twenty-five, the daughters of poor farmers, fiancees of seamen, and young widows. These women, with such "old fashioned country names" as Samantha, Leafy, and Almaretta, girls with yearnings for town culture and independence from their families, were easily convinced that both could be found in the mills.

Each woman had her own reason for entering the mills. One mill girl described the women working beside her.

> One, who sits at my right hand at table is in the factory because she hates her mother-in-law. . . . The one next to her has a wealthy father, but like many of our country farmers he is very penurious, and he wishes his daughters to maintain themselves. . . . The next has a "well-off" mother, but she is very pious and will not buy her daughter so many pretty gowns and collars and ribbons . . . as she likes. . . . The next one has a horror of domestic service. The next one has left a good home because her lover, who has gone on a whaling voyage, wishes to be married when he returns, and she would like more money than her father will give her.[2]

Most of all, the women came to earn wages. Mill owners paid $1.25 a week for the girls' board and a flat 55 cents in salary a week, with piecework rates applied beyond a minimum. A few very fast workers managed to earn $4 a week above board, but the average wage was two dollars and change. In the 1830s that was the best salary a working woman could earn. Teaching, seamstressing, and domestic work—the only other jobs available to women—paid considerably less.

Some mill workers needed wages to help support widowed mothers or "drunken, incompetent, or invalid fathers." Others worked to "secure education for some *male* member of the family." Many of the women, however, used their wages to support themselves. Harriet Robinson, a mill worker who later wrote of her experiences in Lowell, described what earnings meant to unmarried women of the time. "In almost every New England home could be found an unmarried woman, sitting solitary, sometimes welcome, more often unwelcome. . . . From a condition of almost pauperism, they could earn money and spend it as they pleased. . . . At last they were no longer obliged to finish out their faded lives a burden to their male relatives."[3]

In Lowell, Fall River, Dover, Waltham, and other mill towns operatives were at work by 5 A.M., and except for a half-hour break for breakfast and another for dinner, they kept working until sunset. Girls ten years old and younger worked this twelve- to thirteen-hour day. They were called "doffers" because they replaced used doffers or bobbins on the spinning wheels. Teenage and adult operatives worked either as spinners or as weavers.

All the mill jobs were similar to work done at home making cloth, but in the factories the labor was subdivided into many stages and was mechanized. "I never cared much for the machinery," wrote one worker. "The buzzing and hissing and whizzing of pulleys, and rollers and spindles and flyers around me often grew tiresome."[4] Another woman described the first time she tried to operate a power loom.

> She felt afraid to touch the loom and she was almost sure she could never learn to weave; the harness puzzled and the reed perplexed her; the shuttle flew out and made a new bump on her head; and the first time she tried to spring the sathe she broke out a quarter of the threads. It seemed as if the girls all stared at her, and the overseers watched every motion, and the day appeared as long as a month had at home. . . . At last it was night . . . There was a dull pain in her head and a sharp pain in her ankles; every bone was aching, and there was in her ears a strange noise, as of crickets, frogs, and jewharps, all mingling together.[5]

The work was monotonous, requiring only minimal skills, but during the first years of the factory system workers were not pushed too hard. "Help was too valuable to be mistreated," according to Harriet Robinson. The relationship between overseers and operatives was friendly. Women worked one or at most two looms, and there was time to rest at intervals.

During these early years women workers were treated to a heavy dose of paternalism. Mill owners were eager to show the public that factory labor and life in the mill towns would not damage the morals of young women. To "protect" the women, they watched over them at all times, outside the mills as well as within them. All mill girls were required to live in company-built boarding houses, each housing twelve to thirteen workers. The atmosphere within the boarding house was like that in a strict girls' seminary. Widows who leased and managed the houses were instructed to report the names of any girls who stayed out late (after 10 o'clock at night) or complained in any way about their work or life in the mill towns. Anyone who was reported was promptly fired.

Women workers were lectured on the importance of honesty, cleanliness, frugality, and punctuality. Workers in Lowell, the show place of the textile industry, were expected to uphold the company's reputation. They were required to sign contracts promising to demonstrate "on all occasions, both in their work and by their actions . . . that they are penetrated by a laudable love of temperance and virtue and animated by their moral and social obligations."[6] They were also required to attend church regularly. Those who did not purchase pews had their pay docked and were refused mail service at the company post office.

For the most part the first generation of mill girls complied with the rules and regulations. They came from Yankee, Puritan families and had been reared on hard work, duty, and usefulness. Before they could enter the mills, they had to convince their parents that they would not succumb to the temptations of town life such as fine clothes, dancing, or gossiping.

When the mills were new, many of the women who worked in them felt a pioneering spirit—a sense, as Harriet Robinson noted, that they were contributing to the widening of woman's sphere. They were opening the way for unmarried women to live on their own, independent of parents or husbands. Most important, these first factory women thought of their work as temporary. They hoped to stay in the mills for a few years, save money, and move on. Some wanted to continue their educations, some to find better work, others to marry.

This feeling of impermanence among mill workers was extremely beneficial to mill owners. As long as women did not think of themselves as permanently bound to the mills, they did not spend much time questioning the inequities of the factory system. As long as they had families to return to, they could leave the mills when they were worn out or ill. "Upon any embarrassment," wrote one Lowell company backer, "they return to their country homes and do not sink down here a helpless caste clamoring for work, starving unless employed, and hence ready for a riot."[7]

So long as mill girls could leave the factory, they did not think of themselves as being very different from the majority of American women, who lived on farms. But factory women were aware that they were not members of the new class of town ladies; very often they wrote about being "mistaken for ladies" when they went to church or walked about the town. Concerning this awareness, Lucy Larcom remarked, "We did not forget that we were working girls, wearing coarse aprons, and that there was some danger of our becoming drudges."[8]

In whatever ways they could, the early mill girls sought to guard themselves against that danger. Women who worked in the mills for four, five, or even eight years insisted that "at longest our employment was only to be temporary." They clung to the belief that they as much as any American women had the right to be ladies. And they nurtured the hope of finding prosperous middle-class husbands who would support them in ladylike style.

Many of the early mill girls spent their hard-earned wages on fashionable clothing, so that in church no one could tell the difference between them and "the daughters of the first families of the town." They read *Godey's Lady's Book* and spouted all the pious, romantic and domestic sentiments espoused by Sarah Hale. Their advice to men, wrote Harriet Robinson, was, "Treat every maiden with respect, for you do not know whose *wife* she shall be."[9]

Becoming a lady through marriage was one way of guarding against the "danger of becoming drudges." The other way was through self-improvement. In the early days mill girls believed fervently in the power of religion, culture, and learning. Eager for education and determined to benefit from life in the towns, they devoted themselves to numerous self-improvement activities. They read avidly, even in the mills where books were forbidden. Lucy Larcom tore pages from her Bible, sneaked them into the mills, and read them at her loom whenever the overseer was not watching.

In the evenings, after twelve to thirteen hours of work, mill girls somehow found the energy to meet in groups where they studied literature and foreign languages. They flocked to lectures, making up two-thirds of the Lyceum audiences in Lowell throughout the 1830s and 1840s. On Sundays, their one free day, the girls went both to church and to church school. In 1843 Lowell had fourteen religious societies. Ten of these were Sabbath Schools, containing over five thousand teachers and students. Three-quarters of these were mill girls.

Nowhere was the theme of self-improvement more touted than in the pages of the Lowell *Offering,* a monthly magazine edited by two former mill operatives, which began publication in 1841. Editor Harriet Farley believed that as long as workers achieved learning and culture, they did not need to worry about conditions in the factory. The purpose of the *Offering* was "to provide mill girls with sweetness and light" and to prove to the world that there was "Mind Among the Spindles."

The *Offering* claimed to be the voice of the mill girls, but as a rule it spoke for factory owners. Some operatives did submit stories and poetry; only those that stressed virtue and gentility were printed. By the 1840s mill girls had a message to communicate which the *Offering* would never publish.

The mill owners viewed the early cultural and religious activities of the women, followed by the later moral voice of the *Offering,* as the best sort of publicity and advertising. Again and again they used the fact that their workers were exceptional to sell their goods, justify their profits, and win their campaigns in Congress for high protective tariffs. If mill workers attended lectures and wrote poetry after a long day in front of machines, did it not follow that they, the founders of this benevolent factory system, deserved the highest of praise—and the freest opportunity to expand their business as they saw fit?

Visitors to the showcase town of Lowell were usually impressed by the "neat boarding houses" and the "pretty," "healthy," "well-dressed workers." The mill girls' literary talents added frosting to the cake. When Charles Dickens visited Lowell in 1841, his most favorable impressions were of the *Offering* and the piano he saw in a boarding house. Later one of the mill girls noted that only a handful of workers bothered to subscribe to the *Offering* and only a very few boarding houses had pianos.

Not all visitors to the mills were taken in by appearances. Catherine Beecher wrote a scathing critique of the factory system after she visited Lowell in 1845. The 13-hour work day, said Beecher, left eleven free hours in a mill girl's day. Eight of these were needed for sleep; that left a total of three hours for mending, sewing, shopping, recreation, social intercourse, and breathing fresh air. Beecher concluded that all the cultural activity "is probably done in hours which should have been given to sleep." She urged mill girls to rest more and attend night school less.

When Beecher took a look into the "neat" boarding houses, she discovered that girls were often sleeping six to a room, two to a bed. There was absolutely no privacy. Operatives "live in a perpetual buzz of machinery or conversation from month's end to month's end." What sort of religious devotion, asked Beecher, could girls achieve in an environment that outlaws solitude? As far as the work went, the piece-rate system "pushes girls to work as much as possible every day . . . everything goes under the stimulus of rivalry, ambition, and the excitement of gain."

Finally, Beecher had angry words for Dr. Elisha Bartlett, a company-hired physician who claimed that mill work was healthier for women than country living. Bartlett attempted to prove his thesis by comparing the death rate in Portsmouth, New Hampshire, with the lower death rate in Lowell. Beecher countered him with one simple fact: the death rate in Lowell was bound to be lower because the population was much younger. In reality one-third of the girls who worked in Lowell were less healthy than when they had first arrived, and if they were seriously ill, they went home to die. Beecher concluded her appraisal with an appeal to female operatives to leave the mills and become teachers.[10]

Orestes Brownson, a transcendentalist and early foe of the factory system, agreed with Beecher that "the great mass [of mill girls] wear out their health and spirits and morals, without becoming one whit better off than when they commenced labor." Brownson, however, did not tell mill girls to become teachers. Instead, he told them to become the owners of the mills. "I would put the plough into the hand of the owner and also the spindle and the loom. . . . I wish you, the operatives, to be not only the operatives but the owners."[11]

Brownson was one of a small but outspoken group of reformers who blamed the long hours and low wages of mill girls on the nature of capitalism. A few owners, explained these reformers, had gained control of the means of production and used this control, not for the welfare of workers, but for their own gain. Whenever profits fell, workers were thrown off the job or their wages were slashed, so that owners could make up the loss and guarantee themselves and their backers a substantial profit. With the profits they made in this way, capitalists extended their economic power by investing in new industry and thereby gaining control over larger and larger portions of the national economy.

In 1845 Theodore Parker, explaining the tactics of the owners of the textile industry, wrote, "This class is the controlling one . . . it mainly enacts the laws of this state and the nation. . . . It buys up legislators. . . . It can manufacture governors, senators, judges to suit its own purposes. . . . This class owns the machinery of society . . . the ships, factories, shops, water privileges."[12]

Parker was not wide of the mark. By the 1840s the Boston magnates who owned Lowell, Lawrence, Chicopee and Waltham had extended their interests far beyond the mills. With the profits they earned from the mills they bought land, founded insurance companies, controlled New England's shipping industry and most of the banks in Boston.

While the mill owners expanded their field of operation, life for workers became more difficult. New mills and shantytowns gobbled up all the open space in what had once been rural villages. Mill girls no longer looked out on green fields or trees. New mill towns, such as Lawrence, Massachusetts, were thrown up quickly and were slums from the start.

Conditions in the mills were deteriorating as well. Owners were demanding more work from each operative. Processes were speeded up, and women now had to tend three and sometimes four looms each. While new machines, such as the crank-driven loom, speeded up production, they also increased heat, lint, and noise. Whenever more efficient machinery was introduced, owners reduced the piece rate. Operatives thus produced more while earning less.

In addition, wages were cut every time market prices declined. During the national depression of 1837 prices fell. To keep their profits high, mill owners lowered piece rates paid to workers by a larger percentage than the overall decline in prices. As a result, workers suffered a cut in real wages. A similar tactic was used by industrialists every time a depression occurred, which was the case virtually every twenty years throughout the nineteenth century.

The end result for mill girls in the 1840s was that they had to tend more machines, for longer hours, at lower wages than ten years earlier. In addition, mill owners introduced the premium system by which those overseers who got the most work out of girls were rewarded with bonuses. Rules became oppressive. Grounds used by overseers to fire girls in the 1840s included "impudence," "levity," "disobedience to orders," "cautiousness," and "hysteria."

The most significant criticism of the factory system came not from reformers, but from the workers themselves. Even in the beginning, during the brief "golden period" of the mill towns, occasional protests erupted against long working hours, wage cuts and speed-ups. In 1828, 400 women in Dover, New Hampshire, walked off their jobs, protesting the fines they were charged for lateness. This was the first strike by women and the second recorded strike of factory workers in America (the first had been called several months earlier by children who worked in the mills of Paterson, New Jersey).

Throughout the 1830s women staged sporadic walkouts. Perhaps the most dramatic occurred in 1836, after a wage cut, when 1,500 Lowell workers marched through the town singing.

> Oh isn't it a pity, such a pretty girl as I
> Should be sent into a factory to pine away and die
> Oh I cannot be a slave
> Oh I will not be a slave
> For I'm so fond of liberty
> I cannot be a slave

The Lowell girls were starved into submission. Evicted from their boarding houses, with no means of support, they held out for a month and then were forced to return to the mills. Their leaders were fired and blacklisted.

Though none of these early strikes achieved any tangible gains for workers, they were significant for the labor movement. During the 1820s and 1830s workers in various trades—such as shoemaking, carpentry, mechanics and bookbinding—first began to organize. When mill girls went out on strike, they introduced the idea of trade unionism into the factories.[13]

These early mill strikes show that women organized first as workers, not as women. Twenty years before the first women's rights convention women workers were protesting in public. "It required some courage," wrote one observer, "for Yankee 'young ladies' to brave public opinion and develop strike tactics at this early period. . . . It was felt that young women should not march about the streets, making a spectacle of themselves. . . . And yet, they were prepared to do this . . . whether it was conventional or not."[14]

By the 1840s some mill girls were beginning to realize that they might be stuck in the mills for much longer than they had imagined. Many girls no longer had families to return to, as their fathers had lost their farms during the depression of 1837. At the same time, the deteriorating conditions in the factories did away with the dream of self-improvement as an escape. By the 1840s few mill girls had the money to buy church pews, let alone the energy to attend study groups in the evenings.

Harriet Farley, editor of the *Offering*, insisted that if mill girls would arm themselves with learning and culture, they could protect themselves from the "power of the machine." Most of the women saw this argument as a whitewash of factory conditions. But Farley refused to print the many articles stressing the need for factory improvements. Wages and hours, Farley insisted, were matters over which "workers have no control." Improvements would come in time as a result of the kindheartedness of the owners.[15]

At this juncture several mill girls denounced the *Offering* as a company mouthpiece and began publishing their own "Factory Tracts" in which they could write freely. Such papers as the *Factory Girl,* the *Factory Girls' Album,* and most especially the *Voice of Industry,* begun in 1845 and for a time edited and managed by Lowell workers, marked the beginning of the American labor press. These journals encouraged mill girls to think about the inequities of the factory system. "What glorious privilege we enjoy in this boasted republican land," wrote one girl. "Here I am a healthy New England girl, quite well behaved, bestowing just half of all my hours, including Sundays, upon a company for less than two cents an hour."[16] This and similar articles helped to promote a new organization among mill workers—the Female Labor Reform Association. Twelve workers in Lowell started the first association in 1845. Within six months it had five hundred members, all rallying to their motto, "Try Again."

Sarah Bagley, a weaver who had worked in the mills for eight years, was elected president. She was a highly effective leader, who played a major role in organizing women in Lowell and many other New England mill towns. When owners tried to blacklist Association members, Bagley used the *Voice of Industry* to trumpet her outrage.

> "What! Deprive us after working thirteen hours of the poor privilege of finding fault—of saying our lot is a hard one! Turn away a girl unjustly persecuted as men have been persecuted . . . for free expression of political opinions! We will make the name of him who dares the act stink with every wind from all points of the compass."[17]

Soon there were Associations in Manchester and Dover, New Hampshire, and in Fall River, Massachusetts. The groups kept in touch with each other, joined together for mass labor rallies, and resisted wage cuts and speed-ups. When the Lowell corporation ordered weavers to tend four instead of three looms, at the same time reducing the piece rate, Association members refused. They threatened to publish the names of any weavers who complied. As a result, not a single weaver complied, and the mill owners were forced to rescind the order.

The Association also joined the New England Workingmen's Association to lobby for a ten-hour workday. One of the first alliances between male and female workers in the labor movement, this union began as a fairly equal one. Women mill workers attended meetings, gave speeches, and proposed resolutions. Women and men launched petition campaigns and lobbied before the Massachusetts legislature for the ten-hour day. Along with five other women and three working men, Bagley testified that the twelve- to thirteen-hour work day in the mills destroyed workers' health.

The Massachusetts legislative committee members who heard the testimony refused to take action. "We think that it would be better if the hours for labor were less,—if more time was allowed for meals, if more attention was paid to ventilation and pure air in our manufactures," they wrote in their report; "but we say," they added, "the remedy is not with us. We look for it in the progressive improvement in art and science, in a higher appreciation of man's destiny, in a less love for money, and a more ardent love for social happiness."[18]

Women who worked in the cotton mills of Pittsburgh and Alleghany City organized a militant strike as a more direct demand for the ten-hour day. They went from mill to mill, smashing gates and doing battle with the police. The purpose of their attack was not to capture the mills but to get at "scabs." Female strikebreakers who had remained at their machines were seized and tossed into the streets.

When employers in Pennsylvania stated that they would never shorten the workday until hours were reduced in the New England mills, Pennsylvania women called on mill workers in New England for help. Women in Lowell and Manchester discussed the idea of a general strike. In the end, however, there was no unified action for a ten-hour day in the 1840s. Most of the leaders of the New England mill workers' movement urged reliance on petition campaigns and legislative action. The labor movement was not strong enough, they feared, to fight the owners through strikes.

During the 1850s several states passed laws mandating the ten-hour work day. Employers circumvented these laws easily by forcing workers to sign contracts committing them to work overtime. Wherever they could, employers influenced state legislators to vote down laws limiting the workday. Massachusetts did not approve a ten-hour workday until 1873.

The Female Labor Reform Association, like most of the other small, independent unions, was short-lived. Early unions were easily broken by management. One mill owner had a ready answer to his workers' demand for a ten-hour day. "If twelve hours labor in twenty-four will not sustain us, we can and we will work fourteen."[19] Organizers in the mills were blacklisted and forced out of the industry. During the 1840s Sarah Bagley was the victim of a smear campaign designed to break her spirit and deter her followers. Mill girls continued to offer their support, but Bagley herself suffered an emotional collapse and withdrew from the mills. Without her leadership the Female Labor Reform Association soon fell apart.

Like future generations of working women, the mill girls lacked time, money, and power to sustain their association. Working women who tried to organize could not count on the support of either working men or other women.

Though working women sought alliances with working men in such groups as the New England Workingman's Association, and though they supported the struggles of men to win economic rights, men did not consider women equals in this struggle. There were a number of reasons why working men failed to support their female counterparts. Many men believed that economic justice would be achieved when they could afford to keep their daughters and wives out of the factories. The object was to rid factories of women rather than improve conditions for them. Other trade unionists were convinced that because working women were paid one-third to one-half of men's wages, they were underbidding male salaries and threatening jobs for men. The easiest solution to this imagined threat was to drive women from the trades and bar them from unions. That is exactly what happened when national unions began emerging at the time of the Civil War. Of the thirty such labor groups that existed in 1873, only two admitted women.

In reality few women posed a threat to men's jobs. Women did not work in such heavy "central" industries as railroads, steel, or mining, and jobs in factories and the manufacturing industries were sex-segregated. When employers hired women, they hired them for the least skilled jobs, which were marked "Female Only." Some working men understood the situation, but they failed to recognize the importance of organizing the lowest level of workers. Only a few far-sighted working men realized that their own success depended on "strengthening the weakest part of the labor forces, for the main strength of the capitalist class consisted in the divisions existing in labor's ranks."[20]

Unfortunately the women's rights movement was equally blind to the predicament of working women. In 1848, while the Female Labor Reform Association was dying, the women's rights movement was being born. In her Declaration of Rights and Sentiments, Elizabeth Cady Stanton spoke out for the rights of working women. Several female factory workers and women in the home manufacturing trades, such as Charlotte Woodward, attended the Seneca Falls convention. However, none of the founding feminists made contact with women workers in the mills and other industries, nor did Bagley and her followers get in touch with feminists. The interests of feminists and working women were different. Feminists wanted rights their men already had, while the central issue for working women—economic inequity—was one they shared with their men.

The myth of the comfortable and healthy life led by women who worked in the mills survived for twenty years. By the late 1840s no one believed any longer that factory work was a blessing. The population of factory workers was changing; and with that change, conditions deteriorated further.

Millions of new immigrants were beginning to arrive in America. Among them were Irish men and women driven out of their country by the catastrophic famine of 1846. The availability of poor Irish women enabled mill owners to get rid of native-born operatives, who had begun to assert themselves. Between 1845 and 1850 the population in the mills changed dramatically. In 1845, 90 percent of the mill girls were native-born, and only 7 percent were Irish. Five years later, 50 percent were Irish.[21]

In time Irish mill workers fought for improved conditions just as the Yankee operatives had, facing many of the same difficulties. Irish-American working women in other industries—such women as Augusta Lewis of the typesetters and Kate Mullaney of the Troy collar and cuff workers—followed in the tradition of Sarah Bagley, becoming leaders of the women's labor movement in the decades following the Civil War.

As women's traditional work moved from the home to the factory, women moved with it. During the course of the nineteenth century women became workers in a variety of other industries—the garment trades; food-processing plants; cigar, shoe, and glass factories; laundries, and the metal trades. Within these industries women were the most oppressed and least strongly organized group of workers. Because they were both women and workers, they had special problems and few allies.

Not until the late 1800s did male unions and middle-class women's organizations begin to acknowledge the problems faced by working women. In turn, working women, supported by women reformers and feminists, gained the strength to sustain militant organizing drives. Eventually their efforts instilled new life both into the labor and women's movements.

The Civil War and the
Movement Westward

9

Homespun Blue and Gray

During the Civil War, as in the Revolutionary War, women were confronted with many new responsibilities. While the men were away fighting, women became managers, decision makers, heads of families, and income earners—roles that had usually been assumed by men. Women, proud of their wartime contributions, applauded themselves as strong, competent, persevering citizens, vital to the war effort. Few women, however, saw the contradiction between their wartime self-image and their traditional place as the subservient sex. Only a small group of Northern feminists demanded equal rights in payment for helping to fight the war.

The war divided many families. Three brothers of Mary Todd Lincoln—the president's wife—fought and died for the Confederate Army, and Varina Davis—the wife of the president of the Confederacy—had relatives in the Union Army. Annie Carter Lee, Robert E. Lee's daughter, left her family because she supported the Union cause.[1]

During the decade of debate that preceded the war many women spoke for peace. If differences between the North and South led to war, wrote one woman, "men's passion and fanaticism" would be to blame. "I think both parties are wrong in this fratricidal war," wrote Mrs. Robert E. Lee. "I see no right in the matter." But when the fighting began, women were as partisan as men. A Virginian woman who before the firing at Fort Sumter had decried the coming war, wrote a few weeks later, "We must all work for our country . . . the ladies assemble daily by the hundreds, for the purpose of sewing. They are fitting out company after company."[2]

North and South, women were an important part of the war machine. They raised money, recruited soldiers, and provisioned them with food and clothing. Over 20,000 female aid societies were formed to work for the armies.

Throughout the war women cared for the sick and wounded. At least 3,200 women made a career of nursing, and tens of thousands more volunteered their services. The work was exhausting and disheartening. The hospitals were dirty and crowded; there were not nearly enough doctors nor enough medicine, surgical instruments, and anesthetics.

Kate Cumming of Mobile, Alabama, who volunteered for service in the nursing division of the Army of Tennessee, described one field hospital.

"Nothing that I had ever heard or read had given me the faintest idea of the horrors . . . here. . . . . Men mutilated in every way, lying on the floor, just as they were taken from the battlefield; so close together it was almost impossible to walk without stepping on them. . . . The foul air from this mass of human beings at first made me giddy and sick, but I soon got over it . . . when we give the men anything, we have to kneel, in blood and water. . . . It was common to have amputated limbs thrown into the yard. . . . I daily witness the same sad scenes, men dying all around me."[3]

Though there was a desperate shortage of nurses, women were not at first welcome. Many army doctors preferred unskilled male nurses to skilled female ones. The thousands of women who insisted on volunteering in spite of this attitude soon overcame male prejudice. Eventually it was the women who created order and cleanliness out of the filth and chaos Kate Cumming had described.

In the north, Dr. Elizabeth Blackwell pioneered in training women as army nurses. Her efforts sparked the formation of the Sanitary Commission, which coordinated the care of soldiers, staffed and supplied hospitals, and with Dorothea Dix as Superintendent of Nurses, trained women for the army medical corps.

In the South, nurses received less formal training, but the care they gave equaled that of Union nurses. Many Southern women tenderly nursed the Confederate sick and wounded in their homes. Of the 1,300 soldiers Sally Louisa Tompkins nursed in a friend's home in Richmond, only seventy-three died. In recognition of her service, the Confederate government made her a captain in the army.[4] Phoebe Yates Pember, a widow from South Carolina, who became a superintendent in Richmond's largest hospital, was another asset to the Confederacy. Mrs. Pember was a brilliant administrator "with a will of steel under suave refinement," who fought against waste, thievery, and indifference to keep her patients alive and her hospital well supplied and efficient.[5]

Other women traveled with the armies to care for the wounded near the front lines. Mary Bickerdyke, known as "Mother" to the soldiers she nursed in General Sherman's army, made war on lazy or incompetent doctors. General Sherman himself bowed to her rulings. When a ward surgeon whom she had dismissed because of repeated drunkenness appealed to Sherman for help, the general refused to reinstate him because "She [Mary Bickerdyke] ranks me."[6]

Clara Barton spent four years nursing soldiers on both sides, working at the sites of the war's worst battles. Her belief that the army medical corps should be neutral —offering help to all who needed it, regardless of which side they fought for—led her after the war to establish the American and International Red Cross.

Though the care women provided to the victims of the war elevated nursing to a new professional status, women found it difficult to win recognition for their services. Not until 1892 did Congress pass a bill granting Civil War nurses a pension of $12 a month.

As in the American Revolution, some women joined the fighting. An estimated 400 women, disguised as men, served for various lengths of time in the Union and Confederate armies.

Scores of Union and Confederate women were spies, saboteurs, scouts, and couriers. The most effective and daring of these female guerrillas was Harriet Tubman, the former slave who had led hundreds of slaves to freedom prior to the war. Tubman was an invaluable asset to the Union side. Her nineteen journeys leading runaway slaves out of the South had given her an invaluable knowledge of Southern terrain.

Tubman first joined the Union forces as an unpaid nurse on the front lines. She labored tirelessly to ease the pain of the wounded soldiers, black and white. After a full day of work she returned home, slept for a few hours, and woke well before dawn in time to bake pies and cakes. She supported herself by selling these homemade products.

When epidemics of dysentery, small pox and other dread diseases broke out in Union camps, Tubman treated the victims with traditional slave remedies, made from herbs and roots. She herself, having never suffered from any of these diseases, was not immune; but as always, she paid little attention to the danger.

As a spy Tubman was without peer. Able to travel into and throughout the South with ease, she had allies in many Southern towns and on hundreds of plantations. Wherever she went, she was able to win the trust of blacks. Southern whites, underestimating the desire of their slaves for freedom, often spoke freely of the war effort in the presence of blacks. The vital information divulged in this way made its way to Tubman.

As a kind of unofficial representative of the Union Army, Tubman also helped to convince slaves that the Northern side was sincere in its concern for blacks. Because of her, many slaves joined up as soldiers in the Union Army. In her wake, groups of blacks deserted their plantations, helping to undermine the will of the white South.

Tubman headed numerous raids, serving both as guide and as military leader, and earning the title of General Tubman. On one trip she led Union gunboats down a labyrinth of rivers to a bridge which rebels had fortified with torpedoes. The fortifications were successfully removed. She led other raids as well, destroying railroads and bridges and helping to clear the way for the eventual Union invasion.

Tubman's faith in the Union side was not always repaid. After the war it took years for Congress to agree to grant her a pension. Even more disturbing was the Union's treatment of Tubman's army of plantation blacks. In her attempts to fortify the will of frightened slaves during the war Tubman had sung a song to them of her own making.

> Of all the whole creation in the East or in the West,
> The glorious Yankee nation is the greatest and the best.
> Come along! Come along! Don't be alarmed,
> Uncle Sam is rich enough to give you all a farm.[7]

The promise of free land for freed blacks, which Tubman believed in, was never fulfilled by the Union government.

White women were also sometimes treated shabbily by the victorious Union government. Anna Ella Carroll, for example, the daughter of a former governor of Maryland, made invaluable political and military contributions to the

Union cause, for which she never received recognition.

During the spring of Secession, when it looked as if Maryland might join the Confederacy, Carroll lobbied hard and successfully among her state's politicians to keep Maryland in the Union. Her political pamphlets were so astute that the federal government reprinted them for mass distribution.

In 1861 she traveled to the Union Army's western front. Army generals, among them an unknown named Ulysses S. Grant, were devising plans to gain control of the Mississippi River, through a juncture at the Ohio river. Carroll reportedly suggested an alternate route.[8] The Tennessee and Cumberland rivers, less than fifty miles up from the Ohio, offered parallel routes into Tennessee, Alabama, and Mississippi that could be more easily captured. Seizure of the two Confederate forts on these rivers would open a waterway into the enemy's center. Her plan was ultimately used by General Grant in the 1862 Tennessee campaign that made him a national hero and marked a turning point in the war.

Throughout the war Carroll met with members of Lincoln's cabinet, but she was never recognized as the originator of the Tennessee campaign. In 1870 she filed a claim for compensation for her wartime services. Though several Senators supported her, Carroll's claim was denied.

Most women fought the war at home, with married women filling the places left vacant by their husbands. They kept up farms and plantations and managed family businesses. Many returned to the tradition of colonial women as keepers of stores, inns, and saloons. Some learned new trades, such as printing and blacksmithing. Single women took jobs in arsenals, munitions factories, and textile mills. Women monopolized the teaching field.

For the first time women were hired in government offices. Many Americans disapproved of the situation, but replacements for men were needed, and women were willing to work for lower pay. Most of them were dismissed as soon as the men returned from the war. Though the entrance of women into offices during the Civil War established a precedent, only a small number of women worked in offices throughout the nineteenth century.

In the South especially the war disrupted women's

lives. The North's advantage, both in the size of its labor force and in materials, was clear from the start. In the South every man who was not too old or infirm was needed to fight. By 1864 the Confederacy was conscripting all able-bodied men between the ages of seventeen and fifty. Women of the South were left on their own, with the responsibility to produce enough food to feed the Confederacy. Under their management cotton fields were transformed into acreage bearing wheat and other foodstuffs.

From the start of the war the South was cut off from northern manufactured goods. With the Union naval blockade of Southern ports, it also had to forgo goods imported from abroad. Women learned to do without and to make do. They turned their homes into factories and devised all sorts of substitutes for goods no longer available. Parthenia Hague, who lived out the war in southern Alabama, described how the women of her region cultivated indigo for dye, gathered the sap of berries and roots for medicine—"a soothing and efficacious cordial for dysentery . . . was made from blackberry roots . . . The berries of the dogwood tree were taken for quinine"— and even grew poppies from which they made opium. They used okra for coffee, raspberry leaves for tea, and the oil of cottonseed and ground peas in place of kerosene.[9]

Leather was scarce in the South, and the little that was available was saved for soldiers' boots. Some women knitted shoes, while others wrapped their feet in cloth. One woman made shoes from an old carpet, another from parts of a canvas sail, another from tanned squirrel skins. Seventeen-year-old Susan Bradford wrote about her invention.

Today I have on railroad stockings and slippers. Guess what these slippers are made of? Whenever I go to Uncle Richard's I see an old black uncle, hard at work, plaiting shucks and weaving the plaits together into door mats. It seemed to me a lighter braid might be sewed into something resembling shoes, so I picked out the softest shucks and soon I had enough to make one slipper. So pleased was I that I soon had a pair of shoes ready to wear. They are a little rough so I have pasted inside a lining of velvet. Everybody laughed, but I feel quite proud.[10]

All over the South women returned to handweaving and spinning. One woman recalled how "old spinning wheels and handlooms were brought out from dusty corners, and the whirr of the wheel became a very song to us." Many settlements revived the old tradition of spinning and sewing bees. "Wheels, cards and cotton were all hauled in a wagon to the place appointed. . . . Sometimes as many as six or eight wheels would be whirring at the same time in one house."[11] Once the cloth was spun, the women sewed everything from clothing to flags, bandages, and tents.

During the first two years of the war Southern women kept the home front working well. Food production rose as women planted corn and wheat instead of cotton. By mid-war, however, want and poverty were widespread. The tightening blockade caused a scarcity of even such essentials as salt. Inflation and war profiteering drove prices up tremendously. In 1863, immigrant and free black women in Richmond rioted for bread. One woman remarked on the situation.

> I am for a tidal wave of peace—and I am not alone. Meantime we are slowly starving to death. Here, in Richmond, if we can afford to give $11 for a pound of bacon, $10 for a small dish of green corn, and $10 for a watermelon, we can have a dinner of three courses for four persons. . . . Somebody, somewhere, is mightily to blame for all this business, but it isn't you nor I nor yet the women who . . . were only hungry . . . it is all so awful.[12]

Southern women saw and felt the war as fully as the men who fought it on the battlefield. Battles raged in their towns and villages. Their men, wounded and dying, collapsed at their doorsteps, and occupying soldiers invaded their homes.

Mary Ann Loughborough was in Vicksburg, Mississippi, visiting her soldier husband, when General Grant's army began shelling the city in April 1863. Refusing to leave in spite of the Confederate Army's order to evacuate all civilians, Mrs. Loughborough lived out the terrible forty-seven day siege in a cave dug out of the side of a steep hill. Her journal gives a graphic picture of what the cave dwellers of Vicksburg endured.

Terror stricken, we remained crouched in the cave, while shell after shell followed each other in quick succession. I endeavored by constant prayer to prepare myself for the sudden death I was almost certain awaited me. My heart stood still as we would hear the reports from the guns, and the rushing and fearful sound of the shell as it came toward us. As it neared, the noise became more deafening . . . and as it exploded, the report flashed through my head like an electric shock.[18]

As the war became more harrowing, Southern whites began to view blacks in a new way. Suddenly whites were afraid. During the first two years of the war, when there was little action, blacks had generally remained on their plantations, biding their time. But as the Confederacy began to decline, blacks began to act. Many simply walked away from captivity. Some joined the Union Army, some worked for the Yankees in a civilian capacity, others took to the road. Acts of sabotage were common.

When blacks began to act in their own self-interest, whites felt at a loss to explain what was happening. Early on in the war Mary Chestnut had captured this disturbing ambiguity in black-white relations.

Not by one word or look can we detect any change in the demeanor of these negro servants. Lawrence sits at our door, as sleepy and respectful and as profoundly indifferent. So are they all. They carry it too far. You could not even tell that they even hear the awful noise that is going on in the bay [during the firing on Fort Sumter] though it is dinning in their ears night and day. And people talk before them as if they were chairs and tables, and make no sign. Are they stolidly stupid or wiser than we are, silent and strong, and biding their time.[14]

Throughout the war Southern women had shown great courage and stamina in adapting to the Union occupation of their towns and homes. The final Union invasions of the South were different. Utter desolation covered the entire Shenandoah Valley after Sheridan swept through with his cavalry. When General Sherman marched his army from Chattanooga to Atlanta, thousands of women, their homes and crops destroyed, became refugees, fleeing the invaders and seeking shelter in the homes of relatives and friends. Families were split apart as mothers sent their children to pockets of the South the Yankees had not yet reached.

Thousands more, unable to flee, faced starvation in a wasted countryside. After Sherman's army had burned Atlanta and the surrounding region of Georgia, "every larder was empty, and those with tens of thousands of dollars were as poor as the poorest and as hungry too."[15] Mary Ann Gay offered an account of her feelings as she stood on a battlefield outside Atlanta, gathering leftover munitions that she hoped to barter for food.

> In a marshy place, encrusted with ice, innumerable bullets, minie balls, and pieces of lead seemed to have been left by the irony of fate to supply sustenance to the hungry ones. . . . It was so cold! Our feet were almost frozen, and our hands had commenced to bleed and handling cold, rough lead cramped them so badly. . . .
>
> Lead! Blood! Tears! O how suggestive! Lead, blood, and tears, mingled and commingled! In vain did I try to dash the tears away. They would assert themselves and fall upon lead stained with blood. . . . I cried like a baby, long and loud.[16]

Northern women did not experience the war so immediately. The fighting was far away, and their homes were not invaded or destroyed. The effect of the war on their lives depended in large part upon their economic class.

The first draft law in the United States, passed by Congress in 1863, put poor men in uniform while enabling middle-class and wealthy men to avoid serving if they so chose. The law made all white men between the ages of twenty and forty-five subject to military service, but a man could "buy out" by paying $300 or evade service for himself by hiring a substitute. Poor men, who could not afford either of these alternatives, had no way of avoiding conscription. Once they were drafted, their families were deprived of a means of support. Soldiers' pay was extremely low and did not include allotments to families.

The wives and daughters of poor Union soldiers had to manage on their own. Many took jobs in textile mills and munitions factories. The manpower shortage made such jobs plentiful; but when women were hired, wages were slashed.

Many of these women shared their men's resentment of the class inequity expressed in the draft law. The riots following the first draft call in 1863 in New York resulted in the death of several hundred persons and a million dollars' worth of damage. Irish workers, unable to pay for exemptions and afraid of losing their jobs to blacks, ran wild for four days, sacking shops and homes, and lynching blacks who fell into their clutches. Women behaved as violently as men, and when order was finally restored, several hundred women had been arrested and were tried and jailed.

In the end it was middle-class Northern women, rather than the government, who provided some relief to the wives and children of poor draftees. The Sanitary Commission, established first to care for the wounded and sick soldiers, eventually expanded into an enormous civilian relief organization. Thousands of middle- and upper-class women raised money and collected and distributed food and clothing to the poor. For these civic-minded women, the first organized "volunteers," the war provided a chance to participate in a national enterprise. Their work boosted their self-confidence and broadened their view of the world.

Feminists postponed their struggle for women's rights and turned to the issues raised by the war. While approving of women's charity work for soldiers and needy civilians, Elizabeth Cady Stanton and Susan B. Anthony believed that women should have a voice in the politics of the war as well. "In nursing the sick and wounded, knitting socks, scraping lint, and making jellies," they wrote, "the bravest and best may weary if the thoughts mount not . . . to some noble purpose. . . . Woman is equally interested in and responsible with man in the final settlement of this problem of self-government."[17]

The noble purpose mentioned by Stanton and Anthony was freedom for all slaves. Emancipation was the first and foremost reason for the war, they believed. Along with other abolitionists, they criticized Lincoln and the Republican party for putting preservation of the Union above and before the "slave's cause."

For Lincoln, emancipation was a matter of timing. He chose to wait until the eve of the great Union victory at Antietam, when he perceived a spirit of generosity among his countrymen and women. Only then did Lincoln proclaim that "slavery must die that the nation might live." On January 1, 1863, Lincoln issued the Emancipation Proclamation. Much later in her life Stanton wrote, "I now see the wisdom of his [Lincoln's] course, leading public opinion slowly but surely up to the final blow for freedom."[18] At the time, however, she and her fellow abolitionists felt that Lincoln had neither acted quickly enough nor gone as far as he should. The Proclamation freed all slaves in the rebel states but not those in the Union slaveholding states of Maryland, Missouri, West Virginia, Tennessee, Kentucky, and Delaware.

The Proclamation gave Stanton and Anthony a political mission. With other feminists they formed the National Women's Loyal League, an organization with one goal—circulation of a petition asking Congress for a constitutional amendment that would end slavery in Union as well as Confederate territory. Speaking tours were arranged, and such old-time feminist speakers as Anthony, along with a brilliant new orator, eighteen-year-old Anna Dickinson, rallied public support for the future Thirteenth Amendment. All told, the women collected 400,000 signatures for their petition.[19]

In the South the end of the war did not mean an end to hard times. "The war was prosperity compared to what peace has wrought," wrote one woman.[20] Everywhere, especially in rural districts and areas devastated by Sherman's army, poverty and desolation reigned. Atlanta had been burned to the ground, and other major Southern cities were largely in ruins. Transportation lines had been destroyed. Fields lay barren, and there was no cash to buy seed and machinery, no livestock, none of the essentials needed to begin farming anew. In the years following surrender thousands of impoverished white Southerners relied on relief provided by the Freedmen's Bureau, an agency set up to help blacks.

Many Southern women realized that they would have to face the postwar times alone. Of the ten million men who had served in the Confederate Army, one-fourth were dead. Many young soldiers who survived the fighting moved westward, depleting the Southern male population even further. In virtually every Southern community women far outnumbered men.

War widows became heads of their families. Single women, with little hope of finding young men to marry, also looked for ways to earn money. Schoolteaching was the most common occupation sought by single women, while widows with children often turned to sewing or operated inns, restaurants, and schools in their homes.

In rural areas women labored to eke a living from ruined and depleted land. The lower a woman's class, the harder her lot. Poor white women, the wives and daughters of small tenant farmers, who had barely survived the war, experienced further deterioration after the fighting stopped. One Southern writer told of a North Carolina woman reduced to hitching herself to a plow driven by her eleven-year-old son and of a Virginia woman driving a plow to which she had hitched her two daughters.[21]

Many white Southern women saw themselves as the stronger sex. But though they acknowledged their independence, physical strength, and fortitude, they never questioned the traditional image of woman as wife and mother. When 1870 census takers asked Southern women their occupations, a majority replied that they "kept house." Many of these women were in fact breadwinners and heads of families.[22]

Southern women did not attempt to redefine their social and political roles to match their new economic status. Class and race hatred kept Southern women divided from each other. The view held by women of the planter class, who associated women's rights with the hated abolitionists, persisted for at least twenty-five years following the war.

Land remained the basis of wealth in the South, and those who owned it were the most powerful class. Within time some planters were able to restore the productivity of their land and make a profitable living off of it. Poor whites remained poor, and blacks for the most part became sharecroppers.

The dream of most former slaves following the war was a simple one: to own a farm, to make a decent living from it, to educate their children, to live without the threat of white attack. That dream remained unfulfilled for the great majority. Southern whites were determined to keep blacks "in their place" by keeping them poor. In some regions of the South there were some black landowners, but most were not able to purchase land.

After the war many slave owners offered blacks wages for staying and continuing to do the field work they had always done. But instead of wages, former slaves re-

ceived only a portion of the crops they farmed. Sharecroppers were chronically indebted to white landlords,
who provided them with seed and other necessities. In effect sharecropping perpetuated white planter-class control
of the land, preventing poor whites and blacks from gaining a foothold.

Sharecroppers rarely made enough money to support
an entire family. Men and women often sought additional
work in order to get by. Some black women resorted to
domestic work. Under slavery whites had relied on black
women to raise their children, nurse their sick, and cook
and clean for them. This pattern continued after the war.
The wages paid for this kind of work were pitifully low,
but black women had few alternatives. Most of them still
worked in the fields.

Black men, with the support of black women, attempted
to use their postwar right to vote meaningfully. If white
terrorism had not put an end to their access to the political system, it is probable that the blacks would have made
good use of their newly acquired political rights. In some
areas—most notably the South Carolina low country—
blacks did assert considerable political and economic power.
A number of very strong and capable leaders emerged,
many of whom were drawn from the quarter of a million
free blacks who lived in the South before the war. Black
women, of course, like white women, were denied the
right to vote, but they tried to influence the political
choices made by their men.

Frances Ellen Watkins Harper, a black writer from
Baltimore, traveled extensively throughout the South after
the war, speaking and writing about the experiences of
freed blacks. Harper took a special interest in black wom-
en. Her book, *Iola Leroy, or Shadows Uplifted*, which
told the story of an octoroon girl in the postwar South,
was the first novel published by a black American woman.

According to Harper, black women understood "that
the colored man needs something more than a vote in his
hand. . . . A man landless, ignorant and poor may use
the vote against his interests; but with intelligence and
land he holds in his hand the basis of power and elements
of strength." Black women, wrote Harper, urged their
men to acquire land and were "the levers which move in
education. The men talk about it, especially around election time, if they want an office for self or their candidate,

but the women work most for it . . . they make great sacrifices to spare their children during school hours." In the same way black women urged their men to use their votes for black interests. Harper detailed the method in her poem "Deliverance."

> You'd laugh to see Lucinda Grange
> Upon her husband's track
> When he sold his vote for rations
> She made him take 'em back.
>
> Day after day did Milly Green
> Just follow after Joe
> And told him if he voted wrong
> To take his rags and go.
>
> I think that Curnel Johnson said
> His side had won the day
> Had not we women radicals
> Just got right in the way.[33]

White Southerners were determined to overthrow Republican occupation of their land and to prevent blacks from exercising their newly won political rights. Even before congressional Reconstruction began in the South, white Southerners resorted to terrorism. Carpetbaggers found themselves targets of "accidental shots." Blacks were dealt with by secret societies, the most famous of which was the Ku Klux Klan. White terrorism increased when black men were granted the vote. The Klan became an "invisible empire," policing blacks and using violence to force black men to give up their power as political persons.

Northern Republicans at first retaliated by placing regions of the South under military occupation. But the Klan violence—usually perpetrated by poor whites but supported by the planter class—continued. By the early 1870s Republican rule in the South began to collapse. The Northern public was no longer interested in championing the cause of freed blacks. Northern politicians active in the South, their own ranks broken by corruption and factionalism, packed up and went home.

Blacks were left alone to face the reign of terror instituted by white supremacists. Many black Reconstruction leaders were killed. Black schools and self-help institutions were destroyed. Black men were lynched while black women were raped; both were murdered.

In the testimony from one of the few congressional investigations of Southern white violence against blacks during Reconstruction, black women described how they were raped and how their lives and the lives of their husbands and children were threatened. Ellen Parton of Meridian, Mississippi, described how the Klan broke into her home repeatedly, stole and destroyed all her possessions, and "committed rape on me."

> I called upon Mr. Mike Slamon, who was one of the crowd, for protection; I said to him, "Please protect me tonight, you have known me a long time"; Mr. Slamon had an oil-cloth and put it before his face, trying to conceal himself and the man that had hold of me told me not to call Mr. Slamon's name anymore . . . he then took me in the dining room and told me I had to do just what he said; I told him I could do nothing of that sort; that was not my way, and he replied, "By God, you have got to" and threw me down . . . I yielded to him because he had a pistol drawn; when he took me down he hurt me of course; I yielded to him on that account; he . . . hurt me with his pistol.[24]

The rape of black women was an attack on black men as well as on black women, who were warned not to call on their men for protection unless they wanted to see them lynched and murdered. Rape was used to reinforce a sense of powerlessness in black men and women—to strip blacks of the very sense of personal and political power they had been given when they had been emancipated. As historian Gerda Lerner has written, "the sexual oppression of black women is not only an end in itself, it is also an instrument in the oppression of the entire race."[25]

Black women often viewed with trepidation the move of their daughters into adulthood. As one black woman put it, "A colored woman, however respectable, is lower than a white prostitute." Another woman noted that "few colored girls reach the age of sixteen without receiving advances . . . maybe from a young upstart and often from a man old enough to be their father. . . . I dread to see my children grow. . . . Where the white girl had one temptation, mine will have many."[26]

Black women's attempts to resist sexual abuse demanded

a tremendous amount of courage. One woman described what happened when she refused "to let the madam's husband kiss me."

> Soon after I was installed as a cook, he walked to me, threw his arms around me, and was in the act of kissing me, when I demanded to know what he meant, and shoved him away. I was young then, and newly married, and didn't know then what has been a burden to my mind and heart ever since, that a colored woman's virtue in this part of the country has no protection. I at once went home, and told my husband. . . . When my husband went to the man who had insulted me, the man cursed him, and slapped him, and had him arrested! The police fined my husband $25.[37]

The sexual and economic exploitation suffered by black women in the postwar South were links in the chain of racism that kept blacks in "yet another form of slavery." Black women were subject to all the restrictions whites imposed on blacks in general. In addition, they suffered their own special oppression as sex objects for white men and cheap labor for white families. As mothers, too, they were destined to suffer from the effects of the South's (and later the North's) pernicious racism. Black women had to teach their children how to get along in a white world that denied them their personhood.

Black women consistently identified with their men and sought with them to maintain their families and their culture. Throughout the end of the nineteenth century black women founded and staffed black schools and colleges. They fought for education for their children and encouraged them to leave home when it appeared that greater economic opportunity was available in the North. Above all, black women taught their children to resist white oppression as best they could.

10

From Women's Rights to Woman Suffrage

Of all the women who had served the Union and Confederacy during the Civil War, only feminists active in the Northern women's rights movement asked for recognition and for what they considered a fair reward. During the war, feminists claimed, women had proven their political abilities and importance to the nation. After the war, they felt sure, politicians would express their gratitude.

The reward feminists expected was the vote. When Republican Congressmen proposed suffrage for black men during Reconstruction, feminists demanded the same right for women. Not only was the vote women's due for having helped to fight the war, but it was also woman's natural right. Reconstruction, according to feminists, was the time to grant "equal rights to all that the ideal of the Founding Fathers be now made a fact of life."[1]

Republican reconstructionists, however, cared little about equal rights for women or for blacks. The men who formulated Reconstruction policy were interested in their own political power. By giving black men the vote, Republicans hoped to control the South. They never seriously considered woman suffrage.

This bias was clearly revealed in section two of the Fourteenth Amendment, which specifically referred to "male inhabitants" and "male citizens" in the section dealing with the right to vote. For the first time the Constitution contained the word "male" instead of speaking simply of "the people" or "citizens." With that word the amendment introduced the principle of discrimination by sex into the Constitution, with the implication that women were not citizens.

Before the Civil War women were denied the vote by state law alone. With ratification of the Fourteenth Amendment, women needed another amendment to the Constitution before they would be able to vote in federal elections. "If that word 'male' be inserted now," wrote Stanton, "it will take us a century at least to get it out again." Anthony, Stone, and other feminists joined Stanton in protesting the Fourteenth Amendment. But none of their appeals to Republicans was successful, and Stanton's prediction was not so wide of the mark. The Fourteenth Amendment was ratified in 1868; the Twentieth Amendment, granting women the right to vote in national elections, did not come until 1920, half a century later.

On the heels of the Fourteenth Amendment came the Fifteenth, stipulating that suffrage could not be denied on the basis of "race, color, or previous condition of servitude." Feminists urged that the word "sex" be included. But again, Republicans would not change their plan to give the vote only to black men. In reaction, many feminists came to feel that male-legislated justice was no justice at all, and they acquired a deep and lasting distrust of politicians and political parties. In the fifty years it took women to win the vote, feminists continued to seek the support of individual politicians while they adopted a strictly nonpartisan policy. Never again would they endorse or support one political party, as they had during the Civil War.

Abolitionists also refused to support woman suffrage. After the war abolitionists stood with Republicans and organized a national campaign in support of black male suffrage. They expected feminists to join them, once more postponing the demand for their own rights. This rejection by a former ally hurt feminists most deeply.

It was the "Negroes' hour," feminists were told, and women would have to wait their turn. Such abolitionist leaders as Wendell Phillips reasoned that the nation could handle only one reform at a time. Northern and western politicians were ready to give black men the vote, but no section of the nation was ready to enfranchise women. If feminists rashly insisted on the vote for themselves, abolitionists stated, they would only jeopardize the hardwon chance of black men.

Abolitionists justified their rejection of woman suffrage during Reconstruction by claiming that the vote was more important for blacks than for women. "I am engaged in abolishing slavery," wrote Wendell Phillips to Elizabeth Cady Stanton, "in a land where abolition of slavery means conferring or recognizing citizenship, and where citizenship supposes the ballot for all men." Stanton was quick to point out that emancipation applied to black

women as well as black men. "Do you believe the Afri-
can race is composed entirely of males?" she asked.[2]

Not even Stanton's appeal on behalf of black women
could change the minds of abolitionists. Race came before
sex. Black men needed the vote to reclaim the manhood
they had been denied under slavery. Frederick Douglass,
who had seconded Elizabeth Cady Stanton's demand for
woman suffrage at the 1848 Seneca Falls Convention, stated
the general case.

> When women, because they are women, are dragged from
> their homes and hung upon lamp-posts; when their children
> are torn from their arms and their brains dashed to the
> pavement; when they are objects of insult and outrage at
> every turn; when they are in danger of having their homes
> burnt down over their heads; when their children are not
> allowed to enter schools; then they will have an urgency to
> obtain the ballot.[3]

Sojourner Truth was one of the few blacks who spoke for
women as well as men.

> There is a great stir about coloured men getting their
> rights but not a word about coloured women; and if col-
> oured men get their rights and not coloured women theirs,
> you see, coloured men will be masters over the women.
> . . . I wish woman to have her voice.[4]

But most blacks agreed with Douglass.

Enfranchisement did not protect black men from the
systematic enforcement, by violent means, of white male
rule in the South. Abolitionists failed to realize that the
vote alone would not bring racial equality. Feminists had
a similarly inflated idea about suffrage. They believed that
once black men got the vote, they would assume the
power and privileges of white men, and to this belief
they reacted with racist anger.

Tragically, feminists made black men the scapegoats
for their disillusionment with white male politicians and
reformers. Though Stanton wanted both blacks and women
to have the vote, she also felt and stated that it was "degrading" for educated Anglo-Saxon women to remain
voteless while "two million ignorant men are being ush-
ered into the legislative halls. . . . What can we hope for
at the hands of the Chinese, Indians, and Africans?" she

protested.[5] The analogy feminists had once drawn between the plight of women and slaves was forgotten. After Reconstruction the women's movement no longer spoke for black freedom.

The Republican and abolitionist rejection of woman suffrage during Reconstruction changed the course of the women's movement. Winning the vote became a kind of obsession to which other aspects of women's struggle for equality lost out. A few feminists, particularly Stanton, did not place so much faith in the ballot, but many feminists began to refer to their movement not as women's rights, but as woman suffrage.

The failure of feminists to win the vote had the further effect of splitting apart the women's movement. When abolitionists broke their ties with feminists, feminists broke with each other.

All feminists felt betrayed by abolitionists, but Lucy Stone, Julia Ward Howe, and others who lived in Boston remained intimately connected with the Boston-based abolitionist movement. They could not and would not sever their ties with such old friends and neighbors as Phillips and Garrison. Reluctantly they agreed that women should wait to win suffrage until black men were safely enfranchised. Though Stone wrote that there were tears in her eyes and that a nail went through her breast when abolitionists forgot about women, she accepted the antislavery priorities. If there could be "only one great moral victory at a time," she noted, then black men should come first. "I will be thankful if *any*body can get out of the terrible pit."[6]

Elizabeth Cady Stanton and Susan B. Anthony would not wait. They deplored the Boston group's resignation to the will of male abolitionists. The cause of woman suffrage, they insisted, should be led by women who put their sex first.

Stanton and Anthony had both moved to New York City during the war, but they still commanded the support of feminists from small towns in western New York and the Midwest, where the women's movement had originated. They used this support to force a break with the abolitionist establishment. In 1869 Stanton and Anthony withdrew from the Equal Rights Association and called a secret meeting of their own followers to form the National Woman Suffrage Association (NWSA). A year later

Stone and other Boston feminists who had been excluded from NWSA retaliated by forming a second organization, the American Woman Suffrage Association (AWSA).

The split lasted for twenty years. The divisions between the two groups went far deeper than the clash between votes for blacks and votes for women. The basic disagreement concerned the means and ends of the women's movement.

The American wing of the woman suffrage movement, led by Stone, adapted the moderate reform tactic of concentrating on one issue. This faction believed that women could most effectively win the vote if they made it their only cause. The Americans considered it an unrealistic tactic to work for a federal amendment to the Constitution before they had gained greater public support for woman suffrage. Accordingly, they settled down to the long, hard task of establishing local and state suffrage groups. Only delegates from these "approved" groups were seated at their meetings. This strategy attempted to eliminate members who might speak to other women's issues, thus diverting attention from suffrage. Henry Blackwell, Stone's husband, called attention to the risk. "Some insist upon dragging in their peculiar views on theology, temperance, marriage, race, dress, finance, labour and capital. No one can estimate the damage . . . the cause of woman's enfranchisement has already sustained by the failure of its advocates to limit themselves to the main questions."[7]

Blackwell's criticism was directed at the rival National wing, particularly its first president, Elizabeth Cady Stanton. More than any other nineteenth-century feminist leader, Stanton sought to understand the roots of women's oppression. In her thinking the vote was never an end in itself but a tool women could use to gain other rights.

If Stanton was the theoretician, Anthony was the tactician of the National wing. Anthony believed more strongly than Stanton that the vote would produce equality for women. But under Stanton's tutelage Anthony perceived the vote as a means toward woman's social and economic emancipation. Both feminists led the Nationals to adopt a broad liberal platform that linked woman suffrage to numerous other women's issues. They attracted the support of diverse followers, welcoming anyone who would speak for women. One such supporter was George Train, a Democrat and known racist, whose passionate concerns ranged from greenback currency to freedom for Ireland. Lucy Stone called Train "morally unsound" and "mentally unbalanced." When he denounced Republicans and abolitionists for not supporting woman suffrage, however, Stanton and Anthony joined him on a speaking tour. When Train offered to finance a feminist newspaper, they accepted his money. The paper became the vehicle for publishing the "peculiar views" Henry Blackwell thought so "damaging."

The paper was called the *Revolution;* its motto was, "Men their rights and nothing more; women their rights and nothing less." Train supplied both the name and the motto, but aside from his financial columns, the paper was controlled and run by editors Stanton and Parker Pillsbury (a male abolitionist who supported the Nationals) and manager Anthony.

The sixteen-page weekly *Revolution* was angry, irreverent, well-written, and humorous. It touched on every aspect of women's lives, from food, fashion, and health to marriage, maternity, and work. The *Revolution* reported news by, for, and about women covered by no other paper—news of women in professions, trades, and trade unions, women inventors and innovators, women abroad, women writers and lecturers. One news item congratulated a woman who, after helping her author husband research and edit a book, had delivered it to the publisher with a preface of her own refuting many of his opinions.

The *Revolution* was also a forum for feminist theory and practice. Its columns and editorials directed the women's movement to issues far beyond woman suffrage. The *Revolution* insisted that "the ballot is not even half a loaf; it is only a crust, a crumb."[8] The paper urged its female readers to become economically independent, to exercise and develop muscles, to educate themselves, and to stand by each other. When Sophia Smith gave $30,000 to a male seminary, the *Revolution* commented, "Why will women persist in endowing seminaries and colleges that treat their own sex with contempt? Rich women of America . . . we entreat you to remember your fellow *women.*"[9]

Marriage and divorce remained Stanton's consuming interests, and she used the pages of the *Revolution* to explain why she opposed the present marriage system. False religious dogma and restrictive laws against divorce, Stanton stated, were keeping "men and women together who loathe and despise each other. . . . Such marriages are crimes against the individual and the State." Stanton used the sensational Richardson-McFarland murder case to illustrate her point. Richardson was a well-known journalist who had befriended the divorced Mrs. McFarland. When her estranged husband learned of their friendship, he shot and killed Richardson. The press made much of the case, expressing sympathy for the "outraged husband" and reviling his divorced wife. Stanton used the columns of the *Revolution* to denounce the double standard exhibited in this affair.

> I rejoice over every slave that escapes from a discordant marriage. . . . One would really suppose that a man owned his wife as the master his slave and that this was simply an affair between Richardson and McFarland, fighting like two dogs over one bone. . . . This wholesale shooting of wives' paramours should be stopped. . . . Suppose women should decide to shoot their husbands' mistresses, what a wholesale slaughter of innocents we should have.[10]

The *Revolution* also spoke for working women, endorsing equal pay for equal work. When Congressmen debated whether to raise the wages of female clerks in Washington, D.C., the *Revolution* commented, "Members of Congress know very well the cost of living in Washington. They were probably thinking of this very thing when they increased their own salaries. . . . [Congressman Ben] Butler said a woman can support herself and those dependent on her at $900 per annum. . . . Of course she can after a fashion. . . . I know women who support themselves on less; washerwomen for instance who make $1 per day. . . . But they live in a wretched hovel."[11]

Despite their championship of reforms for working women, Stanton and Anthony were at their weakest when discussing woman's economic plight. They never understood that class, rather than sex, determined the priorities of working women. Both Stanton and Anthony believed in the vote more than in unions, while for working women economic justice came before political rights. In a popular lecture, ironically titled "Woman Wants Bread, not the Ballot," Anthony conceded that "capital, not the vote, controls the labor of women"—and then went on to say that if working women voted, they would be able to overcome economic exploitation. In the *Revolution* Anthony and Stanton supported the unionizing efforts of women printers while at the same time hiring a nonunion, "rat," printing shop for their newspaper. They never noticed that this action betrayed working women as much as abolitionist support of the Fourteenth and Fifteenth Amendments had betrayed woman suffrage.[12]

The *Revolution* did not win working women over to the cause of universal suffrage. It did, however, attempt to broaden the base of the women's movement. If Stanton and Anthony did not fully understand the concerns of women outside their own middle-class reform circle, at least they were two of the handful of feminists who tried. The *Revolution* called attention to women from diverse situations—housewives, factory workers, prostitutes, prisoners. In so doing, it asked women to understand their common oppression.

All too soon the *Revolution* folded. When Train was arrested in Ireland for aiding the nationalist cause, the paper lost its backing. For a time Anthony assumed financial responsibility. In Boston Henry Blackwell was financing a paper for the AWSA, the *Woman's Journal*, with money he had earned in business. Anthony did not have Blackwell's background of a secure personal income. By 1870, already $10,000 in debt, she was forced to sell the *Revolution*.

The end of the *Revolution* did not dishearten Stanton and Anthony. They continued to address themselves to a variety of controversial issues, and they continued to ally themselves with radical and unconventional figures, some of whom proved unacceptable to middle-class Americans. Probably the most dramatic, and to some minds the most damaging, alliance they ever made was with Victoria Woodhull.

During the late 1860s and early 1870s Victoria Woodhull was a member of the avant-garde fringe of the American reform movement. She and her associates spoke for socialism, an end to the nation state, and most daring of all, free love. In a period of rigid sexual repression Woodhull spoke and wrote explicitly about female sexuality. Her brief alliance with the National wing of the woman suffrage movement presented an opportunity for feminists to deal with the "marriage question" more fully than they had ever done before, but the alliance was fraught with difficulties, and the opportunity was never fulfilled.

Victoria Woodhull did not work her way up the feminist ranks—she began at the top. In 1871 she appeared suddenly in Washington, D.C., to address the House Judiciary Committee on the subject of woman suffrage. No other feminist had ever been granted that privilege. Some months before she had met and charmed Congressman Ben Butler, who invited her to appear before his committee.

Anthony and other National feminists, who were in Washington at the time for their annual convention, were chagrined to learn that a woman unaffiliated with their movement was going to speak before Congress about woman suffrage. They rushed to attend her presentation. What they heard was impressive. Woodhull argued that woman suffrage was already an implied right in the Constitution because of the word "person" in section one of the Fourteenth Amendment and the use of the word "citizen" without reference to sex in the Fifteenth Amendment. This logical and persuasive argument was just what the Nationals needed to press their point that suffrage for black men and women should be granted together. They invited Woodhull to repeat her Congressional address before their convention that same day.

Woodhull was not completely unfamiliar to feminists. They knew that she and her sister, Tennessee Claflin, had recently earned a considerable fortune (reportedly $70,000 in three years) as Wall Street's first female stockbrokers. Railroad tycoon Commodore Vanderbilt, it was said, had bankrolled the brokerage firm and supplied the sisters with the very best stock tips. Feminists had heard about, and some perhaps had read, the sisters' radical newspaper, *Woodhull and Claflin's Weekly,* in which Victoria had announced herself a candidate for president of the United States. The weekly regularly carried articles on prostitution, abortion, and venereal disease and was the first American periodical to print Karl Marx's *Communist Manifesto.*

Victoria Claflin Woodhull was not at all like the educated, middle-class reformers in the woman suffrage movement. Born in 1838 in a small town in Ohio, she had known little stability and respectability in her young life. Victoria's family survived on its wits, most of the time managing to stay just this side of the law. Her father, Reuben Buckman Claflin, commonly known as Buck, was something of a confidence man and a drifter, who never managed to support his large family. Her mother, Roxanna, was given to hysterical tirades and supernatural visions. Woodhull was trained in mysticism and the occult by her mother. As a child she heard voices and saw spirits. While still in her teens she claimed to have been visited by a noble-looking man in a tunic who told her, "You will know wealth and fame one day. You will live in a city surrounded by ships, and you will become a ruler of your people."[13] Victoria believed in the vision as her true destiny.

Growing up in the Claflin household was like being part of a traveling circus. Buck was always getting into trouble and moving on. Victoria and her sister, Tennessee, were a prime means of support for the family. They were the star attraction of the Claflin medical road show, offering miracle cures at a price.

At fifteen Victoria married a middle-aged physician, Dr. Channing Woodhull with whom she had two children. Woodhull was an alcoholic who periodically abandoned his wife and children. Eventually Victoria returned to the Claflins. Working as spiritualists, she and Tennessee earned enough to provide for the entire family. Every so often Dr. Woodhull, sick and destitute, would return and Victoria would take him in.

On the road Victoria acquired a second husband without divorcing the first. Like Victoria, Colonel Harvey Blood was already married. He was a believer in free love, and in Victoria he found both a lover and a convert. Victoria, who had lived so long outside of middle-class society, knew little about Victorian morality. A passionate woman, she did not care whether or not her lovemaking was legal. Blood left his wife, child, and respectable job as city auditor of St. Louis to join the Claflin family in their wanderings.

Before she met Blood, Victoria had felt despised. On the road she and Tennessee had been called "prostitutes" and "charlatans." Blood talked to Victoria about the "false" and "repressed morality" behind these labels. Armed with Blood's teachings, Victoria began to think of herself as one of an important group of freethinkers who would lead the way to new social freedoms. She had another vision in which the noble-looking man—this time he identified himself as Demosthenes—told her to move to New York City. She followed his advice, and her family and Colonel Blood followed her.

It was not long before Demosthenes' "prophecy" started to unfold. Part of Woodhull's gift for winning the help of powerful men and using their talents to further herself was her beauty; she was petite and blue-eyed, with lovely skin and a genteel demeanor. Though unschooled, she had learned to dress and speak with elegance.

No doubt after all those years on the road telling fortunes and selling cures, Victoria and Tennessee had become accomplished actresses. Though always willing to help Victoria, Tennessee was a different sort of person. Where Victoria was dignified, Tennessee was natural. Victoria was driven; all Tennessee ever really wanted was to have a good time. It was Tennessee who first met and charmed Commodore Vanderbilt and thus started Victoria on her way.

Vanderbilt helped Woodhull to become wealthy. Stephen Pearl Andrews helped her to become famous. Andrews was a brilliant philosopher who had synthesized an enormous body of knowledge. From his study of languages —he knew thirty of them—Andrews created a universal language he called Alawato. His study of history, politics, and government led him to devise a blueprint for a new universal government—or Pantarchy, as he called it. Andrews was one of the first Americans to advance the ideas of Karl Marx. Along with an economic revolution, Andrews called for a social revolution. He detested everything about Victorian morality. Sex, he claimed, was a natural instinct, and men and women had a right to follow their instincts freely, unrestricted by laws or religion. When Woodhull adopted Andrews as her intellectual guide and mentor, Andrews found a spokesperson for his most radical sexual views. With the assistance of Colonel Blood, Andrews supplied the rational arguments for free love. Woodhull and Tennessee Claflin supplied the passion and the drama.

Free love, as Woodhull and Claflin defined it, meant simply the right of any person, man or woman, to enjoy sexual relations outside of marriage. Why should a marriage license, they asked, make sex right, while its absence made it wrong? Men and women who loved and desired each other would continue to live together even if marriage was abolished. Those who needed marriage to keep them together ought not to be married in the first place. "Marriage," Woodhull declared, "is an assumption by the community that it can regulate the sexual instincts of individuals better than they can themselves—and they have been so regulated there is scarcely any natural instinct left in the race."[14]

Woodhull and Claflin challenged virtually every nineteenth-century assumption about sex. They based their theory of free love on an explicit understanding of female sexuality. They claimed for women and men alike the same standards and rights. What was evil, Woodhull and Claflin claimed, was not human sexuality, but its repression. "From the moment the sexual instinct is dead in man and woman, from that moment a person begins to die." Sex not founded in love and mutual desire was demoralizing, and no marriage law could compel two people to love each other. In fact, Woodhull noted, most people married for reasons that had nothing to do with love. "There are thousands of men who marry simply because they can't afford a prostitute. And there are thousands of women who would leave their husbands if they had another means of support."[15]

Woodhull and Claflin claimed that for most women marriage was legalized prostitution. Women married not for love, but for economic survival. "Women have not equal chances with men of earning and winning anything; . . . They must entice, and seduce, and entrap men, either in the legitimate way, or in the illegitimate way, in order to secure their portion of the spoil." In marriage a wife "yielded control of her sexual organs to a man, to insure a home, food, and clothing."[16] In some ways she was worse off than a prostitute, who could refuse a customer; a wife was expected to submit to her husband's desires regardless of her own.

Sex without pleasure, Woodhull asserted, was a "crime." "A wife who submits to sexual intercourse, against her wishes or desires, virtually commits suicide, while the husband who compels it, commits murder, and ought just as much to be punished for it as though he had strangled her to death for refusing him."[17] Moral reformers and many feminists had similarly denounced the law which gave a husband legal ownership of his wife's body. Lucy Stone argued that a wife had a right to abstain from sex and should teach her husband to do likewise. Woodhull's message was very different. She urged women to enjoy sex as much as men did. Mutual pleasure, rather than abstinence, was her answer.

According to Woodhull, men had no right to assume that women lacked sexual feelings. "Every man needs to have it thundered in his ears until he wakes to the fact that he is not the only party to the act, and that the other party demands a return for all that he receives; demands that he shall not be enriched at her expense; demands that he shall not, either from ignorance or selfish desire, carry her impulse forward on its mission only to cast it backward with the mission unfulfilled, to prostrate the impelling power and to breed nervous debility or irritability and sexual demoralization."[18]

In Woodhull's view, "one-half of all women seldom or never experienced any pleasure whatever in the sexual act." It is not clear where she got that figure, but she used it to make a very important point. Denying women the right to enjoy sex was a basic means of male control. Preachers, teachers, doctors, and men in general, Woodhull declared, denied women knowledge about their own sexuality, distorted the truth, and feigned ignorance themselves. Women who somehow managed to become knowledgeable about their bodies and claimed pleasure for themselves were considered immoral. The entire weight of Victorian social attitudes worked against women's discovering their own sexuality. "Men," wrote Woodhull, "know that if women had knowledge about sex, male domination would cease."[19]

Fear of venereal disease and unwanted pregnancies dominated the sexual lives of many nineteenth-century women. Wives worried that their husbands would infect them with VD contracted from prostitutes. Woodhull and Claflin brought the "unspoken fear" into the open when they discussed prostitution. Without condoning the practice, they recognized that "it exists and will continue to exist as long as society maintains its present ideas and organization. As it cannot be extinguished, its evils should be palliated." They recommended that prostitutes receive weekly medical examinations, as was then the custom in Europe.[20]

Finding a solution to the problem of unwanted pregnancies was more difficult. There were as yet no safe and effective methods of contraception. Abortion was the most common form of birth control, but crude medical procedures of the time made it extremely dangerous. Other methods such as douching were not very effective.

To compound the problem, most doctors were ignorant of the process of conception. Until the 1840s it was assumed that women were most fertile near their menstruation. This theory was refuted in 1849 by a British professor who had studied the fertility cycles of the wives of sailors. According to this scholar, the supposed "fertile period" for women was in fact the time they were most safe from pregnancy. His findings, published in American medical books in the 1850s, offered the first accurate information about the female fertility cycle.[21] Middle-class women, who had access to this information, were able for the first time to practice a natural form of birth control—the rhythm method. It was rhythm which Woodhull and Claflin, both of whom opposed abortion, seemed to suggest to women when they urged women to gain control of their "maternal functions."

Not until the twentieth century did sophisticated knowledge about female physiology and more reliable methods of birth control become available to American women, but Woodhull and Claflin took a step in the right direction when they defied Victorian silence about sexuality and challenged women to learn about their own bodies. "There should be as much attention paid to breeding children," said Woodhull, "as to horses and cattle. . . . Sexual union for the propagation of children should be consummated under the highest and best knowledge." Woman's "sexual slavery" would end only when there was no more "enforced pregnancy."[22]

In 1871, when Woodhull was embraced by the National wing of the woman suffrage movement, she had not yet declared all her views about sexual freedom. She had revealed enough, however, to give feminists a clue. Victoria Woodhull, they knew, was no lady.

The Nationals were willing to overlook that fact after they heard Woodhull declare that woman suffrage was an implied right in the Fourteenth and Fifteenth Amendments. Overnight she became the darling of the faction. Invited to reappear at their next convention, she received a standing ovation for her "Great Secession" speech. Woodhull had threatened that unless Congress gave women the vote, they would set up a new government. "We mean treason, we mean secession, and on a thousand times grander scale than was that of the South. We are plotting revolution; we will overthrow this bogus Republic and plant a government of righteousness in its stead."[23]

In the excitement that followed her speech, the Nationals called for reforms in virtually every aspect of government. One resolution demanded that "all laws shall be repealed which . . . interfere with the rights of adult individuals to pursue happiness as they may choose." Not until the convention was over did they realize that they had passed a resolution in favor of free love.

Conservative feminists from the American wing denounced the National-Woodhull alliance. The cause of woman suffrage, claimed Lucy Stone, would be set back a decade or more if it was linked in any way with free love. In spite of the criticism, many Nationals defended Woodhull's contribution to their movement. When several disgruntled feminists called Woodhull an infamous woman, Anthony retorted, "I would welcome all the infamous women of New York if they would give speeches for freedom."[24] Stanton was even blunter in her support of Woodhull. "If Victoria Woodhull must be crucified," she wrote, "let men drive the spikes and plait the crown of thorns."

> We have already enough women sacrificed to this sentimental, hypocritical, practicing purity, without going out of our way to increase the number. This is one of man's most effective engines for our division and subjugation. He creates the public sentiment, builds the gallows and then makes us hangmen for our own sex. We have crucified the Mary Wollstonecrafts, the Fanny Wrights, the George Sands, and the Fanny Kembles of all ages. Let us end this ignoble record and stand by womanhood.[25]

Until this time Woodhull had conducted herself in public with nearly-perfect ladylike decorum. She might have kept up the appearance had it not been for her family. The Claflins were accustomed to airing their differences openly. Roxanna Claflin did not like her new life in New York City, and she blamed the situation on Colonel Blood. If not for Blood, declared Roxanna, the Claflins would all be together in the Midwest, earning money as spiritualists and clairvoyants. When Roxanna dragged Blood to court and accused him of threatening her life, the press learned about Woodhull's disreputable family and scandalous living arrangements. Woodhull, reported the press, was living with both her first and second husbands!

Attacked as a "brazen" and "unsexed woman," Woodhull felt compelled to explain herself to the public once and for all. She hired Steinway Hall to talk on "The Principle of Social Meaning Involving the Question of Free Love, Marriage, Divorce, and Prostitution." On the podium Woodhull began speaking from a prepared text, but her audience was not interested in theory. "Are you a free lover?" shouted a heckler. Woodhull responded with a stunning, extemporaneous outbrust. "Yes. I am a free lover. I have an inalienable, constitutional, and natural right to love whom I may, to love as long or as short a period as I can, to change that love every day if I please: And with that right neither you nor any law you can frame have any right to interfere." Free love meant, not promiscuity, but sexual union based on mutual desire and love. It was her right to love when and whom she chose, and it was, she told her audience, "your duty not only to accord it but as a community to see that I am protected in it."[26]

Woodhull was denounced by the press and pulpit. Old supporters vanished. Business in the brokerage firm declined. She and her family were evicted from their house and evicted again. No landlord wanted to rent to Woodhull and her "gang of free lovers." Some friends remained. In an unexpected gesture of loyalty, National feminists invited Woodhull to their next convention. On the platform she was seated between Stanton and Lucretia Mott. No one mentioned her Steinway Hall proclamation.

As long as Woodhull did not discuss free love at woman suffrage meetings and as long as she followed the priorities of the movement's leaders, she had a place on the National platform. But Woodhull would not keep still. Somehow she managed to convince Stanton that the Nationals ought to form a political party of their own and nominate her,

Woodhull, to run for president of the United States in the 1872 elections. Anthony vetoed the plan on the ground that Woodhull was trying to use the Nationals to enhance her own power. "Persistently she means to run our craft into her port and none other." Anthony further criticized Woodhull because she spoke, not for women, but for men. "She is wholly owned and dominated by men spirits, and I spurn the control of the whole lot of them," Anthony wrote to Stanton.[27] Though the criticism was not entirely unfounded, it is probable that Anthony believed that any woman who called for female sexual freedom was voicing a male opinion. Single all her life, Anthony was not interested in changing the private relations between men and women. Women, she consistently maintained, did not need men, only each other.

At the 1872 National convention Anthony broke the Woodhull spell. When Woodhull tried to gain control over the meeting, Anthony ousted her and her followers from the hall. Then she adjourned the convention. Woodhull was never invited back again.

By this time Woodhull had virtually no money and was looking for vengeance. Why, she asked, should she suffer for doing openly what a great many "respectable" Americans did secretly? She would teach them a lesson about hypocrisy. Woodhull decided to tell all she knew about the Beecher-Tilton affair.

Henry Ward Beecher was the most famous liberal preacher of his day, and Elizabeth Tilton was one of his parishioners. She was also the wife of Theodore Tilton, a Beecher protegé and staunch supporter of the woman suffrage movement. Woodhull, an intimate of all three, happened to know that Beecher had had an affair with Elizabeth Tilton. On November 2, 1872, a special edition of Woodhull's *Weekly* published the secret.

It was the scandal of the century, and its repercussions were felt for years. Eventually Theodore Tilton sued Beecher for misconduct with his wife. Tilton himself was accused of adultery with Woodhull. The reputations of both Tiltons were ruined. Beecher denied everything and was acquitted, by a hung jury. Beecher was the only one who came through unscathed.

Woodhull and her copublishers, Tennessee Claflin and Colonel Blood, were the first to feel the effects of the tidal wave they had released. The famous preacher had powerful and influential friends, men who had invested in his church and his publishing empire. Eager to keep Beecher's name clean, these backers found a front man of sorts in vice suppressor Anthony Comstock.

As head of the YMCA's Committee for the Suppression of Vice, Comstock crusaded zealously against the publication of anything that did not meet his standards of purity. Obscene literature, Comstock asserted, was the root of all evil. His first target was Woodhull and Claflin's *Weekly*.

Congress had recently passed a law making it illegal to send obscene literature through the mails. Comstock used the new statute to get Woodhull and Claflin arrested. Bail was set at $20,000. According to the district attorney, Woodhull and Claflin were guilty of more than circulating an obscene publication; they had committed "gross and malicious libel" against one of the "purest and best citizens of the United States."[28]

Feminists who had once befriended Woodhull and Claflin offered no support to the jailed sisters. Their silence was extremely telling. Woodhull had first heard of the scandal from Stanton, Anthony, Davis, and Beecher's sister Isabella; for years they had all whispered about it. When Beecher said that all of Woodhull's revelations were "entirely false," Anthony reportedly said, "If the Lord ever struck anyone dead for telling a lie, surely he should have struck then." But while they knew that Beecher had, in fact, committed adultery, he was still one of their circle, far more so than was Woodhull. Only Stanton dared to publicly rebuke Beecher and defend Woodhull. "Woodhull has done a work for Women that none of us could have done. She has faced and dared men to call her names that make women shudder." But Stanton predicted that Beecher would maintain his powerful position while Woodhull would "sink into a dismal swamp."[29]

Released from jail and cleared of the obscenity charge, Woodhull suffered an emotional collapse and underwent a religious conversion. In place of social freedom, she lectured on "sacred truths." What happened next was painfully ironic. In 1876 Woodhull sued Colonel Blood for divorce charging him with adultery. Both she and her sister moved to England, and married well, Tennessee Claflin becoming Lady Cook and Woodhull turning into Mrs. Martin, the wife of a rich businessman. Tennessee enjoyed her new life; but Victoria became obsessed with the past. She spent years trying to "vindicate her name" and "set the record straight." Victoria Claflin Woodhull Martin died in 1927 at the age of eighty-five, convinced that she had never supported free love or women's rights.

While it is undeniable that Woodhull's personal weaknesses detracted from her most important ideas, it was also inevitable that Woodhull and Claflin would be censured and isolated because of those ideas. Few Americans in 1871 were willing to insist, as these two women did, that "sex be recognized as a fact of life." Fewer still would admit that women had as much sexuality as men. Female emancipation and sexual freedom of the kind discussed by Woodhull and Claflin was not proposed again for another fifty years.

Most nineteenth-century middle-class women, both feminists and nonfeminists, could not accept the idea of woman's sexual freedom within marriage, let alone outside it. In their view Woodhull's belief that husbands and wives should enjoy mutually gratifying sex would turn the home into a brothel.

Even those feminists who, like Stanton, privately agreed with Woodhull would not publicly support her sexual views. In discussing the "marriage question," Stanton continued to call for more liberal divorce laws; but she never talked about a wife's right to consummation, as Woodhull did.

In opposing the double standard, feminists took a very different direction from that chosen by Woodhull. Men, feminists claimed, should be more like women, not the other way around. Men should imitate the superior moral restraint of their wives. This standard reinforced the Victorian code they felt oppressed by in the first place, but in its own circular way, it was a means of exerting female power. By the end of the nineteenth century middle-class American women were using their clubs, civic organizations, and reform movements in an attempt to turn the whole world into a Victorian home.

In the wake of the Beecher-Tilton scandal, the National wing of the suffrage movement concentrated on winning the vote, as did the American faction. Together, both groups numbered no more than ten thousand members. Though they stuck to the "main question" of suffrage, they convinced few Americans that women had the right to vote. Those who were convinced first came not from the established East, where the women's rights movement had originated, but from the untamed Far West.

In 1869 women in the new territory of Wyoming gained the right to vote. That same year northern politicians and abolitionists refused to support the feminist bid for suffrage. While feminists in New York and Boston protested the Fourteenth and Fifteenth Amendments, women in Wyoming went to the polls. Feminists were inspired by this distant victory, and some began to base their hopes for women's rights on the freedom of the West.

Between 1869 and 1881 Stanton and Anthony, traveling extensively through pioneer country on their yearly eight-month lecture tours for the Lyceum Bureau, were impressed by what they saw. The East was fast becoming urbanized and industrialized. The West was similar to the rural, small-town society of early America that Stanton, Anthony, and other feminists upheld as the ideal democracy. Out West, women could regain the status of colonial women while still being revered as Victorian ladies.

11

The Maverick West

When Elizabeth Cady Stanton and Susan B. Anthony went west in the 1870s, they found a new kind of American woman who was very much to their liking. Women in the West combined eighteenth-century hardiness with Victorian high-mindedness. As in the case of their colonial grandmothers, women in the West were accustomed to working long and hard. As did their sisters in the East, Western women had a highly developed sense of morality. Conditions on the frontier offered this new breed of women the chance to put their moral values to work, building communities and civilizing a "barbaric" land.

The ideas of the Victorian age about women in the East and the West were theoretically the same, but in practice they varied widely. Both regions idealized women as morally superior, gentle rather than aggressive, home-loving rather than worldly. But while in the East women were seen as a symbol of social stability and moral rectitude, in the West women put their superior traits to work. Unlike her eastern sister, the frontier woman was defined as a worker. Her role as housewife and mother was unabashedly active, and as the backbone of the family, she insured the permanence of western settlements and the continuation of civilized values.

The pattern of settlement in the West was very similar to that of colonial times. The first settlers were single men who lived like nomads. Fortune hunters, cowboys, miners, and outlaws congregated in frontier outposts. It was when men and women went West together that roots were put down. Where families settled, communities were organized, the economy was stabilized, churches and schools were built, and law and order were introduced.

After a trip to the West the New England writer Margaret Fuller observed that it was generally men's choice to migrate, and "women will follow as women will, doing their best for affection's sake but too often in heartsickness and weariness."[1] For men the West held out the

176

promise of independence and liberty in a new land. Women who went West often did so with great sadness. Pulling up stakes meant abandoning the comforts of one home and starting over again, often with next to nothing. It also meant leaving an affectionate world of family and friends for the loneliness of an uncharted destiny.

Nevertheless, as the frontier moved westward, women moved with it. They were along on exploring parties crossing the Rockies, with the first wagon trains into California and Oregon, with homesteaders settling the desolate Great Plains. Clinging to a few treasured possessions, souvenirs from their past lives, women accompanied their men across the continent, sharing the dangers and backbreaking difficulties of the journey.

Women drove wagons, fought prairie fires, forded streams in icy water, and walked day after day across the country in burning heat, in rain storms, and in early freezes. They did "woman's work" as well, tending campsites and preparing three meals a day. They faced births and deaths and illnesses along the route. Sometimes the men died, leaving women and children to continue on alone.

One traveler described the scene of such a frontier death on the Great Plains in 1852. "An open bleak prairie, the cold wind howling overhead, bearing with it the mournful tones of that deserted woman; a new grave, a woman and three children sitting near by; a girl of fourteen summers [years] walking round in a circle, wringing her hands and calling upon her dead parent; a boy of twelve, sitting upon the wagon tongue sobbing aloud; a strange man placing a rude headboard at the head of the grave."[2]

Hardships were not over at journey's end. For many women the isolation of life on the frontier was intolerable. Anna Howard Shaw, a leader of the woman suffrage movement, was a little girl when she and her mother went to join Anna's father in the backwoods of Michigan. As they arrived at their destination, her daughter later remembered, Mrs. Howard's eyes were alive with the hope of finding some settlement or at least an inhabited clearing. Instead she found a crude log house, with a dirt floor and holes where the windows and doors should have been. The cabin was surrounded by forest, and there was no sign of any other human life. As Anna recalled, "I shall never forget the look my mother turned on the place. Without a word, she crossed the threshold, and standing very still, looked slowly around her. Then something within her seemed to give way, and she sank upon the floor . . . her face never lost the deep lines those first hours of her pioneer life had cut upon it."[3]

Life on an isolated farm, wrote one woman from Iowa in 1870, "was mighty easy for the men and horses, but death on cattle and women." The men, wrote this farm woman, went often to market and to town for business, but the women were constantly in their homes.[4] A man could feel free in his own fields, but a woman, tied to a cabin and the garden patch beside it, often felt trapped by mud and dirt.

Another woman described the loneliness that almost drove her mad. Her hands, she noted, were busy all day, but her mind was idle. There were no people to see and little to read. "I would keep thinking of the same things over and over, until they nearly drove me crazy. . . . There were weeks in our long winter, when I scarcely left the house."[5]

Ranch women in the Far West experienced the same sense of desolation described by their farming sisters. Agnes Moreley Cleaveland, who recalled her experiences as a ranch woman in a book appropriately titled *No Life for a Lady*, wrote of the "moral stamina" needed to survive in nearly total isolation. Cattlemen rode the range for months on end, while women waited patiently at home, doing back-breaking chores with only small children to keep them company. "Men walked in a sort of perpetual adventure, but women waited—until perhaps lightning struck." This same commentator recalled the "unspectacular heroism" of women on the range. She described the awful journey of one woman whose three-month old baby had just died. The mother was being driven to town by a neighbor because her husband was away. "Halfway across the plains one of the team [of horses] dropped dead from overdriving. All night, the mother sat with the dead child in her arms, while the man riding the other horse bareback went on . . . to fetch a fresh team."[6]

Other women hated the drudgery. Abigail Duniway, a schoolteacher who married an Oregon farmer and later became the leader of the woman suffrage movement in the

Northwest Territory, resented the never-ending work and the life without social or intellectual amenities. Mrs. Duniway bore two children in her first two years of marriage. She was responsible for churning thousands of pounds of butter a year for the market. Her life, she wrote, was full of "washing . . . scrubbing . . . churning . . . or nursing the baby . . . preparing meals in our lean-to kitchen . . . to sew and cook, and wash, and iron; to bake and clean and stew and fry"—in short, to be what Mrs. Duniway called a "general pioneer drudge, with never a penny of my own."[7]

While some women were defeated by the day-to-day struggle, others came alive in the freer air of the West. Away from "civilization" some found they could be courageous and self-reliant, qualities Eastern society neither required nor valued in women.

When white women went West to settle, nobody cared about their past, who their parents were, how much money or social position they had enjoyed in the East. In the West the ability to survive, to work, to help one's neighbors were what mattered. Nannie Alderson, a transplanted southern lady who migrated to Montana in 1883 with her new husband, took delight in the frontier's egalitarian spirit. "The West," she wrote, "was very tolerant towards the lesser faults of conduct. It was even willing to overlook the greater if they were not repeated. A man's past was not questioned nor a woman's either. The present was what counted. . . . Half the charm of the country for me was its broad-mindedness."[8]

Such women as Nannie Alderson, who thrived on the hard work and absence of social conventions in the West, helped forge the legend of the rough-and-ready frontier female. Women of this temperament were probably a minority in the West, but they left their mark, not just on the region, but on the nation's imagination.

Agnes Moreley Cleaveland was of this legendary type. In her memoirs she recalled the freedom of her girlhood on a New Mexico ranch and noted with sadness the change in social customs the passing of time had brought to the West. Although young Agnes rode sidesaddle, her one bow to propriety, as a girl she did ranch chores "side by side with men, receiving the same praise or censure for like undertakings." "There was no double standard on the ranch," she noted. Her major achievement was as a rider.

"I enjoyed a local reputation in the one field where reputations most counted—that of good horsemanship. To prove it, I cherished for years a clipping from . . . an early newspaper. . . . It informed that Miss Agnes of the Datils and Three-fingered Pete are the best riders in the country."[9]

Another hardy woman was Elinore Rupert, a Denver widow who took in washing to support herself and her young daughter. In 1909 Mrs. Rupert decided to try homesteading in an unsettled area of Wyoming. At first she worked as a housekeeper for a Wyoming rancher because he could "give me advice about land and water rights." Along with Clyde Stewart's advice went a proposal of marriage. Mrs. Rupert accepted but persevered with her original plan to obtain land of her own. "I would not for anything allow Mr. Stewart to do anything toward improving my place," she wrote, "for I want the fun and experience of my own." Elinore Rupert Stewart wrote of the many pleasures her new life gave her. "I have tried every kind of work this ranch affords, and I can do any of it. Of course, I am extra strong, but those who try know that strength and knowledge come with doing. I just love to experiment, to work out, and to prove out things so that ranch life and 'roughing it' just suit me."[10]

Whatever men did in the West, there were always a few women who, out of necessity or a love of adventure, did the same. The West had women bronco busters, women sheriffs, women gamblers, women who drank and smoked, and women outlaws. While it was quite common for women to do men's work, occasionally the role reversal went the other way. Nannie Alderson, for example, learned to cook, not from her mother, but from the bachelor cowboys who worked on her Montana ranch. Born in the South to a family with servants, cooking had not been part of Nannie's education. That men could cook, she wrote, "was something new under the sun to me, but men in Montana could and did, and most of what I learned during my first years as a housewife I learned from them."[11]

The West democratized chivalry. In the East there was a narrow line of "ladylike" behavior; if she crossed it, a woman was excluded from the respect bestowed upon ladies. In the West respect was given not for good behavior, but in an appreciation of "womanhood." Virtually all white females in the West were objects of reverence. In practice this freely given admiration allowed women extraordinary leeway in their behavior—a woman might go galloping across the plains and still be a "lady." What a woman did in the West did not cancel out the fact of who she was—a member of the more moral sex, the sex needed to implant home virtues and to domesticate the crude frontier.

Throughout the nineteenth century men outnumbered women in most of the western territories. In 1865 California had three men to each woman; the territory of Washington had a ratio of four to one; Nevada had eight men for every woman; and the ratio in Colorado was twenty to one. A Colorado miner commented on life without women. "We were all in the habit of running to our cabin doors in Denver on the arrival of a lady, to gaze at her as earnestly as at any other rare curiosity."[12]

Single women were, of course, the most sought after. They could pick and choose their suitors much as rich young men chose brides in the East. "The parlour maid," wrote one Californian in a letter dated 1857, "who weeks ago had cooked, charred and washed laundry, has become the wife of a banker or rich merchant, because she has a nice face."[18] Some married women discarded one husband when they found another more to their liking.

Saloon girls, prostitutes, and actresses populated frontier towns during the days of the "wild" West, offering affection, warmth, and companionship to lonely cowboys and miners. The legend of the saloon girl with "the heart of gold" is part of western folklore. Many of these women became famous and rich; others married and settled down to lives of anonymous domesticity. The distinction between saloon girls and prostitutes on the one hand and "respectable" women on the other was nevertheless universally recognized. According to the frontier code, the very existence of a "bad" woman was to be kept secret from "good" women, and a "good" woman's name was never to be mentioned in a saloon.

Nonwhite women did not enjoy the high regard lavished on their white sisters. Some Indian women were raped, murdered, and mutilated by white men. Later, Mexican and Chinese women received similarly brutal treatment from whites.

Sometimes Indians also raped white women. Whenever

Indians raided white settlements, they murdered many inhabitants and carried off female captives. An abducted woman was usually seized as a "wife" by a particular brave; he had the "right" to rape her but generally prevented other men from doing the same. White men often retaliated for the rape of "our women" with raids on Indian camps, killing as many braves and children as possible and then gang-raping and murdering Indian women. White men often mutilated the bodies of the Indian women they had raped and murdered. They rarely took female captives and had little interest in nonwhite wives.

In her important study of rape, *Against Our Will,* Susan Brownmiller notes that Indian and white men in the West had a similar view of females in regard to rape.[14] Rape committed by men of both races was first and foremost seen as an attack upon the men of the other race. The horrible crimes committed against Indian and white women, as Brownmiller points out, had little to do with sex and everything to do with property rights. Women of both races were pawns in the war between Indians and whites to control Western territory. Indians attacked settlements and seized women in an attempt to drive whites off Indian land. White men used the crimes committed against "our women" to justify turning Indians off the land they had inhabited for centuries.

White women held captive by Indians often tried to cover up the fact that they had been raped. These women knew that if they admitted having been the victim of rape, they would become object not of pity, but of scorn among white men. Any woman who was raped, whatever her race, was considered tarnished.

The contribution of white women in settling and civilizing the West was affirmed in law and educational practices. As western colleges and universities emerged, they were generally coeducational, offering women equal training and degrees. In addition, most western territories granted women some legal rights, including ownership of property, control of their own wages, and in some specific instances, dissolution of marriages.

In the Homestead Acts of 1860 and 1890, the federal government tried to provide for women. This legislation gave free land to both men and women, unlike similar acts passed in colonial times, in which any land granted to a married woman was the legal property of her husband. A western homesteading wife could control the title to her own land. The object of Congress in granting land to women was to encourage the migration and settlement of families. A husband and wife who went West together were guaranteed 640 free acres; a single person was given half that amount.

In theory, the Homestead Acts offered single women the chance to be economically independent. A poor eastern widow or spinster could go west and lay claim to 320 acres of land. She could attempt to develop it herself or sell it once she had established residency and won title. In 1890 a quarter of a million women were running their own farms and ranches; most of these, however, were widows who had gone west with their husbands and who carried on alone after their husbands' deaths.

While the Homesteading Acts ultimately failed both men and women, for a few women free land was a solution to "poverty's problems." Elinore Rupert Stewart wrote that she was "very enthusiastic about women homesteading." A former washerwoman herself, Mrs. Stewart declared that it was easier for a woman to support herself and her children on a ranch or farm than by taking in washing.

> I realize that temperament has much to do with success in any undertaking, and persons afraid of coyotes and work and loneliness had better let ranching alone. At the same time, any woman who can stand the beauty of the sunset, loves growing things, and is willing to put in as much time at careful labor as she does standing over the washtub, will certainly succeed; will have independence, plenty to eat all the time, and a home of her own in the end.[15]

The most radical legal right granted to western women was the vote. The four states to enact woman suffrage in the nineteenth century and the first seven to do so in the twentieth century were western states. For the first time women won a measure of political equality.

The fact that woman suffrage was achieved first in the West has been linked to the existence of frontier egalitarianism, to the value granted pioneer women as workers and community builders, and to the high status women enjoyed in the areas where women were scarce. Certainly all these factors contributed to the enfranchisement of Western women, but it should not be supposed that the motivation for granting women their political rights was solely, or even mostly, idealistic. In his study *The Puritan Ethic and Woman Suffrage,* historian Alan P. Grimes has shown that woman suffrage in the West was a product of special-interest politics.[16]

In 1869—the year Stanton, Anthony, and Stone formally launched the woman suffrage movement—the Wyoming territory gave its female citizens the vote, making them the only legally enfranchised women in the world. The Wyoming victory was largely the work of Esther Morris, a transplanted New York milliner and a follower of Anthony. Morris convinced Wyoming legislators that women voters could help in the fight to establish law and order in the barely civilized territory.

In the 1860s Wyoming was noted for its rough terrain and sparse population. Permanent settlers were outnumbered by pioneers pushing toward Oregon and California, cowboys, miners, gamblers, and thousands of railroad workers laying the tracks for the transcontinental line. The railroad population—made up of Chinese laborers, newly emancipated blacks, and soldiers mustered out of the Union and Confederate armies—was so disorderly that Wyoming natives called them the Hell-on-Wheels.

The newly organized territorial legislature was eager to control the transient population and to lure permanent settlers to the region. Prior to the first legislative session Esther Morris gave a tea party at her frontier shack, which was attended by the new lawmakers. She urged them to introduce a bill for woman suffrage, arguing that votes for women would increase the voting strength of progovernment, law-and-order citizens. She stressed that woman suffrage would "prove a great advertisement . . . attract attention to the legislature and the territory," and draw more families to settle in Wyoming.

Morris' arguments were convincing. At their very first session legislators passed a bill mandating woman suffrage, married women's property rights, and equal pay for male and female teachers. When the governor signed it, woman suffrage was achieved in Wyoming without the help of an organized woman suffrage movement or any movement at all.

Even before women had a chance to cast their ballots,

the effect of woman suffrage was felt. By virtue of being voters, women became eligible for jury duty, and Esther Morris of South Pass City became Wyoming's first woman justice of the peace. Women were a strong moral force on juries. The first female panelists in Laramie, Wyoming, indicted every saloon keeper for staying open on the Sabbath. "The presence of ladies" in courtrooms is said to have brought about "the most perfect decorum" in the once rowdy chambers of justice.[17]

At the polls women's presence had a similarly cooling effect on male rowdiness. The election of 1870, the first in which women participated, was not only more orderly, but according to observers, considerably more honest than elections in the past. One Wyoming resident, used to election day drunkenness and rioting, noted that "It seemed more like Sunday than election day."[18]

Vastly outnumbered by men, women voters in Wyoming possessed little political strength. Moreover, they did not, as had been expected, vote as a block. Women turned out to be just as susceptible to party politics as did men. They did not use their votes to gain additional rights or political power.

When Wyoming applied for statehood in 1890, many United States Congressmen opposed woman suffrage. But men in Wyoming refused to annul the law. The Wyoming legislature wired Congress, "We may stay out of the Union for 100 years, but we will come in with our women." Wyoming was admitted as the first woman suffrage state by a narrow margin.

If woman suffrage in Wyoming helped to establish government, in Utah it was used to retain the government in power. Mormon political control in Utah was threatened by an influx of "gentile" settlers who arrived in the wake of the transcontinental railroad. At the same time the federal government was considering a law banning the Mormon practice of polygamy, which allowed male church members to marry as many women as they could support. In response to both these threats to Mormon hegemony, the church-controlled legislature adopted woman suffrage.

Female Mormons did what they were told and voted to uphold polygamy. Mrs. Fanny Stenhouse, one of the few Mormon women to openly express opposition to plural marriage, noted, "I have often seen one solitary man driving into a city a whole wagon load of women of all ages and sizes. They were going to the polls, and their vote would be one."[19]

For a time woman suffrage in Utah kept church leaders in control of the territory and forestalled federal anti-polygamy laws. Eventually, however, Congress devised a means of ousting the Mormon regime. In 1887 the Edmunds-Tucker Act prohibited polygamy and abolished woman suffrage in Utah. Without women, the Mormon vote was cut by more than 50 percent, and anti-Mormon politicians were elected to office. The Mormon Church, bowing to pressure, renounced plural marriage.

In 1896 Utah was granted statehood under a constitution that reinstated woman suffrage. Once the power of the Mormon Church had been checked and Mormons in Utah agreed to conform to conventional marital practices, the issue of woman suffrage was no longer disputed.

Utah was the third state to enfranchise women. Three years before, in 1893, Colorado women had been granted the vote. Men had actually gone to the polls and passed a referendum for woman suffrage. As one pioneer woman noted, "Whenever [Colorado] undertook to do anything, it acted in a most whole-hearted way."

Several factors were involved in the Colorado vote in favor of woman suffrage. Bordering Wyoming and Utah, Colorado residents could see at first hand that women's votes aided community interests. In addition, during the severe economic depression of the 1890s many farmers and small-town citizens turned to such reform groups as the Populist Party and the Farmers Alliance, both of which supported woman suffrage. Populists believed the woman's vote would bolster the strength of the small town fighting against capitalist interests in Denver and the mining camps and against liquor and saloons.

Neither big business nor antisuffragists campaigned against the vote for women in Colorado, because they did not believe it could pass. Carrie Chapman Catt, an aggressive young Westerner who led the woman suffrage campaign, was more than they had bargained for. Catt taught Colorado women how to organize and to lobby. Woman suffrage was enacted largely through the support of farmers and small townsmen; it appeared to be a true victory for reformers in Colorado.

In the same year that Utah became a state with woman

suffrage, Idaho also enfranchised women. As in Colorado, Idaho was influenced by neighboring Wyoming and Utah. Here, too, Carrie Catt led the campaign. In 1896 Idaho voters cast their ballots for the Populist Party's presidential candidate, William Jennings Bryan, and for woman suffrage. Bryan lost the national election, but woman suffrage remained in the Idaho state constitution.

When women won the vote in Wyoming in 1869 and became eligible to sit on juries, they used their political rights to establish law and order. The civilizing influence of the first women who voted in the frontier territory of Wyoming differed from the effect women exerted when communities, towns, and government became established in the West. By the 1890s, when Carrie Catt campaigned for suffrage in Colorado and Idaho, western women were exerting their moralizing and civilizing power in a highly organized way.

Nowhere can the evolution of women's influence in the West be seen more clearly than in the history of women's fight against alcoholic beverages. The fight to ban liquor, commonly known as the temperance movement, emerged in the West in the early 1870s quite haphazardly, but within twenty years women had established a national organization of formidable scope, which campaigned not only against alcohol but in favor of a dozen seemingly unrelated social reforms.

Western women were not the first to blame alcohol for most of society's ills; many Protestant denominations had long preached against alcoholic beverages. As early as 1840 temperance workers, including Susan B. Anthony, had sought to convince drinkers to swear off intoxicating beverages. Temperance, however, remained a relatively minor issue in the reformers' panoply until the women of the West threw their considerable energies into an attack on "demon Rum."

"The Crusade" swept like a tornado through hundreds of small towns during the early 1870s. Armies of singing and praying women invaded and closed thousands of saloons "in the name of all that is holy." In Hillsborough, Ohio, home of the first Crusade, women exhorted liquor dealers to repent "In the name of our desolated homes, blasted hopes, ruined lives, widowed hearts, for the honor of our community, for our happiness, for the good of the town, in the name of God who will judge you and us, for the sake of our souls which are to be saved or lost."[20]

Kneeling in the streets of Hillsborough outside the town's saloons, the women prayed and called upon the publicans to "cleanse yourself from this heinous sin and place yourselves in the ranks of those who are striving to ennoble and elevate themselves and their fellowmen." Either because they were overcome with remorse or because they were simply outnumbered, many saloon keepers poured their stock into the gutter and joined the women in praying and rejoicing. Similar scenes occurred in towns throughout the area. It should be noted, however, that most of the saloons did not remain closed for very long.

The most famous "Crusader" was six-foot-tall Carrie Nation (1846–1911) who spent her time marching into saloons with an axe, smashing bars, liquor bottles, glassware, mirrors, and anything else that stood in her way. Most women lacked Carrie Nation's zeal, not to mention her sense of drama. In lieu of the axe, they chose organization, and in 1874 the Woman's Christian Temperance Union was born.

During the next several years hundreds of thousands of women joined the WCTU. The Union was the first truly national woman's organization; its members could be found in all parts of the country and in all ranks of life. While its greatest strength was in the Midwest, the group prided itself on bringing together on one platform Jew, Catholic, Unitarian, Methodist, and Baptist, all "joined in one pulse, a protected home and a reformed America."[21] Hardly a woman in the nation remained untouched by the WCTU's network of organizations and activities.

In official terms WCTU members were disciples of Christ, dedicated to "enthroning His spirit in the world" by redeeming men from evil. At their meetings members prayed and sang hymns, but that was not the extent of their activities. From the beginning WCTU members imbibed politics along with their religion. While the Union was a national organization, its political voice was regional. The agrarian, antiindustrial spirit of Populism, strong in the Midwest and West in the 1870s, underlay early WCTU thinking.

While the Union's attack on the saloons was carried out

in the name of temperance, other less obvious factors were at work. The saloon was not simply the place where men got drunk. For example, in the nation's eastern cities the saloon was also the meeting place of local political bosses and their followers, many of whom were foreign born. By attacking the saloon, temperance women were striking at the heart of Democratic machine politics, the urban bosses who ran the machine, and the immigrants who voted the machine into office.

Frances Willard, who lead the WCTU for twenty years, devised a highly effective organizational strategy designed to change the world.[22] Willard divided the Union, which she called "the great society," into forty separate departments. Each department was headed by a woman leader who had an assistant in every state. Supporting the upper reaches were ten thousand local branches of the WCTU.

Willard was able to make the Union an extremely effective agent of social change. While always working under the banner of temperance, Willard was basically interested in any reform that would help women and children. During her long stewardship she encouraged the Union to campaign for kindergartens, prison reform, child labor laws, laws to protect working women, and woman suffrage.

Willard drew women who had not previously been receptive to women's rights into the temperance movement and then won them for woman suffrage and other feminist causes. Women's rights, she insisted, were necessary to protect woman's traditional role as wife and mother. She convinced WCTU members they could not protect their homes and families from the evil influence of liquor without having a voice in public affairs. The ballot and legislative programs to benefit women, she declared, were "necessary weapons for home protection." Though the Union had been established for one purpose, she coined the motto, "Do Everything."[23]

Willard had hit upon a clever tactic when she advocated women's rights in the name of home, purity, and God. By doing so, she converted thousands of women to the feminist cause. The cost was high, however. By acknowledging that the home was indeed woman's chief concern, Willard was undermining the very principles for which feminists were fighting. By using the sphere theory to justify women's rights, Willard was using antifeminist arguments to promote feminist positions. This tactic, which was later adopted by suffragists, had a debilitating effect on the entire woman's movement for many years to come.

During her lifetime Frances Willard's method inspired women and won support for woman suffrage, but after her death WCTU leaders abandoned woman suffrage even on the rather limited grounds championed by Frances Willard. The later generation of WCTU leaders, convinced that temperance was more important to the home than were the ballot and child welfare, concentrated entirely on winning prohibition.

Even after the WCTU divorced itself from the woman suffrage cause, in the popular mind woman suffrage and temperance remained linked. Many men who might otherwise have supported woman suffrage opposed it on the grounds that voting women would cast their ballots in favor of prohibition. Moreover, by aligning themselves with the WCTU, suffragists earned the undying enmity of the powerful liquor lobby, which waged a war of propaganda against votes for women for fifty years.

Industrialization and Urbanization

12

Immigrant Mothers and Daughters

Thirty-five million Europeans left their homelands to settle in America in the century between 1820 and 1920. One-third of these newcomers were women. The first to immigrate were several million northern Europeans from Ireland, Germany, and Scandinavia. Beginning in 1880 a much larger wave of immigration began. Twenty million men, women, and children arrived in the forty years prior to 1920. The newer immigrants—Poles, Italians, Jews, Slovaks, Bohemians, Greeks, and Armenians—came primarily from southern and eastern Europe.

Most of the new arrivals were peasants. In Europe they had worked the land, where their way of life had changed little over a dozen generations. Within each small and semicommunal village every inhabitant was known and linked to every other by ties of marriage, shared religious beliefs, customs, and class obligations.[1] Everything in a peasant woman's life—work, marriage, child rearing and ways of thinking and behaving—followed prescribed patterns handed down from generation to generation. A peasant woman tending a vegetable garden knew instinctively that her mother, grandmother, and great-grandmother before her had tended a vegetable garden in much the same way as she did, on the same soil, in the same village.

Peasant society was organized along patriarchal lines. Women had no separate legal existence apart from their fathers or husbands. Property was passed from fathers to sons. At the same time women exerted a significant amount of power within the family. As workers and mothers, their contributions to family well-being were recognized and respected. On a deeper level, in most cultures peasant women were viewed as the emotional, spiritual, and moral centers of their households. The influence of women on their families was transplanted to the New World.

Most of the women who migrated to America came

with other members of their families. Many wives and mothers followed their husbands and older sons, who had come ahead to work and save money to pay for additional passages. Some teen-age daughters came before their parents, but these girls usually traveled with other relatives and, on their arrival, joined brothers, married sisters, or aunts and uncles who had settled earlier. Only among the Irish and Scandinavian immigrants were there numbers of young, single women who settled in America on their own.

Most of the immigrants hoped to buy and live on small farms of their own in America. While some of the early arrivals, especially Scandinavian and German families, were able to fulfill their dreams, by the end of the 1800s, as the Western frontier filled and the price of land rose, new immigrants discovered that they had come too late or were too poor to buy farms. They spent the rest of their lives in American cities.

The new immigrants changed the landscape of the United States. As late as 1870 most Americans, native and foreign-born alike, lived in communities of no more than 2,500 people. Then, in a single decade—from 1880 to 1890—the urban population of the United States leaped from 14 to 22 million.[2] Millions of immigrants turned such towns as Milwaukee, Detroit, Cleveland, and Buffalo into cities, and such cities as New York, Chicago, and Boston into huge urban centers.

The presence of immigrants fed the process of industrialization as well as urbanization. Each shipload of immigrants provided factory owners with a new supply of workers. Immigrant women did not work in heavy industry, the mines, or construction, but like immigrant men they became part of the lowest class of industrial labor. Women worked in mills and factories, producing textiles, clothing, food, and appliances.

Immigrants clung to traditional values and customs. This was especially true for those who migrated as adults. Change was often tenaciously resisted. In face of the new, old values and customs were needed to provide life with a sense of continuity and meaning.

The children of immigrants were more readily absorbed into the American culture. This process often led to painful conflicts between parents and children. The gap between immigrant mothers and their daughters was especially acute. Girls who had arrived as children or been born in the United States learned to view themselves as individuals, separate from their families. Such a view of the self had not existed in Europe, where women and men were defined by their place in the family and where such concepts as individuality and personal happiness were close to meaningless.

In the United States unmarried women enjoyed greater freedom than they did in their European homelands. Girls went to school for at least a few years, and many worked outside the home. When it came time to marry, some exerted their own choice of whom they would marry and even whether they would marry at all. "I am not living in Russia, I am living in America," declared a young girl in a story written by immigrant novelist Anzia Yezierska, who lived her heroine's words. "I'm not hanging on anybody's neck to support me. In America, if a girl earns her living, she can be fifty years old without having a man and nobody pities her." In America, a woman could "make herself a person."[3]

Much as some immigrant daughters rebelled against the past, they were also deeply affected by it. While they absorbed the American value of individuality, they were also committed to the Old World emphasis on loyalty and duty to the family. Attending school and working did not necessarily take them away from home. Many were employed in family-owned shops or in factories where relatives worked. Many of them fell back into traditional roles when they married. Whether they rejected the ways of their mothers or not, these second-generation women often felt torn between the old ways and the new.

The first years in America were years of shock and struggle. In densely populated immigrant "ghettos" the lives of women were bound by the tenement and the slum street. Each block was lined with ten or more tenements on either side, easily housing more people than a peasant woman had ever before known.

Tenements of the mid-nineteenth century were usually extremely narrow, five-story structures built between two alleys. One row of tenements could house five hundred people. The "dumbbell" tenements, which later in the century lined block after city block, were even more capacious. These structures were six, sometimes eight, stories high and narrower at the center, giving them their name.

The structure of "dumbbells" made it possible to crowd two hundred people into a single building and almost a thousand on an acre.[4]

In smaller cities, such as Pittsburgh and Buffalo, the density was less oppressive. Immigrants in these places lived in three- and four-story structures that contained a dozen or so households, but conditions in these smaller, boxlike houses were no better than those in the tenements.

Even minimal standards of sanitation and safety were lacking in immigrant neighborhoods. Garbage and refuse flowed through the streets in open drains. The stench of rotting things poisoned the air in the summer, and in the winter snow turned black as soon as it hit the pavement. Indoor plumbing was practically nonexistent in the 1870s and 1880s. Water often had to be drawn from a street pump or hydrant, and in the poorest sections whole blocks sometimes shared one pump. More "modern" tenements had water closets in the hallways and toilets in the basements, which occasionally flushed by water. During the 1890s matters had improved in the large cities of the East coast to the extent that indoor cold running water was common, and most tenements had one toilet per floor. Even then, however, only 50 of nearly 4,000 tenements in New York had private toilets, and only 306 of 225,000 residents had access to bathtubs.[5]

The average tenement flat in the late 1800s and early 1900s consisted of three or four rooms—a parlor, a kitchen, and one or two bedrooms in between. At best only one room had a window on the street. The rest faced back-alley airshafts. Rooms were not only dark and stuffy, they were also extremely tiny. Bedrooms were like "coops," with space for no more than a bed. Kitchens might contain a "broken stove with a crazy pipe from which the smoke leaks at every joint, a table of rough boards propped up on boxes, piles of rubbish in the corner."[6] Flats such as these often housed families of eight, ten or twelve people.

To perform even their traditional jobs in these new surroundings immigrant women had to make major adjustments. In the old country women did much of their work outdoors; here they were confined to close and cramped quarters. To keep order in a room filled with eight people where there was barely space for one to walk, to organize kitchens so that they could also serve as workrooms, laundries, living rooms, and bedrooms, took skill and endless work. So too did maintaining even minimal cleanliness. In the old country women had swept refuse into the garden or fed it to livestock. In America garbage served no purpose. What difference did it make, then, if instead of walking down several flights of stairs to deposit garbage in already overflowing pails, a woman simply tossed it out the window?

American kitchens were unfamiliar at first. Many peasant women, who had been used to open hearths and fireplaces, did not know how to cook on a coal stove. They were accustomed to providing food from their own gardens and farmyards; now they had to purchase food with cash.

Newly arrived immigrants were invariably overwhelmed by the neighborhood marketplaces, where there was "pushing, struggling, babbling and shouting in foreign tongues, a veritable Babel of confusion." If one could make one's way through the clamor of the crowds, anything could be bought from "bandannas and tin cups at two cents, peaches at a cent a quart and damaged eggs for a song" to "frowsy looking chickens and half-plucked geese." One immigrant described his mother's purchase of "twenty pounds of black bread and several white challas [white bread used for the Sabbath]." She was accustomed to buying bulk amounts of staple goods, like salt and flour, but she had never before bought perishable goods like bread.[7]

To stretch their money as far as possible, women had to be aggressive bargainers. Jewish women who had worked as merchants and peddlers in the marketplaces of eastern Europe used their skills on New York's Hester Street and Chicago's Maxwell Street, turning both buying and selling into an art form of sorts. Here is how one woman bargained with a peddler.

The woman stops with a sneer, pokes contemptuously at the merchandise, insults it and the salesman, underbids him by half. He tries to prove that he would die of starvation if he yielded to her disgusting bid. She implies he takes her for a fool. In a moment he is telling her he hopes her children may strangle with cholera for trying to make a beggar of him. She answers that he is a thief, a liar, a dog. . . . She makes as if to spit on his wares; he grabs them from her and throws them back on the heap. At length a sale is made and she moves on to the next bout.[8]

Everything—food, clothing, furniture, and household appliances—was stretched. Women sewed their own and their children's clothing from scraps of material. A tea kettle would also boil the wash. One woman made a table from "a board placed over a potato barrel and a clean newspaper over that." "A bed fit for the president" was a "spring over four empty pails."[9]

At night every corner and piece of floor in the tenements became a sleeping space. Women created such privacy as could be had by hanging sheets from ropes to halve and quarter rooms eight feet by seven feet. When the newspaper on the table was covered with "white oilcloth, a remnant from a lace curtain tacked around the sink, to hide away the rusty pipe, and a ten-cent roll of gold paper for the chandelier to cover up the fly dirt so thick you couldn't scrub it away," a flat in the slums became "like a palace."[10]

Women also fought disease. The slums were breeding grounds for tuberculosis, pneumonia, diphtheria; such common childhood illnesses as measles were dangerous. There was no space to isolate the sick. When disease struck, it passed from one family member to another and from one household to the next. "The track of an epidemic through the slums," wrote Jacob Riis, could be as clearly traced as "the track of a tornado through a forest."[11]

In the tenements of New York's Lower East Side, Riis frequently observed scenes like this one, of a "child dying of some unknown disease" which turned out to be "starvation."

With the "charity doctor" I found the patient on the top floor stretched upon two chairs in a dreadfully stifling room. She was gasping in the agony of peritonitis that had already written its death sentence on her . . . face. The whole family, father, mother, and four ragged children, sat around looking on with the stony resignation of helpless despair. . . . "Improper nourishment," said the doctor, which translated . . . meant starvation.[12]

Few immigrants had money for doctors, and most of them were frightened of hospitals. Mollie Linker told of her attempt to conceal a leg wound.

I fell in the basement of the glass factory. I injured my leg. And about six weeks later, I felt I couldn't walk. . . . If I had waited two more days, I would have had the leg taken off.

We didn't have money for a doctor, so my mother took me to the clinic. As I was sitting there, there's about twelve young students and a head doctor. As they're examining me, I'se getting red in my face, I was so embarrassed, and I point and I says, "It's my foot."[18]

When epidemics struck, women often nursed entire neighborhoods. Mollie Linker recalled that her mother kept an apron in every home and was on call day and night during the flu epidemic of 1918. "She would call me through the window and say, 'Molly, come take the temperature of so and so . . . she'd wash my hands, put something over my shoes, and take the temperature, take the bedpan. See, women, they were not afraid."[14]

Though most immigrants were in the prime of life, between the ages of fourteen and forty-five, they died more readily than the native-born. Their children, and especially their babies, died even more frequently. In one Chicago precinct at the end of the nineteenth century, three out of every five babies born each year died before they reached their first birthday. Elizabeth Stern recalled that each year her mother had another baby, and each year another baby died. "Mother became a mother eleven times. Only the first four children lived. Perhaps this told of her economic story."[15]

Immigrant women had a higher birth rate than did native-born middle-class women. For every thousand married women of native parentage in 1910, there were 3.396 births; for immigrant women the figure was 4.275 births per thousand.[16]

Immigrants did not subscribe to Victorian ideas about sexuality; abstinence as a way to control pregnancy was not considered proper behavior for wives. When a woman in the old country married, she was expected to conceive and bear as many children as God willed and her husband gave her. Catholicism and Judaism, the religions of most immigrants, preached such a view and supported the ideal of large families. The Catholic Church sanctified sexuality in marriage only insofar as it led to children. As a female ideal, the Church presented the chaste virgin, the Madonna.

Peasant women had a tendency to transform the Madonna into a woman they could more easily identify with. While virginity was demanded before marriage in peasant societies, the true female ideal was the mother. Southern Italians, who worshiped the Madonna as they did the Holy Trinity, considered her the creator of life and mother of all. When they told stories to their children, Italian women described the Madonna as an ordinary woman at her loom while her child Jesus tangled up her weaving. She was, like them, a mother who had problems bringing up her child.[17]

While Judaism sanctioned sexual activity for pleasure as well as procreation and declared that a woman's sexual drive was at least equal to that of her husband, in practice Jewish wives were expected to help their husbands fulfill their religious obligation to procreate. "Give the man plenty of children," was the injunction heard by Jewish women.

In the United States many immigrant women continued to accept yearly, unregulated pregnancies, seeing them as God's will and nature's course. In the face of poverty, however, pregnancy became not simply a duty or a blessing, but also a curse, leading some women to rebel. Emma Goldman and Margaret Sanger, the two women who originated the movement for birth control in the early twentieth century, traced their concern to what they had seen and heard in the homes of immigrants. Both women were trained as professional nurses and had worked as midwives in the tenements of New York City. Both had witnessed the fear and despair immigrant women expressed during childbirth. Mothers entreated them to perform abortions and provide information on contraception. According to Goldman, "most of them lived in continual dread of conception; the great mass of married women submitted helplessly, and when they found themselves pregnant, their alarm and worry would result in determination to get rid of their expected offspring. It was incredible what fantastic methods despair could invent: jumping off tables, rolling on the floor, massaging the stomach, drinking nauseating concoctions, and using blunt instruments."[18]

In addition to raising children and caring for their homes, immigrant women were wage earners. Immigrant men were paid such low wages that family survival required many members to work and pool their earnings. Sons and daughters often found jobs by the time they were twelve or fourteen, and they could not afford to leave home until they married and established families of their own. Mothers of small children looked for ways to earn money within the home.

The most common opportunity was piecework for one of the manufacturing trades that still employed homeworkers. Different ethnic groups tended to gravitate toward different trades. Bohemian and German women rolled cigars in their homes; Italian women manufactured artificial flowers, paper boxes, and trimmings for hats; Jewish and Italian women sewed in their homes for the needle trades, which included manufacturers of coats, dresses, millinery, shirtwaists, and underwear, known as "white goods."

Next to domestic service, the needle trades were the largest employers of immigrant women. Unmarried women sewed in shops and factories while married women stitched in their tenement flats. Homework was controlled by a contractor, or middleman, who picked up bundles of cut garments from "outside" manufacturing shops and farmed them out to workers in various ways. Sometimes contractors bought whole blocks of tenements and leased them to families who worked together stitching, basting, finishing, and ironing, "morning, noon or night, it makes no difference."

Similar conditions prevailed in the cigar industry. Jacob Riis has described tenement-house cigar-making.

> Take a row of houses in East Tenth Street as an instance. They contain thirty-five families of cigarmakers. . . . This room with two windows giving on the street and a rear attachment without windows . . . is rented at $12.25 a month. In the front room a man and wife work at a bench from six in the morning till nine at night. They make a team, stripping the tobacco leaves together; then he makes the filler, and she rolls the wrapper on and finishes the cigar. For a thousand they receive $3.75, and can turn out three thousand cigars a week.[19]

In addition to leasing tenement blocks and employing entire families, contractors in the needle trades also farmed out unfinished garments to subcontractors who in turn set up sweatshops within their own tenement homes. Subcontractors employed a few workers—usually the most recent immigrants, who were willing to work for the lowest wages. The subcontractor himself worked alongside his employees, enduring the same long hours and crowded conditions. Additional bundles were also farmed out to women in their homes. A typical sweatshop at the turn of the century employed thirteen "inside" workers of both sexes and six "outside" female workers. The low wages he paid enabled the subcontractor to make a small profit.

Such work was seasonal. During the peak times a home-worker might earn about $3.00 a week if she worked quickly and steadily for twelve hours a day. Few home-workers earned more. Contractors and manufacturers often played shop workers off against homeworkers. When legislation gradually abolished homework in the early 1900s, women in shops had a better chance to achieve solidarity and to organize for better wages and working conditions. The end of homework created a dilemma for housewives and mothers, however, as one factory inspector noted in 1899.

On the one hand we have a 3-year-old child helping its mother to fix trimmings on women's dresses in the home— never out of sight—always where mother could attend to its wants and allay its fears and sufferings. While on the other hand we see the mother compelled to desert her three little ones . . . going out to the shop to work, because the law prohibits her bringing the work into her home. As a result, these unfortunate little ones . . . are left alone in a tenement, shut up in a fireless room.[20]

Working at home, women could alternate paid chores with everyday household tasks or do both at once. They would spread out bundles on the kitchen table, and between cooking and cleaning they would sew, press flowers, or roll cigars. They kept their children busy and supervised by putting them to work with them.

To complete the work, many women awoke at dawn or labored late into the night, while their families slept. Many immigrant children recalled that the first thing they saw in the morning and the last thing at night was their mother sewing. Elizabeth Stern wrote, "I can never remember my mother in my childhood in any other way than . . . standing at the stove cooking or sitting in the corner, her foot rocking the cradle, and her hands stitching, stitching."[21]

Another important source of income for some immigrant housewives was to take in boarders. Because of the disproportionate number of male immigrants, husbands without wives and sons without families were always seeking lodging in the homes of immigrant families. Not all ethnic groups were equally eager to take in boarders. Male boarders were common in Jewish households, for example, while they were rare in Italian homes. In Jewish households, women crowded their own families into two rooms and rented the third for a few dollars a month. For a little more, they cooked and cleaned for the boarders.

Some makeshift boarding houses and restaurants evolved. When word of a good cook spread in a neighborhood, men without families would ask to take meals in the woman's home. Soon she might be feeding eight to ten people each night. Among immigrants who settled together in one building or house, as Poles often did, one of the wives usually created a job for herself cooking and cleaning for the single men of the group. One Polish immigrant wrote to his parents of his brother's good fortune in having such a wife. "In the beginning he did not do very well, but now everything is going very well with him. His wife keeps eight persons boarding in his home, and he earns $2.50 a day."[22]

Unfortunately the boarder-wife-husband triangle became a common discordant theme in immigrant culture. The files of social agencies were filled with cases that told of marriages disrupted and sometimes broken by a boarder. Immigrants' letters to newspapers described the "troubles" boarders had brought into their homes. One such letter told a typical story.

My wife took in a boarder, a landsman [man from the same native town] who had a wife and three children in Europe. Soon he became chummy with my wife. She told me he wanted to buy her a hat and a skirt. At first I couldn't believe my ears, then I became jealous.

One morning after I had left the house to go to my laundry, the boarder tried to attack my wife, but she escaped and locked him in the apartment. She came running to the laundry. I was furious but waited till I had calmed down. Then we went home, I took two sticks, and we beat him so hard he couldn't go out for eight days. He gave us $80 and made us promise not to write to his wife."[23]

Occasionally wives preferred the boarders. When a wife left her husband for the other man, it was often because the marriage had been bad to begin with. In one such case, a Mrs. Kupczyk from German Poland, despised her husband and felt despised by him. He had, she said, tried to "sell her" to another man and promised her a "nice suit of clothes for it." When John Hubner, a "big, strong, very quiet, stronghearted" Bohemian came to board in the Kupczyk home, Mrs. Kupczyk and Hubner fell in love.

When Mr. Kupczyk discovered that the two were having an affair, he blackmailed Hubner. Finally Mrs. Kupczyk appealed to the United Charities of Chicago for help. She wanted her husband out of her home, but she was "too afraid of him to tell him so." She begged the charity worker to help her get a divorce so she could marry John Hubner. The charity worker, however, discouraged divorce "because the Church forbids it." Unable to receive help and hounded by her husband, Mrs. Kupczyk seems to have resolved the problem on her own; she "quietly disappeared" with her boarder, probably to marry him under a different name.[24]

When husbands deserted wives, many women, out of shame and fear, failed to report this occurrence. Others sought to locate their spouses by placing notices in immigrant newspapers. The Yiddish *Forward* published a "Gallery of Missing Husbands" and printed notices like the following.

I am looking for my husband, Nathan Cohen, known as Note Moshe Mendel Shenker from Hashelsk, Russia-Poland, umbrella peddler, 22 years old, the little finger of his right hand is bent. He abandoned me and a five-month-old baby in great need. Whoever knows of him should have mercy on a young woman and infant and get in touch with Bessie Cohen, 1415 Snafman Street, Chicago.[25]

Many wives were deserted before they ever arrived in the United States. Their husbands came ahead, and after spending a few years apart from their families, they formed liaisons with women they met in the new country. When their wives arrived from Europe, the husbands found their traditional ways and appearance embarrassing. Some of these husbands rejected their "old country" wives for "Americanized" mistresses.

Social service agencies, such as United Hebrew Charities and United Charities of Chicago, found the most common reasons for desertion by immigrant husbands to be "another woman"; "immorality of husband or wife or both"; "temperamental incompatibility"; "shiftlessness and drunkenness"; "economic factors like unemployment and financial depression"; "illness"; and "family interference." The individual case records collected by the agencies supported these findings. "She had come to America with her husband six years before. She said that she had been married 13 years and that her husband treated her well in Poland but was much worse since coming to America. . . . He began to run around with other women here." "He insisted that he loved his wife dearly but could not live with her. She had admitted to him having relations twice with some man and he simply could not forget that." "He never supported his wife nor their three children properly . . . and deserted her after four years of marriage." "He was suffering from tuberculosis and was sent to the hospital. When discharged, he went to his mother's home and his wife complained . . . his mother would not let her see her husband."[26]

Some husbands deserted their wives only temporarily, but others left for good. Of the 591 desertion cases handled by the Conference on Jewish Charities in an eight-month period of 1905–1906, 165 husbands were located, leaving 426 husbands, or close to two-thirds, missing.[27]

The "boarder problem" and desertion rate of husbands were just two indicators of the difficulties immigrants experienced in the face of poverty and dislocation. Alcoholism, postitution, and juvenile deliquency, along with a relatively high rate of mental illness and suicide among the foreign born, were further signs of the pressures on immigrants. Problems of this dimension were unknown in the old country. While every village had its thief, its good-for-nothing, its drunkard, the deviance had been contained to a few. In America, all were threatened.

Most of the immigrants managed to maintain their

physical and mental balance. Crime and pathology were at the edges, not the center, of immigrant life. Yet most immigrants could understand the feelings of anxiety and loneliness that drove some to drink, madness, or life in the streets.

Native Americans who were free from these pressures were less understanding. Native-born charity workers took a different view of the immigrants' problems. Their approach to those who turned to them for help was often impersonal and totally at odds with tradition. American "help" could turn out to be more trouble.

One woman applied for financial relief from a state-run charity group to maintain a home for herself and two children. The agency decided that it would be more efficient to send the woman to a poorhouse and the children to orphanages. Why give the woman money which she would probably mismanage? In the end, the family was split apart—and the agency expected the woman to be grateful. Instead, she expressed an anger and despair at American-style "help" which must have been felt by many.

> I don't ask you to put me in the poorhouse where I have to cry for my children. I don't ask you to put them in a home and eat somebody else's bread. You only want people to live like you but I will not listen to you no more. . . . I can't live here without Helen and John [her children]. I am so sick for them. I listened to you and went to the hospital. I could live at home and spare good eats for them. What good did you give me?[28]

To a remarkable extent, most first-generation immigrants resisted pressures to alter their traditional family patterns and beliefs. When faced with new problems, most of them turned, not to "outsiders," but to others like themselves—relatives from native villages, fellow immigrants from the same parish or block—who understood their ways and could provide a supportive kind of help.

Many of the self-help groups that emerged within immigrant communities were begun informally by women. In the tenements, where families lived on top of each other, shared the same water and toilet facilities, and congregated on the stoops and rooftops, women could not help meeting each other. They became aware of each other's problems, and in times of crisis or need they came to each other's aid.

Mollie Linker recalls that women like her mother "got together and collected goods. When they saw a woman in the butcher shop or the grocer not buying enough, and they knew how many children she had, my mother would go to a few neighbors, collect money, bring food and put it under the door and walk away."[29]

Another major source of self-help in immigrant communities was organized along religious lines. Every immigrant congregation made an attempt to help its needy members. Religious charity was often managed by women, who belonged to one or more of the women's leagues organized within each parish.

Christian religious leaders encouraged women to participate in church activities as well as attending services. In turn, the church gave women an outlet beyond their homes. An immigrant wife might hesitate before attending night school or socializing in a settlement house; her husband might refuse to let her go. Church activities, however, were entirely permissible. Festivals, bazaars, saint's days, evening church groups—these might offer an immigrant wife her only opportunity for venturing outside her home alone.

Immigrant women's church and community activities were extensions of the roles they played within their families. Just as they labored to keep their families alive in America, they struggled to keep family relationships intact. In a recollection of his mother that was typical of many immigrant children, Alfred Kazin wrote, "The kitchen was her life. Year by year, as I began to take in her fantastic capacity for labor and her anxious zeal, I realized it was ourselves she was stitching together."[30]

Many immigrant wives and mothers were preservers of the past. In the cities of America their traditional roles as spiritual centers of their families took on new importance. Wives and mothers were usually the last members of their families to learn about life in America beyond their homes and "ghetto" communities. They had fewer opportunities to learn English or absorb American culture than did their husbands, who often worked outside the home, or their children, who went to school. Their isolation kept them in the old ways longer, making them more than ever the "heart and souls" of family life. As Mollie Linker described it, "The father went out to earn a living. The mother was the backbone of everything."[31]

Among Italians there was an old proverb, "If the father is dead, the family suffers; if the mother dies, the family cannot exist." Italian women brought with them to America a tradition of relating exclusively within the context of their families and of "sacrificing" in "service to the family."[32] In southern Italy, the region from which most of them came, allegiance to the family was the only important consideration in life. Each person was treated according to the status of his or her family and place within it. Each had a definite role to fulfill to protect the family's well-being. Next to nothing was owed anywhere else. Richard Gambino has discussed this pattern in his study of Italian Americans, *Blood of My Blood*.

> The only system to which the *contadino* [southern Italian peasant] paid attention was *l'ordinare della famiglia*, the unwritten but all-demanding and complex system of rules governing one's relations within and responsibilities to his own family.[33]

Italian women in America maintained their traditional allegiance to the family and continued to relate to men as the heads of the family. In their studies of Italian working women, Mary Van Kleeck and Louise C. Odencrantz noted that Italian wives and daughters turned their pay envelopes over to husbands and fathers without ever opening them, while Italian sons controlled their pay envelopes, contributing only a portion of their earnings to the family income. Elizabeth Hasanovitz observed that the Italian women she worked with in one garment sweatshop were all related to each other. Mothers, sisters, sisters-in-law, and daughters did piecework side by side, watching over each other in the shop. These women were commonly escorted to and from work by their male relatives.[34]

While Italian women deferred to male authority in public, in the privacy of their homes they spoke their own minds and often exerted a strong voice in family decisions. When an Italian husband became old, for example, his oldest son was expected to become head of the household.

In many such households mothers actually dominated the family—although in public they pretended to take orders from their sons. One Italian American recalled this process within his family.

> When my father got old we obeyed our mother more than before. My brother, who became the head of the household, had to take orders from her. But that was done only in our home. On the street, he tried to impress everybody that he was boss of the family. As I remember now, it was laughable to see him give my mother commands in the presence of other people and then, five minutes later, to listen politely to what my mother had to say at home. . . .
>
> Also as I remember, I could never make out why my mother would tell untrue things to other women on the street. She would always complain how strict our oldest brother was. She would say: "Oh my Rocco does not want me to do this" or "Oh no, I must first ask Rocco." And so on. And she said all these things while we knew perfectly well that Rocco would probably at the very same time complain to my uncle . . . "Oh, if I only had the power, what I wouldn't do."[35]

Customs varied from group to group. The patterns of Jewish women, for example, differed considerably from those of Catholic women from peasant backgrounds. Jewish women were more likely to assert themselves outside the family as well as within it. The Jewish women from eastern Europe brought along a conflict between their religious obligations and their economic importance. A Jewish wife's duty was to ease her husband's spiritual journey by taking care of his material needs. In the shtetls of eastern Europe these women had kept small shops, worked as artisans, and peddled goods in the marketplaces. By serving as breadwinners for their families, they left their husbands free to study the Torah and fulfill the religious obligations that provided life's greatest meaning.[36]

In the more secular, material culture of the United States, God's law no longer kept Jewish women in their place. Some of them, already accustomed to dealing with the secular, non-Jewish world, made an easier transition into American life than did their devout husbands. Others no longer considered themselves blessed to work all day so that their husbands could pray. In Yezierska's *Bread Givers* Mrs. Smolinsky explains the situation to her husband.

> Does it ever enter your head that the rent was not paid for the second month. That today we're eating the last loaf of bread that the grocer trusted me? . . . You're so busy working for Heaven that I have to suffer here such bitter hell.

At the same time Mrs. Smolinsky and women like her upheld their husbands' deep religiosity and drew comfort from their piety.

> From the kitchen came Father's voice praying. . . . Mother's face lost all earthly worries. Forgotten were beds, mattresses, boarders. . . . Father's holiness filled her eyes with light.[37]

It was more difficult for immigrant women to maintain traditional relationships with their children than it was for them to keep up their standing in regard to their husbands. When the children were young and completely in her care, an immigrant mother could raise them in the old ways. Through daily example and moral storytelling, she could transmit "old country" values and beliefs. As soon as the children went to school, however, the process became reversed. Once in school, children were more apt to listen to their American teachers than to their foreign-born mothers. Schoolchildren brought America home to their mothers and began to educate them. They answered in English to their parents' Italian, Yiddish, or Polish. This system, wrote Harry Golden, "gave rise to the ghetto proverb: In America the children bring up the parents."[38]

In the old country a child who did not obey or respect his parents was ostracized by the entire community. One Italian recalled the uproar that ensued in his native village of Bitetto, in Apulia, when a child named Giovanni slapped his mother.

> I am not exaggerating when I say that it caused a profound shock in my family and among our neighbors. Although Giovanni was a *straniere* [stranger], no relative of ours and lived at the other end of the village and was little

known to us, my family felt as if something terrible had occurred under our own roof. "May Satan pull out all his guts!" was the curse for this devil of a son.

A year later Giovanni's mother died from tuberculosis. The whole town attended her funeral, agreeing she had died from a broken heart. . . .

After the funeral my mother was in great spirits. We, the older children were surprised and remarked about her being happy. This is what she said: "Giovanni's mother was no close friend of mine. I have no interest in her, but I am glad she is dead because it proves what a disrespectful son may do to a mother."

. . . Giovanni meantime became quite sick and got very thin. He was hated by everybody in the village and was called Giovanni Tapeworm. Parents pointed him out as an example to their children. "See what happens to children who do not respect their parents." Giovanni finally left for South America, for he could not stand the hatred of the people.[39]

In the United States children were more likely to point out the wrongs of parents. Broughton Brandenburg, who studied the migration of Italians to America, recorded the following conversation between a mother and child, which he had overheard in an Italian-American home.

—"You shall speak Italian and nothing else if I must kill you, for what shall your grandmother say when you go back to the old country, if you talk this pig's English?"

—"Aw, gawn! You's tink I'm going to talk dago 'n' be called a guinea. Not on your life. I'm 'n' American, I am.[40]

Anzia Yezierska recorded a similar situation in her description of an immigrant daughter criticizing her parents' table manners.

"Oh, mother, can't you use a fork. . . ."

—"Here Teacherin mine, you want to learn me in my old age how to put a bite in my mouth?" The mother dropped the potato back on her plate, too wounded to eat.

—"Yankev," she said bitterly, "stick your bone on a fork. . . ."

—"All my teachers died already in the old country," retorted the old man. "I ain't going to learn nothing new no more from my American daughter. . . ."[41]

Mothers were often confused in their wishes for their daughters. They wanted the daughters to be like themselves, and yet they wanted them to lead easier lives. Mollie Linker described her mother as always wanting "something better for the children, especially for the girls."[42]

When their daughters were young, mothers could keep them close to home and prepare them for their future roles as wives and mothers. At the same time they could learn from their daughters some of the new ways of America. Daughters introduced their mothers to new foods, such as salads, to such amenities as different toothbrushes and towels for every person, and to the books they studied in school. Elizabeth Stern has related that when she was a child, "mother and I were always chums."

> Though she could read not one word of English, there was not one book I read of which she did not know the narrative. She knew my marks at school. She knew my friends. She hated and loved my teachers as I did. It was as if she lived my life with me."[43]

By the time their daughters reached adolescence, however, mothers could no longer keep up with their American ways. They realized that in leaving behind the European past, their daughters were leaving them. They worried that American freedoms could do their daughters more harm than good.

Peasant women, who as young girls in the old country had prided themselves on their strong muscular bodies and red cheeks, watched with horror as their daughters laced themselves into tight corsets and spent their wages on "fancy style Five and Ten Cent Finery." They worried about their daughters' virtue. Boys in America seemed to have no respect; they would take advantage of girls without fear of parental reprisals. Mothers forbade their daughters from going to the dance halls and nickelodeons. The daughters went anyway.

Italian mothers relied on their sons to watch over their sisters whenever the girls left home. In southern Italian culture, brothers rather than fathers controlled the daughters of the family. While some brothers demanded that their sisters wait on them and obey their orders, for the most part brothers acted as chaperones, guarding and protecting their sisters' virtue. "When they [sisters] go out in the street or somewhere else," said one Italian brother, "it is my business to see that they keep up the good name of the family."[44]

In Italy the brother as authoritative guardian of his sisters served a real function. He protected the young women's virtue to insure for them a good and early marriage. Sisters who did not marry were not only a "disgrace to the family," but also an economic burden. "I as the eldest brother," wrote one Italian, "knew well that if I married and my father died, my unmarried sisters would park in my family and I would have to support them . . . as long as they remained single they constituted a hindrance to my own marriage."[45]

In the United States, where girls worked at paying jobs and had at least the possibility of financial independence, brothers did not have to be as concerned with whether and when their sisters married. Yet the old tradition of male domination, handed down from fathers to sons, did not die easily.

Brothers could accommodate the old forms of male domination to American culture more easily than could fathers. In Italy a brother would never allow his sister to speak to a man outside the home; in America this same brother would not object if his sister had a boy friend, provided "I know the fellow and he is okay by me. . . . If I ever find out that my sister went out with a fellow I don't approve of I will break her neck."[46]

The relationship between brothers and sisters kept Italian girls restricted to their traditional roles in the family longer than the girls among other immigrant groups. A Jewish or Irish girl growing up in America could more easily rebel against an old-world father than an Italian girl could rebel against a brother who was as Americanized as she.

In most cases these girls' rebelliousness went no further than asking for the right to make their own choice of a husband. Many dreamed of finding romantic love. Their ideal was the handsome, native-born male who would rescue them from the ghetto and make them ladies "with nothing to do but stay home."[47]

In time some immigrant daughters did attain middle-class status, but the climb out of poverty was slow and

WOMEN
IN
AMERICA

FOUNDING MOTHERS

Top: The beginning of a New England settlement
in the early 1600s. (Library of Congress)

Bottom: Hard at work in a colonial kitchen. (Brown Brothers)

Top: Busy at their embroidery in a
late colonial sewing room. (Brown Brothers)

Bottom: A portrayal of the Salem witch trials. (Brown Brothers)

DAUGHTERS OF LIBERTY

Molly Pitcher at the battle of Monmouth. (Library of Congress)

Abigail Adams (Culver Pictures)

BLACK BONDAGE—
WHITE LADIES

A housewife and a lady. Ambrotype, *ca.* 1855.
(Courtesy of Matthew R. Isenberg, Hadlyme, Connecticut)

Woman whipping
female slave. Woodcut
published in 1834.
(Library of Congress)

Selling black women
by the pound. Woodcut
published in 1834.
(Library of Congress)

ORIGINS OF FEMINISM

Lucy Stone
(Brown Brothers)

Susan B. Anthony
(Courtesy of the
Rochester Public Library)

Amelia Bloomer wearing
her innovative costume.
Daguerrotype, *ca.* 1850.
(Courtesy of the Seneca
Falls Historical Society)

Sojourner Truth
(Sophia Smith Collection,
Smith College)

Elizabeth Cady Stanton.
Ambrotype, *ca.* 1855.
(Courtesy of the Seneca Falls
Historical Society)

THE FIRST FACTORY WOMEN

Above: Hand sewing in the sewing room of
A. T. Stewarts, New York City. (Culver Pictures)

Opposite, top: Power loom weaving.
(Courtesy of the Merrimack Valley Textile Museum)

Bottom: Women shoemakers on strike in Lynn,
Massachusetts, 1860. (Library of Congress)

HOMESPUN BLUE AND GRAY

Above: Nurse with
Union soldiers wounded at
Fredericksburg, May 3, 1863.
(Library of Congress)

Opposite, left: Civil War nurses.
(Brown Brothers)

Right: Harriet Tubman when
she worked as a Union spy.
(New York Public Library —
Schomberg Collection)

HARRIET TUBMAN.

"Would-Be Voters — A Bevy of Strong-Minded Amazons
Makes a Sensation at a New York Uptown Polling Place."
(Historical Pictures Service)

Above: "A lady delegate (Victoria Woodhull) reading her argument in favor of woman's voting on the basis of the 14th and 15th Constitutional Amendments" before the Judiciary Committee of the House of Representatives, January 11, 1871.
(Library of Congress)

Right: Victoria Woodhull
(Culver Pictures)

Osage Indian mother and infant.
(Kansas Collection, University of Kansas Libraries)

Top: "The Emigrant Train Bedding Down for the Night."
(Artist: Benjamin Franklin Reinhart. In the collection of the
Corcoran Gallery of Art, gift of Mr. and Mrs. Lansdell K. Christie)

Bottom: The Chrisman sisters near Goheln settlement on Lieban Creek, Custer County, Nebraska.
(Solomon D. Butcher Collection, Nebraska State Historical Society)

Top: Schoolmistress and her school in Hecla, Montana. (Library of Congress)

Above, left: Carrie Nation (Culver Pictures)

Right: Wyoming women got the vote in the Wyoming constitution of 1869. Wyoming later refused to enter the union without woman suffrage. (Frederic Lewis Photographs, Inc.)

IMMIGRANT MOTHERS AND DAUGHTERS

An Albanian woman arriving at Ellis Island in 1905.
(Lewis Hine, International Museum
of Photography at George Eastman House)

Top: Children of immigrants saluting the flag in the Mott Street Industrial School, *ca.* 1889-90. (Jacob A. Riis, Jacob A. Riis Collection, Museum of the City of New York)

Left: Immigrant woman carrying a bundle on the Lower East Side of New York City. (Lewis Hine, Courtesy of Mrs. William Cahn)

Top: A family in its rear
tenement bedroom,
New York, East Side, 1910.
(Lewis Hine, International
Museum of Photography at
George Eastman House)

Right: A public health
nurse from the Henry Street
Settlement in New York
City visits a woman and
her family in a slum
district in the early 1900s.
(Courtesy of the Visiting
Nurse Service of New York)

LABOR AND UNIONIZATION

BOOK-KEEPER'S STENOGRAPHER'S AND ACCOUNTANT'S UNION · 12646 ·

TRADE UNION LEAGUE

Opposite, top: Strikers' children exiled from Lawrence, Massachusetts, 1912. (Brown Brothers)

Middle: A child laborer at her loom in a southern mill in the early 1900s. (Lewis Hine, International Museum of Photography at George Eastman House)

Bottom: Typists in the Industrial Audit and Policy Division of Metropolitan Life Insurance Co., Orange, New Jersey, 1896. (Courtesy of the Metropolitan Life Insurance Company)

Above: Rose Schneiderman, union organizer. (Brown Brothers)

Left: Mother Jones, "Hell-raiser" of the labor movement. (Culver Pictures)

VOTES FOR WOMEN

Top: Women's suffrage demonstration, New York City. May 16, 1912.
(Library of Congress)

Right: Alice Paul, leader of the Woman's Party.
(Brown Brothers)

Far right: Cartoon, "Congratulations," concerning the 19th Amendment.
(C. D. Gibson in "Life," 1920.)
(Historical Picture Service)

THE SEXUAL REVOLUTION

Left, top and bottom: 1926 and the "new woman,"
the flapper, is in full swing. (Courtesy of Mrs. John Held, Jr.)
Right: Emma Goldman (Courtesy of the Photography Collection,
University of Washington Libraries)

FEMALE WORKING CLASS

Migrant farm worker, July 1940, Berrier County, Michigan.
(John Vachon, Library of Congress)

Left: Two women welders at the Landers, Frary, and Clark plant, New Britain, Connecticut, June 1943.
(Gordon Parks, Library of Congress)

Bottom: The card index section of the Federal Bureau of Investigation in Washington, D.C., May, 1943.
(Wide World Photos)

THE NEW FEMINISM

Top: Susan Brownmiller speaking to an ad hoc meeting of NOW. (Betty Lane)

Bottom: July 12, 1971, delegates to the National Women's Political Caucus at a Washington news conference. Seated from the left are Gloria Steinem, Representative Shirley Chisholm, Betty Friedan. Standing is Bella Abzug. (Wide World Photos)

difficult. More often it was the grandchildren and great-grandchildren of immigrants, not their children, who became middle-class. Nor did most immigrant young women marry native-born men; rather, their husbands were fellow immigrants and children of immigrants of their own ethnic group, whom they met in the factories and the ghetto.

Even this choice had to be fought for. Parents from the old country, whose own marriages had been arranged, thought it madness to allow daughters to choose for themselves. In the old country marriage had been an economic and social institution, not a romantic alliance. Only a daughter who was "arrogant, obsessed, or shall we say crazy"—as one Italian father put it—would refuse to follow her parents' advice concerning a prospective mate. "Either you listen to what I say or you go out of this house," screams Sara Smolinsky's father in *Bread Givers*. "Such shameless unwomanliness as a girl telling her father *this* man I want to marry." Then, turning to his wife, he asks, "Did you ever know of such nonsense in the old country? Did you ever give a look on me or I on you till the wedding was over?"[48]

But the daughters believed in the American form of marriage. "It's a terrible thing to marry someone you don't love," said one woman who married and later divorced a man chosen by her brother-in-law. "It's like living with a man just to take care of him, to cook for him and wash for him. I gave. That's all. Never got anything. So I left him." Subsequently she contracted a happy marriage with a man of her own choosing.[49]

In every ethnic group there were girls who were not content with the right to love and be loved. They wanted something of their own, something their mothers in the old country had never been allowed—a degree of freedom outside the family. They fought for personal independence by staying in school as long as they possibly could in order to find decent work afterward.

Some found allies in their mothers. Elizabeth Stern described the support her mother gave her, against the authority of her father, in her wish to belong to America.

My father did not approve of my continuing high school. It was time for me to think of marrying a pious man. He and mother disagreed about it—their one quarrel.

It was perhaps due to my going to high school, my mother said gently and dubiously, that I wanted something new. I wanted to dance, to play, to have fun just like the other girls in my class. I didn't mean to go to work at fourteen, marry at sixteen, be a mother at eighteen, an old woman at thirty. I wanted a new thing—happiness.

My mother drew her fine dark brows together. She took my face in her little hands, round and soft in spite of constant work. "You shall learn to dance," she said, "my daughter."[50]

Eventually Elizabeth went to college and became a social worker and writer. As her father had predicted, she "became an alien" to her family. She turned her back on her Jewish immigrant background to embrace her native-born husband's world. Her mother and husband, she wrote, "had no common place on which to meet, no common thought nor interest nor memory. . . . Mother said goodbye to me. I went from her to a stranger whose language she did not understand, into a life she did not know. I left her as she had left her mother when she went on a far voyage to America."[51]

Mothers sometimes regretted having helped their daughters rebel against the past. An Italian mother who had sent her daughter through college so that she could become a teacher feared that her daughter would leave home. That thought was intolerable. "A girl cannot go out alone away from her family. The Americans who send their girls away from home don't know what they are doing. We Italians oppose the idea—all of us. . . . It is simply impossible." This mother lay awake nights "thinking of the terrible mistake my husband and I made. We should have followed the good customs of our native village. Send them to work soon to help out the family and then arrange for them to get settled and raise a family."[52]

Daughters also felt the anguish of breaking their ties with the past. The attempt to define for themselves who they were and how they would live was a difficult and painful process. Most who tried were on their own, fighting family restrictions against female independence every step of the way. One Italian American described the difficulties of girls in general and the struggle of one girl in particular to put herself through college.

> The girls have a much harder time than boys. . . . The boys were and still are the favored ones in Italian families. They are catered to, hand and foot. . . . With regard to education, again the boys are favored. Girls are meant to take care of the home, cook, and get married. I know of a family of five boys and a few girls. The oldest girl decided to become a teacher. Everything under the sun was done to dissuade her. . . . The daughter couldn't ask for carfare even in the worst weather for she never got it. In fact, the father cursed the day he came to America, because if he had stayed in Italy, no daughter of his would have the desire to become a teacher.[53]

Rebellion against the old ways led to a new kind of pain—a feeling of a rootlessness in the world, of being without family or community. Daughters of immigrants who fought for freedom and independence often described themselves as "orphans" and "foster children." Living between two worlds, they were a part of neither.

No one described this feeling more poignantly than Anzia Yezierska, who called her generation the "children of loneliness." Through one of her characters, an immigrant's college-educated daughter who leaves home, Yezierska voiced a cry many women of her generation knew well.

> I'm one of the million of immigrant children, children of loneliness, wandering between worlds that are at once too old and too new to live in. . . . I can't live with the old world, and I'm yet too green for the new. I don't belong to those who gave me birth or to those with whom I was educated.[54]

Elizabeth Stern sought and won the American dream; Anzia Yezierska recognized the dream's shortcomings. The material wealth offered by the new country was often gained at the expense of spiritual well-being. Leaving home meant leaving behind disease, poverty, and close quarters where one could never be alone, but it also meant abandoning the warmth and closeness of ghetto communities. Becoming Americanized made one feel proud and self-assured, but also self-doubting and self-critical. Could one ever be as clean, as neat, as soft-spoken as a real American? Sara Smolinsky, the heroine of *Bread Givers,* voices her mixture of elation and despair when, after years of toil, she finally enters college.

> This was the beauty for which I had always longed. For the first few days I could only walk about and drink it in thirstily. . . . Beauty of houses, beauty of streets, beauty shining out of the calm faces and cool eyes of the people. Oh—too cool. They had none of that terrible fight for bread and rent that I always saw in New York people's faces. . . . What a sight I was in my gray pushcart clothes against . . . the fine things these young girls wore. . . . The simple skirts and sweaters, the stockings and shoes to match. . . . And the spick and span cleanliness of these people. It smelled from them the soap and the bathing. . . .
>
> I looked at these children of joy with a million eyes. I looked at them with my hands, my feet, and with the thinnest nerves of my hair. By all their differences from me, their youth . . . their carefreeness, they pulled me out of my senses to them. And they didn't even know I was there.[55]

Yezierska's quest for identity as a woman pitted her against the restrictions of the new world as well as those of the old. To "make herself a person," Yezierska rejected her father's belief that "only through a man can a woman have existence." She also challenged the American version of female dependence on a husband and family when she obtained a "room of her own" and became a writer.[56]

To define her own life, it was necessary to fuse the best of the old with the new. In her youth she had cursed her father's curses. Yet, like Sara Smolinsky in *Bread Givers,* Yezierska ended her life identifying more with her father than with the "clean" American college girl she once aspired to be. She found her voice as a writer in the ghetto, and from her early struggle to survive in America she derived strength to live on her own.

Yezierska rebelled alone. Other immigrant women joined together to rebel as a group. These were women who were stimulated by the trade-union activities in the factories and radical politics in the ghetto. Most of these women were of the generation that was halfway between the daughters who had been born and raised in America and the mothers who had lived most of their lives in the old country. They came to America as teenagers with hopes for education, independence, and a good life. Instead, they found themselves in the factories, working twelve hours a day for six or seven days a week. The promise of America disintegrated quickly, but they did not easily forget or forgive the death of their dreams.

13

Social Housekeeping:
Women in Progressive Reform

By the late nineteenth century the theory of female moral superiority had become a truism of American public and private life. Native-born white women accepted without question the premise that they were members of the better sex—gentler, more virtuous, more fair-minded, more concerned for the general welfare than men. Statements concerning the moral superiority of women were to be found everywhere: among prosuffragists and antisuffragists, among party hacks and reform politicians, among Easterners and Westerners, among educators, muckrakers, vice fighters, social workers, churchmen, medical men.

It was a short step from a recognition of women's superior qualities to the belief that women were needed to purify society. At the end of the century native-born Americans perceived the nation as stricken with severe problems. Rapid changes in the social order, they believed, had caused moral decay; government and business had become corrupt. According to many of the most "progressive" minds, what was required was the moralizing and stabilizing influence of woman.

Women used the issue of corruption as their wedge into the world of men and power. We who have kept American homes pure, they declared, are needed to cleanse the world at large. In this time of social crisis, they said, women can no longer "selfishly" remain at home when they are so obviously needed in the larger world. The sphere theory was not discarded but extended—the needs of society were too great to allow the better sex the luxury of remaining silent.

Reform became women's byword. Millions of women participated in reform movements in one way or the other. Suffragists demanded the vote so as to be able to reform the political structure, but the vote was only a small portion of the picture. Women sought to reform America in literally hundreds of ways. Among the issues they addressed were prohibition of alcoholic beverages; ending prostitution; sterilization of criminals; improvement of prisons; physical education for girls and boys; sex education as a means of ending "vice"; pure food laws and the cleaning up of food-processing plants; child labor; public sewers; antitrust laws; tax reform; public utilities; wiping out political machines; vocational training for girls and boys; good nutrition; free libraries; parks and recreation; protecting historical landmarks; public transportation; and peace.

Most of the issues with which reformers concerned themselves were political and economic, but their perception of these issues was almost always moral. Even in the 1910s, when women allied themselves with the Progressive Party and sought legislation to cure social ills, they did not abandon their moral bias. As Puritans in colonial times had sought to make themselves "good," so the reformers of the late nineteenth century sought to impart "goodness" to the society. In the long run they saw politics as inseparable from morality.

Feeding the nineteenth-century passion for reform were social Darwinist beliefs about the perfectibility of society. Social Darwinists described society as an organism in the process of evolving to a higher state. Reformers who believed that they could speed the process of evolution through their own activities to improve society saw their work as steps toward the perfection of human society. "Perfection of the race" was a frequently used phrase.

Reformers never doubted that history moved in a straight line toward one goal—the betterment of humankind. Because they believed absolutely in the idea that the world was getting better and better, they never questioned the inconsistencies in their own program. They could advocate a measure as conservative as the sterilization of criminals while supporting such liberal issues as the end of child labor.

Social Darwinist ideas added to the prestige of women in reform movements. The theory held that women were more highly evolved than men. Proof of this assertion lay in woman's apparent lack of "low" and "animalistic" sexual drives and urges. It was believed that when society was perfected, men as well as women would be without lust. For the time being it was up to women reformers to try to teach chastity to men. The goal was a single sexual standard under which men and women would be celibate except for the express purpose of procreation. While Dr. Bronson Alcott in the 1850s had told American couples to limit copulation to once a month, late-nineteenth-century moralists told Americans to abolish copulation unless a child was wanted. The WCTU, with nearly one million members, and the YWCA, with half a million, embraced this view, as did many other late-nineteenth-century moral leaders and professional reformers.

One of the curious by-products of moral reform in this period was the introduction of sexual subjects onto the lecture podium, the pulpit, and other public forums. So eager were vice crusader Anthony Comstock, WCTU lecturer Mary Teats, and others like them to cure the ills created by "sexual excess" that they were willing to overthrow traditional modesty and discuss sexual topics in public. Once the subject was broached, however, the sexual discussion moved in a very different direction from the one championed by Victorian moralists.

During the last decades of the nineteenth century millions of women were drawn out of their homes to participate in reform work of one sort or another, through membership in women's clubs and local civic associations. While the women's clubs have been denigrated as frivolous—one critic called the clubs "a body of women banded together for the purpose of meeting together"[1]—there is no doubt that they accomplished much good within their communities. Often a town or city's pure drinking water, improved school system, orphanage, scholarship fund, library, or home for wayward girls existed only because of the efforts of the clubs. Moreover, club activities changed the perceptions middle-class women had of themselves.

While the extension of the sphere theory justified middle-class women's activities outside the home, at least on a part-time basis, certain practical factors were also at work. Toward the end of the century married women of the middle class had less to do. The birth rate among native-born women was lowered substantially, making child-rearing less time-consuming. Moreover, the influx of immigrants guaranteed the availability of servants for middle-class women. Even more important were the changes technology had wrought in housekeeping.

Factory-produced goods were replacing many of the products women had formerly made at home. Women no longer spun fabric; they bought it ready-made. Mass-produced underwear and outerwear for adults and children was diminishing the amount of time middle-class women spent sewing. Bakery-made breads and cakes; canned goods and other processed foods; mass-produced soaps, powders and cleaning potions—all were becoming staples in the life of the American middle class.

Equally important were the modern appliances that took some of the drudgery out of home care. Indoor plumbing, running hot and cold water, gas and coal stoves were introduced into many middle-class homes. The gas light and later the electric light, electrical appliances of all sorts, the ice box and centralized heating systems all eased middle-class woman's work load. Home care was still a job that could be done well only by the expenditure of much time and energy, but most women could now spare a few hours a week for themselves.

There were three kinds of clubs, although their purposes and memberships often overlapped. First were the local groups. These tended to be garden clubs and ladies' associations which devoted themselves to what was known as "self-culture." Members sat through interminable lectures on Japanese flower arrangements and other arcane subjects. Hundreds of male and female lecturers made a living by traveling the women's-club circuit, addressing these local groups. Almost all local clubs had at least one pet project designed to improve their communities in one way or another.

Second were the national groups. Very often local women's clubs were affiliated with larger state, regional, and national associations. The women who ran the national organizations were usually full-time careerists, although they generally did not get paid. National leadership tended to see the mission of the clubs, not as cultural, but as one of service. In 1904 the newly elected president of the General Federation of Woman's Clubs, Sarah Platt Decker, announced to the audience, "Ladies, you have chosen me your leader. Well, I have an important piece of news to give you. Dante is dead. He has been dead for centuries, and I think it is time we dropped the study of the Inferno and turned the attention to our own."[2]

Finally there were the specific women's reform agencies, such as the Women's Christian Temperance Union, the Women's National Committee for Law Enforcement, and the Southern Women's Educational Alliance. These groups were often the most effective in bringing about local and national reform, such as child welfare laws and improved working conditions for women. Many of the organizations maintained lobbyists in Washington. Many of the women who led the reform agencies were married to prominent men who supported their work.

Charlotte Perkins Gilman, the most influential feminist thinker of the early twentieth century, hailed the woman's club movement as "one of the most important sociological phenomena of the century." Gilman applauded the clubs, not so much for the good work they did, as for the beneficial effect they exerted on their members. "The woman's clubs," she wrote, "reached almost everyone and brought her out of the sacred selfishness of the home and into the broader contact and relationship so essential to social progress. . . .Now the whole century is budding into woman's clubs. The clubs are united and federating by towns, states, nations. . . . The sense of unity is growing daily among women."[3]

Yet the attempt of women's organizations to embrace "almost everyone" created problems. The policy of the General Federation of Women's Clubs (GFWC), the largest and most prestigious of the organizations, was to attract the mass of conservative middle-class housewives. Numbers, leaders thought, would give the GFWC power and influence. Unfortunately, to sustain its huge membership—by 1910 the GFWC had one million members—the national leadership was forced to moderate its own basically progressive social program. In order to appeal to conservative women, the Federation itself became conservative and sacrificed some of its founding principles.[4]

While many of its leaders were suffragists, the GFWC did not endorse woman suffrage until 1914, when a national victory for woman suffrage was already close at hand. Even more indicative of the GFWC's cautiousness was its response to the race issue. Clubwomen were proud of their democratic sentiments, and many of GFWC's founding members had served in the Union's Sanitary Commission during the Civil War. Julia Ward Howe was the Federation's most distinguished member, and her "Battle Hymn of the Republic" was sung at meetings. Yet when Josephine St. Pierre Ruffin, a black clubwoman from Massachusetts, sought delegate status at the 1900 national convention, she was denied a seat.

The Federation was more intent on keeping its Southern membership than on overcoming racial prejudice. By adopting an antiblack policy, the GFWC managed to hold onto the Southern women within its ranks. Though Southern clubwomen failed to secure their ultimate goal, a "whites only" clause in the Federation's constitution, they won the right to veto the admission of any club whose racial composition they found "offensive."

The proliferation of women's organizations in the period between 1880 and 1920 is often cited to indicate a high point in feminist activity. In fact, however, the vast majority of organized women during this period did not consider themselves feminists, and the women's club movement did little to advance the cause of equality for women.

Perhaps the major disappointment of the club movement was the degree to which it deflected women's energies into every cause but their own. Early feminists had argued that until women had the power to control their own lives they could wield little power in society. Feminists believed equality to be a prerequisite for effective social action. Few clubwomen grasped or agreed with this fact. They did not see women's rights as a pressing need but were content to be different from men, morally superior, and less in need of personal autonomy.

Just as the club movement failed to realize the most basic fact of women's lives—that they were neither free nor equal—so did it fail to work out a cohesive ideology suitable for long-term goals. For most women the clubs remained a pastime rather than a vehicle for self-realization. The clubs provided middle-class women with an avenue of escape from boredom at home, but for the most part they did not ask why it was so many women were bored.

An answer to that question was found by a pampered daughter of an upper-middle-class family. Jane Addams, who opened a new way for women to use their talents and ambitions in the world, was reared to be a lady of leisure. Born in 1860, Jane grew up in a small town in Illinois, where her father, a successful businessman and Republican politician, was the most prominent citizen. As a member of this first family Jane was reared to feel a sense of moral and social responsibility to others, but as a woman she had no avenue to fully express her wish to do something important with her life.

The college education Jane received at Rockford Seminary in Illinois intensified the conflict between her expected role as a woman and her need to do important work. While her education reinforced Jane's ambitions for a career, she later discovered that it in no way prepared her to have one.

Addams was among the first generation of college-educated women. A few young women had attended Oberlin and Mount Holyoke before the Civil War, but not until the founding of Eastern women's colleges—Vassar, Smith, Wellesley, Bryn Mawr—and Midwestern coeducational universities in the 1870s and 1880s did college become available to more than a handful of women. Some people felt strongly that a college education endangered women. In 1874, just four years before Addams entered Rockford, Dr. Edward Clarke, a professor at Harvard Medical School, argued that college would injure, perhaps even destroy, a woman's reproductive organs.[5]

Jane Addams and many of her classmates were not troubled by Clarke's theory. Many women who sought college degrees in the late nineteenth century were unabashedly not interested in fulfilling their sexual roles. Half of the first generation of college women never married; the rest married late. The upper middle class, from which most college women emerged, was a bastion of the most repressive Victorian sexual attitudes. College attendance enabled women to remain chaste and delay a confrontation with their sexual identities. Those who later chose careers were very well aware that they were choosing not to marry.

College extended and reinforced the feeling of belonging to an exclusive woman's world. Women at Vassar, Smith, Rockford formed what were to become lifelong emotional attachments. At Rockford, Jane Addams met a fellow student, Ellen Starr, the woman who understood her conflicts in the difficult years after college and helped her to resolve them.

The atmosphere at Rockford was like a cloister.

No one could leave the campus without special permission. Girls rose at 6:30 each morning, attended daily chapel and were expected to spend at least one hour a day doing domestic chores. Each girl kept an account book and turned it in for inspection once a month.

Anna Sill, who had founded Rockford in 1847, had modeled the school after Mary Lyons' Mount Holyoke. Sill believed that "the chief aim of woman's education is not simply to shine in society but to elevate and purify and adorn the home . . . and to teach the great Christian lesson, that the true end of life is . . . to give oneself fully and worthily for the good of others."[6]

Anna Sill was an old woman when Jane Addams met her, and Rockford was changing. Following the lead of Eastern women's colleges, Rockford began to place greater emphasis on mathematics, Latin, Greek, and literature than it did on domestic science and Bible study. Jane and her sixteen classmates helped transform Rockford from an advanced finishing school into an accredited four-year college.

Many of these first-generation college women believed in the theory of female moral superiority. They were, however, eager to play a more direct role in the world than was available to club women and civic reformers. They were convinced that higher education would provide them an entry into the male world of politics and the professions. As women, they were already pure and pious; as college graduates they were also "rational," "scientific," "intellectual." Jane Addams stressed this theme in her graduation essay when she argued that more than feminine intuition was needed if women were to fulfill their civilizing mission. Woman's mind, she declared, "must grow strong and intelligible by the thorough study of at least one branch of physical science, for only with eyes thus accustomed to the search for truth could she . . . learn to express herself without dogmatism." In another speech Addams stated that woman's education had "passed from accomplishments and the arts of pleasing to the development of her intellectual force and her capabilities for direct labor."[7]

The hardest time for Addams, and for women like her, came after college. The historian William O'Neill has written that "graduation was often a traumatic experience for these young women who had been educated to fill a place that did not yet exist. Their liberal education did not prepare them to do anything in particular, except perhaps teach, and the stylized, carefully edited view of life it gave them bore little relation to the actual world."[8]

Addams would have agreed with O'Neill. In her autobiography, she called her education "the snare of preparation."

> I have seen young girls suffer . . . in the first years after they leave school. She finds "life" so different from what she expected it to be. . . . She does not understand this apparent waste of herself, this elaborate preparation, if no work is provided for her.[9]

For eight years after college Addams drifted, unable to settle on a career. Teaching did not appeal to her. She thought of becoming a doctor and enrolled in the Woman's Medical College in Philadelphia. But finding medicine unsatisfactory, she dropped out after one term. The longer she was unable to find a suitable career, the more she felt useless, "a failure in every sense." To her friend, Ellen Starr, she wrote, "I have been idle . . . just because I had not enough vitality to be anything else. . . . I have constantly lost confidence in myself and have gained nothing, improved in nothing."[10]

Hardest of all for Addams during these years was what she later called "the family claim." Her family gave her none of the support or encouragement concerning a career that she had gained from her friends at college. In fact, her family actively discouraged her from moving in any direction. Now that she was educated, they expected her to be content to stay at home and make herself useful by caring for relatives. They were not concerned that she might never marry; she was financially secure, with enough money to last a lifetime.

Like many women of her class, Addams responded to the "family claim" by becoming ill. A chronic spinal disease kept her bedridden for six months and in an elaborate straight jacket—made of leather, steel, and whalebone—for two years. She also suffered through numerous periods of exhaustion and "nervous" prostration.

During one of these bouts Addams took the rest cure at Dr. S. Weir Mitchell's Hospital of Orthopedic and Nervous Diseases. Mitchell specialized in treating women who suffered from "nervous complaints." Some of his patients were partially paralyzed, some had convulsions, some experienced fits of weeping, and many, like Jane Addams, suffered aches and pains and fatigue. Mitchell was fully aware that many of these women were experiencing what he called "breakdown through overconformity." Their symptoms were simply exaggerations of traits Victorian men admired in women—helplessness, frailty, submissiveness.

Mitchell does not seem to have shared his insights with his patients. He prescribed for them more of what they already had—rest and total seclusion. No visitors, no books, no papers were allowed in his clinic. The "cure" made Addams feel even more depressed. The longer she stayed in bed, the more she began to think of herself as an invalid.

When Addams was not ill, she was put into service as a companion to her stepmother. The two women went to Europe in pursuit of "culture." Jane visited art galleries, took music lessons, studied French and German. She became convinced that the pursuit of culture for its own sake was an empty one, but she felt at a loss to find a preferable occupation.

In 1887 Addams traveled to Europe again, this time with her friend Ellen Starr. It was during this trip that she finally found a way out of her "sense of futility and misdirected energy." In London she visited Toynbee Hall, the original settlement house. Located in the slum district of London's East End, Toynbee Hall served as a home for young college graduates who lived among the poor and dedicated themselves to aiding the victims of urban poverty.

Addams was inspired. Back in the United States, she and Ellen Starr bought an abandoned mansion in the slums of Chicago, formerly owned by a wealthy real estate dealer named Charles J. Hull, and founded the first American settlement.

Addams always insisted that Hull House was an answer to her personal needs more than to the needs of those she planned to serve. "I should at least know something of life at first hand," she wrote, "and have the solace of daily activity." When she sought a contribution for Hull House from a wealthy woman, she described it as "a place for invalid girls to go and help the poor." Addams was well aware that in establishing Hull House she was creating a solution for countless other women who were "absolutely at sea so far as moral purpose was concerned." "It has always been difficult for the family to regard the daughter otherwise than as a family possession. . . . She is told to be devoted to her family, inspiring, and responsive to her social circle. . . . But where is the larger life of which she has dreamed so long? Her life is full of contradictions."[11]

By 1910 there were four hundred settlement houses in eastern and midwestern cities. Three-quarters of the thousands of young people who resided in them were women.

In the beginning Addams was ignorant about the immigrant Italians, Germans, Poles and Bohemians she chose to live among. She turned the so-called inferior traits that native-born Americans often ascribed to immigrants into what were considered superior qualities. The "pushy," "dirty," "ignorant" immigrants became to her "vital," "colorful," "earthy," and "natural." In other words, Addams romanticized the stereotypes.

She began her activities by trying to perform "good works." Though her charity was tempered by the candid admission that Hull House was also serving her needs, it was affected by her naivete about immigrant cultures and the problems immigrants faced in America. One evening she and Ellen Starr invited a group of Italians to see slides of Florentine art. One of the Italians who came said it was one of the strangest experiences in his life.[12] Just as unconnected to the center of immigrant life was the Labor Museum Addams established, where immigrants were invited to come and make native handicrafts. These projects had little to do with the immigrants' basic problems of economic and emotional survival, nor did they help them maintain the part of their old-world culture—their family structure and religious beliefs—which many sought to keep.

Eventually Addams came to know the people among whom she lived and was able to offer more meaningful services. Kindergartens, English classes, dances, union meetings, athletics for young people were all part of the subsequent Hull House program.

One of Addams' most remarkable skills was her ability to attract diverse and talented people to the settlement. Throughout her life she was able to live with, work with, and learn from people whose experiences, views, and politics were strikingly different from her own. One visitor described Hull House as "a salon of democracy." Through its drawing rooms, he wrote, passes

> a procession of Greek fruit vendors, university professors, mayors, aldermen, club women, factory inspectors, novelists, reporters, policemen, Italian washerwomen, socialists looking hungrily for all persons yet unconverted, big businessmen finding the solution to industrial problems in small parts, English members of Parliament, German scientists, and all other sorts and conditions of men.[13]

Several early women residents changed Addams' goals for Hull House. In his biography of Addams, *American Heroine,* Allen F. Davis notes that before the arrival of these women, Addams thought of Hull House as a first-aid station. Under the influence of her new associates she came to realize that her main job was "to eliminate poverty rather than comfort the poor."[14]

No one influenced Addams more than Florence Kelley who, like Addams, came from an upper-class home (her father was Congressman William D. Kelley, who had supported high tariffs to protect the iron and steel industries) and one of the first generation of college-educated women. There the similarity ended. Kelley had never felt removed from life or at a loss about what to do. After graduating from Cornell University, Kelley did graduate work at the University of Zurich. There she became a socialist, produced the first English translation of Friedrich Engels' *The Condition of the Working Class in England in 1844,* and married a Polish-German socialist who was also a doctor. After returning to New York with her husband, Kelley worked for the Socialist Labor Party, wrote, lectured, and bore three children. When her marriage began to fail, she left her husband and moved to Illinois, where it was easier to obtain a divorce than in New York. She had heard of Hull House and thought it might be a pleasant place to begin her new life in Chicago. She described her arrival.

> One snowy morning between Christmas 1891 and New Year's 1892, I arrived at Hull-House, Chicago, a little before breakfast time, and found there Henry Standing Bear, a Kickapoo Indian, waiting for the front door to be opened. It was Miss Addams who opened it, holding on

her arm a singularly unattractive, fat, pudgy baby belonging to the cook, who was behindhand with breakfast. Miss
Addams was a little hindered in her movement by a super
energetic kindergarten child, left by its mother while she
went to the sweatshop for a bundle of cloaks to be finished. We were welcome as though we had been invited.
We stayed.[15]

Kelley was not at all like the proper, reserved Miss
Addams. She was, wrote one friend, "explosive, hot tempered, determined . . . no gentle saint."[16] Moreover, her
needs were very different from those of Addams, Ellen
Starr, and Julia Lathrop, another friend from Rockford.
Kelley came to Hull House not to escape boredom, but
because she needed a place to stay while she looked for
work. She needed a job to support her children.

Kelley was an activist. In 1892 she was appointed to
the State Bureau of Labor Statistics to conduct an investigation of factories in Chicago. Though she continued
to support socialism in theory, she devoted the rest of her
life to practical reform agitation.

While Kelley liked and respected Addams, she challenged many of her ideas. She found the Hull House art
lessons, evening prayer meetings, and scholarly lectures
amusing, and she said so. She thought social investigation
and political work on behalf of the poor more relevant to
their needs. More than anyone, wrote Allen F. Davis,
"Kelley made Hull House a center for social reform
rather than . . . a place to hear lectures on Emerson. . . .
More than anyone, she turned Jane Addams from a phi-
lanthropist into a reformer."[17]

Other women who educated Addams to the conditions
of immigrants and the working class taught from their
first-hand experience. Mary Kenny O'Sullivan, a bookbind-
er, was in the process of organizing the first women's
union in her trade when she came to Hull House. At first
O'Sullivan thought the settlement workers were "rich and
no friends of working girls."[18] Gradually, however, she
interested Addams in the problems of working women and
their need for unions. Through her, Addams met other
working women and with her organized a cooperative
apartment house for working women, which became
known as the Jane Club.

Many of the women who came to Hull House drew
sustenance from the settlement community and used it as

a training ground for new professions. Like Mary Kenny O'Sullivan, other working women went on to become organizers in the labor movement, Middle-class women created new careers in government and the universities. Kelley went from her job as a factory investigator to become head of the National Consumers League, a group that investigated a variety of industries, tried to influence employers to adapt fair labor practices, and fought for maximum-hour and minimum-wage laws for working women. Doctor Alice Hamilton developed the field of industrial medicine. Grace Abbott was director of the Immigrant's Protective League, while her sister Edith became a professor at the Chicago School of Civics and Philanthropy, one of the first schools of social work in the nation.

Addams became a writer, scholar, administrator, business manager, and above all, a reformer. She was at her best when presenting the problems of the cities and the plight of the poor and foreign born to middle- and upper-class Americans. She became an anthropologist in America's own backyard and was one of the first native-born Americans who recognized and respected the distinct values and cultures of the immigrants. "Immigrant colonies might yield something very valuable to our American life," she wrote, "if their resources were intelligently studied and developed."[19] Immigrants, she declared, were not inferior just because they did not look, act, speak, or think like native-born Americans.

Addams also strongly opposed Social Darwinists who claimed that the poor were poor because of innate character defects, such as laziness and stupidity. Environment, she insisted, was a much more powerful determinant than heredity. The poor were not to blame for the meager wages they earned or the slums they inhabited.[20]

Addams was more interested in tackling immediate problems and fighting for practical improvement than in dealing with the underlying causes of poverty. She was more apt, for example, to try to improve garbage collections than to theorize about the nature of capitalism. She believed that with better housing, decent schools, and improved factory conditions it was possible to achieve equality in America. These improvements could be won through better legislation.

This belief led Addams to become a leader of the Progressive Party. In 1912 these reformers, who believed, as Addams did, that social justice could be achieved legislatively, drew up a platform which advocated an eight-hour day and six-day work week; abolition of tenement manufacture; improvement of housing; prohibition of child labor under sixteen; careful regulation of employment for women; a federal system of accident, old-age, and unemployment insurance; and woman suffrage. Much of the Progressive platform anticipated the New Deal legislation of the 1930s. Theodore Roosevelt was nominated to run as President on the Progressive ticket. Many people chided Addams for supporting such a "militarist," "imperialist," and "anti-suffragist" as Roosevelt. In response, Addams declared that the platform was more important than the candidate.

By the early 1900s Addams had become the most famous woman in America, revered as a national heroine. It is ironic that one of the few American women who ever attained such a prominent role in public life was respected more for her imagined than for her real qualities. To the public Addams was the model of feminine virtue and benevolence, the "Mother Superior" of America. It was, in a way, easier to explain her work as "charity" than to answer her demands for social change. It was less threatening to view her as "good" than to recognize her as the independent, strong-willed woman she was.[21] Many of Addams' most developed talents were all but ignored. She was a gifted scholar, a brilliant administrator, a shrewd tactician, and a marvel of a businesswoman, who handled an annual budget of several hundreds of thousands of dollars. But people kept insisting that she was a saint.

Florence Kelley once advised Addams, "Do you know what I would do if that woman calls you a saint again? I'd show her my teeth, and if that didn't convince her, I would bite her."[22] But, as Allen F. Davis suggests, Addams did not fight the image. She liked being admired and loved. Though her life was a testament to woman's ability to compete with men and share an equal role in public life, Addams did not overtly challenge the idea of woman's separate place or her "special," "superior" qualities.

As long as Addams advanced beliefs that Americans felt they too supported, she remained a heroine. But as soon as she opposed a very popular cause, the image reversed itself. During the First World War, a period of intense patriotism and nationalism, when Addams became a leader of the international peace movement, she was abruptly toppled from her pedestal. She was no longer "Saint Jane" but a "villain" who posed a "serious threat" to the nation's security.

While Jane Addams used her experiences in the slums of Chicago to educate the middle and upper classes, other women who went to live in the slums devoted their time primarily to forming alliances with the poor and the foreign born. In 1903 Margaret Dreir Robbins was one of several people who organized the Woman's Trade Union League in an effort to help working women organize unions and bridge the gap between women in the labor movement and women in middle-class reform groups. Robbins believed that working women could state their case with more eloquence than could reformers. She correctly predicted that large numbers of working women could and would join together to demand social and economic equality.

14

Bread and Roses

By 1900 there were five million female wage earners in the United States, making up one-fifth of the nation's total work force. Two million of these women were domestics—maids, cooks, nurses, and laundresses, who worked in private homes. In the South this servant class was made up primarily of black women. In the North the presence of millions of immigrant girls, many just off the boat from Europe, also made household help cheap and accessible.

Aleksandra Rembienska found a job as a domestic soon after she arrived in Chicago in 1911. She wrote to her parents in Poland, "I have fine food, only I must work from 6 o'clock in the morning to 10 o'clock at night, and I earn $13 a month." Her second domestic job paid $16 a month, but Aleksandra had to wash and iron three hundred pieces of linen each week in addition to cleaning eighteen rooms and cooking.[1]

Domestic workers who lived with their employers rarely had the chance to get away from their jobs. One Russian girl related that in six months of service for a family who had paid her passage to America, she had been allowed out only two or three times, was forced to work from five in the morning until eleven at night, and had never received any wages. This girl finally appealed to the Immigrant's Protective League of Chicago for help in finding another job. Aleksandra Rembienska wrote poignantly about the isolation of her job. "I am in America, and I do not even know whether it is America. . . . It seems to me as if there were only a single house in the whole world and nothing more, only walls and a very few people."[2]

Attitudes toward domestic work varied. Scandinavian women, for example, sought jobs as domestics, while Jews and Italians preferred factory work even though the wages were less once room and board had been deducted. After 1880, with the influx of immigrants from southern and eastern Europe, factory work became the second most common kind of employment for women. Immigrant girls helped to feed the industrial labor supply. Between 1900 and 1910, a decade of massive immigration, the proportion of women in the labor force increased from 20 to 25 percent.

The typical immigrant girl began working in the factory by the time she was fourteen, keeping the job for five to ten years. When immigrant women married, they usually left the factory to return to more traditional roles, although many did piecework at home or took factory jobs when their husbands were out of work or they were unable to make ends meet.

Many immigrants from peasant backgrounds had difficulty adjusting to factory work. Even women who had worked in factories in the old country, in the emerging garment trades of Italy and Russia, were unfamiliar with the American system of industrial labor.

In Italy women who worked in the needle trades did skilled dressmaking or fancy hand embroidery. Each worker made a whole garment or an entire piece of work from start to finish, working at her own pace. Craftsmanship counted for more than speed. The American system of subdividing the production of one item into many parts, so that one woman made buttonholes all day long while another basted seams, denied women a feeling of pride in their work. One woman complained, "They only do cheap work in this country. Everything must be done in a hurry. In Italy it would take six months to do a pillow and here it must be done in three or four hours. Cheap work!"[3]

Besides objecting to the lack of craftsmanship and stress on assembly-line methods in American factories, women spoke out against working conditions. In garment factories in Russia at the end of the nineteenth century, for example, many Jewish women had come in contact with the labor and socialist movements that predated the 1905 uprising in Russia. They brought their new awareness as workers to America. The anarchist Emma Goldman was one of these women. She recognized the common problems confronting workers in Russian and American factories.

In the St. Petersburg glove factory where Goldman had worked, one room contained six hundred workers. In 1885, when she was sixteen years old, Goldman found a job in an overcoat factory in Rochester, New York. Here, she said, there was more "elbow room," but the work in

Rochester "was harder and the day [twelve hours] with only a half hour for lunch seemed endless. The iron discipline forbade any free movement (one could not even go to the toilet without permission), and the constant surveillance of the foreman weighed like a stone on my heart."[4] Years later Goldman recalled the foreman's reaction when a fellow worker, a frail girl named Tanya, fainted from overwork.

> Without even asking the reason for the commotion, he shouted: "Back to your machines! What do you mean stopping work now? Do you want to be fired? Get back at once." When he spied the crumpled body of Tanya he yelled: "What the hell is the matter with her?" "She has fainted," I replied, trying to control my voice. "Fainted nothing," he sneered, "she's only shamming."[5]

Immigrant women took factory jobs that were listed as "female only." By the end of the nineteenth century all but nine of the 369 industries listed by the U.S. Census Bureau employed women, but in all of them job categories and wages were sex segregated;[6] women were hired only for the most unskilled jobs.

In the needle trades, men usually held the more skilled jobs of cutting and pressing garments, while women were hired for the unskilled finishing tasks of sewing on buttons and basting seams. In the cigar industry the relatively well-paid job of hand rolling expensive cigars was monopolized by men. The second best category—machine rolling cigars—went to men and native-born American women. Bohemian women, many of them skilled cigar makers, were relegated to the task of stripping tobacco leaves. In food-processing plants, such as the National Biscuit Company of Pittsburgh, men did the baking while women frosted and packaged the cakes. The tasks assigned to women were not necessarily those requiring less physical strength. In the steam laundries only women and blacks were hired for the physically exhausting job of shaking and wringing hundreds of pounds of wet linen. "D'ye think any white man that calls hisself a man would work in a place as this, and with naygurs?" commented one woman.[7]

Most female factory workers were paid by the piece rather than receiving a fixed weekly wage. Women workers, who counted the pennies earned with each shirt they basted or box they pasted, pushed themselves hard to produce as much as possible. When a nimble worker managed to produce enough to earn a decent living, she often found that her piece rate was reduced. She would then have to work even more quickly, producing more to earn the same or less than she had before. Frequent adjustments in piece rates added stress to jobs that were already arduous.

For ten to twelve hours a day a woman factory worker might "concentrate mind, body, and soul, itself, literally on the point of a needle" or sit on a stool feeding shoes, one by one, into a machine that punched lace holes or stand at a table and press covers on thousands of thousands of jars or glue linings into an endless number of boxes.[8] One woman interviewed by the magazine *The Independent* told what it was like to work in a garment factory in Brooklyn, New York.

> I get up at half-past five o'clock every morning and make myself a cup of coffee on the oil stove. I eat a bit of bread and perhaps some fruit and then go to work.
> At seven o'clock we all sit down to our machines, and the boss brings to each one the pile of work that he or she has to finish during the day, what they call in English their "stint." This pile is put down beside the machine and as soon as the skirt is done it is laid on the other side of the machine. . . .
> The machines go like mad all day, because the faster you work the more money you get. Sometimes in my haste I get my finger caught and the needle goes right through it. It goes so quick though that it does not hurt much. I bind the finger up with a piece of cotton and go on working. We all have accidents like that. . . . Sometimes a finger has to come off. . . .
> All the time we are working the boss walks about examining the finished garments and making us do them over again if they are not just right. So we have to be careful as well as swift.[9]

In the cotton mills of New England and the South women and children were hired as spoolers; they fed yarn into a high-powered, quick-whirling machine and retrieved it once it had been wound. All day spoolers walked up and down alongside their machines. Their arms and sides ached until they grew numb.

The mills were among the few industries that hired entire families. Mothers, fathers, children signed up for work, earning together just enough to enable them to keep on working. Mill hands were often paid, not in cash, but in coupons which could be exchanged for food at the company-owned store and paid to the landlord for company-owned housing. Thus the company was able to govern virtually every aspect of its workers' lives.[10]

Married women who worked in the mills had a second full-time job. "When the whistle blew and toilers poured out of the mills and hurried to their homes," wrote one mill investigator, Rhetta Childe Dorr, ". . . the women of the mills went on working. They cooked and served meals, washed dishes, cleaned the house, tucked the children into bed, and after that sewed or mended or did a family washing."[11]

Another early investigator of the mills was Marie Van Vorst, a wealthy socialite who, pretending to be a poor working woman, took a job in a South Carolina mill. In the mill Marie Van Vorst met children as young as five, six, and seven years old. She described some of what she saw.

Through the looms I catch sight of Upton's, my landlord's little child. She is seven; so small that they have a box for her to stand on. She is a pretty, frail, little thing, a spooler, "a good spooler tew." Through the frames on the other side I can see only her fingers as they clutch at the flying spools; her head is not high enough, even with the box, to be visible. . . .

"How old are you?"

"Ten."

She looks six. It is impossible to know if what she says is true. The children are commanded both by parents and bosses to advance their age when asked.

"Tired?"

She nods without stopping. She is a "remarkable fine hand." She made 40 cents a day. See the value of this labor to the manufacturer—cheap, yet skilled; to the parent it represents $2.40 a week.

Here is a little child, not more than five years old. . . . She has on one garment, if a tattered sacking dress can be so termed! Her bones are nearly through her skin, but her stomach is an unhealthy pouch, abnormal. She has dropsy.

It is eight o'clock when children reach their homes—

later if the mill work is behind and they are kept over hours. They are usually beyond speech. They fall asleep at the table, on the stairs.[12]

Children also worked in Northern mills, sweatshops, and coal mines. In 1900 Pennsylvania employed 120,000 children in mines and mills. The same year New York reported some 92,000 employed children under fifteen years old.

The ten- to twelve-hour work day of women and children was spent in factories and mills that were dirty, noisy, dark, smelly, and dangerous. Hundreds of workers were jammed together in dimly lit rooms that were stifling hot in summer, cold and drafty in winter. The moist, lint-filled air in the cotton mills bred tuberculosis. In other industries women breathed dangerous fumes of paint and naptha, tobacco, and glass and brass dust. Materials were flammable, and factory buildings were firetraps. Machines were cleaned and adjusted while they were running. As the woman garment worker from Brooklyn noted, workers often lost fingers and even hands in accidents.

Women's unskilled work never provided them with a living wage. The piece-rate system, combined with the sex division of jobs, made women the cheapest pool of workers in the labor force. Studies of working women in the late nineteenth and early twentieth centuries show that women received one-half to one-third the wages of working men. A female tobacco stripper in 1900 earned about $5 a week to a male cigar roller's $10. A seamstress in the needle trade earned $6 or $7 compared to a cutter's $16.[13]

Discrepancies in wages paid to men and women were not simply the result of differences in jobs. Even when men and women did the same work, women were paid considerably less. Employers often justified unequal pay by claiming that women were only working for "pin money." The wages earned by most of the immigrant girls were, in fact, very much needed by their families. In addition, tens of thousands of women factory workers without families were attempting to live on salaries that hardly ever matched the bare minimum needed for subsistence.

Elizabeth Hasanovitz provides a clue to how working women without families survived. She budgeted her $2.55 a week this way: $1 for rent, 60 cents for carfare, 6 cents for newspapers, and a variable amount for a diet of bread and butter, milk, beans, and sugar. Hasanovitz tried to save something every week toward bringing her parents to America. After nine weeks on this budget she attempted suicide. "Does it pay to live, after all," she later wrote. "Work, work, and never earning enough for a living, eternal worry how to make ends meet."[14]

Most of the women factory hands held seasonal jobs. During the rush seasons women worked overtime, but as soon as the slack season set in, they were laid off. In her first four years in America, Elizabeth Hasanovitz held forty jobs. "My head reels from that eternal repetition—slack, busy, slack, busy," she wrote.[15]

Bosses regularly made "mistakes" in computing piece rates. A worker who was paid for only twenty-five hat trimmings when she knew she had made thirty or forty usually did not argue. She was frightened of losing her job, and unless she could multiply and divide quickly, it was difficult to figure out the correct amount.

Some employers deducted a large part of the pay for supposedly imperfect work. Others "fined" women for being a few minutes late or for singing, talking, laughing, or washing. In the garment industry seamstresses were charged for everything they used, from machines, electricity, needles, and thread to drinking water and washrooms. The International Ladies Garment Union claimed that these charges to workers constituted a net profit to manufacturers. Owners, declared the union, charged workers 20 percent more than they paid for electricity and 25 percent more than they paid for needles and electric bolts. Fines for imperfect work ran 300 to 400 percent above the cost of the material.[16]

Male as well as female workers suffered these fines and salary "mistakes," but women in factories were bullied, insulted, and humiliated in special ways. Some bosses locked women in while they worked, presumably to keep them from going on strike. Others searched women at the end of the day to make sure that they had not stolen any materials. Frequently women workers were required to finish their week's labors by scrubbing the factory floor. To enforce their demands, bosses simply withheld pay until the women did as they were told. The union leader Rose Schneiderman recalled one hat-making shop where she worked. On Saturday, a half day, men were paid at noon, while women were kept waiting for their pay until four o'clock in the afternoon.[17]

Wherever they worked, women were sexually harassed by male workers, foremen, and bosses. Learning to "put up" with this abuse was one of the first lessons on the job. Fannie Shapiro described how her naivete cost her her first job.

On the day the machine broke . . . I had to get up on the table to reach it . . . So when I went up on the table reaching and the boss, an old man, he went and pinched me so I gave him a crack and he fell. He was very embarrassed; so the whole shop went roaring. He thought I would keep quiet. I was so naive . . . so he fired me.[18]

It was common practice for male employers to demand sexual favors from women workers in exchange for a job, a raise, a better position. In her autobiography, *One of Them,* Elizabeth Hasanovitz talked openly about the physical and psychological intimidation men used on women. On one occasion, after a long stretch of unemployment, Hasanovitz asked her new boss to advance her some of her salary. The boss agreed but attempted to make her "come across" before giving her any money.

The boss sat at his desk writing. I had no courage to disturb him, so I sat and waited. At last he stood up, straightened himself and smiled at me.

"So you are in hardship—too bad, too bad."

Then he took my pay, looked at it, fixed his eyes on me and asked: "Is that all you get?"

"No, I get thirteen, but this is only for two days and a half," I said, already regretting to have aroused his pity.

"But my dear girl, that would not be enough for you. . . . Wait a minute, I will give you more."

But no more had I time to refuse when he grasped me in his arms.

I screamed and with superhuman strength threw him from me and ran into the hall. . . . How I hated men, all of them without exception! I stood up before the mirror and studied my face, trying to find out if there was anything in it that awakened men's impudent feelings toward me.

If I could only discredit that man so that he would never dare insult a working-girl again. If only I could complain of him in court. But I had no witnesses to testify the truth; with my broken English I could give very little explanation. . . . So I left him alone and never went to collect my money, although I was in frightful need.[19]

Women such as Elizabeth Hasanovitz placed not only their jobs in jeopardy but their reputations as well. A boss could easily deny the incident or claim that the woman had solicited his attention. This tactic of blaming women for permitting or provoking seduction kept women quiet and compliant. To avoid the shame of exposure many women agreed to their bosses' propositions.

Some women accepted the typical male explanation for harassment ("I couldn't help myself—you're so pretty") and flattered themselves on their own appeal. Others blamed themselves. Elizabeth Hasanovitz ran from her boss's embrace to a mirror to wonder what was wrong with her face. Other girls came to view sex in general and their own sexuality with fear and loathing. One girl who was raped by a boss said, "He might better have killed me," and then added, "please forgive me."[20]

Some women tried to fight the problem of sexual harassment through unionization. In 1912 women striking a corset factory in Kalamazoo, Michigan, complained that the company foreman blackmailed them for sexual favors. Strike organizer Josephine Carey stated, "The girls are compelled to pay for their thread and this is quite an item. It is common practice for the foreman to forget to charge them for the thread for several days and then suggest to them a way in which the girls might repay him for his act of kindness."[21]

Rose Schneiderman heard of a shop where the owner had a "habit of pinching the girls whenever he passed them, and they wanted it stopped." When Schneiderman told the man that "the girls resented it," he replied, "Why Miss Schneiderman, these girls are like my children." The shop chairwoman who had filed the complaint responded, "We'd rather be orphans."[22]

Not all union leaders were as willing as Schneiderman to investigate women's complaints of sexual harassment. Some ignored the problem, others thought that women should handle it individually, still others blamed it on the women themselves. One woman organizer acknowledged that in virtually every factory, "Men will talk to the girls, take advantage of them if the girl will let them, the foreman and superintendants will flirt with the girls and this is nothing new." Yet this woman preferred to believe that it was the women who needed reforming.

> True, I have seventeen affidavits in my possession now, but I read them over and you find the same old story, that the foreman asked a girl to come into his office and hold hands, etc., etc. This to my mind can be done away with by educating the girls, instead of attacking the company.[35]

Most unions failed to act upon or even perceive the special problems of working women. Because women retired from factories when they married—though for many of them retirement was only temporary—union men did not consider women worth organizing.

Women's unskilled jobs further reduced their worth. Their problem was shared by many immigrant men. As industries became more and more mechanized, unskilled assembly-line jobs replaced skilled craft labor. By 1880, 70 percent of all workers, men and women, were concentrated in unskilled jobs.

Skilled workers, many of them native-born men, feared that their jobs would be mechanized and that they would be replaced by cheaper immigrant labor. When skilled workers tried to organize, they usually formed exclusive trade or craft unions. Skilled hand cigar rollers, for example, unionized with men who did the same work rather than with machine cigar rollers and tobacco strippers, who shared the same factory and boss.

Unskilled workers recognized the need of organizing all workers in an industry, regardless of skills or job categories. Industrial unions, as they came to be called, were more willing to help working women organize than were the segregated and exclusive craft unions.

In 1881 the Knights of Labor emerged as a national union offering support to working women. The Knights called itself a "universal brotherhood of workers, a federation that would embrace unskilled as well as skilled workers, blacks as well as whites, women as well as men." "An Injury to One is an Injury to All," proclaimed the Knights. The union's platform advocated an eight-hour day; an end to convict and child labor; health and safety regulations; and arbitration instead of strikes. The Knights was the first and for a long time the only national labor group to advocate equal pay for equal work. It actively recruited women members.

Leonora Barry, a women's organizer for the Knights, noted that "apathy was ingrained among working women, as was the habit of submission and acceptance of terms offered them, with a pessimistic view of life in which they see no ray of hope."[24] Yet within five years the Knights had chartered 113 women's assemblies and claimed a female membership of more than fifty thousand. Women Knights were delegates at national assemblies, and they joined men in strike actions.

Several events led to the decline of the Knights by 1886. During that year the labor movement as a whole suffered a major setback when leaders of the movement for an eight-hour day were accused of throwing a bomb during a rally in Chicago's Haymarket Square. Though there was little evidence to support the charge, eight men were convicted and four were hung. The Haymarket affair frightened many men and women away from joining unions.

In addition, there was division within the Knights of Labor. T. V. Powderly, chief of the Knights, deplored strikes and actively worked against some that were started by his own members. As a result, many rank-and-file members felt betrayed, and membership shrank as fast as it had grown. When the Knights fell apart, working women lost an important ally.

In place of the universal brotherhood promoted by the Knights came the conservative trade unionism of the American Federation of Labor. Found in 1886, the AF of L was not interested in helping working women, or for that matter, the majority of working men. Its effort was on behalf of the minority of skilled workers who could be organized into independent craft unions. The AF of L won gradual improvements for its members in wages and working conditions. Unskilled working men and women did not share in these benefits.

By the early 1900s many workers and intellectuals had come to feel that the plight of unskilled labor could be alleviated only by a drastic change in the economic system. "The issue is socialism versus capitalism," Eugene

Debs declared. "I am for socialism because I am for humanity."[25]

Debs' Socialist Party, organized in 1901, envisioned a cooperative society in which workers would share in the profits of their labor and government would assume ownership of industry. The Socialist Party won a voice through the established political system by accumulating votes and electing its members to public office. Socialists also worked within the ranks of organized labor. Many tried to get the AF of L to abandon its craft-union policy and engage in a far-reaching, more militant labor struggle. While individual socialists won the backing of some AF of L locals, especially in the female dominated garment trades, AF of L President Samuel Gompers vehemently fought socialism.

Some radicals gave up hope of changing the AF of L and, in 1905, formed their own union, the Industrial Workers of the World (IWW). Members of the IWW—called Wobblies—were among the most militant unionists in American labor history. The IWW platform declared, "The working class and the employing class have nothing whatsoever in common." Wobblies advocated industrial unions and militant strikes.

Working women benefited from and helped to bring about gains made by the left wing of the labor movement. The socialist, anarchist, and militant unionist camps included several remarkable women leaders.

Mary Harris Jones, known as Mother Jones, was the female "hell raiser" of the labor movement. Born in Ireland, she came to the United States as a child, worked as a dressmaker in Chicago, and married an iron moulder. When her husband and four children died in a yellow fever epidemic in 1867, Mother Jones found a second purpose in life. She became an organizer for the Knights of Labor and, later, for the United Mine Workers and Industrial Workers of the World. Her motto was, "Pray for the dead and fight like hell for the living."

For 50 years Mother Jones was in the center of the bitter and often bloody struggles of mine workers. When soldiers barricaded a bridge that led to striking miners, she waded through an icy river to get to them. She organized "armies" of miners' wives to chase scabs with brooms, mops, and dishpans. When a group of women picketers were arrested and sentenced to thirty days, she advised them to bring their babies to jail and "sing to them all night long." For five days the women sang and the babies howled, until they were released to the relief of the sleepless town. On another occasion Mother Jones marched a group of mill children from Pennsylvania to the nation's capitol to show President Theodore Roosevelt their crippled hands. At a Congressional hearing Mother Jones was asked, "Where is your home?" She answered, "Sometimes I'm in Washington, then in Pennsylvania, Arizona, Texas, Alabama, Colorado, Minnesota. My address is like my shoes. It travels with me. I abide where there is a fight against wrong."[26]

Mother Jones once told a meeting of suffragists, "You don't need the vote to raise hell. You need convictions and a voice." When one of the women present called her an "anti" [suffragist], she replied, "I am not anti to anything which will bring freedom to my class. . . . The women of Colorado have had the vote for two generations and the working men and women are still in slavery." Finally she offered a word of advice to suffragists—"No matter what your fight, don't be ladylike."[27]

Kate Richards O'Hare, Rose Pastor Stokes, and Elizabeth Gurley Flynn also allied themselves with the left wing of the labor movement. Like Mother Jones, they identified with the working class rather than with the reforming middle class, and they put class identification above their identification with other women. Each of them spoke for a socialist revolution, a radical redistribution of wealth, and an end to private property. They saw the feminist struggle for women's rights contained in the larger class struggle.

Kate Richards O'Hare, an active socialist speaker and writer who ran for Congress on the 1910 Socialist Party ticket, expressed her belief in the following words.

I as a Socialist most emphatically state that I demand Equal Suffrage not merely as a Sex Right but also as a Class Right. I demand not only better laws for MY SEX but more particularly for MY CLASS.[28]

Elizabeth Gurley Flynn grew up imbibing socialism. Her Irish revolutionary grandfather was called "Paddy the Rebel," and her parents were active in working-class politics. By the time she was fifteen, Gurley Flynn was addressing audiences on the street corners of New York. She entitled her first speech "What Socialism Will Do for Women." She chose that topic, she subsequently recalled, so that "my father would not interfere too much. He thought they [the Harlem Socialist Club] should have asked *him* to expound on Marxism, on which he considered himself an expert."[29]

In her autobiography, *Rebel Girl*, Gurley Flynn recalled that she had spoken about

> the possibility, at least under socialism, of industrializing all domestic tasks by collective kitchens, and dining places, nurseries, laundries and the like. . . .
> I referred to August Bebel's views of socialist society. . . . He foresaw . . . the right of every woman to be a wife, a mother, a worker, a citizen. . . . I was fired with determination to work for all of this.[30]

Gurley Flynn believed that a capitalist society would always deprive women of equal opportunity. Her speeches on behalf of the working class discussed the woman's cause. One reporter in 1906 heard her tell a street corner audience that

> the state should provide for the maintenance of every child so that the individual woman shall not be compelled to depend for support upon the individual man while bearing children. The barter and sale that go under the name of love are highly obnoxious.[31]

For herself Gurley Flynn wanted freedom from woman's traditional roles in marriage. At eighteen she married a miner and fellow agitator in the labor movement; at twenty, she gave birth to a son. By then she had decided that "a domestic life and possibly a large family had no attraction for me."

> My mother's aversion to both had undoubtedly affected me profoundly. She was strong for her girls "being somebody" and "having a life of their own." . . . I saw no reason why I, as a woman, should give up my work for his [her husband's]. I knew by now I could make more of a contribution to the labor movement than he could. I would not give up.[32]

Gurley Flynn had no "state" to turn to for child support. Nor could she depend on her husband or other male socialists to understand her wish for both a personal and a public life. The sexual equality she and other radical women sought under socialism was rarely offered by the men in the socialist camp. Gurley Flynn relied on her mother to help raise her child so she would be free to raise "the worker's cause."

Like Mother Jones, Gurley Flynn traveled the nation, organizing workers for the Wobblies. Between 1906 and 1926 she participated in some twenty strikes and was arrested fifteen times.

Other women unionists emerged as labor leaders within their specific trades. Women such as Emma Steghagen of the shoemakers, Agnes Nestor of the glovemakers, Mary Kenny O'Sullivan of the bookbinders, and Leonora O'Reilly, Bessie Abramowitz, and Rose Schneiderman of the garment workers became convinced of the need of unions for women by their personal work experiences. These women had grown up in factories. Most of them were foreign-born or the daughters of immigrants. They used their first-hand knowledge to reach other women and to speak on their behalf. They knew that working women were not going to be handed their rights without a struggle. "There is no harder contest," noted Rose Schneiderman, "than the contest for bread."[33] That contest involved the courage to risk one's job and face down employer and police violence on picket lines.

Most women unionists began their careers as teenagers, organizing in the factories where they themselves worked. Some of them subsequently formed alliances with middle-class reformers whom they met in the settlement houses.

By the time she was thirteen, Rose Schneiderman was the major breadwinner for her family. Born in Russia in 1888, she was brought to the United States when she was two. When her father died two years later, Rose's mother did home sewing and took in a boarder. Unable to make ends meet, she went to work in a factory, placing her children in orphanages for several years.

The family was reunited when Rose went to work. As an errand girl for a department store, she worked sixty-four hours a week for $2.16. Three years later Rose advanced to a job in a more fashionable department store, which paid $2.75 a week. Because factory work was better paid, Rose called on a friend who made linings for caps for help in getting a job as an apprentice. Within a year Rose had formed the first female local within the United Hat and Cap Makers Union. The following year she was elected to the general executive board, becoming the first woman in the trade union movement to hold such a high position.[34]

Few women ever reached eminence of this sort in their unions, but thousands of women made the existence of union executive boards possible. Like Rose Schneiderman, working women waited at factory doors before and after work, talking up the union. They collected dues, obtained charters, and formed bargaining committees in their shops. Women laid the foundations of unionism in industries that employed a majority of female workers, most notably the garment and textile trades.

When women shirtwaist makers went on strike in New York City in 1909, they transformed the International Ladies' Garment Workers Union (ILGWU) from an obscure organization with a handful of members into a force of tens of thousands. Like many previous strikes in the needle trades, the Great Uprising, as it came to be called, began as a small walkout of workers from one shop. By the time the strike was over, it had changed the course of the labor movement and organized more women than had ever been unionized before.

The strike started when the Triangle Shirtwaist Company, one of the largest manufacturers of women's blouses in New York City, fired workers suspected of supporting unionization. The company claimed that the measure was necessary because there was not enough work for all, but workers discovered that the company was in fact advertising for new workers. They called a strike and were joined by workers from the Leiserson Company.

Workers from both these shops picketed daily for the right to organize and to bargain collectively with bosses for improved wages and working conditions. Triangle hired prostitutes to taunt the strikers; Leiserson called in professional thugs to beat them up. The strikers withstood the abuse and violence, but after two months they were tired and hungry. Finally Local 25 of the ILGWU and the United Hebrew Trades, a coalition of Jewish socialist unions, called a meeting of all shirtwaist makers in New York.

At the time more than thirty thousand such workers were employed in various shops throughout the city. Eighty percent were women, and 70 percent were between sixteen and twenty-five years old; 65 percent of the women employed in the trade were Jewish, 26 percent were Italian, and 8 percent were native-born, with the remainder composed of a sprinkling of Poles, Germans, and Irish.

Thousands of these shirtwaist makers met to discuss a general strike of the entire trade. Various labor leaders and organizers debated the proper course to take. Then sixteen-year-old Clara Lemlich, a striker from the Leiserson Company who had been beaten up on the picket line, made her way to the platform. Speaking in Yiddish, she called on her fellow workers to be done with the talk and take action.

I am a working girl and one of those who are on strike against intolerable conditions. I am tired of listening to speakers who talk in general terms. What we are here for is to decide whether or not we shall strike. I offer a resolution: that a general strike be declared—NOW.[85]

Clara Lemlich's appeal was greeted with cheers, applause, and shouts of "Yes." When the chairman asked those present, "Do you mean faith?" everyone in the hall rose to recite together an old Jewish oath—"If I turn traitor to this cause I now pledge, may this hand wither from the arm I now raise."

It was originally thought that about three thousand workers would join the strike; instead, between twenty and thirty thousand responded. "From every waist-making factory in New York and Brooklyn, the girls poured forth, filling the narrow streets of the East Side, crowding the headquarters at Clinton Hall and overflowing into twenty-four smaller halls. . . . It was like a mighty army rising in the night, and demanding to be heard."[36]

For thirteen weeks the women picketed, held mass meetings, and built their union, sometimes at the rate of a thousand members a day. Yiddish, Italian, and English speakers had to be found for each of the twenty-four union halls. Committees were appointed from each shop to settle on a wage list.

On the picket lines hundreds of women were beaten and clubbed by police and hired thugs. Hundreds more were dragged off to jail in "Black Maria" police vans. One judge sentenced a striker to jail with the words, "You are on strike against God and Nature, whose prime law it is that man shall earn his bread in the sweat of his brow. You are on strike against God."[37]

The women returned to the picket lines carrying placards with such slogans as, "We are Striking for Human Treatment." Their courage and determination won them new allies. Wealthy and middle-class women philanthropists, club leaders, and suffragists, who had never before considered the plight of working women, contributed money for bail funds and relief. Caroline Woelshoffer persuaded her mother to convert family real estate into bonds, posted herself at the door of the Jefferson Market Court House, and entered it with every group of arrested women to offer bonds as bail security. Mrs. O. H. P. Belmont posted her mansion as bail security.

A link between the strikers and women philanthropists was provided by the National Women's Trade Union League (NWTUL). During the strike the NWTUL raised an estimated $60,000 (a fortune at the time), provided legal counsel, operated relief kitchens, and joined workers on the picket lines. Mary Dreier, president of the New York WTUL was arrested and taken to the station house. When she gave her name, the police officer shouted, "Why didn't you tell me you was a rich lady? I'd never have arrested you in the world."[38]

Shirtwaist makers used the strike to educate the public about conditions in the factories. "We work eight days a week," said one woman. "This may seem strange to you who know that there are only seven days in the week. But we work from seven in the morning until very late at night, when there's a rush, and sometimes we work a week and a half in one week."[39]

When the strike was finally settled, workers had won some improvements in wages but no formal recognition of the union, for which the ILGWU had held out. Nonetheless the strike was a liberating event for working women.

In *The Women's Garment Workers* Louis Levine wrote that the Great Uprising "inspired workers in other branches of the industry. It showed 'big' things could be done in the way of organization, that large masses of workers could be marshalled . . . deep emotions of enthusiasm awakened. It popularized the idea of a general strike."⁴⁰

The revolt of New York City shirtwaist makers was repeated elsewhere—in Philadelphia, Baltimore, countless small cities in the Midwest, and in another massive general strike in Chicago, this time of garment workers who made men's clothing.

As in New York, the Chicago strike started with a walkout against intolerable conditions by a small group of unorganized workers from a Hart, Schaffner and Marx shop. Soon it had spread throughout the trade, until forty thousand women and men of nine nationalities were out for fourteen weeks. Once again the NWTUL joined strikers on picket lines and raised money from wealthy women; and once again working women displayed remarkable stamina.

During the course of the walkout 1,250 babies were born to women strikers and wives of strikers. Margaret Dreir Robbins, president of the NWTUL, told of her visit to the bedside of one of these mothers, a young Italian woman who lay beside her newborn infant, surrounded by three other children. They had been without food for days, yet the woman was proud of her husband's refusal to go back to work. "It is not only bread we give to our children," she told Robbins. "We live by freedom and I will fight till I die to give it to my children."⁴¹

Only workers from the Hart, Schaffner and Marx shop won an agreement from bosses. They returned to work after a three-member arbitration committee was appointed to bargain with employers. One of the three was Bessie Abramowitz, a fifteen-year-old Russian Jewish immigrant who had led the initial walkout.

For four years after the Chicago strike, Bessie Abramowitz worked to keep the local union in her shop alive and to gain recognition from the AF of L's United Garment Workers. The recognition never came. The United Garment Workers were interested only in organizing skilled cutters, a small minority in the trade. Alienated by this policy, Abramowitz moved to form an independent union that would represent all forty thousand workers in the men's clothing trade. In 1914 she, her future husband Sidney Hillman, and other activists founded the Amalgamated Clothing Workers of America, one of the first unions to provide members with health care, housing, adult-education courses, school scholarships, and day care centers for the children of workers. Abramowitz held that unions should raise the self-esteem of workers as well as their wages.[42]

Most histories of the American labor movement designate Sidney Hillman as the founder of the Amalgamated. Until feminist historians began writing about women's role in the labor movement, Bessie Abramowitz was all but forgotten. Though she continued to work alongside her husband in the organizing drives of the 1930s, her position in the leadership hierarchy of the Amalgamated, the union she had helped to found, became secondary to the men's.

Abramowitz was only one of the women leaders in the labor movement who was not given her full due. There were thousands of other women organizers whose names have gone completely unrecorded. Rank-and-file working women were discriminated against by the very unions they played a central role in establishing. Women made up the majority of workers in the garment industry. Their militant strike actions in the early 1900s made labor history. Yet when it came time to settle these strikes, men took over. Women were refused roles as arbitrators and excluded from positions on executive boards.

In 1913 the ILGWU signed the famous "Protocol in the Dress and Waist Industry," the first contract between labor and management arbitrated by outside negotiators. This contract formalized the trade's division of labor by gender, reserving the more skilled, more highly paid jobs for men. Only men could be hired as cutters and pressers; women were assigned the less skilled jobs of draper, joiner, examiner, finisher, and cleaner. The lowest paid male worker was to earn more than the highest paid female. Men were to be paid more even when they did the same work.[43]

Some of women's most important demands for health and safety regulations in the factories were ignored. The importance of these demands was brought home in a tragic way, when many of the women who returned to the Triangle Company after the Great Uprising were killed two years later in a fire that took the lives of 146 people.

The Triangle Company was located on the top three floors of a ten-story building. There were only two elevators and two narrow staircases, and the door to one of the staircases was kept locked. Fire hoses in the building were unconnected. Once the fire broke out, it spread rapidly. On that day five hundred workers were at their machines, sewing highly inflammable materials. Some workers managed to leave by the elevators before they jammed, and some made their way down the staircase. Others escaped to the roof and then jumped to the roof of the adjacent building. The rest were trapped in the burning building. Many jumped to their deaths from the windows, their bodies already on fire. Others burned and suffocated inside.[44]

In New York—especially on the Lower East Side, where most of the victims of the fire had lived—there were scenes of hysteria, mass protests, demonstrations. Uptown, in a wealthier section of the city, the NWTUL rented the Metropolitan Opera House for a memorial meeting, which was attended by many of the women philanthropists who had contributed money to the Great Uprising. Rose Schneiderman was also present. Called on to speak, she choked out the following words.

I would be a traitor to these poor burned bodies, if I came here to talk good fellowship. We have tried you good people of the public and we have found you wanting. The old Inquisition had its rack and its thumbscrews and its instruments of torture with iron teeth. We know what these things are today: the iron teeth are our necessities, the thumbscrews the high powered and swift machinery close to which we must work, and the rack is here in the fireproof structures that will destroy us the minute they catch fire.

This is not the first time girls have been burned alive in the city. Every week I must learn of the untimely death of one of my sister workers. Every year thousands of us are maimed. The life of men and women is so cheap and property is so sacred. There are so many of us for one job it matters little if a hundred forty-three of us are burned to death.

We have tried you citizens; we are trying you now, and you have a couple of dollars for the sorrowing mothers and daughters and sisters by way of a charity gift. But every time the workers come out in the only way they know to protest against conditions which are unbearable, the strong hand of the law is allowed to press down heavily upon us. . . .

I can't talk fellowship to you who are gathered here. Too much blood has been spilled. I know from my experience it is up to the working people to save themselves. The only way they can save themselves is by a strong working-class movement."[45]

Mill workers in Lawrence, Massachusetts, agreed with Schneiderman that it was up to working people to save themselves. In January 1912 workers in the Lawrence mills opened their pay envelopes to find that their wages had been further reduced. It was one pay cut too many.

The majority of workers in Lawrence were women and children. A state law had just been passed reducing their hours from 56 to 54 per week. To get around the law, bosses speeded up the looms. When they cut the pay in addition, workers revolted. "Short pay, short pay," was heard from loom to loom, and the cry echoed from mill to mill. Thousands of workers poured into the streets to declare a strike.

"Better to starve fighting than to starve working," became their battle cry, shouted in a score of languages. The fourteen thousand Lawrence workers came from at least thirty different countries, and they spoke some forty-five different languages. The largest groups were Italians, Germans, and French Canadians. There were also Poles, Lithuanians, Franco-Belgians, Syrians, Letts, and Turks. Only eight percent of the mill workers were native-born.

For over fifty years mill owners had used cheap foreign-born labor in the mills and kept out foreign business competition. A high protective tariff prevented foreign-made textiles from entering the country. This system produced high profits for the mill owners and stockholders, and they enjoyed them a great distance away from the mill towns. When muckraker Ray Stannard Baker traveled to Lawrence to report on the strike, he discovered that "not a single large stockholder in the Lawrence mills lives in Lawrence, not one."

A textile town is not a pleasant place to live in—dirty wooden buildings, dirty streets, unlovely looking people, cheap goods, no good society. . . . So the owners live in Boston . . . representatives of . . . the strong old families of Massachusetts. . . . Many . . . are interested in all good works. . . . But about conditions in the dark alleys of Lawrence, where their own money comes from—apparently they know very little nor do they want to know."[46]

Though Lawrence mill workers earned less than did factory workers in New York, they paid higher prices for rent and food. "There is an appalling amount of underfeeding . . . many young people looked (and they were) stunted. . . . Thousands in this city, which often suffers from overproduction of cloth, go underclad."[47]

The Lawrence workers were neglected not only by their absentee owners, but also by the unions. The AF of L's United Textile Workers had organized only a handful of the skilled mill workers; the vast majority—women, children and unskilled men—had never been approached.

When the Lawrence strikers called on the UTW for help, the union's president John Golden ignored their request and attempted to break the strike by sending his members back to work after making a separate deal with mill owners. But the majority of workers stayed on strike. When Golden ordered the WTUL to stop providing relief, Margaret Dreier Robbins charged that "many of those in power in the AF of L seem to be selfish and reactionary and remote from the struggle for bread and liberty of unskilled workers."[48] Nonetheless the League complied and stuck to its policy of working only in AF of L-sanctioned strikes.

Lawrence strikers next appealed to the Industrial Workers of the World. The Wobblies had done most of their organizing in the West, among migrant farm workers, miners, and lumbermen, but they were eager to reach industrial workers in the East. The Wobblies sent in twenty-one-year-old Elizabeth Gurley Flynn; Joseph Ettor, who could speak to workers in Italian, English, and Polish; and Arturo Giovanniti, a poet as well as a labor organizer.

The Wobblies held meetings for every language group in every part of town. A strike committee of women and men from every mill, every department, and every nationality was elected. Each day all the strikers were rallied to meet on the Lawrence Common, so that they could feel "their oneness and strength."

"Big" Bill Haywood, head of the Wobblies, came to Lawrence to encourage the strikers to organize "One Big Union." The workers, wrote Elizabeth Gurley Flynn, "roared with laughter and applause when he said: 'The AF of L organizes like this!'—separating his fingers as far apart as they would go, and naming them—'Weavers, loom-fixers, dyers, spinners.' Then he would say: 'The IWW organizes like this!'—tightly clenching his big fist, shaking it at the bosses."[49]

No union had ever before tried to unify workers of such diverse nationalities. Gurley Flynn told of the Wobblies' emphasis on the workers' shared immigrant experience.

> We spoke to nationalities who had been traditionally enemies for centuries in hostile European countries, like the Greeks and Turks and Armenians. . . . We said firmly: "You work together for the boss. You can stand together to fight for yourselves."[50]

Gurley Flynn and Haywood also held special meetings for women, encouraging them to make the strike their own. Many of the Jewish women who had led the garment strikes were familiar with labor activities from Russia. The Italian, Polish, and other East European Catholic women of Lawrence had little knowledge of the labor movement and were more closely tied to "the old-world attitude of the man as lord and master." Gurley Flynn noted the hostility.

> There was considerable male opposition to women going to meetings and marching on picket lines. The women wanted to picket. They were strikers as well as wives and were valiant fighters. We knew that to leave them at home alone, isolated from the strike activity, a prey to worry, affected by the complaints of landlords, priests, and ministers was dangerous to the strike. We did not attack their religious beliefs but . . . we pointed out that if workers had more money they would . . . put more in the church collections. The women laughed and told it to the priests and ministers the next Sunday.[51]

As soon as the Lawrence workers walked off their jobs, the town of Lawrence became an armed camp. The governor sent 1,400 militiamen to back up police and state troopers. One officer remarked, "Our company of militia went down to Lawrence during the first days of the strike. Most of them had to leave Harvard to do it; but they rather enjoyed having a fling at these people." Another officer gave orders to "strike the women on the arms and breasts and the men on the head."[52]

Clashes took place daily between the militia and strikers. When a young woman striker named Annie Lo Pizzo was killed, organizers Ettor and Giovanitti were arrested and charged as accessories to the murder because they had advocated picketing.

The Wobblies were attacked by mill owners and the press as "outside agitators" and "anarchists" who were stirring up "contented workers." The passion and determination of the workers showed something quite different. Reporters who descended on Lawrence discovered a vital, intense commitment, an almost "religious spirit" among workers. "It was a new kind of strike," wrote journalist Mary Heaton Vorse.

> There had never been any mass picketing in any New England town. Ten thousand workers picketed. It was the spirit of the strikers that seemed dangerous. They were confident, gay and released, and they sang. They were always marching and singing.[58]

Large groups locked arms on the sidewalks and marched through the town, bearing their message in song and signs. When a group of women carried a picket sign which read "WE WANT BREAD AND ROSES TOO," James Oppenheim was inspired to write the following evocation of the spirit of the women strikers:

> As we come marching, marching in the beauty of the day
> A million darkened kitchens, a thousand mill lofts gray
> Are touched with all the radiance that a sudden sun discloses
> For the people hear us singing: Bread and roses! Bread and roses!
>
> As we come marching, marching, we battle too for men
> For they are women's children, and we mother them again,
> Our lives shall not be sweated from birth until life closes;
> Hearts starve as well as bodies; give us bread, but give us roses!
>
> As we come marching, marching, unnumbered women dead
> Go crying through our singing, their ancient cry for bread.
> Small art and love and beauty their drudging spirits knew.
> Yes it is bread we fight for—but we fight for roses too!

As we come marching, marching, we bring the greater
days.
The rising of the women means the rising of the race.
No more the drudge and idler—ten that toil where one
reposes,
But a sharing of life's glories: Bread and roses! Bread and
roses!

The strikers had no money, and the Wobblies had no
treasury. Food and fuel supplies diminished. The strikers
decided to send their children to the homes of strike supporters in other cities. The first group of evacuated children arrived in New York City weary, ragged, and on the
verge of starvation. These children aroused support for
the strikers as nothing else had. Mill owners refused to
allow more children to leave Lawrence. When the strikers
tried to evacuate another group, troopers surrounded
the railroad station, clubbed the children and their mothers, and then arrested them. The mothers were charged
with "neglect" and "improper guardianship."

Public reaction turned to the side of the strikers. Congress was pressured to open an investigation. Mill owners,
fearing that Congress would rescind their tariff protection,
decided to accept the strikers' demands. Two months after
the initial walkout the Lawrence workers returned to the
mills with an increase in wages of 5 to 20 percent. The
highest percentage of this increase went to women and
children.

The Wobblies soon left Lawrence. They were organizers
who traveled around the nation to scenes of strikes, not
workers who remained in one place. Elizabeth Gurley
Flynn admitted that "most of us [the Wobblies] were won-
derful agitators but poor union organizers."[54] Without
ongoing organizing help it was extremely difficult for mill
workers to maintain the union structure that had emerged
during the strike.

Gurley Flynn described another incident that lost support for the Wobblies in Lawrence. During the labor
parade after the strike, an unknown group unfurled a banner with the words, "No God, No Master." The atheism
proclaimed in this sign disturbed many workers, a majority
of whom were devout Catholics. Gurley Flynn claimed
that the Wobblies were not responsible for this sign, but
the words "No God" came to be associated with them, and
support for the Wobblies in Lawrence fell away.[55]

Emma Goldman understood the social as well as the economic factors that kept many women from rebelling against their secondary place in the labor force. "But a very small number of the vast army of women workers look upon work as a permanent issue in the same light as does man. No matter how decrepit the latter, he has been taught to be independent and self supporting."

The woman considers her position as worker transitory, to be thrown aside for the first bidder. That is why it is infinitely harder to organize women then men. "Why should I join the union? I am going to get married, to have a home." Has she not been taught from infancy to look upon that as her ultimate calling? The most tragic part, however, is that the home no longer frees her from wage slavery; it only increases her task.[56]

The fact that most men who led the labor movement considered women not worth organizing reinforced working women's apathy. Discrimination against women in the labor movement discouraged many women from remaining active. It took a lot of energy to fight, not only bosses, but also male labor leaders. "After four years I was too tired to rebel any more," wrote Elizabeth Hasanovitz.[57]

In *All for One* Rose Schneiderman charged that union men never treated women as equals. They never fought for the right of women to perform the same work as men at the same pay. Rather than work for the male-dominated American Federation of Labor, Schneiderman chose to work with the female-led Women's Trade Union League, which by 1915 concentrated on winning improvements for working women through protective legislation. The League, noted Schneiderman, offered to help the AF of L whenever it was asked, yet AF of L unions were condescending when it came to helping the League.

The few unions that helped us looked upon us as children look upon their parents. The help they gave us was first of all not enough and second it wasn't given graciously, the way we gave our services to them. There was never any question of our helping when we were needed.[58]

Women in the socialist movements had similar problems. Female membership in the Socialist Party was never more than 15 percent. Most socialist women were segregated into female auxiliaries, which organized "social" functions; political decision-making was handled by men.

At its founding meeting in 1901 the Socialist Party resolved merely to "favor equal political and civil rights for men and women." The party did not endorse woman suffrage until 1910, after a great deal of pressure from women who threatened to desert the socialist ranks for the woman suffrage movement.[59]

Socialist men in the labor movement and political left argued in theory for women's total equality, but in practice they failed to support the idea of a special women's movement to fight for and win that equality. In their personal relationships with women, moreover, these men often behaved in extremely conservative ways. Elizabeth Gurley Flynn noted that many union and socialist men expected their wives to stay at home, "in the background," managing the household and bringing up the children, leaving the men free to work for the movement.

Radical women wanted both personal relationships and activity in the world. Many found it extremely difficult to have both. Their struggle foreshadowed a conflict felt by many women in the twentieth century.

Gurley Flynn titled one chapter in her autobiography "Not Much Personal Life." When her thirteen-years-long relationship with anarchist Carlo Tresca was breaking up, his friends "tried to tell me that if I would only stay home and 'keep house' for Carlo all would be well. But I rejected the solution. I said: 'He had a good Italian wife who cooked spaghetti and was a model housekeeper. Why didn't he stay with her?' They knew the answer and so did I then. Carlo had a roving eye."[60]

Emma Goldman arrived at the harrowing decision not to have children because she feared that she would not be able to be a good mother and still carry on her work. Goldman's efforts to combine relationships with men and her work were difficult enough. She described how she "hungered for someone who would love the woman in me and who would also be able to share my work. I had never had anyone who could do both. Sasha had been too obsessed by the Cause to see much of the woman who craved acceptance. Hannes and Ed, who had loved me profoundly, had wanted merely the woman in me. . . . All the others had been attracted by the public personality."[61]

The promise of the radical labor movement was never fulfilled. During and after the First World War, leftists were violently persecuted by the government. Many of the strongest leaders, including Emma Goldman, were jailed and deported. In addition, there was bitter internal dissension between those leftists who supported the Communists in the newly established Soviet Union and those who did not. These factors made it extremely difficult for radical women to find and assert their voices within the left.

For women in the labor force at large, the First World War created new opportunities. As in the Civil War, when men had enlisted or been drafted into the armed services, women were recruited to take their places in the labor force. During the First World War, women worked in factories assembling explosives, armaments, machine tools, electrical appliances, and railway, automobile, and airplane parts; they took jobs in brass and copper smelting factories, oil refineries, and steel foundries; thousands of additional women were hired in the textile mills to produce uniforms for the armed services.

The number of women who took jobs in heavy industry during the First World War was small compared to the numbers so employed during the Second. Nevertheless, the numbers of occupations in which women could be found working in 1917 and 1918 increased dramatically. The presence of women in jobs that had formally been restricted to men challenged the view that women were capable of performing only limited kinds of work. It also led to increased government regulation of the conditions under which women worked.

The Women's Bureau of the Department of Labor, established in 1920 and headed first by Mary Anderson, emerged out of the Women's Division of the Ordinance Department, which regulated conditions of women workers in munitions and ordinance plants during the First World War. By the time the war was over, the women who had headed this effort, Mary Van Kleeck and Mary Anderson, had convinced government officials that all working women, in peacetime as well as wartime, needed the protection of labor laws. To the present day the Women's Bureau remains an important ally of working women, lobbying for improved conditions for women in the labor force and equality with men.

Though the period 1910–1920 was a highpoint of labor activity for working women, the overwhelming majority of working women were still unorganized and remained in the lowest paid, least skilled jobs. Those who had moved into more remunerative positions in heavy industry during the war were fired when men returned home and were forced to return to their prewar female-only jobs.

In subsequent years more working women joined unions and won gradual improvements in wages and working conditions, but they never won equality with men on the job or in the labor movement. The major changes of the following years dealt with where women worked and how long they stayed in the work force.

The Modern Women

15

Votes for Women

In 1890 a merger was made between the two wings of the woman suffrage movement—one based in Boston, the other in New York. By joining together, suffragists hoped to revitalize their cause. Despite the growing activism of middle-class woman toward the end of the century, the suffrage movement had remained small. Women's clubs and temperance organizations had millions of supporters, but suffrage measured its adherents only in the thousands. Even suffrage victories in the West had failed to arouse public interest on a mass level.

The formation of a united movement, the National American Woman Suffrage Association (NAWSA), signaled a new era in woman's fight for the vote. By the time the NAWSA was formed, woman suffrage was in fact no longer a truly radical issue, and the women who fought for it no longer held radical social views. The old leaders, who were far more obstreperous in their demands than were newer generations of feminists, remained on the scene for a time, but their influence was on the wane.

Elizabeth Cady Stanton, the first president of the NAWSA, served for two years only. She continued to regard woman suffrage as one among many reforms essential for women. In the early years of the movement Stanton had singled out the laws and customs related to marriage as the most important cause of woman's oppression. As Stanton grew older, she came to hold the Bible and organized religion most responsible for woman's inequality. When she resigned the presidency of NAWSA in 1892, she set out to expose the role of religion in fostering and maintaining the oppression of women.

Working with a committee of feminists, Stanton produced a feminist commentary on scripture called *The Woman's Bible*. Her analysis of woman's treatment within the Old and New Testaments was based on her belief that the Bible was a human, not a divine, document.

She saw in many Biblical pronouncements an antifemale bias which, she believed, had a very strong influence on "modern" thinking about women.

Stanton's scriptural objections began with Genesis and extended to Revelation. Stanton did not accept the version of creation reported in Genesis according to which Eve was created from one of Adam's ribs. Stanton was convinced that God had created men and women to be equal. The way the Bible portrayed creation, the origin of womankind, she said, was reduced to "a petty surgical procedure." Of the Old Testament in general Stanton wrote that it "makes woman a mere afterthought in creation; the author of all evil; cursed in her maternity; a subject in marriage; and all female life, animal and human, unclean." The story of Ruth, "who believed in the dignity of labour and self-support," was one of the few she admired.[1]

Anticipating clerical opposition to *The Woman's Bible*, Stanton was nevertheless unprepared for the storm of protest emanating from her own comrades in the suffrage movement. At the 1896 NAWSA convention, suffragists introduced a resolution which declared "That this Association is non-sectarian and that it has no connection with the so-called *Woman's Bible* or any other theological publication." Susan B. Anthony, who had become president of the NAWSA following Stanton's resignation in 1892, was almost alone in opposing the resolution.

Anthony was no enthusiast for *The Woman's Bible*, which she thought "flippant and superficial," but she was appalled that the movement could censure her old friend. In a speech to the convention Anthony reminded suffragists of Stanton's enormous contribution to the movement. "This resolution, [if] adopted, will be a vote of censure upon a woman . . . who has stood for half a century the acknowledged leader of progressive thought and demand in regard to all matters pertaining to the absolute freedom of women."

Anthony continued, calling on suffragists to allow "the right of individual opinion for every member."

When this platform is too narrow for people of all creeds to stand on, I shall not be on it. . . . If you fail to teach women a broad catholic spirit, I would not give much for them after they are enfranchised. You had better organize

one woman on a broad platform than ten thousand on a
narrow platform of intolerance and bigotry.[a]

Anthony's plea for a "broad platform" was rejected,
and the "Bible Resolution" passed. Thereafter Stanton
no longer worked for the NAWSA.

Anthony was a far more acceptable leader to the newer generation of suffragists than Stanton had been. She
shared with the younger women in the movement a single-minded concern with winning the vote. Anthony,
however, was unable to unite the movement. She believed the most efficient way to win woman suffrage to
be through an amendment to the federal constitution.
Younger suffragists, especially from the West and South,
opposed federal action.

The success of suffrage campaigns in Colorado and
Idaho led Western suffragists to believe that they could
win the vote on the state level. Women from the South
also preferred to work state by state; their reasoning was
based on their awareness that women had no chance of
winning the vote in the South unless suffrage was presented
as a "states' rights" issue.

White southerners, using the argument of states' rights,
had been able to carry out a racist program which in
effect nullified the Fourteenth and Fifteenth Amendments.
"Jim Crow" laws made it impossible for blacks to vote.
Southern suffragists, who fully supported Jim Crow, certainly did not want to work for a federal woman suffrage
amendment that might raise anew the specter of the
Fourteenth and Fifteenth Amendments.

Anthony lost the strategy fight. Following the suffrage
convention of 1894, attempts to win a federal amendment
were dropped. Instead the movement was decentralized,
and suffragists, under new leadership, devoted themselves
to winning state referendums.

The women who led the suffrage movement to victory
between 1890 and 1920 were realists rather than vision-
aries, tacticians rather than radical ideologues. These
leaders believed that if women could vote, they would
need nothing else to achieve full equality. Their goal was
to win the support of the mass of middle-class women,
and in this effort they were willing to purge the woman's
movement of its most unconventional leaders and radical
positions.

The two women who succeeded Anthony in the presidency of the NAWSA—Anna Howard Shaw and Carrie Chapman Catt—were prototypes of this second generation of suffragists. Both came from pioneer families in the Midwest. Both were among the growing number of college-educated women. Both had experienced at first hand the difficulties facing women who needed to earn a living and wanted professional careers. In their personalities and talents, however, they differed sharply.

Anna Howard Shaw (1847–1919) spent much of her youth in poverty on a farm in the Michigan wilderness.[3] She decided early that she wanted something more out of life than her family could offer. She taught school to earn money for college. Eventually she decided to become a minister—a career choice that was opposed by her family, her friends, and the academic community. The ministry was still an almost unheard-of vocation for females, although in the early part of the century a few women, such as Antoinette Brown, had managed to become ordained preachers.

Shaw's determination was unbending. She fought her way into Boston University's theological school, and she fought her way through the school's program. Denied the financial assistance given to male students, throughout most of her stay she suffered from malnutrition. On completion of her training she was ordained by the Methodist Church in 1880.

Shaw became a pastor in two churches, but the work was not satisfying to her. Inspired by Elizabeth Blackwell, she decided to become a doctor. For the next several years, while serving as a minister, she studied medicine. In 1886 she earned a medical degree from Boston Medical School.

Shaw's ambition, which drove her to become a doctor as well as a minister, gives support to an idea of historian Andrew Sinclair. The first women in the professions, Sinclair has written, were less interested in the law or medicine than in the enormous challenge of winning acceptance in a profession. Throughout their lives these women seemed to have had a burning need to overcome obstacles.[4] Shaw, like Blackwell, set enormously high standards for herself and set out to prove to herself and to the world what she could do.

Medicine and the ministry were not enough. Shaw next

turned to reform work. She became a lecturer for the Women's Christian Temperance Union and was said to be without peer as a public speaker. It was through the WCTU that Shaw became interested in suffrage and was introduced to Susan B. Anthony. The two formed a very close friendship. Shaw idolized Anthony and believed she understood the old leader better than did any other of the new generation suffragists. She hoped to assume the presidency of the NAWSA when Anthony retired.

The fact of the matter was, however, that Shaw was not cut out to lead the movement. She was a brilliant spokesperson and a woman of enormous intellectual gifts, but she had no talent whatsoever for organization. By 1900, when Anthony retired, the movement needed an organizer, a job which Carrie Chapman Catt was better equipped to handle than Shaw.

Carrie Lane Chapman Catt (1859–1947) grew up in Wisconsin and Iowa and studied at Iowa State College.[5] After graduation she quickly rose from teacher through high-school principal to the Superintendent of Schools in Mason City, Iowa, the first woman to hold such a high administrative position in the public school system. She resigned to marry Leo Chapman, a journalist who died a few months after their marriage. Catt turned to lecturing and suffrage work to support herself.

The difficulties Catt experienced as a young widow trying to earn a living added passion to her prosuffrage feelings. When she married again in 1890, she drew up a contract with her second husband, George Catt, specifying that she would have several months of the year during which she could devote herself solely to suffrage work. George Catt, a wealthy engineer, gave his wife the same kind of financial and emotional support Henry Blackwell had given Lucy Stone.

As a full-time worker for woman suffrage, Carrie Chapman Catt soon won a reputation in the Western states as a brilliant strategist and organizer. After leading Colorado and Idaho to woman suffrage victories, she was appointed chairwoman of the NAWSA's organization committee in 1896; this post won her recognition from the national leadership.

Catt designed a plan which she was sure would win women the vote. She regarded the decentralization of the NAWSA as a temporary necessity. Campaigns for state amendments were important, she thought, in order to win the kind of grass roots support she knew would be needed to secure a federal amendment. Catt understood that the yearly suffrage conventions the movement favored as a method of winning support produced nothing but the conversion of the already converted. She recommended that suffrage adherents take to the stump, carrying "our question into every town meeting, caucus and primary, for it is there," she noted, "that the rank and file voters go. They won't come to our meetings."[6]

Catt's executive abilities led Anthony to support her bid for election over Anna Howard Shaw to become the third president of the NAWSA. As soon as Catt took over from Anthony in 1900, she began to put her reorganization plan into motion. She was hampered, however, by disunity within the movement and a number of personal problems. Her husband, George Catt, was ill with a fatal disease, and in 1904 Catt was forced to retire. Her withdrawal opened the position to Anna Howard Shaw.

Anthony was both pleased and displeased to see Shaw assume leadership of the movement. Though fond of Shaw, Anthony was worried about Shaw's ability to produce a victory for woman suffrage. Just before Anthony's death in 1906, she secured a promise from other suffragists that they would support Shaw financially, leaving her free to devote all her time to suffrage work.

Despite this aid, Shaw's presidency was not successful. During her eleven-year incumbency—from 1904 to 1915 —woman suffrage made few gains. Until 1910 no new states granted women the vote, and only six state referendums were held.

Shaw did not have the gift for inspiring loyalty, and she tended to quash all initiatives which did not stem directly from her. Both her personality and her policies created friction and hostility both among the NAWSA officers and the rank and file.

While the national organization floundered, a profound change was taking place on the local level. Second-generation suffragists were discarding the old prosuffrage argument for one that proclaimed women to be the morally superior sex. The early theorists had claimed for women nothing more or less than full equality. Stanton in particular had argued that before women were wives and mothers, they were individuals and citizens, possessing the same rights and obligations of all citizens.

The new leaders were no longer content with equality. Women were no longer like men, *entitled* to the vote; women differed from men and therefore *deserved* the vote.[7] These suffragists cheerfully agreed with antisuffragists that woman was the moral, pure, virtuous sex. They argued that only women possessed the peaceful instincts and moral strengths needed to combat the increasing corruption of government by big business and political machines.

There is no doubt that by changing their argument on the issue of equality women speeded their victory for suffrage. By accepting the notion of the moral superiority of women, suffragists placed themselves comfortably within the camp of high Victorian social attitudes and beliefs. At the same time, by proclaiming themselves better than men, they claimed the vote as a reward for being so good. This argument undermined the political strength of their movement.

At a time when large numbers of women were working in factories and growing numbers were attending college and establishing careers, suffragists were emphasizing women's special place in the home as support for their claim to the vote. Within their sphere, suffragists declared, women had developed traits necessary to government. To protect their sphere, moreover, women would have to engage in politics. In an industrialized and urbanized society, such as America was becoming, suffragists asserted, home and world were no longer separated, and women were needed to be housewives to the world, straightening up the mess male leaders had made, cleaning up the filth spawned by corruption. One prosuffrage leader explained the stand in the following words.

> When anti-suffragists declare that woman's place is in the home we grasp them by the hand and say amen most earnestly. . . . The woman's place is in the home. But today would she serve the home she must go beyond the house. No longer is home compassed by four walls. Many of its most important duties lie now involved in the bigger family of the city and state.[8]

When antisuffragists argued that women were already involved in serving society through the network of wom-

en's clubs and charitable organizations, Anna Howard
Shaw retorted, "Thank God, once women vote . . . there
will not be such a need of charity and philanthropy."[9]
Suffragists truly believed that when women won the vote,
they would naturally support the kind of enlightened programs that could eradicate social problems and make charity unnecessary.

Jane Addams, who endorsed woman suffrage in 1897
and became a vice president of the NAWSA in 1911,
tempered this view slightly. Women were not men's su-
periors, noted Addams. "We have not wrecked the railroads nor corrupted the legislatures, nor done many
unholy things that men have done, but then we must
remember that we have not had the chance."[10] But women
were different from men, Addams stated, and they could
use their special feminine traits to the benefit of society.

Addams was fond of arguing the political-housekeep-
ing theory. To keep their homes clean and feed their
families pure food, women required a voice in affairs
outside the home. Addams, more than other suffragists,
emphasized industrial, urban conditions.

> In a crowded city quarter . . . if the street is not cleaned
> by the city authorities, no amount of private sweeping will
> keep the tenement free from grime; if the garbage is not
> properly collected and destroyed, a tenement mother may
> see her children sicken and die of diseases from which she
> alone is powerless to shield them, although her tenderness
> and devotion are unbounded. She cannot even secure un-
> tainted meat for her household . . . unless the meat has
> been inspected by city officials . . . in the interests of public
> health. In short, if woman would keep on with her old busi-
> ness of caring for her house and rearing her children, she
> will have to have some conscience in regard to public af-
> fairs lying outside her home.[11]

Two other arguments, both viciously undemocratic,
were used by women seeking the vote at the end of the
century. Racist and antiimmigrant feelings were cited as
justifications for woman suffrage. Northern suffragists
claimed to feel threatened by laws made by ignorant,
foreign-born men. Carrie Catt made this argument in an
1894 speech in Iowa.

> This government is menaced with great danger. . . .
> That danger lies in the votes possessed by the males in

the slums of the cities, and the ignorant foreign vote which
was sought to be bought by each party, to make political
success . . . There is but one way to avert the danger—
cut off the vote of the slums and give it to women.[12]

Ten years later Anna Howard Shaw went even further.

No other country has subjected its women to the humiliating position to which the women of this nation have been
subjected by men. . . . In Germany, German women are
governed by German men; in France, French women
are governed by Frenchmen; and in Great Britain, British
women are governed by British men; but in this country,
American women are governed by every kind of a man
under the light of the sun. There is no race, there is no
color, there is no nationality of men who are not the
sovereign rulers of American women.[13]

The feeling implied in Shaw's statement—that white
American women would have nothing to complain of if
their rulers had been white American men—shows the extent to which suffragists had changed since the early days
of the movement.

Suffragists seized the opportunity to suggest that the
votes of native-born women could counter the "foreign
menace." First they repeatedly cited statistics to show
that native-born women outnumbered foreign-born men
and women combined. Thus, even if all women were enfranchised, the votes of native-born women would out-
number the total immigrant vote. Next suffragists began
suggesting that unfit voters be disenfranchised. An educational qualification for voting, they claimed, would insure
rule by the native-born white portion of the population.

Surprisingly, Stanton was among those who advocated
an educational requirement. In the 1890s she began to
declare that there was a growing feeling among intelligent
people that thousands of "uneducated foreigners landing
every day on our shores," should not be so quickly enfranchised. A literacy test and the requirement that a
voter understand English would "limit the foreign vote"
and "decrease the ignorant native vote by stimulating the
rising generation to learning."

Not all suffragists went along with this ill-disguised bigotry. Opposing voices argued that each class was entitled
to speak for itself at the polls, that education did not

necessarily instill a sense of justice, and that the concept of a privileged ruling class went against the basic tenets of American democracy. Harriet Stanton Blatch criticized her mother's assumption that foreigners were "ignorant" and unqualified to voice their opinions on how they should be governed.

> I do not call the man ignorant or wanting in an understanding of Republican principles who, under the grinding of economic conditions of the Old World, stints himself to lay by, little by little, his passage money across the Atlantic, hoping to find in America a broader freedom for himself, but I do call ignorant and a real danger to the State, the educated man, born and bred in a Republic, who devotes his highest energies to money getting and neglects his every duty as a citizen[14]

Jane Addams reinforced and expanded Blatch's position. Addams was one of the few NAWSA leaders who spoke for immigrant women's rights to suffrage. "The statement is sometimes made," she wrote, "that the franchise would be valuable only so far as educated women exercised it. This statement totally disregards the fact that those matters in which women's judgment is most needed are far too primitive and basic to be largely influenced by what we call education."[15]

Addams pointed out that Scandinavian women had voted in municipal elections in their native countries. She told of "illiterate" immigrant housewives who made intelligent and sensible choices at the polls after they were granted the vote in city elections in Chicago. She argued that immigrant women, needed the vote to protect their families far more than did middle-class women.

Addams' belief changed the minds of some suffragists. Furthermore, by the time the woman suffrage campaign ended, many in the NAWSA realized that the votes of immigrant men in the cities were necessary to win suffrage in the industrial East. Suffragists began to draw on the support and organizing skills of immigrant working women. Yet when suffragists campaigned in middle-class neighborhoods, many continued to voice antiforeign feelings.

The antiimmigrant sentiments of Northern suffragists marched hand in hand with the racist sentiments of Southern suffragists. The enfranchisement of women, claimed

Southern suffragists, would greatly increase the white electorate in the South and insure the hegemony of whites. Though Southern women who became suffragists were motivated by more than the race issue, they supported white supremacy and made it their most important rallying point.

Some Southern suffragists, such as Kate M. Gordon of Louisiana—a state where blacks outnumbered whites— proposed that woman suffrage be limited to white women only. Others, such as Laura Clay of Kentucky, quoted statistics to show that most states contained more white women than black men and women combined. Still others, including Belle Kearney of Mississippi, pointed out the need for an alliance between Northern and Southern whites in face of the "threat" posed by foreigners and blacks.

> The civilization of the North is threatened by the influx of foreigners and their imported customs; by the greed of monopolistic wealth and the unrest among the working classes. . . . Some day the North will be compelled to look to the South for redemption of these evils on account of the purity of its Anglo-Saxon blood . . . so surely will the South be compelled to look to its Anglo-Saxon women as the medium through which to retain its supremacy of the white race over the African. [16]

The NAWSA conventions of 1899 and 1903 marked the final separation of the woman suffrage movement from the black cause. There were in fact black suffragists, but the movement did its best to discourage their involvement. At the 1899 convention Mrs. Lottie Wilson Jackson, a black delegate from Michigan, offered a resolution "that colored women ought not to be compelled to ride in smoking cars and that suitable accommodations should be provided for them." Mrs. Jackson explained to the meeting that in some parts of the South it was almost impossible for black women to travel. Not only were they assigned to filthy quarters, but they were also likely to be insulted by whites and sexually harassed by white men.

White southern delegates denied the existence of the conditions Mrs. Jackson had described, adding that they were illegal if they did exist. Alice Stone Blackwell, Lucy Stone's daughter, was among the northerners who spoke in favor of the Jackson resolution. Anthony put an end to

the debate by asserting, "We women are a helpless disenfranchised class. . . . while we are in this condition, it is
not for us to go passing resolutions against railroad corporations or anybody else." Her argument—that women
could do nothing until they got the vote and that they
should do nothing for the time being but try to win the
vote—swayed many delegates, and the Jackson resolution
was defeated.[17]

The final push for woman suffrage began in 1910, when
the state of Washington passed a woman suffrage amendment, the first state in fourteen years to do so. The victory
stimulated the movement, and it was quickly followed by
the passage of woman suffrage in California, Oregon, Arizona, Kansas, Montana, Nevada, and Illinois (where wom-
en won the right to vote in presidential elections only). In
addition, around 1910 several American women returned
to the United States from England, bringing with them the
militant tactics of the radical wing of the British suffrage
movement.

British suffragists had begun later than their American
counterparts, but once they started, they were far more
militant. Emmeline Pankhurst and her daughters Christa-
bel and Sylvia led the British radicals. The Pankhursts dismissed the idea of winning the vote through "gentle
persuasion." They believed that the only way to win was
through civil disobedience and confrontation with the ruling class.[18]

The Pankhursts were not adverse to violence. They
hounded political figures and battled police. They chained
themselves to the gates of public buildings and gave prosuffrage speeches until policemen sawed them free. They
climbed into the rafters above Parliament and lay there
for hours, springing up at dramatic moments to join the
debate. They burned down buildings, including churches
and castles, and mutilated art objects in museums. They
stormed the House of Commons and blew up mailboxes.
All their activities were an effort to coerce the British
government.

The suffragettes used mass marches on Parliament in
hopes of convincing male leaders to at least consider the
woman question. On one occasion marching suffragettes
(in England the term "suffragettes" was used; in America,
"suffragists") tried to sneak into Parliament by jumping
from a truck that drove near the massive doors of the

legislature's chamber. They were joined by women who sailed up the Thames in boats and cried out, "Rise Up Women" as they passed near the Parliament building.

British suffragettes were arrested and imprisoned by the hundreds. Behind bars they organized hunger strikes and were subjected to forcible feedings, a brutal business that had the effect of swaying public opinion in their favor.

Among the American women who worked with the Pankhursts was Harriet Stanton Blatch, Elizabeth Cady Stanton's daughter. When Blatch returned to the United States in 1907, after the death of her British husband, she found the American suffrage movement "completely in a rut. . . . It bored its adherents and repelled its opponents," she wrote.[19]

Blatch saw little hope of revitalizing the NAWSA. She organized her own group and started the famous woman suffrage parades in New York City, the first outdoor demonstrations by American suffragists. Blatch also succeeded in recruiting some working-class women into the movement by forming an alliance with the Women's Trade Union League.

Many of the factory women Blatch recruited were among the most effective lobbyists for woman suffrage. They used the skills they had developed on the picket lines and at mass labor meetings to call for votes for women. Rose Schneiderman in a 1912 speech debunked the myth that women would lose their beauty and purity if they voted.

We have women working in the foundries, stripped to the waist. . . . They . . . stand for thirteen or fourteen hours in the terrible steam and heat with their hands in hot starch. Surely these women won't lose any more of their beauty and charm by putting a ballot in a ballot box once a year than they are likely to lose standing in foundries or laundries all year round.[20]

More militant than Blatch was Alice Paul (1885–1977). As a graduate student in England, the Quaker-born Paul participated in the Pankhurst demonstrations, spent time in jail, and joined the hunger strikes. Inspired by her experiences among British suffragettes, she returned to the United States determined to revive the dormant American movement.

Paul began by organizing a demonstration of ten thou-

sand in Washington, D. C., on the day before President
Woodrow Wilson's inauguration in 1912. She was eager to
show the new president that thousands of women were
expecting to win the vote during his administration. After
the demonstration Paul established the Congressional Union
as an auxiliary to the NAWSA.

She devised a simple strategy for winning suffrage. She
announced her determination to hold the party in power
—in this case the Democrats, led by President Wilson—
responsible for women's being denied the vote. She proposed to harass the Democrats until they found it politically disadvantageous to continue their opposition to woman
suffrage.

At the time Paul organized the Congressional Union,
four million American women already possessed the vote,
and woman suffrage states made up one-quarter of the
electoral college. Paul wanted women to use their votes
to further woman suffrage. When the Democrats lost votes
because women refused to support them, she argued,
the party would change its position on suffrage. Eventually,
she hoped, both parties would be forced to compete for
women's votes, and in this way a federal amendment could
be achieved.

The NAWSA leaders disliked Paul's plan for a number
of reasons. Officials complained that since neither the
Democrats or the Republicans controlled the two-thirds
majority in Congress needed to pass a federal amendment,
the plan could not possibly work. In addition, Paul's program ran counter to the nonpartisan policy suffragists had
maintained since Reconstruction. Moreover, many suffragists considered it improper for women to use force, even
in the form of political pressure. As the group that would
purify politics, women had to win the vote in the same
moral, peaceful manner in which they planned to exercise
it. To make woman suffrage a party issue, in the eyes of
many NAWSA chapters, was to lower women and their
cause.

When Carrie Chapman Catt returned to power as president of the NAWSA in 1915, Alice Paul was expelled.
Along with other members of the Congressional Union—
among them Lucy Burns, Chrystal Eastman and Maud
Wood Park—Paul organized a new radical suffrage group.
The Women's Party was not a political party in the traditional sense. It had just one plank—winning the vote for all

American women. Paul and her followers planned to use activist tactics to force Congress to pass a woman suffrage amendment.

Carrie Catt also planned to press for a federal amendment. She hand-picked an executive board to lead and coordinate all state activities. Her goal was ratification of a federal amendment by 1920, but Catt believed that suffragists would first have to win several more Western states, at least one Southern state, and one Eastern state.

Thirty-six state suffrage associations pledged themselves to Catt's master plan. Some groups organized local campaigns. Some pressured legislators to support a federal amendment. Others worked building up the grass-roots support Catt knew would be needed to win ratification.[21] Catt's organizational genius was undeniable. Once she had centralized all the NAWSA's activities, her plan began to unfold exactly according to her predictions.

While Catt watched her strategy unfold, Alice Paul was taking direct action. During the 1916 presidential election campaign the Women's Party worked to defeat Wilson in woman suffrage states. As Paul explained, what mattered was not the outcome of the election, but that women demonstrate their potential political power.

> One thing we have to teach Mr. Wilson and his party—and all on-looking parties—is that the group which opposes national suffrage for women will lose women's support in twelve great commonwealths controlling nearly one hundred electoral votes; too large a fraction to risk.[22]

Peace was the major issue in the 1916 Wilson-Hughes race. The slogan among Democrats was, "Vote for Wilson; he kept us out of war." The Women's Party retorted, "Vote against Wilson; he kept us out of Suffrage."

With a membership of only fifty thousand (as compared to the two million in the NAWSA), the Women's Party campaigned vigorously against Wilson. One Women's Party campaigner, Inez Millholland, toured California day and night, sleeping only on trains. At a San Francisco rally she asked, "Mr. President, how long must women wait for liberty?" And with those words she collapsed and died from exhaustion. Memorial services for her were held throughout the country. Millholland's death, if nothing else, made people think about woman suffrage.

Wilson was reelected, carrying ten of the twelve equal suffrage states. In Illinois, however, the only state where votes were tallied by sex, women voted against Wilson by a ratio of two to one. An important goal had been accomplished—the Women's Party had forced politicians to notice women. Democrats put out as much campaign literature on suffrage as they did on peace.

With America's entry into the first World War the Women's Party stepped up its agitation. Members began picketing the White House. Day after day, around the clock, they stood in silent vigil outside the President's home. Their banners referred to "Kaiser Wilson" and proclaimed that "Democracy should begin at home." Repeatedly the Women's Party accused the administration of hypocrisy in fighting a war, allegedly to guarantee democratic principles abroad, while denying democratic rights to women at home.

Many politicians and much of the press attacked the Women's Party as unpatriotic and "militant." Mrs. H. O. P. Belmont, the rich New Yorker who had provided bail funds for working women during the Great Uprising in the garment industry and who was herself a member of the Women's Party, answered the charge.

> Militant? Why all this tenderness and delicacy about "militancy" in the form of banner-bearing when the Governments of all nations are conscripting their men, including our own nation, to be militant. . . . The sentimental ladies and gentlemen who are so afraid lest we fatigue the President are urged to remember that we ourselves are very, very tired, and perhaps some sentimentalists will confer some pity on the faithful women who have struggled three-quarters of a century for democracy in their own nation.[23]

The woman suffrage picketers remained in front of the White House protesting their unenfranchised state until the Wilson administration began to lose its nerve. After several months police began making arrests. At first the picketers—who had broken no law—were dismissed without sentence. When they returned to the picket lines, the courts began charging them with obstructing sidewalk traffic. Found guilty, the women were sentenced to the notorious Occaquan workhouse in Virginia.

In prison Alice Paul, Lucy Burns, Dorothy Day, and

others, borrowing the tactics of British suffragettes, demanded to be treated like political prisoners and went on a hunger strike. The authorities responded by force-feeding them. Alice Paul's hunger strike lasted for twenty-two days. Prison officials considered her insane and forced her to undergo a mental examination. The doctor reported, "This is a spirit like Joan of Arc, and it is useless to try to change it. She will die, but she will never give up."[24]

The maltreatment of imprisoned women was a mistake on the part of the authorities because it created great sympathy for the Women's Party and the cause of woman suffrage. When the courts invalidated all the arrests and convictions several months later, the imprisoned suffragists were acclaimed as heroines. Released from prison, they returned to the White House to resume their picketing.

Though some Congressmen denounced the tactics of the Women's Party and turned against the suffrage cause, the Rules Committee of the House, which for years had bottled up the suffrage amendment, brought it to the floor for debate. The Women's Party had forced the issue out into the open in Congress. In addition, the Party's demonstrations reinforced the right of Americans to free speech and free assembly—rights which some politicians were willing to abridge in wartime.

The NAWSA never participated in the White House picketing. The association did not defend the right of the Women's Party to picket, nor did it protest its members' treatment in prison. In fact, the NAWSA declared itself in no way affiliated with the party's actions. Carrie Chapman Catt, who was a frequent visitor of President Wilson at the White House, claimed instead that she was gradually gaining his active support for woman suffrage.

Unlike the Women's Party, which had many pacifist members, the NAWSA supported the war. Catt headed the women's committee of the National Manpower Board, which mobilized women for the war effort. She did not, however, repeat the feminists' mistake during the Civil War; war work, she declared, was important, but so was the fight for suffrage. NAWSA members did enough for the war effort to prove their patriotism, but the vote remained their primary objective.

By war's end the question was no longer whether women would win the vote but when. As victory drew near, however, organized opposition grew. Woman suffrage was said to be a radical plot. Racists claimed that woman suffrage would lead to the end of white supremacy. Liquor interests campaigned vigorously against suffrage on the grounds that votes for women were votes for prohibition. Northern political bosses, fearing the reformist spirit of suffragists, also worked to prevent women from winning the vote.

Antisuffrage forces were fairly ruthless in their tactics, bribing politicians, lying about the nature of the woman's movement, and producing scurrilous propaganda. In public, however, the "antis" hid behind a bland facade of a single-minded concern for the sanctity of the American home. Women, averred the "antis," did not need the vote, did not want the vote, could not handle the vote. One "anti" leaflet made the following appeal.

Housewives: You do not need the vote to wash out your sink spout. A handful of potash and some boiling water is quicker and cheaper. Good cooking lessens alcoholic craving quicker than a vote on a local option. Why vote for pure food laws when you can purify your ice box with saleratus water.[25]

One "anti" organization, the National Women's Organization to Oppose Suffrage, claiming to speak for a majority of women, insisted that the vote would be a burden on women. The group produced "evidence" that the suffrage movement was a Boshevik plot aimed at the nationalization of women. The NAWSA exposed this group as containing no women and, in fact, as being a front for liquor-industry moguls.

Suffragists matched the propaganda of the "antis" and held their own against the powerful interest groups. The painstaking work of the NAWSA and the dramatic demonstrations of the Women's Party had won over a majority of Americans. On January 10, 1918, Jeannette Rankin of Montana, the newly elected first woman representative in Congress, introduced the suffrage amendment onto the floor of the House.

The roll call was very close. A New York representative left the deathbed of his suffragist wife to cast his "yes" vote and then returned home to attend his wife's funeral. Another Congressman was carried in on a stretcher to vote for the amendment. The final tally was 274 in favor, 136 against—exactly one vote more than the required two-thirds.

It took another year and a half to win over the Senate. Then began the arduous task of achieving ratification. "Antis" made a last-ditch effort to block woman suffrage. Because the "antis" controlled the deep South, suffragists had to carry practically every other state in order to win ratification.

On August 26, 1920, the thirty-sixth state, Tennessee, ratified, twenty-four-year-old Harry Burns casting the deciding vote. His mother, a staunch suffragist, had sent him a telegram.

> "Hurrah! and vote for suffrage and don't keep them in doubt. . . . I've been watching to see how you stood but have noticed nothing yet. Don't forget to be a good boy and help Mrs. Catt put "Rat" in Ratification."[26]

Harry Burns voted yes, and woman suffrage was achieved after a seventy-two-year struggle. The NAWSA, continuing its nonpartisan stance, became the League of Women Voters. The Women's Party dedicated itself to seeking an Equal Rights Amendment to the Constitution which would guarantee the full equality of women before the law; nearly sixty years later American women were still fighting for it.

16

Flappers, Sex Objects, and Birth Control

By the time the vote was won, many women were active
participants in public life. Some had chosen to devote
themselves to suffrage, social work and reform. Others
had made their way into the male professions. Many had
chosen to remain single. Some of these women used what
they thought of as their moral superiority to men to justify their entry into public life. Once they had taken their
place outside the home, they established a way of life in
which their professional interests and their relationships
with other women were of primary concern.

Many of the young women who came of age in the
1910s and 1920s considered the price professional women
paid for their public life too high. Younger women did
not want to be like Jane Addams, satisfied with a public
life at the expense of marriage and a family. These younger women did not necessarily see themselves as part of a
community of women. The new generation rejected the
single life and the antisexual beliefs of the late Victorian
era as empty and old-fashioned.

One of the most passionate critics of women professionals was anarchist Emma Goldman (1896–1940).
Goldman believed that in gaining careers many women
had sacrificed much that was valuable—passion, sexual
intimacy, love for a man and for children.

The moral preoccupations of late Victorian professionals
and reformers seemed misguided to Goldman. She did not
believe that women had earned their place in the world
because they were more moral than men. Most important,
she held the single, celibate life on which many professional women prided themselves to be emotionally and
spiritually empty. "Our highly praised independence," she
wrote, "is after all, but a slow process of dulling and
stifling woman's nature, her love instinct, and her mother
instinct."[1]

Goldman understood the problems facing reformers
and professional women. She saw that the battles they

fought often consumed their emotional reserves. A professional woman, Goldman wrote, "is often compelled to exhaust all her energy, use up all her vitality, and strain every nerve in order to reach the market value." Even then, Goldman noted, the fight often ended in defeat. "Very few ever succeed, for it is a fact that women teachers, doctors, lawyers, architects, and engineers are neither met with the same confidence as their male colleagues, nor receive equal remuneration. And those that do reach that enticing equality generally do so at the expense of their physical and psychical well-being."[2]

Goldman did not believe that women could emancipate themselves merely by overcoming what she called "external tyrannies." "True emancipation," she wrote, "begins neither at the polls nor in the courts. It begins in woman's soul."[3] She urged women to break loose from the traditional ideas that restricted their ability to experience all life had to offer. In effect, she urged them to reclaim their sexuality. For Goldman emancipation meant being a woman in the most basic sense—free to be sexual and to love a man and yet not become a "subordinate or a slave" to husband and home.

Goldman believed woman's sexual difficulties to have a psychological basis. Because of the way most women were reared, they came to view sex as repulsive and frightening. To rid themselves of this deeply rooted view was not easy, but Goldman believed that until women were free of such attitudes, they could never achieve full emancipation. "Until woman has learned . . . to stand firmly on her own ground," wrote Goldman, "and insist upon her own unrestricted freedom, to listen to the voice of her own nature, whether it calls for life's greatest treasure, love for a man or her most glorious privilege, the right to give birth to a child, she cannot call herself emancipated. How many emancipated women are brave enough to acknowledge that the voice of love is calling, wildly beating against their breasts, demanding to be heard, to be satisfied."[4]

As far as Goldman was concerned, marriage only stood in the way of the kind of emancipation she sought for women. She saw the institution of marriage as an economic arrangement in which women traded their sexual favors and domestic labor for economic support. Marriage, she wrote, "condemns her [woman] to life-long dependency, to parasitism, to complete uselessness, individual as well as social." Because marriage infantilized women, Goldman doubted that love could be sustained within it. "Love," she wrote, "the freest and most powerful molder of human destiny, how can such an all compelling force be synonymous with that poor little State- and Church-begotten weed, marriage?"[5]

Goldman believed that sexuality was a driving creative force within each person. For her, the sexual spirit was the essence of freedom, daring, ambition. Its chief enemy was the state, which attempted to control, limit, and destroy the free individual. Anarchism was her remedy for overthrowing the old state and creating a new political structure in which the individual's essential self, his or her sexuality, would be unencumbered.

Not all anarchists agreed that the sexual question was part of their program. Goldman argued about sex with the aging father of Russian anarchism, Peter Kropotkin. Kropotkin did not agree that woman's enslavement was sexual. "When a woman is man's equal intellectually and shares his social ideal, she will be as free as he," Kropotkin asserted. Goldman disagreed, and when she failed to convince Kropotkin, she commented, "When I have reached your age the sex question may no longer be of importance to me. But it is now, and it is to thousands, millions even, of young people." Kropotkin is said to have been taken aback. He paused and replied, "Fancy, I didn't think of that."

Alix Kates Shulman, one of Goldman's biographers, has commented that the real issue was not Kropotkin's age, but his sex. Men, even radical men, failed to see what to Goldman was obvious—that women were victimized by archaic notions of sexuality. The society defined women almost exclusively by their sexual roles as wives and mothers, and yet the society refused to recognize that women, too, had sexual feelings. A man who visited a prostitute, Goldman noted, was quite acceptable; a woman who was a prostitute was a criminal. A man who had sexual affairs was tolerated and even admired; a woman who had affairs was liable to social ignominy, besides running the danger of conceiving a child.[6]

For herself Goldman sought a relationship with a man with whom she could share both her work and her sexual self. She had many affairs, several of which lasted for a number of years. Though she loved many men, she never found her ideal.

One of the most important relationships in Goldman's life was with Ed Brady, a German anarchist who came to America after serving a long prison sentence. Goldman met Brady when she was in her early twenties. He was nearly twenty years older, and it was he who taught her about sexual pleasure. Before she met Brady, Goldman wrote, "My own sex life had always left me dissatisfied, longing for something I did not know. . . . In the arms of Ed," she continued, "I learned for the first time the meaning of the great life-giving force. I understood its full beauty, and I eagerly drank its intoxicating joy and bliss. It was an ecstatic song, profoundly soothing by its music and perfume. My little flat . . . became a temple of love."[7]

Brady loved Goldman, but not her career. He shared her political convictions, but prison had worn him out. He wanted a quiet life, with her, with a family. "You are a typical mother, my little Emma," he told her. "Your tenderness is the greatest proof of it."[8]

Though Goldman desperately wanted to have a child, she had decided against motherhood. Several years earlier, when a doctor had told her that she would need a minor operation before she would be able to conceive, she had decided against the surgery. She never changed her mind, but she was never totally comfortable with her choice. Ed's wish for a family stirred her. "I could only tell him again of my love . . . of my longing to give him much of what he craved." But she was too afraid. "My starved motherhood," she wrote, "was that the main reason for my idealism?" It was impossible, she believed, for a woman to combine the roles of mother and activist. "I had silenced the voice of the child for the sake of the universal, the all-absorbing passion of my life." It appeared to her that there was an injustice at work. "Men were consecrated to ideals and yet were fathers of children. But man's physical share in the child is only a moment's; woman's part is for years—years of absorption in one human being to the exclusion of the rest of humanity. I would never give up the one for the other."[9]

Goldman and Brady stayed together for seven years, but their relationship was troubled by their different needs. In the end both were bitterly disappointed. Brady came to view Goldman's career as his enemy. "Your interest in the movement," he told her, "for which you are willing to break up our life, is nothing but vanity, nothing but your craving for applause and glory and the limelight. You are incapable of a deep feeling. You have never understood or appreciated the love I have given you." She in turn came to view Brady as an egotist with what she called "the man's instinct of possession, which brooks no deity except himself."[10]

When she finally left him, it was with anger and defiance.

> Under the pretext of a great love you have done your utmost to chain me to you. To rob me of all that is more precious to me than life. You are not content with binding my body, you want also to bind my spirit. First the movement and my friends—now it's the books I love [Brady had ridiculed the work of Nietzsche]. You want to tear me away from them. You're rooted in the old. Very well, remain there! But don't imagine you will hold me to it. You are not going to clip my wings, you shan't stop my flight. I'll free myself even if it means tearing you out of my heart.[11]

Goldman's beliefs were shared by some intellectuals and radicals in the years before the First World War. It was this small group which first discussed Sigmund Freud's important ideas about human sexuality and its effects on identity. Only after the war, however, did an entire generation of American young people rebel and attempt to rid the society of nineteenth-century attitudes toward sexuality. This generation used the ideas about sexuality generated by Freud and popularized by radicals such as Goldman as the starting point of a social revolution against American sexual morals and manners.

What the young people of the 1920s sought to achieve was to tear the cloak of shame and hypocrisy from sexual behavior and from public discussion of sex. Their most basic belief was that sex was natural and "good," while repressive nineteenth-century attitudes toward sex were unnatural and "bad." Artists of this generation (Ernest Hemingway and F. Scott Fitzgerald were probably the most influential) attempted to discuss sexual experience in realistic terms.

Few of the young people who promulgated the sexual

revolution of the 1920s were political radicals, although a fair number considered themselves socialists. The women of this group were all concerned with "the woman question," but in a very different way than suffragists and reformers. Even as they called themselves feminists, they also called themselves New Women. Like Emma Goldman, they believed that woman's emancipation depended upon sexual liberation.

After the first World War many of the young women in the forefront of the sexual revolution congregated in New York City. They were among the first American women to leave home, take apartments, work for a living, and attempt to be truly self-sufficient. Like men, these women claimed the right to enjoy sexual affairs without committing themselves to marriage.

Many of them were naive about the obstacles they faced. They thought that it would be easy to be free —to have beautiful love affairs and stimulating careers. They wanted romantic fulfillment above all, but they did not want it to interfere with their independence. Marriage, many declared, was a trap into which their mothers had fallen, and they vowed never to make the same mistake.

Even the most free-thinking men were often bewildered by the independence these young women demanded. Floyd Dell, the socialist, writer, and male feminist who lived in New York's Greenwich Village, captured this confusion in many of his stories. In a volume entitled *Love in Greenwich Village,* Dell told the story of a young man, a novelist, who falls in love quite against his will with his poetry-writing neighbor, June. Paul has budgeted every cent in order to take a year to write his novel, but when he falls in love, he is willing to give it all up. He asks June to marry him, knowing it will mean going back to a conventional job. But she refuses.

> I don't want to be anybody's wife. I want to write poetry. . . . That must come first always. And so I mustn't try to be a wife to anyone. It's terribly nice for you to ask me to be. . . . And what you say is true. It would be pleasant to be taken care of, and all that; but I'll have to take my chances. Oh, I know I would be happy being your wife. But that's just what I'm afraid of.[12]

The most adventurous women were hungry for experience rather than commitment. Virginity, which had once

been a young woman's most treasured asset, became a
hindrance, something to be discarded so the New Woman
could go ahead with living. The journalist Dorothy
Thompson, who was to become a famous columnist in
the 1930s, was on assignment in Italy in 1919 when she
wrote to a friend, lamenting her virginity. "I want to
stay forever under these gleaming skies. The only thing I
miss in Italy is a lover. To be 27 and loverless in Italy is
a crime against God and man." In Genoa, Thompson met
an Italian leftist, Guiseppe Guilietti. "I was tremendously
aware of him physically every moment I was with him
and felt that he wanted me to be. I noticed every detail
of his person. The way his hair grows." They were separated before anything could come of the attraction.
Thompson mentioned the disappointment in her diary.
"I knew that I should never have resisted him. . . . I'm
not even glad to be saved."[13]

The highest goals of the sexual revolution in the 1920s
were not achieved. It did not lead to a rejection of the
double standard; for women sexual activity outside of
marriage remained highly illicit. Relatively few young
women in the 1920s dared to live openly with their lovers. Affairs had to be kept secret from family, employers,
landlords, and even friends. Marriage alone legitimized
woman's sexuality. Dorothy Thompson, for example, married her first lover rather than live with him because she
did not want her "reputation" tarnished.

SEXY, NOT SEXUAL

While the double standard remained intact, a number
of fundamental changes in the attitude toward female
sexuality did occur in the 1920s. Most significant was the
idea that women by their very nature were sexual and
that they should show their sexuality by looking "sexy."

A new, consciously "sexy" look in women's clothing
became popular, along with a new way for women to be-
have. Women who adopted the new style were called
flappers. They wore their skirts short and left their arms
bare, applied bright red lipstick and tweezed their eye-
brows. Their bodies were slim.

When the flapper first made her appearance in the early 1920s, it seemed to many Americans that the total
emancipation of women was finally at hand. Critics of the
flapper found her morally reprehensible. Supporters ap-

plauded her straightforwardness, her lack of Victorian sentimentality, her daring. Critics and supporters agreed that she was the product of seventy-five years of feminist agitation. She was the new American woman who could vote.

The flapper did accomplish some goals conventional feminists had failed to achieve. Flappers rid themselves of many of the uncomfortable accoutrements of nineteenth-century "femininity." They wore their hair "bobbed" short. They threw out their corsets—though now they bound their breasts to make themselves look flat. In general they insisted upon comfortable clothing in which they could move freely and be athletic.

The flapper's emancipation was often more apparent than real. While more physically comfortable than the old, the new style was in some ways simply a new standard of conformity. While before women had to look pure, now they had to look sexy. They had to wear make-up and the right clothing. Frederick Lewis Allen discovered that before 1920 only two firms in the cosmetic business paid federal income tax. In 1927, 18,000 cosmetic enterprises paid taxes. According to Allen, in the year 1929 the average American woman bought one full pound of face powder and eight separate rouge compacts.[14]

The movement that began as an attempt to liberate the sexuality of women ended with women seeing themselves and being seen by men as sexual objects. What the flapper's "freedom" really signified was an escalation in the war to attract men. To be socially acceptable, to be attractive, to win a husband, to keep a husband, women had to look sexy, free, and available.

But they were not supposed to be available until after they married. Before that occasion women were still expected to fend off the ardent attentions of their beaux. After marriage they were expected to respond enthusiastically to the sexual attention paid them. Many found the transition demanded of them—from alluring but unavailable girlfriend to sexual wife—a difficult one.

Doctors, social scientists, even clergymen agreed that a happy sex life was essential to a healthy marriage. Despite this consensus, almost nothing was written for women or by women explaining in realistic terms how a satisfying sex life in marriage could be achieved.

Women were led to believe that if they married for

love, sexual fulfillment would simply follow. Many women were disappointed, and no wonder—women and men were often ignorant of even the most basic sexual facts. The early discussion of woman's sexual experience was couched in romanticism. Many women still had little sense that they had a sexuality of their own. For these women, as in the nineteenth-century, sex was something they "gave" their husbands—but now they were supposed to enjoy it too.

BIRTH CONTROL

The public discussion of sexuality that took place in the 1910s and 1920s went hand in hand with a growing awareness of birth control. Emma Goldman was one of the first to speak out on the topic.

Goldman recognized that without effective birth control there could be no true sexual freedom for women. The fear of pregnancy inhibited the sexual pleasure of both married and single women. Goldman's efforts prior to the First World War to raise the issue of birth control led to the formation of a highly organized birth-control movement in the 1920s. This movement ultimately made it possible for women to enjoy sex without fear.

Few contraceptive methods were available when Goldman began lecturing on birth control in the years just before the war. Condoms, douching, and withdrawal were all she could offer, and the latter two methods were not particularly effective. Nevertheless, Goldman's discussion of birth control was extremely important. Prior to her lectures most members of her audience were ignorant of even these far from ideal methods. The most widely practiced birth-control procedure was illegal abortion.

It is generally believed that before 1973, when the United States Supreme Court handed down its decision on abortion, at least one million women a year underwent illegal abortions. Between five and ten thousand women are believed to have died each year from the effects of improperly performed abortions.[15] These figures are only for the twentieth century, when other methods of effective birth control existed. It is impossible to estimate how many pregnancies were aborted and how many women died before 1900.

Abortion is a fairly simple procedure, but one requiring great skill. Before the advent of the vacuum aspirator, a curettage or sharp instrument was inserted into the uterus and used to scrape the fetus from the uterine wall. If the curettage pierced the uterus, the woman bled to death. If the instruments were not sterile, a fatal infection often set in.

The more money a woman had, the more likely she was to be able to afford a skilled abortionist. Poor women often attempted to abort themselves. Many of the methods used—folk remedies, charms, patent medicines—were harmless and ineffective. Other methods, however, were both ineffective and dangerous. Sterility, severe illness, and death could be the result of women's inserting coat hangers, shoe hooks, and knitting needles inside themselves. Others douched with deadly soap solutions, which were fatal if they entered the blood stream.

Goldman hoped that birth control would provide women with an alternative to abortion. More important, she expected that birth control would enable women to control their own sexuality. Once women could control whether and when they would have children, Goldman recognized, they could begin to free themselves from their dependence on and domination by men. When Goldman was jailed for giving the first public demonstration of contraceptives, one reporter wrote, "Emma Goldman has been arrested for saying that women need not always keep their mouths shut and their wombs open."

Margaret Sanger, the woman who organized the American birth-control movement, first learned about contraception from Goldman. She played a major role in transforming public attitudes toward contraception from a gutter topic unmentionable in polite society to recognition of birth control as a major public health issue with profound political and economic significance.

Emma Goldman's experiences as a midwife had exposed her to the desperate need of the poor for birth control; in the same way Margaret Sanger had become aware of the situation through her experiences as a nurse. During the early 1910s, when Sanger worked on New York's Lower East Side, one case in particular became a symbol for her of the plight of poor women.

Twenty-eight-year-old Mrs. Sadie Sacks was the pregnant mother of three young children. Her husband, a truck driver, earned a very small wage. Mrs. Sacks attempted to abort herself and became seriously ill with an infection. Sanger cared for Mrs. Sacks for three weeks, and the young mother recovered. During her convalescence Mrs. Sacks asked Sanger how she could prevent becoming pregnant again. Sanger passed her question on to the attending doctor. His answer was typical of what the medical establishment then had to offer women. "Tell Jake [Mrs. Sacks' husband] to sleep on the roof." Three months later Sanger was called back to the Lower East Side. Mrs. Sacks was in a coma following another attempt to abort herself, and she died ten minutes after Sanger's arrival.[16]

Like Goldman, Sanger believed that female emancipation began with a woman's control of her own body. Like Goldman, too, Sanger first presented birth control as a free-speech issue. In her view, the most urgent need was to establish the right of birth-control advocates to write and speak openly on the subject. Once this right had been won, she expected that "experts" would use the public forum to educate women in birth control. Women would then "treat" themselves, buying or preparing at home whatever contraceptive suited their needs. In her early view, doctors had nothing to do with birth control.[17]

By 1915 Sanger had found a new mentor, the scientist and sexologist Havelock Ellis, and a new way of looking at birth control. Ellis trained Sanger in methods of medical research and aided her in the search for advanced contraceptive techniques. It was Ellis who sent Sanger to Holland, where the diaphragm was being dispensed in state-run birth control clinics.

The Mensinga diaphragm, which came in fourteen sizes, was inserted by a woman inside her body. In Dutch clinics each client was examined by a medical worker before she was individually fitted for a diaphragm. The internal examination also often led to the early diagnosis of gynecological problems, thus reducing the maternal death rate.

By using the diaphragm, the Dutch had cut their maternal death rate in half. Along with early detection of illness, the proper spacing of pregnancies was a major reason for the decline. Previously Sanger had been concerned with the number of babies born to a woman. Now she realized that a woman who might not survive the physical rigors of four pregnancies and births in four years might do very well by spacing four births over a ten-year period. After visiting the Netherlands, Sanger came to regard

contraception as a medical issue. She was also convinced
that the diaphragm was the "ideal" contraceptive for
which she had been searching. Not only was it safe and
effective but, unlike the condom, it gave women, rather
than men, control over contraceptive procedures. Since
pregnancy and birth affected a woman's body, not a man's,
Sanger believed that it was important for women, not men,
to be in control of preventing conception.

In 1917, back in New York, Sanger established a clinic
where physicians dispensed diaphragms to poor women.
This first clinic was quickly shut down by the New York
City Police Department, and Sanger and her sister, Mrs.
Ethel Byrne, were indicted for dispensing "obscene" ma-
terials.

Mrs. Byrne was tried first, found guilty and sentenced to
thirty days in prison. Eventually she went on a spectacular
hunger strike, refusing food and drink. After 103 hours she
was weak and very ill. Sanger, who was free pending trial,
did a good deal of press agentry on her sister's behalf. For
days Mrs. Byrne was on the front page of many newspapers. The public became more and more aroused to the
injustice of the case. Finally, with the help of the birth-
control movement's new socially prominent friends, Sanger
won a governor's pardon for her sister. After Mrs. Byrne's
release, Sanger was tried, convicted and served her thirty
days without protest.

During the 1920s the birth-control movement in New
York was able to take advantage of a small but important
legal victory. The New York obscenity law banned the
distribution of birth control material except for the preven-
tion of disease. The "disease" lawmakers had in mind was
venereal disease which could be prevented through the use
of a condom, but the law did not specifically refer to that
device. A liberal interpretation established the birth-control
movement's right to dispense diaphragms to women for
whom pregnancy represented a health hazard.

Sanger established a new clinic in New York City under
the direction first of Dr. Dorothy Bocker and later of Dr.
Hanah Stone. The Clinical Research Bureau (CRB)
stayed within the law, dispensing contraceptives only to
women whose medical histories ruled out another pregnancy. Other women were referred to private doctors who
were sympathetic to the movement.

Drs. Bocker and Stone amassed the first accurate statistical information on contraceptive techniques. By publishing their findings in medical journals, they were gradually able to win the medical establishment over to the side of contraception. Throughout the 1920s, however, many doctors continued to preach abstinence as the only moral and reliable form of contraception.

Ironically, though legally permitted to dispense contraceptives, the CRB was unable to legally obtain them; a federal law still banned the importation of contraceptive devices. Because Sanger and others were forced to smuggle diaphragms into the United States from abroad, only a relatively small number of women could be served. Not until 1936 did a federal court throw out the import ban, ruling that doctors could prescribe birth control for whatever reasons they saw fit.

Until the development of the birth control pill in the late 1950s, the diaphragm, reinforced with spermacidal jelly, was the preferred method of contraception within the birth control movement. Clinics established by Planned Parenthood (as the movement came to be known) dispensed diaphragms, as did public health centers. (Because of widespread fears about the long-range effect of the pill, the diaphram is making a significant comeback in the late 1970s.) Though the diaphragm used with the jelly is an extremely effective contraceptive—experts believe it to be 95 percent safe when used properly—it presented problems for many women.

Some women disliked inserting the diaphragm. The diaphragm, and particularly the spermacidal jelly used with it, is messy. For women living without running water—as many did in the 1920s, 1930s and 1940s—the diaphragm was very inconvenient. Then, too, many women distrusted the device. They found it difficult to understand how it worked. Researchers have discovered that until a woman has an accurate understanding of how conception takes place, she is liable to misuse the diaphragm or use it only occasionally.

Margaret Sanger and other leaders of the birth-control movement tended to be insensitive to the effect of these attitudes on the use of the device.[18] Sanger had begun her birth control crusade hoping to make contraceptives available to the poor, but the movement was extremely slow in achieving this goal. In fact, not until the 1960s were many poor, working-class and nonwhite Americans served by birth-control organizations.

Following the Second World War, sociologist Lee Rainwater was commissioned by Planned Parenthood to find out why blue-collar families were less likely than families of the middle class to use contraception effectively. In talking with working-class wives, Rainwater learned that their attitudes differed markedly from those of middle-class women. The poorer women did not feel that they had control over their lives or over the future. The idea of controlling conception was therefore not one they could accept comfortably.[19] For many working-class people the condom was a better form of birth control than the diaphragm. It was easy to understand, and those using it did not have to plan ahead. One of Sanger's critics has suggested that the birth control movement could have better served poor and working-class women and men by carrying out massive public-education programs in their neighborhoods and then dispensing the condom. Such, however, was not the case.

While poor women most often were not served at all by birth control, middle-class women were often served poorly. During the 1930s Sanger used the resources of what had become a large national birth-control movement in a futile attempt to persuade Congress to pass a law favoring birth control. Emphasis on lobbying in Washington detracted from local public-education programs. Many women still did not know that birth control was available. For those who did, contraception information often did relatively little to help clarify any confusion they might have about sex.

Doctors were part of the problem. Many physicians were as ignorant about sex and just as embarrassed by it as were their patients. A 1930 survey of seventy-five grade-A medical schools in the nation found that only thirteen of them offered courses on contraception. Fewer still offered courses on sexuality.

One woman, a twenty-one-year-old bride in 1941, recalled that prior to her wedding she had asked her doctor if there were any information she should have. The physician seemed uncomfortable and told her if she had any questions after her honeymoon, he would answer them then. When the young woman returned from her wedding trip, she discovered, much to her consternation, that she was pregnant. About her first year of marriage she later commented, "It was awful. We had no time to get to know one another. We didn't have much money. I had grown up so sheltered by my mother. I wasn't prepared for a baby. I swear if I had had anywhere to go that first year, I would have left him."

After the birth of her first child, it was a woman friend, not a doctor, who told the young mother about birth control. She was fitted for a diaphragm, which she used for the next twenty years. She had two more children and one miscarriage. One of the pregnancies was planned, the others were "accidents." Later, when the pill became available, she switched to it.[20]

THE FREUDIAN MYTH

In the decades following the 1920s the idea that women were sexual beings was no longer controversial. Women were also beginning to have access to contraceptive devices. If the kinds of birth control available were not ideal, they did give women more control over their bodies than they had ever had before.

Birth control and the recognition of female sexuality were significant events—but they did not lead to sexual emancipation for women. The ideas about female sexuality and personality that became accepted in the 1930s and 1940s were nearly as destructive as the Victorian ideas they replaced.

Sigmund Freud was then the most powerful authority on the proper female sexual response. Freud's belief that men and women are equally endowed with sexual energy had abetted the overthrow of Victorian morality. Freud's theory of female sexual development, however, placed women in another bind.

Freud believed that women were "anatomically inferior" to men. Girls, he maintained, experienced a sense of loss and envy when they discovered that they lacked the male sexual organ. Females could overcome their feelings of "inferiority" when they reached adulthood, said Freud—but only by embracing their roles as wives and mothers. By giving birth to a son, Freud wrote, a woman came as close as possible to resolving her sense of anatomical inferiority.

While Freud was never entirely satisfied with his understanding of female development, many of his disciples in the psychoanalytic community and the popularizers who presented his work to the public at large accepted his theories without question. By the late 1930s Freudian thinking about women pervaded nearly all levels of American culture. Women did not need to seek psychoanalysis to be affected. Books, magazines, movies, and plays all spouted popularized and often bastardized versions of Freud.

Followers of Freud developed his sexual ideas into a rigid theory of female personality. Helen Deutsch, in her influential work, *The Psychology of Women,* claimed that women who viewed themselves as other than passive were suffering from "masculinity complexes." Deutsch's description of "feminine-passive" and "masculine-active"[21] personalities harkened back to the nineteenth-century sphere theory. It is therefore not surprising that the most extreme Freudians recommended a return to nineteenth-century domesticity. In 1947 psychiatrist Marynia Farnham and sociologist Ferdinand Lundberg published a popularized work entitled *Modern Woman: The Lost Sex,* in which they argued that the desire of a woman to be anything more than a wife and mother as "the desire for the impossible, a desire to be a man."[22]

Such misguided Freudian thinking about female sexuality and personality created many conflicts for women. For example, on the one hand women were told that they were sexual and that their ability to experience sexual pleasure was a hallmark of mental health. On the other they were told that there was only one right form of sexual response and that those women who did not conform to it were "immature" and hadn't made the transition into "true femininity." This misinformation left many women feeling that they were abnormal. Most women's experience did not conform to psychoanalytic theories.

Freud's theories about female sexual development were remarkably influential, and women were often hesitant to discuss the binds in which they found themselves. Many women and a number of men realized that the passive behavior pattern authorized by the Freudians did not match up with reality. Nevertheless, Freudianism remained the accepted public ideology about woman's sexuality and personality. Not until the publication of Masters and Johnson's extensive research on female sexuality and the resurgence of the feminist movement in the 1960s did women in numbers begin to talk about the reality of their lives and feelings.

17

Don't Steal a Job from a Man

The nineteenth-century pattern of discrimination against working women continued into the twentieth century. Women workers were poorly paid, segregated in "female" jobs, and treated as temporary workers by employers, unions, and the public. This discrimination persisted despite the new and larger place women filled in the labor force.

Between 1920 and 1940 the numbers and kinds of women who worked remained fairly stable. Twenty-five percent of American women held paying jobs; most of these working women were young and single. Women did not stay in their old domestic and factory jobs, however. By 1930 a young woman looking for work was more likely to become a secretary, a file clerk, a saleswoman, a waitress, or a hairdresser than a housemaid or factory seamstress.

After the First World War the white-collar and service sector of the economy expanded rapidly. At the same time with the passage of restrictive immigration laws in the 1920s, businesses could no longer count on a steady stream of new immigrants to fill their labor needs. Businesses turned to women, the largest available reserve of labor, and recruited them for work in new white-collar occupations.

One of the most profound changes for working women was the feminization of office work. New technology eased women's entrance into the office. Like the textile loom and sewing machine, the telephone and typewriter were considered "women's machines." By 1902 the Bell system, which was founded in 1876, employed 37,000 women switchboard operators as compared to 2,500 men.[1] When Phil Remington introduced the typewriter to the public in 1873, he hired women demonstrators. Called typewriters themselves, the women created a sensation. Business firms that bought the machines wanted the women operators as well.

Before the invention of the typewriter and the telephone the office had been a male domain. Male clerks handled correspondence, kept the books, and received visitors. When women were hired in offices, clerical work was restructured, and its status declined.

Women were offered and accepted lower pay than that given to men. They were assigned the more routine, less responsible jobs, while male clerks were promoted to new managerial positions. Male clerks were able to turn their specialties into professions, becoming accountants, efficiency experts, personnel managers, and junior executives.[2] Women were typists, stenographers, file clerks, receptionists; those who combined all these skills were personal secretaries.

Women worked for men but not with them. Secretarial pools, reception and switchboard areas, billing and credit departments were all filled with women. Male executives were usually out of sight, in the inner offices, guarded from the public and served by the army of women workers. In 1935 *Fortune* magazine offered a picture of the typical office.

> The male is the name on the door, the hat on the coat rack, the smoke in the corner room. But the male is not the office. The office is the competent woman at the other end of the buzzer, the two young ladies chanting his name monotonously into the mouthpieces of a kind of gutta-percha halter, the four girls in the glass coop pecking out his initials with pink fingernails on keyboards of four voluble machines, the half dozen assorted skirts whisking through the filing cases of his correspondence, and the elegant miss in the reception room recognizing his friends and disposing of his antipathies with the pleased voice and the impersonal eye of a presidential consort.[3]

Frequently office jobs were monotonous and mechanical. Large companies adopted assembly-line procedures. In the 1920s Commonwealth Edison stationed eighty girls along a line processing information.

> Orders are passed along by means of a belt and lights from a chief clerk to a series of checkers and typists, each of whom does one operation. The girl at the head of the line interprets the orders, puts down the number and indicates the trade discount; the second girl prices the order, takes off the discount, adds the carriage charges and totals; the third girl gives the order a number and makes a daily record; the fourth girl puts this information on an

alphabetical index; the fifth girl time-stamps it; it next goes along the belt to one of several typists, who makes a copy in septuplicate and puts on address labels; the seventh girl checks it and sends it to the storeroom.[4]

Office and sales work did not earn a woman a living wage any more than factory work had. Most single women in the job force in the 1920s and 1930s, like factory women of the preceding generation, were helping to support their families. Two out of three gave all their earnings to their parents and then received an allowance for personal expenses. Practically all lived at home and paid for room and board. "Women's so-called pin money," wrote Mary Anderson, head of the Women's Bureau of the Labor Department, "is often the only means of holding the family together."[5]

The married women in the job force usually needed wages even more desperately. Most of the 11.7 percent of wives who worked in 1930 (28 percent of all working women) were married to men whose incomes were below the poverty line. Primarily black or foreign born, they worked as domestics or operatives in garment and canning factories. A Women's Bureau study summarized the situation of women in the labor force.

A vicious circle is set up. Unemployment or low wages of men make it necessary for their wives, mothers, and daughters to go to work. . . . Women who have jobs feel they must keep them at any wage . . . largely unorganized, practically unskilled and victims of a tradition that places less value on women's work than men's, women workers haven't been able to do much toward removing unfair differentials that exist to their disadvantage and to men's advantage.[6]

THE GREAT DEPRESSION

The Great Depression compounded the problems of working women. When the stock market crashed in 1929, blue-collar men in heavy industry were the first to lose their jobs, followed by women who worked in food plants and in garment and textile factories. "Each morning it was the same story," wrote one female textile worker. "Where shall I go? This mill is slowing down, that mill is laying off girls. It just seems as if there was no place for me to go. This last year about 20 mills have gone out of business, making it impossible to get any kind of job at all."[7]

Women in white-collar office and sales occupations were able to hang on to their jobs for a while, but by the early 1930s they too suffered heavy lay-offs. Once out of work, it took women longer to get their jobs back or to find new ones. At the end of the Depression decade, more women than men were unemployed.

Though jobs were very scarce, the number of working wives increased from 11.7 percent to 15.2 percent during the Depression; this was the largest increase since the first decade of the twentieth century, when immigrant wives had gone to work in factories. Married women joined the work force during the Depression because their husbands had been laid off or had suffered salary cuts. Yet they were accused of stealing jobs from men, and they faced job discrimination when they went looking for work.

In some occupations the employment of married women was actually prohibited. Twenty-six states had laws prohibiting the employment of married women. Between 1932 and 1937 the federal government forbade more than one member of a family from working in civil service. Designed to combat nepotism, the law in effect discriminated exclusively against women. The majority of the nation's schools, 43 percent of public utilities, and thirteen percent of department stores refused to hire wives.[8]

Married women sought work anyway, trying to earn what they could to keep their families afloat. Many took off their wedding bands and pretended to be single.

Black women had been poor before the Depression, and they grew poorer during it. In 1932 an appalling 56 percent of blacks were jobless. When they applied for relief, they were turned away or offered only a fraction of the amount granted to whites. In the South blacks faced starvation and terror. Lynchings nearly doubled as white men began violently seizing black men's jobs.

During the First World War, when prosperous war industries had attracted southern rural blacks to northern cities, the North had seemed a place for better jobs and a better life. The Depression destroyed that hope. In urban ghettos blacks were "reduced to living below street level. . . . Packed into damp rat-ridden dungeons, they existed in squalor not too different from that of the Arkansas sharecropper." In the North and the South black women did what they had always done to keep their families alive. They worked as maids, cooks and laundresses. During the 1930s southern black domestics averaged $6.17 for a 66-hour week. Black laundresses were known to do a day's wash in exchange for lunch and a dress or a week's wash for 50 cents.[9]

For America's farm families the economic disaster was compounded by natural disaster. In the summer of 1930 a terrible drought dried up land all the way from Virginia to Arkansas. Tens of thousands of farm families and sharecroppers, having lost their land or their leases, took to the road, joining the migrant workers who followed the seasonal crops.

Middle-class professional women suffered their share of unemployment during the Depression. Barnard College reported that only one-third of the class of 1932 who sought jobs found them. Deans at numerous colleges advised women graduates not to try for careers.[10]

During the 1920s women seemed to be making advances in the professions. The proportion of women professional workers increased from 11.9 percent to 14.2 percent. Only a handful, however, became doctors, lawyers, architects, engineers, scientists, or business executives. Men in business and the professions were unwilling to share their position with women. In the period 1925–1945 American medical schools placed a 5 percent quota on female admissions. In the 1920s Columbia and Harvard law schools still excluded women applicants, and until 1937 so did the New York City Bar Association.[11]

Women who wanted careers ended up where they had always been—in nursing and teaching. During the Depression they found it difficult to get jobs even in these traditional fields. Teaching jobs for women almost disappeared when thousands of men applied for the open positions.

The New Deal

President Franklin Roosevelt's New Deal promised to restore the good life by putting the nation back to work. Working-class women benefited from protective-labor legislation and union organizing drives. Middle-class women carved a place for themselves in FDR's social-welfare administration. On the whole, however, the New Deal was not new enough to significantly alter women's second-class economic status. At the end of the 1930s women still lacked equality with men in the labor force.

Several New Deal laws gave the federal government the unprecedented right to regulate wages and hours for both men and women. The National Industrial Recovery Act (NIRA) of 1933 established industry-wide codes; the Walsh Healy Act of 1936 abolished child labor and set standards for workers in industries holding sizable federal contracts; the Fair Labor Standards Act of 1938, which also abolished homework in most industries, applied the same principle to workers in jobs related to interstate commerce.

Before the New Deal, protective legislation had been directed primarily at women. Though the laws sought to regulate the worst abuses of sweatshop labor, they also singled out women as a special sex in need of separate but not necessarily equal treatment. The precedent of protective labor legislation for women was established in the 1908 case of *Muller* vs. *Oregon*. Louis Brandeis successfully argued that women's working hours needed to be regulated to protect their health. "Woman has always been dependent upon man," read the deciding brief. "Her physical structure and a proper discharge of her maternal functions . . . justify legislation to protect her from the greed as well as the passion of men."[12] The result of this and subsequent labor laws was often to exclude rather than protect women. Employers who were unwilling to hire women could refuse to meet the standards set by the law; they could claim that a job involved night work or heavy lifting.

FDR's administration tried to equalize protective labor legislation, but in the end the equality went only halfway. One out of every four industry codes permitted women to receive a lower minimum wage than men. These were precisely the industries that employed the largest numbers of women.

Women at the very bottom of the economic ladder —laundry workers, seamstresses, textile operatives—received more equitable wages as a result of the minimum-wage statutes. But poor enforcement and resistance by state governments to federal regulations weakened the New Deal. In 1939 twenty-one states still had no minimum-wage laws for women, twenty-nine did not regulate homework, and thirty lacked eight-hour-workday laws.[13]

The revival of the labor movement during the 1930s was another instance of working women making limited gains. The ILGWU launched a massive organizing drive in the garment industry in 1930. Black, Hispanic, and Oriental garment workers were unionized for the first time, and by the end of the decade the union claimed it had increased membership by 300 percent to 800,000 workers.

Women deserved much of the credit for the ILGWU's revival. But once again they were not given their due. In 1940 three out of four ILGWU members were women, but only one woman served on the twenty-four-member executive board. Both the ILGWU and the Amalgamated Clothing Workers, another largely female union, signed contracts permitting unequal pay for men and women.

The formation of the Congress of Industrial Workers (CIO) promised unions for women who had never before been organized. The CIO proposed industrial unions, the kind started by the Wobblies. For the IWW industrial unionism had been a step in a revolutionary struggle to abolish capitalism. The less radical CIO, which did not oppose capitalism, was supported by workers in the big industries—automobiles, steel, electrical appliances, and textiles.

In the textile industry, where women made up 40 percent of the work force, the CIO won a victory over the reactionary United Textile Workers, the AFL union that had opposed the Lawrence strike and refused to represent unskilled women. During the 1930s hundreds of thousands of mill hands joined the CIO's Textile Workers Union of America (TWUA). But in the South, where much of the textile industry had relocated, the union was defeated. Southern bosses ignored New Deal labor laws, fired union members, evicted them from company housing, and hired vigilantes to break strikes. In 1939 the TWUA represented less than 10 percent of Southern mill hands.[14] As late as the 1970s women in Southern textile plants were still struggling to form unions.

The unequal treatment and lack of attention women received from unions that agreed to represent them continued throughout the twentieth century. Jean Tepperman, who wrote about her experiences working in two factories in 1968, described what the "union" meant to her women coworkers.

"Union" is an office where some men in suits work. Your relationship to that union is like car insurance. It is compulsory for you to pay a certain amount of money each year to these people. You do it because you are forced to and also because you have a vague feeling that without it you would be even worse off. . . .

At Mary Ann [another factory], people felt more positive toward the union because it got them more money. On the other hand the main grievance people talked about was the unfair way of assigning tasks, and that was never considered a problem that the union would have anything to do with.[15]

During the New Deal middle-class professional women became involved in politics again. FDR's administration summoned to Washington scores of women reformers whose work had been eclipsed after the 1920 woman suffrage victory. Members of the Women's Trade Union League, the Consumers League, and the League of Women Voters, old-time suffragists, settlement workers, and trade-union women and younger journalists and politicos became advisers to and administrators of New Deal social-welfare programs. No one was more instrumental in helping women make a place for themselves in politics and government than Eleanor Roosevelt. Most women New Dealers thought of her as their "resident lobbyist."[16]

Eleanor Roosevelt saw herself as a social activist, and during her stay in Washington she greatly influenced public policy. Her political convictions, more liberal than FDR's, favored the New Deal's responding to the needs of many groups who had been overlooked by the federal government—blacks and other ethnic minorities, women, unskilled workers.

"I was not," Eleanor Roosevelt remarked later in life, "what you would call a 'yes man,' because that was not what he [FDR] needed."[17] The greatest danger facing her husband as President, she felt, was that he would never hear the truth. She made it her business to be FDR's "listening post," "roving ambassador," and "spur." She toured the country repeatedly, surveying conditions in the coal mines and migrant camps, talking to farmers, the unemployed and minorities. At the White House, she prodded her husband to provide programs for the poor and unemployed.

Eleanor Roosevelt was a consummate politician. At least part of her success as a liberal reformer stemmed from her understanding of party politics and her ability to use the system. "Get into the game and stay in it," she advised women reformers. "Throwing mud from the outside won't help. Building up from the inside will." In the 1936 reelection campaign she worked closely with Molly Dewson, head of the Women's Division of the Democratic Party, helping women to win 50 percent representation on the Democratic platform committee.

One of the most controversial aspects of Mrs. Roosevelt's stay in the White House was her insistence on maintaining a career of her own. She wrote books and a syndicated newspaper column, she lectured and gave radio broadcasts. Because she was paid for this work, she was accused of commercializing the role of First Lady. Eleanor Roosevelt took a different view. She was, she said, more than the wife of the President; she was also a professional woman with activities and opinions of her own.

Having made a place for herself in public life, Eleanor Roosevelt urged other women to join her. She upheld the Progressive belief that women would have a humanizing and moralizing effect on government. At the same time she advised women to leave their "womanly personalities at home" and "disabuse their male competitors of the old idea that women are only 'ladies in business.'" Women must stand or fall "on their own ability, on their character as persons."[18]

ROSIE THE RIVETER

Ten years after women were warned not to steal jobs from unemployed men, they were being told to get a job as fast as possible. The change came about because of the Second World War. The war overturned attitudes about working women and altered women's place in the labor force more radically than any other event in the twentieth century.

When men left their places in factories and offices to take up arms, women were recruited to replace them. The War Manpower Commission realized that women workers were vital to the war effort. Government told industry, "You're going to hire women," and industry told women, "If you can drive a car, you can run a machine." The news media joined the campaign. Such women's magazines as the *Ladies Home Journal* featured cover illustrations of women pilots and machinists. "Why do we need women workers?" asked one broadcaster. His answer was emphatic—"You can't build ships, planes, and guns without them."[19]

Six million women took paying jobs during the war. The proportion of women in the labor force increased from 25 to 36 percent. Two million of these women went to work in offices—half of these for the federal government, handling the flow of paper created by the war. An even greater number of women went into the factories. Heavy industry alone created nearly two million jobs for women during the war.

When the Women's Bureau visited seven airplane factories in 1941, it counted 143 women workers. Eighteen months later the same seven plants employed over 65,000 women. Nationwide women accounted for 12 percent of workers in shipyards and 40 percent in aircraft plants. They also worked in the steel, electrical, and automobile industries.

"Girls who started working during World War II," wrote Caroline Bird, "never learned that some jobs supposedly 'belong' to men and some to women."[20] Former housewives, beauticians, waitresses, saleswomen, and domestics dressed in overalls instead of skirts, tied up their hair in hairnets or bandannas, and showed that they could do any job that needed to be done. They maneuvered giant overhead cranes, cleaned out blast furnaces, handled gun powder, drove tanks off the production line, and used acetylene torches. They riveted, welded, cut lathes, and loaded shells. They worked as stevedores, drill-press operators, and foundry helpers.

Those who did not move directly into the war industries performed hundreds of other "male jobs." During the war women were bus drivers, bell hops, lumberjacks, truck drivers, train conductors, gas station operators, barbers, policewomen, and lifeguards.

Because they were urgently needed, women gained higher wages and better working conditions than ever before. In the war industries the federal government endorsed the principle of equal pay for equal work. Many employers circumvented the equal-pay provision by re-classifying jobs and hiring women for those that paid less. Nonetheless, women who switched from sales, office, or manufacturing work in consumer factories to production in heavy industry doubled their wages.

Black women, older women, and married women bene-fited most from the manpower shortage. Before the war, 72 percent of black working women were domestics, and 20 percent were farm hands. By the end of the war eigh-teen percent of black women were working in factories. Before the war government and industry generally re-fused to hire women who were over thirty-five years old or married. By the end of the war these bans had been lifted.

The war radically changed the composition of the fe-male labor force. Rosie was not only a riveter, but also a wife and mother. Three-quarters of the new women workers were over thirty-five years old, 60 percent were married, and the majority had children of school or pre-school age. For the first time married older women were a majority among working women, and most Americans supported their right to work.

In Britain during the war working wives were offered various special services. They had paid time off one after-noon a week to take care of household chores. Stores stayed open late so women could shop in the evenings. Cen-tral kitchens in England prepared food for three million women each week to take home to their families. Govern-ment-sponsored day-care centers solved the problem of what to do with the children.

American working women had to get along without these services. Child care was the most serious problem. Only one-tenth of the factories producing war materials had day-care programs. The federal government did not provide funding for day care until 1944, and then it appropriated only a small fraction of the funding that was needed. Federal and local day-care programs served only 10 percent of the children of war workers. Most working mothers relied on relatives, friends, and paid baby sitters to care for their children while they were at work.[21]

At the beginning of the war, 95 percent of women workers intended to quit when their men came home. By war's end they had changed their minds. More than 80 percent wanted to continue working, mostly because they needed the income. Women in government, such as Congresswoman Helen Gahagan Douglas, and women professionals supported them. The war worker, wrote economist Theresa Wolfson, "cannot be cast off like an old glove."[22] But cast off they were.

Two months after V-J Day 800,000 workers, most of them women, lost their jobs in the aircraft industry. Layoffs of women in the auto and electrical industries were equally high. Such companies as IBM and Detroit Edison resurrected their prewar policy against hiring married women. By the end of 1946 two million women had been fired from heavy industry.[23]

"The courtship of women workers has ended," wrote *New York Times* reporter Lucy Greenbaum. After five years of keeping the war production lines moving, women were suddenly told that the work was too heavy for them.

THE WHITE-COLLAR GHETTO

Many of the women who were fired from their wartime jobs did not retreat back to their homes. More women were in the work force in 1952 than during the war. The numbers and percentages of working women have continued to grow every year since.

The typical woman worker was no longer young and single. She was over thirty-five and married. Fewer women quit their jobs when they had children, and those who did returned to work after a shorter absence. Between 1940 and 1960 the number of working mothers quadrupled. By the late 1960s almost 40 percent of mothers with children between the ages of six and seventeen were working, as were 30 percent of mothers with children younger than six.

Many working wives and mothers needed their wages to keep their families out of poverty. Others entered the job force to help provide their families with middle-class life advantages. Men, who generally earned twice as much as women, were viewed as "providers" while women were "supplementary workers," enabling their families to live more comfortably.[24]

Business used the fact that many working women had income-earning husbands to justify the low salaries and segregated, low-level jobs they assigned to *all* women. Single women trying to support themselves, and even divorced and widowed female heads of families, were also treated as "supplementary workers."

Women became a working class unto themselves in white-collar occupations. By 1960 they comprised 38 percent of all workers, but 75 percent of these were segregated in "female only" jobs. Clerical work headed the list; nearly one-third of all working women filled two-thirds of all typing and filing jobs.

What Caroline Bird has called the "sex map of the work world" pervaded all levels of the economy. No matter what a woman's class, educational background, or occupation, when she went looking for work, she was offered a "female" job. Usually women were, and are, bookkeepers, not accountants; file clerks, not office managers; salaried sales workers in department stores, not commissioned automobile dealers; teachers, not principals; telephone operators, not repairmen; seamstresses, not garment cutters; operatives of light machinery, not heavy machinery; executive secretaries, not executive vice presidents.

Women were least accepted in jobs that involved travel, risk, high profits, machinery, and negotiations. Most important, they were denied positions of power. "Most managers are men," said one woman clerical worker. "You can always tell who's who just by their sex." Even in "female" fields, such as the cosmetics industry, a man usually sat in the president's chair. All the qualities associated with power, money, prestige, and achievement, were denied to women.[25]

In 1950 women's average earnings were 65 percent of men's, and by 1960 they had fallen to less than 60 percent. Women sales workers earned 40 percent of male sales workers' salaries, and women clericals averaged 44 percent.[26] Of course women earn less, said businessmen —they do different work.

The sexual division of work could be subtle. At times women and men performed work that was identical in all but name and salary. In insurance companies, both men and women processed policy applications, but the higher-paid men were called underwriters while the women were called raters.[27]

One-third of the 1,900 office managers polled in 1961 admitted that they routinely paid men higher salaries than they paid to women in equivalent positions.[28] Few saw anything wrong with the dual pay system. Women did not need as much money as men; and besides, they were worth less. Many businesses placed ceilings on the amount a female worker could earn. A woman who became "too expensive" was sometimes fired and replaced by a man.

Education did earn women better jobs or salaries. Women were expected to be better educated than men for lesser jobs. In the 1950s and 1960s women high-school graduates earned less than men who had not completed eighth grade, and women college graduates averaged less than a male high-school drop-out. "To be an insurance broker a woman will have to have a B.A.," said one woman in the business. "And let's say she's got six years of experience. Here comes some guy, straight out of high school. . . . They tell her, 'Well, Mrs. X, you train Willy here.' She trains Willy, but when there's a management position open, Willy gets it."[29]

Women who achieved even a minimal amount of responsibility were often considered threatening. One woman who fought her way out of the secretarial ghetto to become an insurance bond writer, at half the salary paid to men, described the general refusal to take her seriously.

> People still call and say, "May I please speak with so-and-so," and we say, "Well, he's no longer here. May we help you?" and they say, "Then can I speak to the bond man who *is* there?" And we say, "I'm sorry, *we* are the bond man here." "Well, who is your boss?" "Well, we are our bosses." "OK, well *maybe* you can help me." And every time that we can't get something rushed they say, "Well gee, looks like you don't pull much weight in the company."[30]

Middle-aged women with grown children were called girls in offices. Some companies governed their female employees' every moment. "Working here is just like being in elementary school," said one woman, and another noted that women were always treated "like kids."

> If you got up from your desk you were told to sit down. If you looked around, you were told not to talk. If you went to the ladies' room too many times, they'd tell you. I was told they counted the papers in the wastepaper basket. I

did work with one woman who used to rip up the used papers, put them in her pocketbook, and flush them down the toilet.[81]

At the telephone company, observers were everywhere. Supervisors surreptitiously "plugged in" to operators' conversations with customers. The women who did not converse in exactly the way prescribed by the company—for example, if they said, "Hello," instead of "May I help you, please?"—were given demerits. Enough demerits could get an operator fired.[32]

During the 1950s efficiency experts advised companies to standardize jobs. By applying uniform procedures in every department, subdividing work into repetitive tasks and hiring workers to perform only one chore, businesses could increase productivity while keeping salaries low.

Specialization tended to isolate workers from each other and denied them a picture of how the company functioned. Only top management had an overview of the entire operation. In her article "The Secretarial Proletariat," Judith Ann explained that, as an insurance rater, she spent the day computing policy rates. Once she was done with her pile of papers, they were sent to the typists. "The typists were off somewhere on another floor; I never found out where for sure. Typing was even more lowly work than rating, so a rater never even met, much less mingled with typists."[33]

There were also new technological developments, most notably the introduction of computers. Insurance and banking companies began using computers in the 1950s, and by the 1960s they had spread to numerous industries. While computer automation made women's work more routine, it also created greater stress. Companies hired men "from the outside" for the skilled job of programming and assigned women the "dead end," high-speed job of operating keypunch machines. In one office in the 1950s keypunch operators were described as "nervous wrecks who stay at home often and keep supplies of tranquilizers and aspirins in their desk, at which they are frozen as though it were a spot on the assembly line."[34]

With advanced technology and standardized division of labor, a majority of women's white-collar jobs became very much like factory jobs. "The machine dictates," said one telephone receptionist. "This crummy little machine with buttons on it—you've got to be there to answer it. You can walk away from it and pretend you don't hear it, but it pulls you. . . . Your job doesn't mean anything. Because *you're* a little machine."[35] A woman typist explained that she was time-rated for her work, much as factory women had been piece-rated. "You're supposed to put out *X* numbers of pieces of paper a day. . . . Each sheet has a number that automatically goes on the tape when you push the button. So you can't really cheat."[35]

At the top of the female office pecking order was the personal secretary, whose title was taken quite literally. The personal secretary often spent as much time attending to her boss's personal needs, brewing coffee, dusting his desk, reminding him of appointments, balancing his checkbook, shopping for his Christmas gifts, and remembering his children's birthdays as she spent on company work. Some bosses also expected sexual services. "I finally got the picture," said one woman after she had been interviewed by a lawyer who promised her they would share drinks. "He wanted a maid-cook-bottle washer-companion-whore."[36]

In a job market where women were assigned work on the basis of their sex, sex appeal was an important qualification. Employment agencies used secret codes to rate female applicants on looks and dress. An older woman's experience sometimes counted less than a younger woman's attractiveness. Frances Donovan found this out early in the century, when she investigated the working conditions of waitresses. Most restaurants advertised for young, good-looking women. "There ain't no chance for an old hen, they all want chickens, and they want 'em slender," said one waitress. Another told Donovan. "You'll never make no dough here if you wear a wedding ring."[37]

In a 1962 poll 28 percent of businesses acknowledged that they considered sex appeal a qualification for some jobs.[38] Sales and service industries hired women as display pieces to woo customers and clients. This was especially true in the airline industry. A stewardess described how she was trained to be sexy in "stew school."

> We'd go through a whole week of make-up and poise. . . . They make you feel like you've never been out in public. They showed you how to smoke a cigarette, how to look at a man's eyes. . . .

The idea is not to be too obvious about it. . . . That's the whole thing, being a lady but still giving out that womanly appeal, like the body movement and the lips and the eyes. . . .[39]

Despite their unequal place in the workforce, many women preferred working to remaining at home. Dolores Dante, who became a waitress after her husband left her "with debts and three children," and who was still working in the same restaurant twenty-three years later said, "I won't give up my job as long as I'm able to do it. I feel out of contact if I just sit at home."[40]

What women seemed to like most about working was the chance to join a community outside their homes. Women who worked together often formed close friendships. Jean Tepperman in factories, Frances Donovan in department stores and restaurants, and Eleanor Langer at the telephone company discovered a family feeling among female coworkers. Women helped each other out when the workload was heavy and gave special support to new workers. "Many women kept telling me, 'Don't let anyone push you around,'" wrote Jean Tepperman.[41] Eleanor Langer found the same concerned spirit among women telephone employees.

Their attitude toward new employees was uniformly friendly and helpful. When I first went out on the floor my presence was a constant harassment to the older women in my unit. I didn't know what to do, had to ask a lot of questions, filed incorrectly. As a newcomer, I made their already tense lives far more difficult. "Don't feel bad," one or another would say at a particularly stupid error. "We were all new once. We've all been through it. Don't worry. You'll catch on."[42]

Women refused to be demeaned by work others considered demeaning. Dolores Dante insisted, "I can't be servile. I give service. There's a difference." When people asked her, "How come you're just a waitress?" she asked in return, "Don't you think you deserve to be served by me?" Waitressing, she said, was "an art." "When I put the plate down, you don't hear a sound. When I pick up a glass I want it to be just right.[43]

Strong-willed and self-assured women, such as Dolores Dante, knew their worth as workers, but few women recognized their collective importance and power. The double duty most working women took for granted kept them too busy to realize their economic importance. More than half the women in the job force were wives and mothers. Before and after factory or office hours they cooked, cleaned, shopped, and took care of children. Many were on a constant treadmill.

One working mother, Peggy Sheppard, told *New York Times Magazine* writer Gertrude Samuels about the way she spent her time. Peggy Sheppard was one of the few women with wartime production experience who found a peacetime job in heavy industry in 1951. Her day began earlier than that of women office and sales workers, but in most other respects it was typical.

> Peggy gets up in the dark at 5:30, makes lunch for Leon [her husband] and herself, gets breakfast started; wakes Ricky [her young son] up at 6:15. The Sheppards leave home at 6:30, Peggy driving first to the nursery to deposit Ricky, then to Lockheed, clocking in at 6:55. She leaves the factory at 3:30, drives over for Ricky and gets home by 4:15, bathes the baby . . . and starts dinner. After dinner there are the dishes and baby to be played with until his 7:15 bedtime. Then "I am free to do what I want."
>
> This usually means baking once a week—a chocolate cake or cupcakes for Ricky; Friday is laundry night; another for ironing; another for a drive-in movie or sewing (she makes her own blouses)."

Traditional ideas about "woman's place" helped keep working women in "dead end," low-paying jobs. During the 1950s and early 1960s women were told by husbands, employers, and "experts" that their most important role was domestic. Though more women were working than ever before, the ideal woman stayed at home, creating a nest for her husband and children. It was acceptable for her to work in order to help her family; but if she sought work for her own satisfaction or for financial independence, something must be wrong with her as a woman. Professional women who consciously sought careers were warned that they were destroying their marriages and jeopardizing their children's well-being.

Employers used statements like these to further their own self-interest. Had they really believed in the importance of women's role as wives and mothers, they would have made efforts to adjust women's work schedules and offered the services available to married working women in many other countries—payment for childbirth costs, guaranteed maternity leaves, day care, and child allowances. Instead, they exploited women's sexual roles to justify their unequal treatment of female employees.

Husbands, too, benefited from the belief that women should be wives and mothers above all. So long as women were segregated in second-class jobs, men did not have to fear competition or assume greater responsibility for their homes and children.

American society, commented the historian William O'Neill, "demands that women work, but when they do they and their children must suffer. No other developed western nation has such vicious, irrational and self defeating policies toward working women. Yet American women are continually reminded of the unique blessings national affluence has bestowed on them."[45]

Many working women internalized the very sexual biases that kept them underpaid workers outside the home and unpaid workers in it. Few women questioned the truism that housework and child care were "female jobs," which they had to perform even if they also held full-time paid jobs. Wives with husbands who "helped out" considered themselves lucky. Few women demanded services from their employers or from government, such as adjustments in their work schedules or day care for their children.

Unable to alter either the home or the workplace to meet the needs of their dual role, women often played one role off against the other. Many consoled themselves about their low status, low pay, and lack of opportunity for advancement with the thought that their main identity was elsewhere, as wives and mothers.

Even single women did not take themselves seriously as workers but thought of themselves as potential wives and mothers. They felt no urgency to acquire job experience and advance to more responsible, better-paid positions, as young single men did. Finding a husband was more important. Judith Ann described how she and her coworkers agreed that the best job to advance to was a secretarial position in a "small office with several men and only one or two girls . . . a vast improvement over the rows and rows of women and the female supervisor we had to deal with." The best part of the better job was the opportunity it offered them to meet men.[46]

Since none of these women earned enough to support themselves, they lived at home with their parents. Their wish to leave home made them impatient to marry.

Most single women saw marriage as an answer to all their problems in the workforce. They were certain that once they married, they would stay at home. On the job they were surrounded by older married women, but few stopped to wonder whether they, too, would have to remain wage earners after they wed. They did not realize that if they married, they could expect to spend twenty-five years of their adult lives in the job force, and some forty-odd years if they did not.[47]

The postwar consumer economy had come to rely on a workforce of women who did not think of themselves as workers and who were not taken seriously by their employers. Before working women could effect any change, they would have to confront the double exploitation they faced as both workers and women.

18

Just a Housewife

THE PROFESSIONAL MINORITY

The married woman who worked at a clerical or factory job did not challenge contemporary ideas about woman's role. The ill-paid married female worker was perceived as having extended her role as nurturing wife and mother into the marketplace—she worked to earn money for her family, to make her husband and her children's life more comfortable and secure.

But what about the professional woman? Married women doctors, lawyers, college teachers, journalists, and social workers usually had reasons for working that went beyond simply "helping out." Career women generally sought personal fulfillment in their work. Their motivations were "selfish," not selfless. Married career women challenged the idea that family life offered every woman all the fulfillment and opportunity for self-expression she would ever need.

American society did not accommodate women who wanted to combine the role of wife-mother with a career. Married career women could expect little or no help from professional schools, employers, coworkers, child-care specialists, husbands, or even their friends and relatives. Some did succeed, of course, but for the most part these were women of extraordinary gifts and drive. Often they managed to carve niches for themselves in what could be considered "women's fields"—gynecology, pediatrics, fashion, retailing, teaching, social work, nursing, and so on.

Married career women with children faced two distinct sets of problems—one in the job market, the other within their families. Many employers refused to hire married women with children, and those who did often refused to promote them. On job interviews married career women were frequently asked to explain how they intended to care for their husbands and children. (No professional man was ever asked to describe the care he provided for his family.)

Elizabeth Stern, daughter of Jewish immigrants who worked her way through college to become a social worker in the 1910s, found employers greatly resistant to married job applicants. Mrs. Stern, married to a social-work administrator, had left the job market when she became pregnant. She returned to full-time employment when her husband fell seriously ill. After his recovery she decided to continue working. She was recommended for a high-level job, and the interviewing board demanded to know how she intended to care for her young children. Mrs. Stern refused to answer.

> I don't think . . . I care to speak about my children and the care I give them. It seems to me that if a woman is capable of arranging for the lives of several hundred people, she is equally able to arrange for the lives of those dearest to her. I do not wish to discuss how I plan to do so. That seems to be the personal business of myself.[1]

Mrs. Stern did not get the job.

In some respects the difficulties married women faced within their families were even more severe than the obstacles they encountered in the job market. Like all working women, professional women were expected to assume total responsibility for their homes and families. In addition, professional women faced a complex psychological situation at home.

Elizabeth Stern, who had worked at home as a writer when her children were small, described her husband's attitude toward her literary career and to her professional life in general.

> My husband was modern. He said I must not give up my writing, that I must do anything I wanted to do, just as he did what he chose. Only he added, *he* must earn our living. Whatever *I* did I could do without thinking whether it was successful or not; only whether it made me happy.
>
> I took his hands in mine, I recall, and put his palms against my cheek. But he did not feel how hot my cheeks were against his palms. I kissed him. But as I kissed him then, I know I wished he had said that my work was as *practically* a need of mine, as his—that it was as essential to our life as his.[2]

Husbands often felt threeatened by wives who had careers. Until Elizabeth Stern's husband became successful himself, he felt demeaned by his wife's earning power. Other men—some successful, some not—refused to accept the idea of their wives having careers under any circumstance. Even well-meaning men used various emotional pressures to keep their wives at home. Elizabeth Stern, for example, did not have the courage to seek full-time employment, though she desperately wanted to, until her husband became seriously ill and was unable to work for a year.

Society encouraged men to equate their masculinity in part to their ability to financially "support" women and children. A wife who wanted a career therefore often damaged a man's sense of self-esteem. "If I were a 'real' man," such a man would say to himself, "Jane would stay home like a 'real' woman."

In the 1950s the propaganda against career women took on a particularly scurrilous tone. Women who sought careers were regularly depicted as "castrating" and incapable of loving. In a 1956 issue of *Life* magazine a psychiatrist was quoted as saying, "In New York City the 'career woman' can be seen in fullest bloom, and it is not irrelevant that New York City has the greatest concentration of psychiatrists." The author went on to describe female ambition as a form of mental illness that produced alcoholism and other forms of emotional disturbance in husbands and homosexuality in children.[3]

The woman who persisted in her desire for a career despite the hostile propaganda often paid a large emotional price. Gail Kaplan, the vice president of a major book publishing house, now in her early fifties, remembered the early years of her marriage, when her children were young and she worked as an accountant, as "the years when I was guilty about everything."

> The only person who approved of me in those days was my father. He had encouraged me to be an accountant and whatever I did was all right with him. But my mother thought I was terrible. She used to read newspaper clippings to me about the importance of mothers being home. My husband didn't want me working either. When I got a job he made it clear that I was not to expect him to help me in any way.
>
> Sometimes I don't know how I survived. The first year I had 17 housekeepers. Most of my salary went to pay the housekeeper. Every time I got a good one, she would quit.

Women in the town where we lived used to come up to me and tell me I was doing a terrible thing to my family. Sometimes I used to get up at six in the morning and bake —so no one could say I was depriving my children.

My way of dealing with the whole situation was to drive myself. I had to be the best—the best wife, the best mother, the best cook, the best daughter, the woman with the cleanest house. Everybody and everything came before me.[4]

WOMEN IN THE HOME

Marriage and domesticity, rather than a career, was the path followed by most women after the Second World War. Men and women looked to marriage and the family as a safe harbor against the uncertainties of the postwar years. Inflation was high, and the memory of the Great Depression was still fresh. Experts believed that the economy could not retain female war workers and still accommodate returning servicemen. Women lost the economic ground they had gained during the war.

The postwar desire to return to "normalcy" in the 1950s helped to create a particularly conservative social climate. Americans in general disavowed the social and political activism that had marked the years between the two wars. In particular, the postwar years saw an almost total rejection of feminist programs and awareness; building a home and bringing up a family seemed to be enough for most women.

The female return to domesticity was partially reflected in the postwar baby boom. The American birth rate soared in the 1950s, surpassing that of Japan and nearly equaling that of India. The number of women with three children doubled; the number with four tripled. Women were marrying at a younger age. By the end of the decade the average female married before she was twenty years old; fourteen million girls were engaged by the time they were seventeen.

The women who planned to marry young and have large families were less interested in higher education than were women of earlier decades. The proportion of women attending college (as compared to men) declined, although the number of both men and women attending college rose sharply. By the mid-1950s, 60 percent of all college women were dropping out to marry before they had earned a degree.

Another factor encouraging women to make a "career" out of homemaking was the migration to the suburbs. The young marrieds of the 1950s did not settle in the "old neighborhoods," the small towns and big cities where they had grown up. Millions of them moved to new suburban developments burgeoning outside the cities in what had formerly been rural areas. One planner characterized this trend as "the greatest migration in our country's history and perhaps one of the greatest migrations in the history of man."[5] By the mid-1970s, 40 percent of the American population—roughly eighty million people—was living in twenty thousand suburban communities.

Suburban housewives were encouraged to be "creative" in their homemaking. They sewed curtains, upholstered furniture, laid carpets, wallpapered bathrooms, and when that was done, took up bread making and home canning. Experts discovered that despite the postwar labor-saving devices, women actually spent more time on household chores than had their mothers. One study by a highly prestigious and conservative bank discovered that the average housewife was logging a 99.6-hour workweek.

Added to the suburban woman's work load was the job of chauffeur. Suburban communities rarely had adequate public transportation. While women without automobiles were trapped in their homes all day, women with cars often spent a disproportionate part of their day behind the wheel—driving her husband to the railroad station and picking him up on his way to and from work; going to the supermarket; driving the children to school and picking them up; making afterschool trips with the children to the dentist, to scout meetings, and to music lessons. A woman could easily spend twenty hours a week behind the wheel—half the work hours of a salaried employee.

Suburban communities were made up of nuclear families, usually of the same race and economic class. Old people and single people rarely moved to the suburbs. The result of this homogeneity was to separate suburban women from their unmarried and elderly relatives. Young housewives could no longer rely on members of their extended family to help out, as they often had in the past.

Nor were relatives available as surrogate parents to suburban children. While in earlier times a grandfather or grandmother, an aunt or an uncle might have played a key role in bringing up a child, now almost the entire responsibility fell to the mother.

Even fathers tended to be less available to their children than they had been in the past. If he commuted some distance to work, a suburban father might leave home early in the morning and not return until six thirty or seven in the evening, leaving just enough time to kiss the "kids" good night.

It was the mother, then, who became the dominant influence in her children's lives. In many suburban households she was the nurturer of children and the source of their discipline. In her study of suburban housewives, sociologist Helena Lopata commented on the importance of the mother.

> This is one of the few times in recorded history that the mother-child unit has been so isolated from adult assistance. Responsibility for health, welfare, the behavior and ability of the child is basically unshared. The father is not held accountable for what happens to the children because "he is not home much of the time."[6]

The problems faced by suburban housewives during the 1950s were shared by many nonsuburban middle-class and working-class housewives. The rigors of caring for a home; the heavy workload associated with raising a family, particularly a large family; the sense of loneliness many women experienced within their homes—these difficulties were exacerbated by the isolation of suburban communities, but they were by no means confined to the suburbs.

By the end of the decade it was becoming clear that the role of full-time wife and mother itself created conflicts for many women. Women who had chosen to marry and rear children, women who had expected to remain within the house all their lives, found themselves filled with an intangible discontent. This feeling of disquiet was to be found among housewives in nearly every economic class and geographic region throughout the nation.

WHO AM I?

The image of American women portrayed in the mass media during the 1950s was a well-groomed wife and mother. *She* was the American woman; any other kind was an aberration, as a spate of "experts" proclaimed.

Psychologists, sociologists, writers, and educators had not forced women out of the world and into the home, but the experts reinforced the return to domesticity. They were outspoken in their belief that a woman who failed to find sufficient satisfaction in her sexual roles was neurotic and "masculinized."

As they had in the nineteenth century, experts again spoke of immutable feminine traits. Biology was said to be a woman's destiny; individual personality and individual choice were all but blotted out by physiology. Robert Coughlan summed up this view in a long article appearing in an issue of *Life* discussing American women. "For a woman," wrote Coughlan, "the sexual act itself implies receptiveness and a certain passivity, while the long period of human gestation and extraordinarily long period of a child's dependence implies a need for protection and support for the mother."[7]

Some educators extended the "differences" between the sexes into the area of intellectual development. Lynn White, President of Mills College in California, considered traditional university training a waste of time for women because of what he perceived to be the vastly different intellectual traits of males and females. Men, he believed, were "creative," "egotistical," "individualistic," "innovative," capable of "abstract" and "quantitative thinking." Women, he claimed, possessed none of these qualities, having an "aversion for statistics and quantities" and being incapable of artistic creation on a par with men. What women did possess, in his view, was "intuition," "emotion," and a love for all that is "good, true, beautiful, useful and holy."

Women, White believed, should be educated as wives. All else was irrelevant and even potentially destructive. "Why not," he asked female students in all seriousness, "study the theory and preparation of a Basque paella, of a well-marinated shish kebob, lamb kidneys sauteed in sherry, an authoritative curry, the use of herbs, even such simple sophistications as serving cold artichokes with fresh milk."[8]

The definition of femaleness (and maleness as well) promulgated by such "experts" as Robert Coughlan and Lynn White were remarkably inflexible. These thinkers' underlying message was that human personality and human sexual identity would be shattered unless they were channeled into an extremely narrow course. In their view almost any deviation from the norm, any form of unconventional behavior, was a sickness.

For his *Life* magazine article Robert Coughlan consulted a panel of five male psychiatrists around the country. Each one described the irreparable damage to the human family when women failed to adjust to their sexual role. One psychiatrist Coughlan spoke with referred to a form of mental illness he called the "suburban syndrome." Women who fell into this category remained at home but longed for the kind of "masculine" satisfactions they had known in the job market prior to marriage. Women suffering from suburban syndrome were more or less a menace to themselves and others.

> If she avoids depression . . . her humiliation still seeks an outlet. This may take various forms: in destructive gossip about other women, or raising hell at the P.T.A., in becoming a dominating mother . . . or above all in dominating her husband.[9]

Another one of Coughlan's consultants spoke with distaste of the psychological effects on a family in which both husband and wife are factory workers.

> The factory couple, leaving perhaps on the same bus in the morning, both perhaps wearing trousers, he soldering the radio parts which she later puts together on the assembly line, coming home equally tired to their frozen-food ready-cooked dinners and the television set they bought with their joint earnings, are sexually undifferentiated at all times except in the marital embrace. *Their relationship is mutually insulting to their primary maleness and femaleness.*[10]

Women's failure to "adjust" to their sexual roles became the scapegoat for a long list of social problems. The rising rates of alcoholism, divorce, and juvenile delinquency, were blamed on women.

Women were given a particularly confusing message about motherhood. "Experts" assured them that it was their duty to be constantly available to their children.

Social scientists "proved" that juvenile delinquency resulted when women abandoned their children to work outside the home. At the same time women were roundly
criticized for overprotecting their children, keeping them
dependent, failing to "untie the apron strings."

Despite the emphasis psychologists placed on "good
mothering," and despite the retreat of many fathers from
active parenthood, the 1950s saw a marked decline in the
status of mothering. In fact, during this era *mother* was
becoming something of a dirty word. Among those leading the antimother movement was Philip Wylie. In his
best-selling *Generation of Vipers,* Wylie wrote that modern
man had become a flaccid and pathetic creature, and
"Mom" was the reason. Her possessive and conniving ways
were the root of human destructiveness, Wylie contended.
Curiously, the same "experts" who urged women to
devote themselves heart and soul to their children often
agreed with Wylie that mothers were the source of most
of the nation's social and psychological disturbance.

The "experts" understood that many women had difficulty valuing the lives they were leading and the work
they did. One member of Coughlan's psychiatric panel
commented on the fact that when women were asked
their occupation they often answered, "I'm just a housewife." The word "just" conveyed the message that "I'm not
very important . . . I'm not very interesting."

The psychiatrist who raised this point believed that a
woman who called herself "just a housewife" secretly
yearned to be a man. It never occurred to this doctor
that the problem might stem, not from the inadequacy of
the woman, but from the restrictions of the role she was
expected to play.

Every aspect of the traditional role of wife and mother encouraged women to be what social scientists, following David Riesman's lead, called "other-directed."
Women were told to look attractive for their husbands,
to keep a nice home for their husbands. One woman,
divorced and remarried, remembered her first marriage.
"In twenty years, the only times we ever discussed sex,
were when we talked about what I could do to increase
his pleasure. It never occurred to me that I was a person,
that my needs counted for something."[11]

Child-care practices also emphasized the needs of the

child, often to the exclusion of the needs of the mother. Dr. Benjamin Spock did tell new mothers to get out of the house one afternoon a week to buy a hat or go to a movie. While recognizing a mother's need to "escape" from her home now and then, however, Dr. Spock failed to recognize a woman's deep need for an identity separate from her husband and children.

One suburban mother spoke plaintively of what she would do if she had an hour or two of "peace" a day.

When you are married and with small children, you have a lot of things you would like to do but can't; you don't have the time and facilities. If I could, if I had peace one [or] two hours a day I would continue voice lessons, buy a piano, study. Sometimes I feel lost in the shuffle, confused: not the make-a-meal self, but as if I lost identity. Before, I worked in an office, was career-minded. I would like to be what I am for a few hours a week. My greatest satisfaction does not come from "terrific dinner" as much as from "she sings well."[12]

Middle-class women often felt the conflict about being "just a housewife" most acutely. A middle-class upbringing emphasized competition and achievement for girls as well as boys. Many girls of the middle-class performed at a high level in school and college, and they derived a sense of self-worth from performing well. Marriage and motherhood represented a sharp and startling change to this kind of woman. Cut off from the avenues of self-expression that a middle-class upbringing encouraged, many women felt as if they had lost their identity.

I've tried everything women are supposed to do—hobbies, gardening, pickling, canning, being very social with my neighbors, joining committees, running PTA teas. I can do it all, and I like it, but it doesn't leave you anything to think about—any feeling of who you are. I never had any career ambitions. All I wanted was to get married and have four children. I love the kids and Bob and my home. There's no problem you can put a name to. But I'm desperate. I begin to feel I have no personality. I'm a server of food and a putter-on of pants and a bed-maker, somebody who can be called on when you want something. But who am I?[13]

In 1963, when Betty Friedan published *The Feminine Mystique* it was women such as these she had in mind. Friedan objected to the idea that marriage and motherhood was all a woman needed to be happy. She termed this falsehood the feminine mystique.

OUTSIDE THE FEMININE MYSTIQUE

Working-class Women

Working-class women were affected by "the feminine mystique" in very different ways than were women of the middle class. The wives of blue-collar workers were often defensive toward and uncomfortable with the middle-class style and image. They had neither the money nor the time for a model home, fashionable clothes, domestic and personal accomplishments. They knew that they could never be the sexy housewife-hostess shown on television commercials. Struggling with the problems of basic economic survival, working-class women often found it difficult to sympathize with the "identity conflicts" of middle-class women.

The wives of blue-collar workers were even more dependent than were middle-class women on marriage to provide them with economic security. They could not survive alone or support their children on the salaries they could earn as clerical and factory workers. Working-class men wanted to "support" their wives and children but were often unable to do so. Consequently many of their wives moved in and out of the labor force, taking jobs when their husbands were unemployed or underemployed, leaving their jobs when their husbands were doing better.

Whether or not they worked outside the home, blue-collar wives were expected to defer to their husbands. Frequently the only way working-class men could assert their "masculinity" was by exercising authority over wives and children. Within many blue-collar homes men were seen as having the exclusive right to make important decisions. Further, men had the privilege of leisure time spent outside the home with the "boys," while women were expected to remain at home caring for the children.

Working-class women often spoke of a lack of closeness between them and their husbands. One woman spoke of the wall her husband threw up around himself.

I used to try to ask him when we were first married, why he gets into those real flippy moods, but he used to say nothing was wrong, and asking seemed to make him worse. The more I tried, the worse he'd get. So I found out that if you just don't bother him, it wears off.[14]

Another wife spoke about her husband's lack of communicativeness.

I get angry when he doesn't talk to me—he doesn't like silly conversation—it's no fun for me to go fishing with him —when he goes fishing, he doesn't talk—when he works with his tools, he doesn't talk—of course if I have a great problem that has been bothering me for a while, he says, "Let's sit down and talk it out," but otherwise he is quiet.[15]

A third wife commented on the differences between men's and women's need for companionship. "Men are different. They don't feel the same as us—that's one reason men are friends with men and women have women friends."[16] This woman's claim that men and women have different personalities and little in common voiced a widely held belief among blue-collar men and women.

Many working-class women turned to other women— mothers and sisters in particular, but also neighbors and coworkers—for the closeness and support their marriages lacked. One woman spoke about her relationship with her mother and sisters.

You tell her [your mother] kinds of secrets that you don't tell other people. You tell her secrets that are sort of sad and that she won't tell other people because she'd be ashamed for your sake. Sad things like a sickness, cancer or T.B. or it could be if your husband has been bad, maybe he'd gone with another woman, and nobody else knew it and somehow you found out all by yourself. Then there would be another kind of secret that you wouldn't know whether it was a secret or not, but you asked her advice about it and she'd decide.

You can tell a lot of that kind of secret to your sisters too, and they can give you advice. And then when you got things that are puzzling, close stuff. Like maybe you think your husband's bad, but you don't know, or maybe you wonder if you're pregnant, or maybe you got trouble in the neighborhood and you don't know how to handle it, that kind of thing you can tell your sister when you don't want to bother your mother.[17]

Along with the difficulty some working-class women experienced in communicating their thoughts and wishes to their husbands, some also expressed feelings of inferiority about their traditional female role.

Ye Gods, what do I do with my time? Well, I get up at six. I get my son dressed and then give him breakfast. After that I wash dishes and bathe and feed the baby. Then I get lunch and while the children nap, I sew or mend or iron and do all the other things I can't get done before noon. Then I cook supper for the family, and my husband watches TV while I do the dishes. After I get the children to bed, I set my hair and then I go to bed.[18]

Yet in contrast to middle-class women, working-class women did not often envy their husbands' jobs. They recognized that their men had great difficulty sustaining their own sense of self-esteem on the job. One working-class woman explained it in her own way.

If your husband is a factory worker or a tugboat operator you don't want his job. We're not after the jobs that our men have because we know how our men feel. We know that when they come home from work every day they feel they've been treated like the machines they operate.[19]

Sex roles in working-class marriage were generally well defined. Both husband and wife knew what was expected of them. According to the wives, a "good man" was someone who brought home a weekly paycheck and did not drink or gamble to excess. A "good wife," in the husbands' view, was one who stretched the family income as far as possible, did not nag too much, and kept the children neat and well-behaved. Many working-class couples perceived themselves in a partnership, each contributing to the family's well-being. Strains were put on these partnerships when husbands were chronically unable to bring in an adequate wage.

When working-class women were asked what part of their lives they most enjoyed, they often pointed to the children. Many sociologists have noted that working-class mothers approached their children in ways that differed markedly from attitudes expressed by mothers of the middle class. While middle-class women often demanded that their children win their love by performing well, working-class women tended to look to their children for love. The love that flowed between a mother and her children gave a working-class woman a sense of importance rarely available to her elsewhere.

Undermining the pleasure working-class women took in their children and in other aspects of their lives was the struggle to remain afloat economically. Financial insecurity affected their image of themselves and their relationships in and out of the family. Working-class women realized that their husbands could never provide the kind of income a "real man" was supposed to offer. Nor could they themselves ever meet the image of femininity presented in magazines, movies, television, and advertising. Perhaps most hurtfully, working-class women knew that they and their husbands could not provide their children with the education and other opportunities middle-class children looked forward to.

Black Women

The concepts of "femininity" used to describe white women have rarely been applicable to black women. In every century of American history racist ideas have set black women apart from their white sisters. The realities of black life in America made it impossible for most black women to be "leisured ladies" or "pampered housewives" or any other of the stereotypes used to describe white women. Black women could not, and in some cases had no wish to, shape themselves to match the white definition of femaleness.

Black women are on the lowest rung of the economic ladder. In the United States white men have the highest median incomes; minority men are second highest; they are followed by white women; and minority women come last. Black female workers receive the lowest wages, often for the least desirable jobs. In 1974 more than one-quarter (26.9 percent) of the black female workforce was employed as household laborers. (The median income for all domestic workers in 1970 was $1,700.) Often the meager pay black women earned as domestics, factory workers, and clerical employees did not supplement the family income—it *was* the family income. In 1965 one in four black families was headed by a woman; in 1974 the figure was one in three. Nearly half (45 percent) of all female-headed households lived below the poverty line. While nearly two-thirds of black families contained both husband and wife, the increasing number of female-headed families undercut the economic progress blacks in general made in the 1960s and 1970s.

While white women, even those who worked outside the home, were rarely recognized as workers, such was not the case for black women, either inside or outside their communities. Nevertheless the image of black working women was grossly distorted by racist and sexist ideas.

White social scientists accused black women of twisting the black family out of shape, of creating a "matriarchy" that "castrated" males. Martha Wright, calling for "the right to be black and me," has commented on this allegation.

> Some white man wrote this book about the black matriarchy saying that black women ran the community. Which is bull. We don't run no community. We went out and worked because they wouldn't give our men jobs.[20]

Eleanor Holmes Norton, director of the federal Equal Employment Opportunities Commission denounced the myth that black women were "liberated" because they had "been forced into roles as providers."

> They [black women] have been liberated only from love, from family life, from meaningful work, and just as often from basic comforts and necessities of an ordinary existence. There is neither power nor satisfaction in such a matriarchy. There is only bitter knowledge that one is a victim.[21]

One of the most insidious effects of racism was to drive a wedge between black women and black men. White society systematically denied black men access to jobs that would allow them to support their wives and children. In this way black men were denied a feeling of manhood, and black women were denied the opportunity to rely on their men. Both sexes often felt disappointed in themselves and each other.

Sociologist Carol Stack, writing about an urban black ghetto she called The Flats, has commented on the devastating effects of chronic male unemployment.

> The most important single factor which affects interpersonal relationships between men and women in The Flats is unemployment and the impossibility for men to secure jobs. Losing a job, or being unemployed month after month, debilitates one's self-importance and independence, and for men, necessitates that they sacrifice their role in the economic support of their families. Thus they become unable to assume the masculine role as defined by American society.[22]

Other factors continued the attack on black male-female relationships. Aid to Dependent Children, for example, was not available to women still living with their husbands. Welfare split families apart by forcing men out. Social workers made spot checks to ascertain that women on welfare were not secretly living with their husbands.

The artist and activist Maya Angelou described some of the pressures on black women. "She is caught in a tripartite crossfire of masculine prejudice, white illogical hatred, and Black lack of power." Even when black women managed to overcome the destructive effect of these forces they were denied the respect they had earned.

> The fact that the adult American Negro female emerges as a formidible character is often met with amazement, distaste and even belligerence. It is seldom accepted as an inevitable outcome of the struggle won by survivors and deserves respect if not enthusiastic acceptance.[23]

The situation for black women was one of double jeopardy—they were oppressed both as blacks and as women. Theirs tended to be a world in which every strength was turned into a liability and every act of courage called forth another test. Maya Angelou meditated on the condition of black women.

> The Black woman embodied a contradiction that makes her a living legend. She has nursed a nation of strangers, yet she's supposed to be mean and vicious, and given to

violent, revengeful acts. She's supposed to be obsessive
about the desire to have children out of wedlock, and yet
she's supposed to castrate them and be cold and indifferent
to them. By day she is supposed to be black and beautiful,
by night she is alone. Because she has for over a hundred
years been such a mainstay and such a breadwinner, she's
worked herself into the position of a man-loser. The more
she copes, the more she's asked to cope. So the more she
copes. . . .

Suddenly we are in the position of matriarchal ogres.
That way no one has to deal with this living, breathing,
needful person who wants a family, who wants a man, who
wants a Christmas.[24]

The antidote to racist stereotypes has always been
black pride and solidarity. Black women were a vital part
of the civil-rights movement that emerged in the 1950s
to become a full-scale struggle for liberation from overt
and covert forms of racism.

One of the women who breathed life into this movement was Mrs. Rosa Parks, a Montgomery, Alabama,
seamstress. Her arrest for refusing to give her bus seat to a
white passenger helped to ignite the mass movement
among blacks to end segregation.

The civil rights leader, Dr. Martin Luther King, Jr., described Mrs. Parks' "intrepid" protest.

On December 1, 1955, an attractive Negro seamstress,
Mrs. Rosa Parks, boarded the Cleveland Avenue bus in
downtown Montgomery. She was returning home after
her regular day's work in . . . a leading department store.
Tired from long hours on her feet, Mrs. Parks sat down in
the first seat behind the section reserved for whites. Not long
after she took her seat, the bus operator ordered her, along
with three other Negro passengers, to move back in order to accommodate boarding white passengers. By this
time every seat in the bus was taken. This meant if Mrs.
Parks followed the driver's command she would have to
stand while a white male passenger, who had just boarded
the bus, would sit. The other three Negro passengers immediately complied with the driver's request. But Mrs.
Parks quietly refused. The result was her arrest.

There was to be much speculation about why Mrs.
Parks did not obey the driver. Many people in the white
community argued that she had been "planted" by the
NAACP in order to lay the groundwork for a test case.

But the accusation was totally unwarranted. . . . Mrs.

Parks' refusal to move back was her own intrepid affirmation that she had had enough. It was an individual expression of a timeless longing for human dignity and freedom. She was not "planted" there by the NAACP, or any other organization; she was planted there by her personal sense of dignity and self-respect.[25]

19

The New Feminism

In 1963, when Betty Friedan wrote the *Feminine Mystique* and urged women to "stop giving lip service to the idea that there are no battles left to be fought for women in America," feminism was considered an outdated concept. Few women knew of the battles that had been fought for women's rights. If the nineteenth-century women's movement was remembered at all, it was as a relic, the effort by a few quaint spinsters to win the vote.

Seven years later feminism had resurfaced in fuller form than ever before. On August 26, 1970, tens of thousands of women across the United States went on strike to commemorate the fiftieth anniversary of woman suffrage and to protest the inequality they still faced. Participants called for twenty-four-hour child care, safe abortions for all women who wanted them, and equal opportunities in employment and education.

The strikers noted all the ways in which women were still the second sex, and they demanded change. In half a dozen cities women invaded and "liberated" male bars and restaurants. In New York City feminists visited corporations whose advertising stereotyped women as "servants and sex objects" and threatened to boycott their products. In Boston an office worker marched along chained to an oversized typewriter, and in Los Angeles marching housewives strapped pots and pans to their backs. A little girl carried a sign reading, "I Am Not a Barbie Doll," and stewardesses, protesting the airline industry's refusal to employ women with children, marched under the slogan, "Storks Fly—Why Can't Mothers?"

The contradictions in the lives of twentieth-century American women made the reemergence of feminism almost inevitable. On the one hand women had legal rights and they could vote, but if politics meant power, then women remained disenfranchised. Women had educational opportunities, but they were not expected to use them. They were assured that they were sexual beings, but

341

their sexuality was defined by male standards. Perhaps the largest contradiction of all was the fact that 40 percent of American women held full-time jobs outside their homes, yet they were defined as wives and mothers. The domestic image of women was so ingrained that even though married women with children were moving into the labor force at a greater rate than any other group in society, they were not viewed as workers.

Further setting the stage for the reemergence of the feminist movement was the birth-control pill. With 97 percent effectiveness, the pill relieved women of the fear of unwanted pregnancies. Women who took the pill could be confident that they were controlling conception. This technological advance and the more widespread availability of other contraceptives, like the diaphragm, enabled women to limit their childbearing years to a relatively short span of time. By the mid-1960s the average American woman gave birth to her last child by the time she was twenty-eight. The belief that a woman should derive fulfillment through her biological role now left more than half her life unaccounted for.

Betty Friedan addressed herself to the "strange discrepancy" between the "reality" of women's lives and the "image to which we were trying to conform." She offered a perspective that differed markedly from that of social scientists who, after studying modern woman's "role confusion," told women to adjust to the contradictions and "accept" their femininity. Friedan pointed to society, rather than women, as needing adjustment.[1]

The Feminine Mystique highlighted the problems of middle-class housewives, many of whom told Friedan that they felt "empty," "isolated," "bored," and "useless." They did not seem to know who they were, and though many were young—in their late twenties and in their thirties—they dreaded the future.

It's as if ever since you were a little girl, there's always been somebody or something that will take care of your life: your parents, or college, or falling in love, or having a child, or moving to a new house. Then you wake up one morning, and there's nothing to look forward to.[2]

Friedan declared that women and men shared a basic human need to grow. The "feminine mystique" thwarted women's needs by telling them they never had to grow up. Girls were encouraged to ignore, even flee from, the question of who they were and what they wanted to do with their lives. Unlike boys, girls did not have "to do"; they could simply "be." Ultimately women paid a high price for passivity.

Friedan urged women to begin to develop their own potentials and talents, to go back to college and professional schools, and to find meaningful work of their own. Until they did, she warned, women would remain unfulfilled.

The Feminine Mystique had its limitations. For one, Friedan ignored the satisfactions women derived from homemaking and motherhood. She assumed that the roles themselves limited women's chances for growth when, in fact, some women resented only the lack of recognition of the real importance of these roles. Some women genuinely felt that raising children and homemaking were more gratifying than the jobs their husbands did.

Friedan's solutions were directed almost exclusively to highly educated middle-class women. She had little to offer working-class and poor women who did not have the resources to pursue a career in business or the professions. Working-class women took jobs because they needed the money, and work outside their homes had not freed them from preconceptions about femininity.

Despite its limitations, the *Feminine Mystique* was a compelling book. Friedan not only named a problem, she also challenged women to take action to alter it. The book sold more than 300,000 copies within one year. Many women expressed relief, gratitude, and hope after reading it. They had discovered they were not alone.

WOMEN'S RIGHTS AND WOMEN'S LIBERATION

In 1964 southern and conservative Congressmen were fighting a losing battle to halt passage of a major Civil Rights Bill. An eighty-one-year-old Virginia Congressman, Howard W. Smith, suggested that Title VII of the bill, which outlawed employment discrimination on the basis of "race, color, religion, or national origin" should include the word "sex." His amendment was greeted with laughter.

Smith was not a feminist. A year earlier he had voted against the Equal Pay Act, which stipulated that men and women who did the same work should be paid the same wages. Smith's "sex amendment" to Title VII was a last-ditch effort to undermine the Civil Rights Bill. The idea that women were a "minority" group was considered amusing. If rights for women were linked to rights for blacks, Smith and others reasoned, civil-rights legislation would not be taken seriously.

The joke backfired. The Civil Rights Bill, including the sex amendment, became law, and in the following decade more women than any other group filed discrimination complaints based on Title VII. More immediately, Title VII led directly to the formation of the first activist feminist organization since the woman-suffrage era.

Once Title VII took effect, women realized that they needed an organization to enforce it. The Equal Employment Opportunities Commission (EEOC), the federal agency established to hear complaints under Title VII and issue guidelines to employers, was not eager to do the job. EEOC Director Herman Edlesberg called the sex provision "a fluke . . . conceived out of wedlock."[3] Some initial EEOC guidelines, were promising, however. An employer could not prefer a man or a woman on the presumption that one sex was better suited to a particular kind of job such as the belief that women are good at "detail" work, men at outdoor jobs) or hire a man over a woman "to please co-workers, clients or customers." However, the EEOC saw nothing wrong with classified newspaper advertisements that listed job openings by sex.

Women protested that "Help Wanted—Male" and "Help Wanted—Female" job listings were as discriminatory as those that distinguished between white and black. "It took only a few of us to get together, to ignite the spark," Betty Friedan later wrote, "and it spread like a nuclear chain reaction."[4]

The National Organization for Women (NOW) was established in 1966 with the goal of "taking action to bring women into full participation in the mainstream of American society *now*, exercising all the privileges and responsibilities thereof in truly equal partnership with men."[5] "Participation in the mainstream" was the key phrase. NOW sought to win an equal place for women in the male world of politics, business, and the professions by extending and strengthening women's rights under the law.

At the same time NOW voiced a new kind of feminism.

It proclaimed that for women to share men's sphere, men would have to start sharing women's sphere.

> We believe that a true partnership between the sexes demands a different concept of marriage, an equitable sharing of the responsibilities of home and children and of the economic burdens of their support. We believe that proper recognition should be given to the economic and social values of homemaking and child care.[6]

Another section of NOW's Statement of Purpose sounded very much like portions of the 1848 Declaration of Rights and Sentiments.

> We will protest and endeavor to change the false image of women now prevalent in the mass media and in the texts, ceremonies, laws and practices of our major social institutions . . . church, state, college, factory or office which in the guise of protectiveness . . . foster in women self denigration, dependence and evasion of responsibility, undermine their confidence in their own abilities and foster contempt for women.[7]

Betty Friedan was elected NOW's first president by the three hundred charter members. Most of them were middle-class women who had experienced sex discrimination on their jobs in government, academia, the professions, and organized labor. Quite a few had worked together on President John F. Kennedy's Commission on the Status of Women, the first government-sponsored study of its kind, and on the numerous state commissions that followed the Kennedy Commission's 1963 *Report on American Women*.

The organization established by the charter members reflected their characters. These women with executive abilities created a group that was both stable and flexible enough to sustain itself. National in scope, NOW had elected officers and state and local chapters. Though it was soon challenged by both "conservative" and "radical" feminists, in 1976 NOW remained the largest and most enduring organization in the contemporary women's movement.

During its first decade NOW changed direction a number of times, but it never veered from its basic reformist course. NOW members continued to seek "rights" for women within "establishment" institutions.

At its second national convention in 1967 NOW's Bill of Rights incorporated a resolution supporting "the right of women to control their own reproductive lives." This provision called for the repeal of all laws that restricted access to birth-control information, and more particularly the repeal of all "penal laws governing abortion." This was the first time a woman's group had supported abortion as a feminist issue. NOW advocated a woman's right to control her own body, claiming that the decision of whether or not to bear a child should be hers alone.

Some NOW members considered abortion "too controversial" an issue, with the potential to "damage the image" of women's rights. They resigned to form their own organization, the Women's Equity Action League (WEAL), which adopted a narrow, "conservative" approach to women's issues. WEAL aimed to attract women in the professions and business who would exert a "patient and diplomatic . . . influence on legislation regarding the work and education of women."[8]

Other women's organizations—some new, such as Federally Employed Women (FEW), others already in existence, such as the YWCA and the National Federation of Business and Professional Women—also joined the fight against sex discrimination. Following the lead of NOW, these groups lobbied, litigated, and propagandized for equality in education, employment, and political organizations. Their goals included government-supported child care, paid maternity leaves for working women, and tax reforms that recognized the value of homemaking. By 1970 they had won some important gains.

Women's rights groups turned existing legislation into effective weapons against sex discrimination. They demanded and won liberal interpretations of Title VII and the 1967 Executive Order 11246, which forbade sex discrimination by the federal government and federal contractors. Because of these protests, the EEOC finally outlawed sex-segregated want ads, and Executive Order 11246 ordered federal contractors to take "affirmative action" to end sex discrimination.

Women were next able to use the laws in new ways. In 1970 WEAL filed complaints of sex discrimination against three hundred colleges and universities. The schools were threatened with loss of their federal funding unless they began to hire and promote more women. That same year NOW used the same tactic against 1,300 corporations doing business with the federal government.

The women's rights approach to feminism, which relied on steady organizational work and traditional reform tactics, was only one part of the contemporary woman's movement. A second center of the emerging feminism was far more controversial.

This second focus came to be called women's liberation or radical feminism. The radicals were concerned with the underpinnings of sex discrimination, claiming that unequal laws and customs were the effect, not the cause, of woman's oppression. Underlying sex discrimination was sexism, the male assumption that woman's different biology made her inherently inferior. Because she could bear children, woman was held to be somehow incapable of the strengths, responsibilities, and power assumed by men.

Sexism, operating on several levels, was built into all institutions. Woman's place was in the home and family; the world at large belonged to men. It was evident in many of the ways men viewed women ("She's a dumb broad," "she gets excited over every little thing," "she's an angel/she's a bitch") and related to women ("All a woman needs is a strong man who can show her he's boss"). Finally, and perhaps most damaging, sexism governed the way women saw themselves.

Women had so deeply internalized society's definition of them as "differently made creatures . . . more childlike and less mature" that they were detached from their own talents and strengths. The very qualities society valued and instilled in men—confidence, creativity, aggression, mastery—were discouraged in women. In turn, women's lack of confidence, creativity, aggression, and mastery were used as proof of their inferiority.

Radical feminism had its roots in the student-protest movements of the 1960s. Many of the young women who became radical feminists had traveled South in the early 1960s to campaign for the civil rights of blacks; later in the decade they demonstrated against the war in Vietnam and joined various groups of the new left. Though these movements opposed the prevailing "power structure," they were organized traditionally; men ran the movements while women were expected to make coffee, type papers, and provide sexual favors.

At first women tried to equalize their place with movement men, but they had as little success as had the Grimke sisters and Elizabeth Cady Stanton 130 years before. Like the pioneer feminists, they discovered that men might fight for equality "out there," but they were not willing to give equal treatment to the women they worked and lived with.

When women in SNCC (Student Non-Violent Coordinating Committee) wrote a paper entitled "The Position of Women in SNCC," black-power leader Stokely Carmichael remarked, "The only position for women in SNCC is prone." And when women in SDS (Students for a Democratic Society) demanded a feminist plank at the 1966 convention, they were pelted with tomatoes and expelled from the meeting.

Many movement women made their final break with the new left in 1969, at a peace demonstration in Washington, D. C. One feminist participant described the violent male reaction when women tried to speak.

> Our moment comes. M. from the Washington group gets up to speak. This isn't protest against movement men which is second on the agenda, just fairly innocuous radical rhetoric—except that it's a good-looking woman talking about women. The men go crazy. "Take it off! Take her off the stage and fuck her!" They yell and boo and guffaw at unwitting double entendres like "We must take to the streets." When S., who is representing the New York group . . . announces that women will no longer participate in any so-called revolution that does not include the abolition of male privilege, it sounds like a spontaneous outburst of rage. . . .
>
> I am shaking. If radical men can be so easily provoked into acting like rednecks, what can we expect from others? What have we gotten ourselves into?[9]

The women who split from the left declared that feminism was their first priority. They rejected the male leftist position that women's issues were "part of the larger struggle for socialism." Redstockings, a New York City group formed in 1969, argued that "male supremacy is the oldest and most basic form of domination," the model for "all other forms of oppression," including racism and capitalism and "thus the tapeworm that must be eliminated first by any true revolution." "Men dominate women, a few men dominate the rest," the Redstockings manifesto asserted.[10]

Radical feminists also challenged the moderate goals of women's-rights groups. Though many women believed that the legal campaigns waged by NOW and WEAL were valuable, they argued that formal rights for women were not enough. Robin Morgan compared women's rights activists to the suffragists who had "never dared enough, never questioned enough . . . and wound up having to settle for the vote." The radicals called for a transformed society in which neither women nor men would be assigned or restricted to roles on the basis of sex.[11]

There was never any one women's-liberation group. Radical women rejected the traditional structure of NOW and WEAL. Keeping in mind their goal for feminism to promote equality among all women, they formed small "cooperative" groups. Some groups outlawed leaders, others insisted that all tasks be shared, from making coffee to writing position papers. Though various groups exchanged ideas through a network of personal contacts, newsletters, journals, and conferences, each group remained independent.

Such a format posed problems. The movement was so decentralized that it was difficult to find its core. When members of one group disagreed, they divided to form two or more groups. The attempt to work "collectively" was often impractical. Individual feminists who showed talents as speakers, writers, or organizers were denounced as "elitist." It took some time before feminists began to build stable groups in which the individual contributions of each woman were valued.

Despite these difficulties, the structure of small groups had much to offer. It promoted the idea that feminism was for each and every woman. "Why interview me?" one woman's liberationist asked a female reporter. "Why don't you write about your own oppression?" Most important, the intimate atmosphere within small groups led women to a new understanding of themselves and each other.

THE PERSONAL IS POLITICAL

When feminists met in small groups, they talked about their backgrounds and experiences. Very quickly they discovered that the "problems" each had thought of as uniquely hers were common to other members and to women in general.

The idea that the personal is political was the most important insight of modern feminism. It led to the understanding that women were a caste or class, linked together by their sex. Regardless of the many differences among groups of women—class, race, age, education, life style—all women were subject to sexism. One had only to listen to their everyday experiences to perceive their common plight. Meredith Tax, describing a "woman walking down a city street," noted that "any man, whatever his class or race had the power to make her hate herself and her body." Even if he did not physically assault or hurt her, he could "impinge on her . . . demand that her thoughts be focused on him, use her body with his eyes . . . evaluate her market price . . . comment on her defects and compare them to those of other passers-by . . . make her a participant in [his] fantasies without asking if she is willing . . . above all, make her feel like a *thing*."[12]

Radical feminists agreed that their first task was to awaken women, helping them to explore their experiences and to discover how these experiences conformed to an assigned social role. They called this process *consciousness raising*. "We have to face the fact that pieces have been cut out of us to make us fit into this society," wrote Meredith Tax.

> We have to try to imagine what we could have been if we had not been taught from birth that we are stupid, unable to analyze anything, "intuitive," "passive," physically weak, hysterical, overemotional, dependent by nature, incapable of defending against any attack, fit only to be the housekeeper, sex object and emotional service center for some man or men and children. And then only if we're lucky—otherwise we must act out a commercial mockery of those roles as someone else's secretary.[13]

CONSCIOUSNESS RAISING AND SISTERHOOD

"What's so new about a bunch of women getting together to talk?" asked one woman when a friend invited her to join a consciousness raising (CR) group. "Everyone knows that misery loves company. Why trade wounds? Go out and get an analyst. Or a job. Or a husband." Several consciousness-raising meetings later, this same woman had changed her mind.

> I gave up the protective device of exempting myself from Woman's Condition. I stopped saying and thinking that other women are "them"—because I realized that when anything was said about what women can or cannot do my "objective distance" did not let me out of the dragnet. Like a convert to the female sex, I became "us."[14]

By 1970 CR groups had become "the heart and soul of the women's liberation movement." As both an organizing tool and an analytic technique, the groups were highly effective, providing entry into the feminist movement for thousands of women. Ultimately even women and men who never joined groups were affected by the ideas discussed in them.

The format of CR groups reflected the grass-roots style of women's liberation. Groups emerged wherever several women decided to meet and talk about their experiences. At weekly meetings members usually picked a subject, and the discussion "went around the room" to allow each woman a chance to speak.

Men were excluded from meetings. According to *Ms.* Magazine's guidelines on consciousness raising,

> even well-meaning men tend to adopt an attitude of helpful paternalism and less enlightened ones take over the focus of the group by becoming adversaries—symbolic enemies to be defeated or convinced. . . . Men who really want to be helpful will care for houses and children, so that women may be free to take part, or they will start rap groups of their own, to discuss the ways they are restricted by their "masculine" roles.[15]

The New York Radical Feminists suggested that women in CR groups begin by discussing their earliest childhood memories of sex-role stereotyping ("What did you do as a little girl that was different from what little boys did? Why? Did you ever want to do anything else?") and move through adolescence to adulthood. Though not all groups followed this chronological sequence, most of them explored a wide variety of questions. One group included the following.

—What do you like/dislike about your face and body?
—Do you worry about being overweight, flat-chested, having the "wrong kind" of hair and skin?
—What are your feelings about your mother?
—Do you think women have to sacrifice more to make a marriage work?
—When your husband does a household chore, does he do it because he's helping you with *your* work?
—What do you tell your relatives when they ask why you're still not married?
—If you don't have a date on Saturday night, does it mean you have to stay home alone?
—Can you have a home without a husband?
—Can men nurture children—or does it take a woman to provide nurturance?
—Do you ever have sex when you don't want to?
—Are you able to tell your partner what gives you sexual pleasure?
—Have you ever been sexually attracted to a woman?
—Are you afraid of getting old?
—Did you ever say you'd never work for a woman boss?
—Would you trust a female lawyer (doctor, accountant) as much as a man?

Women in another CR group remarked that "we looked at our present lives and realized how we were perpetuating unequal power relationships between ourselves and men."

We never expected enough time and pleasure in sex. We never respected the questions we asked our doctors, we never expected men to adjust their lives to parenthood as we bore the child for both of us, we never expected men to take on some of the worry about birth control . . . we never respected the support and comfort other women gave us when we needed it. The list was endless.[16]

At the beginning consciousness raising generated "a kind of emotional rush, almost a high." Relieved to learn that their "private" grievances were shared, women sensed the possibilities of change through movement action. They experienced "sisterhood"—understanding, trust, and respect for women. They also experienced anger. They were, wrote one feminist, "clicking-things-into-place angry, because we have suddenly and shockingly perceived the basic disorder in what has been believed to be the natural order of things."[17]

In her article "Cutting Loose," Sally Kempton offered a powerful description of a woman confronting her rage. Kempton understood that her anger was an outgrowth of her dependency. As a woman she was defined "through her man's life and by virtue of having a man." This dependency made her childlike, seductive, manipulative, and angry. It also made her afraid of expressing her anger.

> I had gotten myself into a classic housewife's position: I was living my husband's life, and I hated him for it. And the reason this was so was that I was economically dependent upon him; having ceased to earn my living I could no longer claim the breadwinner's right to attention for my special needs.
>
> My husband told me . . . there were certain realities which I had to face. He was the head of the household: I had never questioned that. He had to fulfill himself: I had never questioned that. . . . Except that it was also necessary for his fulfillment that . . . I adjust to his situation or else end the marriage. It never occurred to him to consider adapting himself to mine, and it never occurred to me. . . . I only knew that his situation was bad for me . . . that it kept me from working. . . .
>
> I used to lie in bed beside my husband after those fights and wish I had the courage to bash in his head with a frying pan. I would do it while he slept, since awake he would overpower me, disarm me. If only I dared, I would mutter to myself through clenched teeth, pushing back the realization that I didn't dare not because I was afraid of seriously hurting him—I would have loved to do that—but because even in the extremity of my anger I was afraid that if I cracked his head with a frying pan he would leave me.[18]

Women's growing anger as they became aware of sexism took two directions. There was anger at men—husbands, bosses, men in the streets, doctors, advertisers. There was also anger that turned inward, asking, "Why have I let this happen, why have I acquiesced for so long?"

Consciousness raising helped some women to admit their anger and to use it as a starting point for change and growth. "Healthy anger," wrote one feminist, "says 'I'm a person . . . I have a right to get what I can for myself without hurting you. And if you deprive me of my rights, I'm not going to thank you . . . I'm going to fight you.' "[19] For this change to occur, women had "to stop participating in our oppression." On the other hand, there were women who simply blamed men ("It's all their fault") and never sought to change.

Groups which supported the "prowoman's line"—the belief that "we do not need to change ourselves but to change men"—could fall into what Robin Morgan called "failure vanguardism."

> What began as a positive idea of standing up for "women who are down" became a glorification of the victim. The more scars one could show, a bad marriage for example, the more "real" one's confrontation with sexism, the more support one deserved.[20]

Furthermore, women who failed to deal with their competitive feelings toward other women might support each other's weaknesses rather than their strengths. "None of us really wanted any one of us to get better," wrote Nora Ephron about her CR group. "There was one woman whose sex life was so awful it made us all feel lucky. . . . I think each of us felt . . . well-I'm-not-as-bad-off-as-I-thought."[21]

Despite these problems, consciousness raising was a powerful and positive vehicle. The very act of meeting together, away from men, was the beginning of change for many women.

> There is often a sense of genuine cultural rebellion in the atmosphere of a Woman's Liberation meeting. Women sit with their legs apart, carelessly dressed, barely made up, exhibiting their feelings or the holes on the knees of their jeans with an unprovocative candor which is hardly seen at all in the outside world. Of course, they are demonstrating by their postures that they are in effect, off duty, absolved from the compulsion of making themselves attractive.[22]

Consciousness raising prompted women to change their day-to-day lives.

> Some women quit their jobs . . . others began job training. . . . Some women started living together, some began living alone for the first time. . . . Some women left their husbands, others began to live with a man, feeling somehow less of a psychological disadvantage than before.
>
> Many women started reading "political" and "scientific" books as passionately as they read novels . . . women stopped giggling and competing with each other for male attention. . . . Many women found they could think. . . . Some women stopped going to beauty parlors . . . They began to value their time; they needed fewer adornments to "make up" for being female.[23]

In addition, consciousness raising led many women into active work for the women's movement. Members of many groups joined together for demonstrations, lobbying, and conferences on a variety of issues.

LIBERATION NOW

Radical feminists used the rhetoric and protest tactics of the new left to bring consciousness raising to the public. They staged dramatic and at times deliberately provocative demonstrations, which they called zap actions, to focus attention on women's need for liberation.

The first and most famous "zap action" occurred at the 1968 Miss America beauty pageant. A small group of women picketed the pageant with signs proclaiming, "Let's Judge Ourselves as People." They crowned a live sheep and dumped girdles, cosmetics, high-heeled shoes, and bras into a "freedom trash can." Some newspapers reported this event as a massive bonfire of brassieres and movement women were subsequently derided as "bra burners."

Feminists dramatized issues by offering "personal testimony." Conferences on abortion, marriage, employment, and rape always included women "speaking out" about their experiences. At an abortion rally, for example, a woman might describe her experience while undergoing an illegal abortion to support the demand for repeal of all abortion laws.

Women's liberationists made men and women aware of

sexism by deliberately defying the prevailing image of
femininity. They opened doors for themselves, lit their
own cigarettes, picked up their own checks in restaurants.
When men whistled and hooted at them in the street,
they whistled and hooted back. Some learned karate and
other self-defense tactics to defend themselves against
muggers and unwelcome males. "Hit her, she's your
equal," one feminist demonstrator shouted to a man under
attack by another feminist during a demonstration. Anne
Koedt responded to charges that feminists were "castrating man haters."

> Men have told me I want to castrate them. This is some-
> thing they never understand: the idea of a female-dominated
> society is as repugnant to me as the idea of a male-
> dominated society. What I want to cut off is the power
> men exercise over women. And if a man associates that
> power with his genitalia, that's his problem.[24]

The power with which feminists defied their critics and
challenged feminine stereotypes startled and at times an-
gered, frightened, and appalled both women and men; but
by refusing to behave according to established etiquette,
feminists caught both sexes off guard, forcing them to consider the question of woman's condition. Consciousness
raising gave men a realization, often discomforting, that
women were dissatisfied and were determined to win
equality. Women reacted more personally. As Ellen Levine
and Judith Hole wrote in *The Rebirth of Feminism*, "the
idea of women's liberation apparently touches a raw nerve
sensitivity in women, regardless of their political orienta-
tion or lack of one."[25]

ISSUES AND IDEOLOGY

Central to the feminist critique was the question of
differences between the sexes. Were there any real ones
between men and women other than those of biology?
Some feminists denied the idea; the emotional, intellectual,
and psychological differences that existed at present were
simply a result of social conditioning. All feminists agreed
that if real differences did exist, nobody would know what
they were until men and women were raised under equal
conditions.

Radical feminists analyzed the methods by which the

sex-role system kept women separate and unequal. As wives and mothers, women took care of the basic everyday needs of men and children. While they served society, they were never allowed to assert their own power or will, as men did. Instead, women were carefully reared to believe that their sex roles were the natural result of their "feminine" personalities. Feminine women were supportive, kind, nurturant, giving, and "in the bargain—pliant and stupid enough never to resent their subservient position."[26]

Feminists noted the advantages men gained by being men in a sexist society. In an article entitled "Why I Want a Wife," Judy Syfers exposed the many services wives provided their husbands.

> . . . I want a wife to make sure my children eat properly and are kept clean. I want a wife who will wash the children's clothes and keep them mended. I want a wife who is a good nurturant attendant to my children, arranges for their schooling, makes sure that they have an adequate social life with their peers. . . . I want a wife who takes care of the children when they are sick. . . . My wife must arrange to lose time at work and not lose the job. . . . Needless to say, my wife will arrange and pay for the care of my children while my wife is working.
>
> I want a wife, who will take care of *my* physical needs. I want a wife who will keep my house clean. . . . A wife who will pick up after me. I want a wife who will keep my clothes clean, ironed, mended, replaced when need be, and who will see to it that I can find what I need the minute I need it. I want a wife who . . . is a good cook . . . a wife who will plan the menus, do the necessary grocery shopping, prepare the meals, serve them pleasantly and then do the cleaning up. . . . I want a wife who will care for me when I am sick and sympathize with my pains. . . . I want a wife to go along when our family takes a vacation so that someone can continue to care for me and my children when I need a rest.
>
> My God, who wouldn't want a wife?[27]

Men, recognizing their self-interests, were not so willing to relinquish traditional forms of marriage. In "The Politics of Marriage," Pat Mainardi illuminated some of the tactics men used to avoid sharing household labor.

> —"I don't mind sharing the housework, but I don't do it very well. We should each do the things we're best at."

MEANING: Unfortunately I'm no good at . . . washing dishes or cooking. What I do best is a little light carpentry, changing light bulbs, moving furniture. (How often do you move furniture?)

—"I hate it more than you. You don't mind it so much."

MEANING: Housework is garbage work. It's the worst crap I've ever done. It's degrading and humiliating for someone of my intelligence to do it. But for someone of *your* intelligence . . . [28]

Feminists wanted new choices—to remain single, without being pitied or ridiculed; to enjoy the intimacies of marriage without having to live through or for one's husband or children; to have children or not, whether married or single. Many experimented with new living arrangements and new forms of relationships. These included cooperative or partnership marriages in which husband and wife split the housework and childbearing; childless marriages; marriages in which a husband took care of the home and children while the wife was the breadwinner; living alone and living in groups; all female households; and households composed of several nuclear families.

The movement also helped lesbian women to accept their sexual preference and to begin living an openly homosexual life.

I don't know if I would ever have come out if it hadn't been for the women's movement. The women's movement first led me to question the naturalness of the male-female roles I had always largely accepted. The movement helped me to reject these roles, and with them every reason for struggling to be heterosexual. I realized femaleness was something I was born with. It was not something others could reward me with when I acted "feminine" or take away from me as punishment. [29]

Feminist issues and ideology were central to lesbians' lives. Because homosexuality was listed as a crime in most states, lesbians looked to organized feminism for help in protesting the legal discrimination they faced in employment, housing, divorce, and child-custody rulings. Moreover, as women who had rejected traditional female roles, lesbians' very right to exist openly depended on overcoming sexist attitudes and customs. In effect, the lesbian need for social acceptance and self-esteem went to the heart of women's liberation, raising the question of whether women in general would be allowed to decide for themselves who they were and how they would live their lives, without being told that they were less than women if their choices seemed unorthodox.

Yet heterosexual ("straight") feminists were slow to support lesbians' rights. Many of them were prejudiced against homosexuality and eager to prove that theirs was a movement of "normal" women. By ignoring gay (homosexual) women, they hoped to dispel charges that feminists were "frustrated man haters." Some claimed that there were no lesbians among them and refused to discuss lesbian issues.

Lesbians in turn formed their own organizations. Some, proclaiming the politics of "lesbian separatism," accused straight feminists of "selling out to men" and argued that lesbians, having rejected "oppressive" heterosexual relationships, were the only true feminists.

The division between straight and gay feminists was healed in time, with women on each side modifying their positions. When straight women came to understand that their antilesbianism was a form of sexism, many lesbians returned to work within groups that had initially rejected them.

The lesbian effort to win equality was part of the feminist discussion of female sexuality. Feminists showed that women's sexuality had always been defined by men and that the contemporary male definition, while perhaps meeting the needs of men, did not meet the needs of women.

William Masters' and Virginia Johnson's *Human Sexual Response,* published in 1968, helped women to understand their sexuality and reject old myths. Masters and Johnson were the first researchers to study the physiology of sexual response. Their findings substantiated what many women already knew but were hesitant to admit—that there is no one right way for women to feel sexual pleasure; rather, "there is an infinite variety of female sexual response."[30] The work of Masters and Johnson undermined the Freudian theory that women should assume a passive sexual role, as well as the notion that women were anatomically inferior to men.

Women's descriptions of their experiences and subsequent research on female sexuality confirmed the findings of Masters and Johnson. Feminists used this information to help women define and enjoy sex for themselves. They encouraged women to trust their sexual feelings, to experiment in order to find out what felt good for them, and to share their likes and dislikes with their partners.

Feminists declared that women ought to be allowed to say "no" as well as "yes" to sex, and when they said "yes" they ought to be able to get the maximum amount of pleasure. Men did not know everything there was to know about sex, and they should not have to please by performing any more than should women.

The right of women to define their own sexuality extended to health care. Feminists rejected the "doctor knows best" attitude of many gynecologists and obstetricians. They expected to be treated with respect and consulted about every aspect of their treatment.

Though many women had at first hailed the birth-control pill, subsequent research showed its potential for serious side effects. Feminists called for the development of new contraceptives that would prevent pregnancy without harming the user's health. While birth control should be available to all who sought it, they deplored government programs that forced contraception and sterilization on poor and minority women.

Without the right to abortion many women felt there could be no true sexual freedom for women. As one proabortionist wrote, "to advocate the right of abortion . . . whether for the single girl or the married woman . . . meant destroying the ultimate punishment of sex and allowing the pleasure of sex for its own sake without the concomitant obligation of childbirth. . . . Abortion stood at the apex of all our nightmares and inhibitions about sex."[31]

In 1973 the United States Supreme Court ruled that women had a constitutional right to abortion during the first six months of pregnancy. While access to abortion during the first three months of pregnancy was virtually unrestricted, the Court did allow individual states to set regulations on second-trimester (four to six months) abortions.

Feminists are still fighting for women's right to abortion. Since the high court's ruling, numerous legislative acts have attempted to limit its scope, and antiabortionists continue to seek a constitutional amendment to outlaw abortion. In 1977 Congress voted to bar Medicaid funding for abortions, thereby making it extremely difficult for poor women to obtain them.

The feminist critique of the medical and legal establishments was part of an overall analysis of institutions. In *Sexual Politics*, Kate Millett noted that women's exclusion from key institutions perpetuated their subservience to men. Women's oppression, she wrote, "is evident at once if one recalls that the military, industry, technology, universities, science, political office, finance, in short every avenue of power within society, including the coercive force of the police, is entirely in male hands."[32]

WORKING-CLASS AND MINORITY WOMEN

Working-class and minority women were largely absent from the early women's movement. Most identified more strongly along class and race lines than they did on the basis of sex. Many felt that they had little in common with the affluent housewives, professional women, and students who were agitating for women's emancipation. They argued that their men needed rights as much, if not more so, than the "already privileged" feminists. Ann Giordano, speaking for working-class women, said:

> It [women's liberation] doesn't relate to us. You can't agitate women without agitating men. It's destructive to the family. Most of us were poverty families—the men were put down as much as women. They need support too.[33]

The poet Gwendolyn Brooks commented on the attitude of blacks toward women's liberation. "Our black men have enough to do without worrying about black women either getting behind or in front of them."

Black and working-class women spoke of feminists as "spoiled children," "not my sister," "man hating," and "wrong in the way they are protesting." Both groups, however, had a vital stake in feminist issues. A majority supported day care, economic equality, and abortion. They agreed that "women are right to be unhappy in their role in American society."[34]

Working-class women depended on their husbands for

support and drew security from their traditional roles in the family. Their changing roles nevertheless led some to seek more equal marital relationships. They wanted recognition for the contributions they made both as breadwinners and as homemakers. They asked for a voice in important household decisions and the right to participate in activities outside their homes.

As Nancy Seifer has shown in *Absent from the Majority,* the social and political problems that beset working-class neighborhoods in the 1970s—school busing, urban renewal, crime, and drug addiction—involved many housewives in community organizing and city politics. These women realized that their families' survival depended on winning funding for and control over community services. They formed such groups as the National Congress of Neighborhood Women. "The difference between this . . . group and NOW," noted one member, "is that it will never just fight for women's rights. It's always concerned with larger social issues of ethnic groups and class."[35]

In some cases working-class women adopted feminist tactics, transforming their neighborhood network of friendships into consciousness raising groups. In one CR group middle-aged housewives from Brooklyn, New York, helped each other "figure out" what they would do with their lives "now that our children have left home." As a result of their discussions, some women found jobs, others went back to school, still others started community projects.

Working-class women were conscious of their differences from more affluent women.

I confess I don't feel much of a sense of sisterhood when I see pictures of Gloria Steinem [founder of *Ms* magazine and a spokeswoman of the movement] with her streaked hair and slinky figure. I feel somehow that these people don't know how it is to be getting older with very little money and education . . . it's not true that we're all in the same boat.[36]

At the same time, they realized that some problems were shared by all women.

Well, there's one thing we all have in common—we're all afraid of muggers and rapists when we walk down a dark street at night. And that's something we have in common with the colored women who live right here . . . even though most of us are better off financially than they are.[87]

Black women, even more than working-class white women, insisted that their own emancipation could not be separated from that of their men. Their liberation, they declared, depended on the elimination of racism and on improving life in the black community. Eleanor Holmes Norton pointed out this reality.

> If women were suddenly to achieve equality with men tomorrow, black women would continue to carry the entire array of utterly oppressive handicaps associated with race. Racial oppression of black people in America has done what neither class oppression or sexual oppression with all their perniciousness have ever done: destroyed an entire people and their culture. This difference is between exploitation and slavery.[88]

But Norton spoke for many women of her race when she added that "black women cannot—must not—avoid the truth about their special subservice. They are women with all that that implies."

As black men in the 1960s and 1970s struggled to achieve their own manhood, there were some who urged black women to take a back seat. In the civil-rights movement, for example, black women who had led sit-ins and boycotts, had integrated schools, and had withstood the violent assault of whites were excluded from positions of leadership. Some black men adopted the white stereotype of black women as "emasculating matriarchs." These men suggested that their own liberation depended on their women adopting a less assertive style.

Black women denied the charge, arguing against the liberation of only half the race. In her article "Double Jeopardy," Frances Beal spoke to the issue.

> If we are going to liberate ourselves as a people, it must be recognized that black women have very specific problems that have to be spoken to. We must be liberated along with the rest of the population.[89]

As blacks and females, black women had experienced more extreme forms of sexual exploitation than had white women. They had been used as sex objects and cheap labor by white society and denied a positive image of themselves as women.

> Where the white woman is the wife, the black woman is the mother on welfare . . . where the white woman is the call girl or mistress the black woman is the street prostitute; where the white woman is married to a man who can afford it, a black woman takes over the care of the home and children for her.[40]

Because racism and sexual exploitation were so completely intertwined, black women developed their own brand of feminism. Their organizations had the double goal of helping black women achieve a positive identity while also combating the oppression of all black people. In 1973 the National Black Feminist Organization was formed with the aim of "strengthening the efforts of the black liberation struggle by encouraging all the talents . . . of black women to emerge, strong and beautiful . . . and assume positions of leadership and honor in the black community."

> The black woman has had to be strong, yet we are persecuted for having survived. We have been called "matriarchs" by white racists and black nationalists. We have virtually no positive self image to validate our existence. Black women want to be proud, dignified, free. . . . We, not white men or black men, must define our own self image as black women and not fall into the mistake of being placed upon the pedestal which is even being rejected by white women. It has been hard for black women to emerge from the myriad of distorted images that have portrayed us as grinning Beulahs, castrating Sapphires, and pancake-box Jemimahs . . . we realized the need to establish ourselves as an independent black feminist organization.[41]

Economic issues were of primary concern to black and working-class women. Both groups were acutely affected by the growing inequity women faced in the job market.

The earnings gap between male and female workers was increasing. In 1956 woman's salaries averaged 63 percent of men's, and in 1973 they averaged only 57 percent. This decrease in women's relative income compared to men's was especially noticeable in the clerical fields, which employed the largest number of women workers. In 1956 female clericals earned 72 percent the wages of male clericals and in 1973 only 61 percent.

Another serious problem for black and working-class women was child care. Black women had long faced the problem of how to provide for their children while they worked outside the home. Increasingly black mothers were joined in the labor force by white working-class mothers. Not only did women with grown children and children in school work outside their homes, but so did women with preschool-age children. By the 1970s these young mothers were the most rapidly growing group in the female labor force. Many of them were heads of families.

As in previous decades, working wives and mothers were offered few services to ease their double workload. Although some six million preschool-age children had working mothers in 1973, there was space for only 640,000 in public and private day-care centers. Not until 1977 were working mothers allowed a tax credit for child care.

While middle-class feminists fought for access to professional and managerial work, black and working-class women fought for decent pay and improved working conditions. "We're on the nitty-gritty level," said one black woman. A working-class woman agreed. "Feminists talk about meaningful work, while we're talking about earning enough to support our families if we have to work." Yet both groups recognized the use they could make of equal employment rulings won by women's rights advocates.

Mildred Jeffries, an organizer for the United Auto Workers (UAW), believed that the women's movement helped to bring about in a few years many of the gains she had spent forty years fighting for. "I don't care what they [women's liberationists] did, burn bras, anything! I'm totally grateful to the young women. . . . The men had to be brought along kicking and screaming every step of the way, but we did it." Jeffries pointed to the UAW's endorsement of equal pay, integrated seniority lists, a day-care policy, and the Equal Rights Amendment.[42]

These gains helped individual women win acceptance into what had formally been "male only" skilled crafts and blue-collar jobs. They became miners, mechanics, painters, carpenters. Telephone operators left their switchboards to become repair and installment workers, police women joined men in patrol cars and on the beat.

Kathy Richter told *The New York Times* some of the difficulties she faced when she "traded her secretary's typewriter for a factory worker's drill . . . on a production line at the Chevrolet gear and axle plant." Her "father and brother bet her that she wouldn't last more than two days"; male coworkers claimed that she "didn't belong to the plant"; and her foreman tried to force her to quit during her probationary period.

Despite male resistance and an eight-month layoff (because women were the last hired, they were the first laid off in a recession), Richter preferred her new job. As a unionized auto worker, she earned almost twice her secretarial salary and spent far less on "job-related expenses."

> After four years at Detroit Edison [as a secretary] I was making $3.85 an hour. . . . And I started out here at $4.65. (Now she earns $6.60.) . . . in an office . . . I had to be dressed . . . my hair done, nylons. . . . It costs money. Here I'm in blue jeans and a sweatshirt.[48]

Few working women earned the salary or benefits granted to Kathy Richter as a member of the UAW. The overwhelming majority, thirty million out of thirty-four million, were nonunionized. The Coalition of Labor Union Women (CLUW), formed in 1974 by three thousand women representing fifty-eight trade unions, hoped to improve the status of all working women. CLUW aimed to "take aggressive steps to more effectively address ourselves to the critical needs of 30 million unorganized sisters and to make our unions more responsive to the needs of all women, especially the needs of minority women."

During the 1970s more women joined and established unions than in any decade since the 1930s. One of the most dramatic union struggles occurred in the Southern textile mills. Poor white and black women joined together in a renewed attempt to establish industrial unions.

Working women's organizing attempts went beyond the factory setting. Domestic workers demanded protection under minimum wage and social security laws. Welfare mothers organized. And even housewives proposed unionization. At a 1970 Consultation on Working-Class Women, sponsored by the National Project on Ethnic America and the National Council of Negro Women, one participant spoke out.

A crazy idea is a union for housewives, and I'm serious about this. The powerlessness that we've been talking about comes from the fact that women, particularly the wives of working-class men, have absolutely no security. What happens if the husband drops dead? They know they can't get along on social security. What happens if he simply gets tired of her nagging and walks out? A union could give some sort of security to those women.[44]

Women office workers waged one of the most significant organizing drives. Beginning with small protests on their jobs, they challenged the myth that clerical work was "woman's work" and that they were "better off" than were blue-collar workers. Many soon moved toward the idea of unionization. One legal secretary explained her views.

Most of us started out with a sort of anti-union attitude because we felt that a union shop . . . would deny your right of free choice. But we tried all other means—petitions, meetings, pressuring management to make certain changes. We saw that if we didn't have any clout, we didn't get respect from the employer.[45]

Female clerical workers in business, government agencies, and universities sought affiliation with unions promoting sex equality. They fought for contracts that included maternity leaves, training and promotion of women, health care and day care, as well as better wages and working conditions. At the same time, groups such as Women Employed of Chicago, "9 to 5" of Boston, and Women Office Workers of New York City organized female clericals on a citywide basis.

Women who organized on their jobs began to change their feelings about themselves.

I don't believe there was one of us . . . who had ever made a speech or written a leaflet or engaged in any type of organizing before. We didn't know we could do it . . . It's the most exciting thing I've ever done in my life.

Women office workers were a majority of all working women, comprising 75 percent of the clerical work force. Their efforts to organize had an impact on both the women's movement and the labor movement. In *Not Servants, Not Machines,* Jean Tepperman wrote about this situation.

It's possible to convince someone that a woman lawyer or college professor is a serious, intelligent person. But many people see those women as exceptions—they're not "just" secretaries or waitresses or housewives, like most women. So when clerical workers begin to organize and assert themselves, it is a much more basic challenge to stereotypes of women. . . .

This movement also challenges the idea that the purpose of the women's movement is to clear the way so that individual women can compete with men to become bank presidents or astronauts. . . . Even if half those top positions were filled by females, it would still leave most women, like most men, doing ordinary jobs. If that were the only change, women would still be getting paid less, treated worse and looked down upon.[46]

THE MOVEMENT BRANCHES OUT

In the 1970s the number and kinds of groups in the women's movement multiplied dramatically. One study estimated that by 1973 between eighty thousand and a hundred thousand women had joined one or another of these groups.

Consciousness-raising groups grew most rapidly. Next to CR, women most frequently organized along occupational lines. Professional women, like blue- and white-collar women, demanded equal treatment at work. Female lawyers, doctors, historians, psychologists, scientists, and artists all protested the sexist thinking of their male colleagues and fought for greater opportunities for women in their fields.

Groups were also formed for specific purposes—to change the portrayal of women in the media, school texts, and children's books and their treatment in schools, churches, and hospitals. Some lobbying groups evolved into feminist institutions. There were health and psychological counseling clinics, centers for rape victims and battered wives, credit unions, publishing firms, magazines, day-care centers, employment agencies, and women's-studies programs. A Boston women's health collective wrote and published *Our Bodies, Ourselves,* a self-help book that included information on everything from nutrition and karate to female physiology and sexuality.

Seeking greater political power, women formed the bipartisan National Women's Political Caucus in 1971. Democratic and Republican women organized to form a power bloc within their political parties. Each group lobbied to increase the number of female delegates to national political conventions and to win planks concerning women's issues in the party platform. They encouraged women to seek political office and supported candidates of either sex who were sympathetic to feminist goals.

As the movement grew, the differences that divided women's liberationists from women's rights advocates diminished. Women from both camps found themselves supporting many of the same goals and working together on a variety of issues. Moderate feminists in NOW began to support the analysis of radical feminists. Articles that discussed the ideas first raised in small groups—such as Anne Koedt's "The Myth of the Vaginal Orgasm," Pat Mainardi's "The Politics of Housework," and Naomi Weisstein's "Psychology Constructs the Female"—changed all women's thinking about the nature and scope of their oppression. Furthermore, as a result of their own work in the movement, many women realized that winning formal rights was only a first step toward the goal of eliminating sex roles. "It's bound to happen," said one woman. "The more you are in the movement, the more aware you become of all the attitudes and values which uphold sex discrimination."

This change could be seen within NOW. In the late 1960s NOW members fought for legal reforms to end sex discrimination in education and employment. They hesitated and debated before affirming that abortion was a women's-rights issue. They tabled motions calling for support of lesbians, and they argued that such issues as female sexuality and women's roles as wives and mothers were "irrelevant" and "nonpolitical." By 1973 NOW had taken a different direction. Members established task forces to work on numerous issues, including women's health and control of their own bodies; marriage, divorce, and family relations; sexuality and lesbianism; minority women; older women; and women and unions.

At the same time women's liberationists were changing as well. The 1960s confrontational style of protest faded. Radical feminists moved from developing theory and staging "zap actions" to attacking specific institutional problems. They became more willing to adopt moderate tactics.

The gains won by NOW and WEAL through legal action raised hopes for achieving change "through the system." Florynce Kennedy, urging women to "stop agonizing and start organizing," commented as follows.

> If you've got a broken leg, you don't get up and win the Olympics. The first step is to get out of bed . . . Some people say they won't work "inside the system"—they're waiting for the revolution. Well, when the ramparts are there, honey, I'll be there, but until then I'm going to go right on zapping the business and government delinquents . . . and all the other niggerizers any way I can. The biggest sin is sitting on your ass.[47]

Because feminists never attempted to unify the movement into one central organization with a uniform ideology, there was room for all women to seek a place for themselves within it. Various feminists believed that equality could be achieved only by ending capitalism or the family structure or women's roles as childbearers or all heterosexual sex. Others supported specific reforms but staunchly defended the nuclear family or the existing economic structure. The movement became a huge umbrella sheltering women of diverse viewpoints and interests.

The underlying message feminists communicated was that women's liberation "is as much a state of mind as a movement." Robin Morgan described it as follows.

> This is not a movement one "joins." There are no rigid structures or membership cards. The Women's Liberation Movement exists where three or four friends or neighbors decide to meet regularly over coffee and talk about their personal lives. It also exists in the cells of women's jails, on the welfare lines, in the supermarket, the factory, the convent, the farm, the maternity ward, the street corner, the old ladies' home, the kitchen, the steno pool, the bed. It exists in your mind and in the political and personal insights that you can contribute to change and shape and help its growth.[48]

The concept that women can be equal to men has taken hold in America. Once the province of unpopular rebels, the idea of women's equality is now supported, at

least in principle, by a majority of "ordinary" women—
suburban housewives, farm women, "white ethnics," minority women, high-school-age women, old women. Men,
too, have agreed that women deserve an equal chance.
In 1975 a Harris poll found that 63 percent of the
American populace favors "most of the efforts to strength-
en and change women's status." In 1970 it had been 42
percent in favor, 41 percent against.

The first goal of the modern feminist movement—to
raise the consciousness of both women and men—has
been remarkably successful. One woman described the
changes she perceived in herself and other women.

Ten years ago, the thing to do at a party was for the
women and the men to break up into groups. Well, they still
do that, but instead of talking about toilet-training and
where they get their hair done, women are talking about
feminism. They discuss what they are *doing*.

During the past ten years women have changed themselves in large and small ways. They have learned to say
"no," to speak up, and to be assertive.

Women have joined the army. Women have become
priests and rabbis. Two women have been elected governors of states. A black Congresswoman was the keynote
speaker at the 1976 Democratic National Convention.

Women are resisting the crime of rape, calling for the
prosecution of rapists and an end to the idea that the
rape victim is the criminal. Girls are competing with boys
in sports and demanding that their athletic programs be
funded. Women are telephoning men to ask for dates;
women are paying half the check. Women who have no
wish to marry feel free not to do so. Friendships between
women have grown deeper. Women are loving themselves
and each other.

The new choices made by women have created more
questions than answers. As author Jane Howard writes,
"we now have the freedom to be confused."

Options—was that what we were saying we wanted?
Okay, here they are, in profusion: home or office, long
skirts or Levi's, chopsticks or fork, kids this year or next or
never, my place or yours, bridal showers or graduate
school or abortions or custody fights, take your pick or try
to take it all.

The old masculine-feminine stereotypes no longer fit. But, as Howard points out, it is not yet entirely clear what will take their place.

Money, fame and power, for example, are nice, but these traditional male indices of "success" don't keep us warm at night, and so are incomplete. Marriage and motherhood often do mean warm nights, which are nice, but these traditional female indices of "success" don't guarantee interesting days. The new definition will have to be more generous, and it might be full of surprises.

While there is no doubt that consciousness about women's inequality has been raised, the goal of emancipation is far from won. The idea of equality for women is supported in the abstract, but the institutional changes needed to make that idea a reality still meet with great resistance.

Woman's place in the family and her position in the labor force remain the cornerstones of her oppression. While feminists have encouraged women to reject traditional sex roles at home and on the job, there has been little change in public policy to bolster women in this effort. Child care and household labor are still viewed as "woman's work."

The destructive effect of sex role stereotyping will persist at least until certain basic reforms—adequate and inexpensive child care; wages for housewives and househusbands—are achieved. In addition, there must be public recognition for the fact that the responsibility for home and children belongs equally to both sexes.

Despite the new activism and visibility of women in the labor force, their overall economic situation has not improved. Though in 1974 women comprised 43 percent of all workers, nearly half remained segregated in ten occupations: secretary, salesworker, domestic, elementary school teacher, bookkeeper, waitress, typist, cashier, sewer and stitcher, and nurse.

Just as the earnings gap between male and female is on the rise, so is the gap between male and female unemployment. In *Born Female*, Caroline Bird notes, "In 1970, our [national] prosperity depends on the labor and earnings of women." But women remain a cheap "labor reserve," still condemned to be the last hired and the first fired.

If women's efforts to achieve emancipation áre to be sustained, they must continue to generate "feminist consciousness" and translate that consciousness into action. Only by keeping the process of self-definition alive will women be able to overcome resistance to their full autonomy.

By joining together to seek new choices and freedoms, women have been able to change their history. Writing sixty years ago, Emma Goldman envisioned limitless possibilities.

> True emancipation . . . begins in woman's soul. History tells us that every oppressed class gains true liberation from its masters through its own efforts. It is necessary that woman learn that lesson, that she realize that her freedom will reach as far as her power to achieve her freedom reaches.

Notes

1: Founding Mothers

Readers concerned with the role of women in colonial America may be interested in the following books: Elizabeth Dexter, *Colonial Women of Affairs: Women in Business and the Professions in America before 1776,* (Houghton Mifflin, 1931). This book is a classic which has been criticized in recent years for painting an overly optimistic picture of the opportunities enjoyed by colonial women. Daniel Boorstin's *The Americans: A Social History of the United States,* (Capricorn Books, 1969) provides a more sophisticated discussion of the professional opportunities—particularly in law and medicine—available to colonial women. Arthur Schlesinger Sr.'s *The Birth of the Nation,* (Knopf, 1968) is a very pleasant and readable social history with a great deal of material about women. Schlesinger was among the very first American historians to treat seriously the role of women in the American past.

1. Julia Cherry Spruill, *Women's Life and Work in the Southern Colonies* (New York: Norton, 1972), p. 3.
2. Ibid., p. 81.
3. Page Smith, *Daughters of the Promised Land* (Boston: Little Brown, 1970), p. 54.
4. Daniel Boorstin, *The Americans: The Colonial Experience* (New York: Random House, 1958), p. 350.
5. Spruill, *Women's Life and Work in the Southern Colonies,* p. 41.
6. J. C. Furnas, *The Americans: A Social History of the United States* (Capricorn Books, 1969), p. 261.
7. Carl Holliday, *Woman's Life in Colonial Days* (New York: Ungar, 1960), p. 197.
8. Boorstin, *The Americans,* p. 229.
9. Holliday, *Woman's Life in Colonial Days,* p. 298.
10. For a full discussion of Margaret Brent's political activities, see Spruill, *Woman's Life and Work in the Southern Colonies,* pp. 236–41.
11. Boorstin, *The Americans,* p. 217.
12. For a discussion of indentured servants see Arthur Schlesinger Sr., *The Birth of the Nation* (New York: Knopf, 1968), pp. 59–61.
13. Ibid., p. 15.
14. Ibid., p. 19.
15. Spruill, *Women's Life and Work in the Southern Colonies,* p. 179–184.
16. Ibid., 180.
17. Ibid., p. 45.
18. Schlesinger, *The Birth of the Nation,* p. 22.
19. Spruill, *Women's Life and Work in the Southern Colonies,* p. 52–53.

2: Suffer Not a Woman to Speak

1. A definitive work on the sectarian establishments in the new world is by Sidney Ahlstrom, *A Religious History of the American People* (New Haven: Yale University Press, 1972).

2. Perry Miller, *The American Puritans* (New York: Doubleday/Anchor, 1958), pp. 48–59.
3. Carl Holliday, *Woman's Life in Colonial Days* (New York: Ungar, 1960), p. 47.
4. Arthur Schlesinger Sr., *The Birth of the Nation* (New York: Knopf, 1968), p. 77.
5. Holliday, *Woman's Life in Colonial Days*, p. 51–59.
6. Alice M. Earle, *Childhood in Colonial Days* (New York: Macmillan, 1927), p. 238.
7. Ibid., p. 238.
8. Julia Cherry Spruill, *Women's Life and Work in the Southern Colonies* (New York: Norton, 1972), pp. 249–51.
9. Mary R. Beard, *Woman as a Force in History* (Collier, 1971), p. 89.
10. Andrew Sinclair, *The Emancipation of the American Woman* (New York: Harper & Row, 1965), p. 84.
11. Leo Kanowitz, *Women and the Law* (Albuquerque: University of New Mexico Press, 1969), p. 39–40.

3: Remember the Ladies

1. See Samuel Eliot Morison, *The Oxford History of the American People*, Vol. 1 (New York: New American Library, 1972), pp. 283–286.
2. Alice Brown, *Women of Colonial Times* (New York: Scribners, 1896), p. 12.
3. Sally Smith Booth, *The Women of '76* (New York: Hastings House, 1973), p. 264–265.
4. Brown, *Women of Colonial Times*, p. 88.
5. Booth, *The Women of '76*, p. 121–170.
6. Ibid., p. 144.
7. Ibid., p. 52.
8. Elizabeth Evans, *Weathering the Storm* (New York: Scribners, 1975), pp. 303–334.
9. Morison, *The Oxford History of the American People*, p. 336.
10. Janet Whitney, *Abigail Adams* (Boston: Little Brown, 1947), p. 87.
11. Ibid., p. 101.
12. Meade Minnigerode, *Some American Ladies* (New York: Putnam, 1926), p. 187.
13. L. H. Butterfield, ed., "The Adams Papers," Series II, *Adams Family Correspondence* (Cambridge: Harvard University Press, 1963), Abigail Adams to John Adams, letter dated March 31, 1776.
14. Butterfield, *Adams Family Correspondence*, John Adams to Abigail Adams, letter dated April 14, 1776.

4: Black Bondage/White Pedestal

1. *Narrative of James Williams, An American Slave* (Philadelphia: Historic Publications, 1838).
2. The concept of the "family, white and black" is discussed in detail by Eugene Genovese in his excellent book, *Roll Jordan Roll*, pp. 133–149. (Random House, 1974; paperback, Vintage, 1976. All references are to the Vintage edition.)
3. Norman Yetman, ed., *Voices from Slavery*, "Ferebe Rogers" (New York: Holt Rinehart and Winston, 1970), p. 257. This book contains interviews with former slaves conducted by the WPA during the 1930s.
4. Francis Anne Kemble, *Journal of a Residence on a Georgian Plantation*, ed. John A. Scott (New York: Knopf, 1961), p. 305.
5. Yetman, ed., *Voices from Slavery*, "Sarah Gudger," p. 121.
6. Kemble, *Journal of a Residence on a Georgian Plantation*, pp. 224–225.

7. Ibid., p. 481.
8. Yetman, ed., *Voices from Slavery*, "Mary Bell," p. 23.
9. Ibid., "Lucy Ann Dunn," p. 101.
10. Ibid., "George Key," p. 110.
11. Ibid., "Sarah Debro," p. 100. Italics were added by the authors.
12. Ibid., "Delia Garlic," p. 133.
13. Harriet Jacobs Brent, *Incidents in the Life of a Slave Girl*, ed. Lydia Marie Child (Boston, 1861; republished by Negro History Press, Detroit), pp. 26–27.
14. Sidney Mintz, *Caribbean Transformation* (Chicago: Aldine Company, 1974), p. 80.
15. Quoted in Genovese, *Roll Jordan Roll*, p. 456.
16. Adolph Niemoeller, *Sexual Slavery in America* (Panurge Press, 1935), p. 77.
17. Williams Wells Brown, *Five Slave Narratives* (New York: Arno Press, 1968), p. 48.
18. Henry Grimke was the brother of Sarah and Angelina Grimke, the famous abolitionists from South Carolina. (See Chapter 6.) After the Civil War the nephews got in touch with their white aunts. A fine relationship ensued, the sisters helping their nephews to earn college degrees and establish themselves in the North. See Gerda Lerner; ed., *Black Women in White America: A Documentary History* (New York: Vintage, 1973), p. 52.
19. Brent, *Incidents in the Life of a Slave Girl*, p. 42.
20. Ibid., p. 60.
21. Ibid., p. 31.
22. Lerner, ed., *Black Women in White America*, p. 51.
23. W. E. B. DuBois, *Darkwater: Voices From Within the Veil* (New York: Schocken, 1968), p. 172.
24. For a general discussion of slave resistance, see Raymond and Alice Bauer, "Day to Day Resistance to Slavery," *The Journal of Negro History*, Vol. 27 (1942), p. 388–419.
25. Ibid., p. 394.
26. Yetman, ed., *Voices from Slavery*, p. 19.
27. Ibid., p. 239.
28. Ibid., p. 239.
29. Sarah Bradford, *Harriet Tubman: Moses to Her People* (Corinth Books, 1961), p. 31–32.
30. Ibid., p. 18.
31. Ibid., p. 30.
32. Anne Firor Scott, *The Southern Lady* (Chicago: The University of Chicago Press, 1970), p. 12. See also Genovese, *Roll Jordan Roll*, pp. 81 ff.
33. Genovese, *Roll Jordan Roll*, p. 79.
34. Mary Chestnut, *Diary from Dixie* (Boston: Houghton Mifflin, 1949), p. 21.
35. Scott, *The Southern Lady*, p. 53.
36. Chestnut, *Diary from Dixie*, p. 44.
37. Ibid., pp. 10–11.
38. J. W. Cash, *The Mind of the South* (New York: Knopf, 1941), p. 83.
39. Ibid., p. 84–86.

5: The Making of a Middle-Class Lady

1. A number of general sources were used to arrive at an understanding of the relationship between women and the commercial and industrial revolution. Among them are Alexis de Tocqueville, *Democracy in America*, ed. Richard Heffner (New York: New American Library, ...56); Mrs. Frances Trolloppe, *Domestic Manners of the Americans*, ... York: Vintage, 1962); and Mary P. Ryan, *Womanhood in*

America, (New Viewpoints, 1975.) Ryan's chapter "Mothers of Civilization," pp. 137–193, was particularly helpful.

2. Historian Anne Firror Scott in *The Southern Lady,* (Chicago: University of Chicago Press, 1970) points out that Dew is not typical of sphere theorists in that he believed "womanly" qualities to be the product of environment and training rather than of nature. Her point is well taken; but for general purposes the most important aspect of Dew is the explicitness with which he described the spheres.

3. Aileen Kraditor, ed., *Up from the Pedestal* (New York: Quadrangle, 1970), pp. 45–46.

4. Ibid., p. 46.

5. *Godey's Lady Book,* July, 1832.

6. Nancy F. Cott, ed., *Root of Bitterness* (New York: Dutton, 1972), p. 141.

7. Barbara Welter, "The Cult of True Womanhood: 1820–1860," *American Quarterly,* XVIII, Summer 1966, pp. 151–174. It is Welter's thesis that these four attributes—piety, purity, submission, and domesticity—defined "true women" in the nineteenth century.

8. Gail Parker, ed., *The Oven Birds* (New York: Doubleday/Anchor, 1972), p. 204.

9. Ibid., p. 187.

10. Welter, "The Cult of True Womanhood," p. 155.

11. William Alexander Alcott, *The Physiology of Marriage* (Hewett and Company, 1856), p. 57.

12. Ibid., p. 53.

13. Milton Rugoff, *Prudery and Passion* (New York: Putnam, 1971). Part One, "The Denial of Eros" (pp. 35–120), contains important information on the manifestations of prudery in the second half of the nineteenth century.

14. Ibid., p. 108.

15. Alcott, *The Physiology of Marriage,* p. 167.

16. Ryan, *Womanhood in America,* pp. 137–191.

17. Barbar Ehrenreich and Deidre English, *Complaints and Disorders: The Sexual Politics of Sickness* (Glass Mountain Pamphlet No. 2, The Feminist Press, 1973), pp. 5–89.

18. Carol Smith Rosenberg, "The Female World of Love and Ritual," *Signs,* vol. 1, number 1 (Autumn, 1975), pp. 1–30. The authors have relied extensively on the research of Ms. Rosenberg in this section.

19. Ibid., p. 14.

20. Ibid., p. 14.

21. Ibid., p. 16.

22. Ryan, "Mothers of Civilization," *Womanhood in America.* See also Phillippe Aries, *Centuries of Childhood* (New York: Vintage, 1962), for the best general discussion of the changing role of the child in the middle-class family.

6: Origins of Feminism

1. Mary Wollstonecraft, *A Vindication of the Rights of Woman* (New York: Norton, 1967), pp. 31–73.

2. Gerda Lerner, *The Grimke Sisters from South Carolina* (New York: Schocken, 1971), pp. 123–124.

3. Ibid., p. 162.

4. Ibid., p. 187. Italics added by the authors.

5. Ibid., p. 146.

6. Aileen Kraditor, ed., *Up from the Pedestal* (New York: Quadrangle, 1970), pp. 50–52.

7. Ibid., p. 52.

8. Lerner, *The Grimke Sisters,* p. 192.

9. Ibid., p. 193.

10. Ibid., p. 4.
11. Ibid., p. 7.
12. Elizabeth Cady Stanton, *Eighty Years and More: Reminiscences of Elizabeth Cady Stanton 1815–1897* (New York: Schocken, 1971: reprint of 1898 edition).

7: The First Feminist Revolt

1. All quoted material on Elizabeth Cady Stanton is drawn from Elizabeth Cady Stanton, *Eighty Years and More: Reminiscences of Elizabeth Cady Stanton 1815–1897* (New York: Schocken, 1971: reprint of 1898 edition), unless otherwise attributed.
2. Theodore Stanton and Harriet Stanton Blatch, eds., "Elizabeth Cady Stanton to Susan B. Anthony, September 10, 1855," *Elizabeth Cady Stanton as Revealed in Her Letters, Diary and Reminiscences,* vol. II (New York: Harper, 1922), pp. 59–60.
3. Alma Lutz, *Created Equal* (John Day, 1940), pp. 16–17, 21–22, 111.
4. Theodore Stanton, "Elizabeth Cady Stanton to Rebecca R. Eyester, May 1, 1847," *Elizabeth Cady Stanton As Revealed in Her Letters,* pp. 147–148.
5. Stanton, *Eighty Years and More,* pp. 147–148.
6. "Declaration of Rights and Sentiments, 1848," in *History of Woman Suffrage,* vol. I (Rochester: Charles Mann, 1881), pp. 70–73.
7. Quoted material on Lucy Stone drawn from Alice Stone Blackwell, *Lucy Stone: Pioneer of Woman's Rights* (Boston: Little Brown, 1930), and Elinor Rice Hays, *Morning Star: A Biography of Lucy Stone* (New York: Harcourt, 1961).
8. *History of Woman Suffrage,* vol. I, pp. 165–166.
9. Ibid., vol. I, pp. 115–117.
10. Stanton, *Eighty Years and More,* "The Albany Register, March 7, 1854," p. 190.
11. Aileen Kraditor, ed., "Gerrit Smith to Elizabeth Cady Stanton, December 1, 1855," *Up from the Pedestal* (New York: Quadrangle, 1968), pp. 125–129.
12. Lutz, *Created Equal,* "Elizabeth Cady Stanton, in *Carpet Bag,* July 5, 1851," p. 65.
13. Ibid., "Henry Stanton to Elizabeth Cady Stanton," p. 66.
14. Theodore Stanton, "Elizabeth Cady Stanton to Elizabeth Smith Miller, June 11, 1851," *Elizabeth Cady Stanton as Revealed in Her Letters* pp. 28–31.
15. Eleanor Flexner, "Elizabeth Cady Stanton to Susan B. Anthony, Feb. 19, 1854," *Century of Struggle* (New York: Atheneum, 1959), p. 84.
16. Theodore Stanton, "Elizabeth Cady Stanton to Daniel C. Stanton, October 14, 1851," *Elizabeth Cady Stanton as Revealed in Her Letters,* pp. 35–36.
17. "Marriage of Lucy Stone Under Protest, *Worcester Spy,* May 1, 1851," *History of Woman Suffrage,* vol. I, pp. 260–261.
18. Andrew Sinclair, "Frank Stone to Lucy Stone, Nov. 28, 1846, Library of Congress;" Luther Stone to Lucy Stone, June 6, 1847, Library of Congress," *The Emancipation of the American Woman* (New York: Harper & Row, 1965), p. 68.
19. Henry Blackwell-Lucy Stone courtship correspondence in the Library of Congress, Blackwell Papers Collection, quoted in Hays, *Morning* ͡͡r, pp. 127–129, 133–143, and Sinclair, *The Emancipation of the ͡rican Woman,* pp. 69–70.
͡ore Stanton, "Lucy Stone to Elizabeth Cady Stanton, October ͡6," *Elizabeth Cady Stanton as Revealed in Her Letters,* pp.
͡zabeth Cady Stanton to Susan B. Anthony, March 1, 1853,"

22. Ibid., "Elizabeth Cady Stanton to Thomas Wentworth Higginson, 1859," pp. 73–74; diary entries, pp. 210, 183.
23. Ibid., "Elizabeth Cady Stanton to Henry Stanton, February 13, 1851, pp. 26–27.
24. Ibid., "Elizabeth Cady Stanton to Lucretia Mott, October 22, 1852," pp. 44–45.
25. Stanton, *Eighty Years and More*, pp. 145–146.
26. Theodore Stanton, "Elizabeth Cady Stanton to Susan B. Anthony, April 2, 1852," *Elizabeth Cady Stanton as Revealed in Her Letters*, pp. 41–42; diary entries, p. 174.
27. Bibliographical material on Susan B. Anthony drawn from Alma Lutz, *Susan B. Anthony* (Boston: Beacon, 1959); Ida Husted Harper, *The Life and Work of Susan B. Anthony*, 3 vols. (Indianapolis, Hollenbeck, 1898–1908); Katherine Anthony, *Susan B. Anthony* (Doubleday, 1954).
28. Theodore Stanton, "Elizabeth Cady Stanton to Susan B. Anthony, June 20, 1852," *Elizabeth Cady Stanton as Revealed in Her Letters*, pp. 61–62. Italics in original.
29. *History of Woman Suffrage*, vol. I, p. 514.
30. Harper, vol. I, p. 104.
31. Theodore Stanton, "Elizabeth Cady Stanton to Susan B. Anthony, September 10, 1855," *Elizabeth Cady Stanton as Revealed in Her Letters*, p. 60.
32. Ibid., "Elizabeth Cady Stanton to Susan B. Anthony, April 2, 1852," *Elizabeth Cady Stanton as Revealed in Her Letters*, pp. 41–42.
33. *History of Woman Suffrage*, vol. I, pp. 458–459.
34. See Yuri Suhl, *Ernestine L. Rose* (New York, 1959), pp. 49–65.
35. *History of Woman Suffrage*, vol. I, pp. 629–630.
36. Theodore Stanton, "Susan B. Anthony to Elizabeth Cady Stanton, 1856," *Elizabeth Cady Stanton as Revealed in Her Letters*, p. 65.
37. Ibid., "Elizabeth Cady Stanton to Susan B. Anthony, June 10, 1856," *Elizabeth Cady Stanton as Revealed in Her Letters*, pp. 66–67.
38. *History of Woman Suffrage*, vol. I, pp. 716–720.
39. Ibid., vol. I, p. 735.
40. Theodore Stanton, "Elizabeth Cady Stanton to Susan B. Anthony, 1860," *Elizabeth Cady Stanton as Revealed in Her Letters*, pp. 82–83.

8: On the Loom

1. Mary Beard, ed., *America Through Women's Eyes* (New York: Macmillan, 1933), p. 133.
2. Hannah Josephson, *The Golden Threads* (Duell, Sloan and Pearce, 1949), pp. 64–65.
3. Harriet H. Robinson, *Early Factory Labor in New England*, 14th Annual Report of the Massachusetts Bureau of Statistics for 1883 (Wright & Potter, 1889), pp. 11–12.
4. Lucy Larcom, *A New England Girlhood* (Boston: Houghton Mifflin, 1892), p. 152.
5. From *Mind Among the Spindles*, a miscellany selected from the *Lowell Offering* (Jordon, Swift and Wiley, 1845), p. 89.
6. Josephson, *The Golden Threads*, p. 72.
7. Ibid., p. 83.
8. Larcom, *A New England Girlhood*, p. 182.
9. Robinson, *Early Factory Labor*, p. 14.
10. Catherine Beecher, *The Evils Suffered by American Women and Children: The Causes and the Remedy* (Harper, 1846).
11. Orestes Brownson, "The Laboring Classes," *Boston Quarterly Review*, July 1840, quoted in Josephson, *The Golden Threads*, pp. 192–194.
12. Quoted in Josephson, *The Golden Threads*, p. 107.
13. See Philip S. Foner, *History of the Labor Movement in the*

States, vol. I (New York: International Publishers, 1949) and Norman Ware, *The Industrial Worker 1840–1860* (Gloucester, Mass., P. Smith, 1959; reprint of 1924 edition), for valuable accounts of women's early involvement in the labor movement.

14. Quoted in Foner, *History of the Labor Movement*, p. 109.
15. *The Offering*, No. III, September 1843, quoted in Foner, *History of the Labor Movement*, p. 194.
16. Bertha M. Stearns, "Early Factory Magazines in New England," *Journal of Economic and Business History*, vol. II, August 1930, quoted in Foner, *History of the Labor Movement*, p. 195.
17. *Voice of Industry*, May 15, 1846, quoted in Eleanor Flexner, *Century of Struggle* (Cambridge: Harvard University Press, 1959), p. 58.
18. Report of the Massachusetts House of Representatives committee on a ten-hour workday, March 12, 1845, reprinted in Nancy F. Cott, ed., *Root of Bitterness* (New York: Dutton, 1972), p. 156.
19. Abbott Lawrence, quoted in Josephson, *The Golden Threads*, p. 176.
20. Josephson, *The Golden Threads*, p. 288.
21. Lynn Cralazar, "Women in the Working Class," *Radical America Pamphlet* (New England Free Press, 1972), p. 5.

9: Homespun Blue and Gray

1. Anthony, Gage, Stanton, *et. al.*, *History of Woman Suffrage*, vol. II (1861–1876) (Rochester, N. Y., 1881), p. 22.
2. Katherine M. Jones, ed., *Heroines of Dixie*, vol. I (New York: Ballantine, 1974, reprint of 1955 edition), pp. 23, 24–25, 33.
3. Ibid., pp. 115–125.
4. Anne Firror Scott, *The Southern Lady* (Chicago: University of Chicago Press, 1970), p. 85.
5. See Phoebe Yates Pember, *A Southern Woman's Story* (G. W. Carleton, 1879).
6. Gerda Lerner, *The Woman in American History* (Reading, Mass.: Addison Wesley, 1971), p. 98.
7. Sarah Bradford, *Harriet Tubman: Moses to Her People* (Corinth Books, 1961).
8. *History of Woman Suffrage*, vol. II, pp. 3–11.
9. Parthenia A. Hague, *A Blockaded Family* (Boston: Houghton Mifflin, 1888), pp. 261–265.
10. Jones, *Heroines of Dixie*, vol. II, p. 71.
11. Hague, *A Blockaded Family*, p. 258.
12. Jones, *Heroines of Dixie*, pp. 119–120.
13. Ibid., pp. 5–21.
14. Mary Chestnut, *A Diary from Dixie* (Boston: Houghton Mifflin, 1949), p. 38.
15. Jones, *Heroines of Dixie*, vol. II, p. 156.
16. Ibid., vol. II, pp. 156–159.
17. *History of Woman Suffrage*, vol. II, p. 53.
18. Theodore Stanton, diary entry of Feb. 12, 1901, in *Elizabeth Cady Stanton as Revealed in Her Letters, Diary and Reminiscences* (Harper, 1922), p. 355.
19. *History of Woman Suffrage*, vol. II, pp. 50–89.
20. Scott, *The Southern Lady*, p. 91.
21. Myrta L. Avary, *Dixie After the War*, quoted in Scott, *The Southern Lady*, p. 98.
22. *Compendium of the Ninth Census* (Washington, 1873), quoted in Scott, *The Southern Lady*, p. 106.
23. Quoted in Gerder Lerner, ed., *Black Women in White America* (New York: Vintage, 1973), pp. 243–249.
24. Ibid., p. 185.

26. Ibid., pp. 167, 158–159.
27. Ibid., pp. 155–156.

10: From Women's Rights to Human Suffrage

1. Speech by Elizabeth Cady Stanton on Reconstruction, 1867, Library of Congress, quoted in Andrew Sinclair, *The Emancipation of the American Woman,* (New York: Harper & Row, 1965), p. 185.
2. Theodore Stanton, "Wendell Phillips to Elizabeth Cady Stanton, May 10, 1865;" "Elizabeth Cady Stanton to Wendell Phillips, May 25, 1865," *Elizabeth Cady Stanton as Revealed in Her Letters, Diary and Reminiscences* (Harper, 1922), p. 105.
3. Frederick Douglass speech, 1869, quoted in Eleanor Flexner, *Century of Struggle* (Cambridge: Harvard University Press, 1959), p. 144.
4. *History of Woman Suffrage,* vol. II, p. 193–194, 225.
5. *The Revolution,* vol. III, February 11, 1869.
6. Lucy Stone to Abby Kelly Forster, January 24, 1867 in Blackwell papers, Library of Congress, quoted in Sinclair, *The Emancipation of the American Woman,* p. 187.
7. Henry Blackwell, *The Woman's Journal,* vol. I, no. 1, quoted in Sinclair, *The Emancipation of the American Woman,* p. 191.
8. *The Revolution,* vol. I, January 8, 1868.
9. *The Revolution,* vol. I, July 23, 1868.
10. Quoted in Alma Lutz, *Created Equal* (John Day, 1940), p. 190.
11. *The Revolution,* vol. III, March 11, 1869.
12. Susan B. Anthony, "Woman Wants Bread, Not the Ballot!" reprinted in Miriam Schneier, *Feminism: The Essential Documents* (New York: Random House, 1972), p. 137. For a discussion of Anthony and Stanton's involvement in the National Labor Union and the relationship between feminists and women in the early labor movement see Philip S. Foner, *History of the Labor Movement in the United States,* vol. I (New York: International Publishers, 1949), pp. 382–388.
13. See Johanna Johnston, *Mrs. Satan* (New York: Putnam, 1967), and Emanie Sachs, *The Terrible Siren* (Harper, 1928), for biographies of Victoria Woodhull.
14. Victoria Woodhull Martin, *Tried as by Fire, or the True and the False* (New York, 1874), pp. 7–8.
15. Ibid., p. 24.
16. Tennessee Claflin, "Which is to Blame?" *Woodhull & Claflin's Weekly,* 1872, reprinted in Schneier, *Feminism: The Essential Documents,* pp. 149–151.
17. Victoria Woodhull Martin, *The Elixir of Life* (New York, 1873), reprinted in Schneier, *Feminism: The Essential Documents,* p. 153.
18. Ibid., p. 153.
19. Martin, *Tried as by Fire,* p. 40.
20. *Woodhull & Claflin's Weekly,* 1871, quoted in Johnston, *Mrs. Satan,* pp. 70–71.
21. Sinclair, *The Emancipation of the American Woman,* pp. 132–134.
22. Martin, *Tried as by Fire,* pp. 5–6.
23. Victoria Woodhull at Apollo Hall, May 1872; see also Johnston, *Mrs. Satan,* p. 91.
24. Susan B. Anthony, quoted in Lutz, *Created Equal,* p. 217.
25. Theodore Stanton, "Elizabeth Cady Stanton to Lucretia Mott, April 1, 1872," *Elizabeth Cady Stanton as Revealed in Her Letters,* pp. 136–137.
26. Victoria Woodhull Martin, *The Principles of Social Freedom* (London, 1894), and Johnston, *Mrs. Satan,* pp. 118–119.
27. Susan B. Anthony to Elizabeth Cady Stanton, March 1872, quoted in Katherine Anthony, *Susan B. Anthony,* p. 270.
28. Johnston, *Mrs. Satan,* p. 146.

29. Susan B. Anthony to Isabella Beecher Hooker, quoted in Lutz, *Created Equal*, p. 224; Elizabeth Cady Stanton in the *Newark Call*, 1875, quoted in Lutz, *Created Equal*, p. 228; Elizabeth Cady Stanton, quoted in Johnston, *Mrs. Satan*, p. 198, p. 215.

11: The Maverick West

1. M. Wade, ed., *The Writings of Margaret Fuller* (New York, 1941), quoted in Andrew Sinclair, *The Emancipation of the American Woman* (New York: Harper & Row, 1965), p. 205.
2. Sinclair, *The Emancipation of the American Woman*, p. 205.
3. Anna Howard Shaw, *Story of a Pioneer* (New York, 1915), pp. 24–26, quoted in Eleanor Flexner, *Century of Struggle* (New York: Atheneum, 1959), p. 7.
4. Sinclair, *The Emancipation of the American Woman*, p. 206.
5. Nannie Alderson and Helena Huntington Smith, *A Bride Goes West* (New York: Farrar & Rinehart, 1942), pp. 122–124.
6. Agnes Moreley Cleaveland, *No Life for a Lady* (Boston: Houghton Mifflin, 1941), pp. 156–157.
7. Abigail Scott Duniway, *Pathbreaking: The Story of a Pioneer* (New York: Schocken, 1971, reprint of 1914 edition), pp. 9–10.
8. Alderson and Smith, *A Bride Goes West*, p. 109.
9. Cleaveland, *No Life for a Lady*, pp. 127, 129–130.
10. Elinore Pruitt Stewart, *Letters of a Woman Homesteader* (Lincoln: University of Nebraska Press, 1961, reprint of 1914 edition), p. 282.
11. Alderson and Smith, *A Bride Goes West*, pp. 40–41.
12. Dee Brown, *The Gentle Tamers* (New York: Putnam, 1958), p. 220.
13. Ibid., p. 222.
14. Susan Brownmiller, *Against Our Will: Men, Women and Rape* (New York: Simon and Schuster, 1975), pp. 140–153.
15. Stewart, *Letters of a Woman Homesteader*, pp. 214–217.
16. Alan P. Grimes, *The Puritan Ethic and Woman Suffrage* (New York: Oxford University Press, 1967).
17. Elizabeth Cady Stanton, Susan B. Anthony, Mathilda Gage, eds., *History of Woman Suffrage*, vol. III (Rochester, N. Y., 1881), p. 737.
18. Ibid., pp. 738–739.
19. Grimes, *The Puritan Ethic and Woman Suffrage*, p. 39.
20. Sinclair, *The Emancipation of the American Woman*, pp. 215–216.
21. Page Smith, *Daughters of the Promised Land* (Boston: Little Brown, 1970), p. 234.
22. Ibid., p. 256.
23. See Mary Earhart, *Frances Willard, From Prayers to Politics* (Chicago: University of Chicago Press, 1944).

12: Immigrant Mothers and Daughters

1. See Oscar Handlin, *The Uprooted* (New York: Grosset & Dunlap, 1951) and Ann Novotny, *Strangers at the Door* (New York: Viking, 1971).
2. Bernard Weissberger, *The American People* (New York: American Heritage, 1970), p. 194.
3. Anzia Yezierska, "Wings," in *Hungry Hearts* (New York: Grosset & Dunlap, 1920), p. 15.
4. Handlin, *The Uprooted*, p. 148; and Jacob Riis, *How the Other Half Lives* (New York: Hill and Wang, 1951, reprint of 1890 edition), pp. 1–15.
5. Mary Ryan, *Womanhood in America* (New York: Franklin Watts, 1976), p. 214.

6. Riis, p. 48.
7. Riis, *How the Other Half Lives*, p. 85. Irving Howe, *World of Our Fathers* (New York: Harcourt, 1976), p. 73.
8. Charlotte Baum, Paula Hyman and Sonya Michel, *The Jewish Woman in America* (New York: Dial, 1976), pp. 101–102.
9. Anzia Yezierska, *Bread Givers* (New York: Braziller, 1975, reprint of 1925 edition), p. 15.
10. Ibid., pp. 37–38.
11. Riis, *How the Other Half Lives*, p. 125.
12. Ibid., p. 126.
13. Sydelle Kramer and Jenny Masur, *Jewish Grandmothers* (Boston: Beacon, 1976), p. 96.
14. Ibid., p. 99.
15. Elizabeth Stern, *My Mother and I* (New York: Macmillan, 1917), p. 55.
16. Ryan, *Womanhood in America*, p. 215.
17. Leonard Covello, *The Social Background of the Italo-American School Child* (Leiden; E. J. Brill, 1967), pp. 118–122.
18. Emma Goldman, *Living My Life*, vol. I (New York: Dover, 1970, reprint of 1931 edition), pp. 185–186.
19. Riis, *How the Other Half Lives*, p. 104.
20. Howe, *World of Our Fathers*, p. 84.
21. Stern, *My Mother and I*, p. 21.
22. William I. Thomas and Florian Znaniecki, *The Polish Peasant in Europe and America* (New York: Knopf, 1927, reprint of 1897 edition), p. 730.
23. *Forward*, March 9, 1903, quoted in Howe, *World of Our Fathers*, p. 178.
24. Thomas and Znaniecki, *The Polish Peasant*, pp. 1684–1687.
25. "Gallery of Missing Husbands," *Forward*, September 4, 1910, quoted in Baum, Hyman, and Michel, *The Jewish Woman in America*, p. 117.
26. Thomas and Znaniecki, *The Polish Peasant*, pp. 1707–1735.
27. Howe, *World of Our Fathers*, p. 179.
28. Thomas and Znaniecki, *The Polish Peasant*, pp. 1683–1684.
29. Kramer and Masur, *Jewish Grandmothers*, p. 98.
30. Alfred Kazin, *A Walker in the City* (New York, 1951), pp. 66–67, quoted in Howe, *World of Our Fathers*, p. 172.
31. Kramer and Masur, *Jewish Grandmothers*, p. 98.
32. Covello, *The Social Background*, pp. 208–209.
33. Richard Gambino, *Blood of My Blood* (New York: Doubleday, 1975), pp. 3–5.
34. Mary Van Kleck, *Artificial Flower Makers* (New York: Russell Sage, 1913), p. 28; Louise C. Odencrantz, *Italian Women in Industry*, (New York: Russell Sage, 1919), pp. 168–180; and Elizabeth Hasanovitz, *One of Them* (Boston: Houghton Mifflin, 1918), p. 150.
35. Covello, *The Social Background*, p. 215.
36. Baum, Hyman, and Michel, *The Jewish Woman in America*, pp. 55–57.
37. Yezierska, *Bread Givers*, p. 10.
38. Baum, Hyman, and Michel, *The Jewish Woman in America*, p. 120.
39. Covello, *The Social Background*, p. 177.
40. Broughton Brandenbourg, *Imported Americans* (Frederick Stokes, 1903), pp. 19–20.
41. Anzia Yezierska, "Children of Loneliness," in *Children of Loneliness* (New York: Funk and Wagnalls, 1923), p. 101.
42. Kramer and Masur, *Jewish Grandmothers*, p. 99.
43. Stern, *My Mother and I*, p. 86.
44. Covello, *The Social Background*, p. 359.
45. Ibid., p. 200.
46. Ibid., p. 359.
47. Yezierska, *Bread Givers*, pp. 75–76.
48. Covello, *The Social Background*, p. 204; Yezierska, *Bread Givers*, pp. 75–76.

49. Kramer and Masur, *Jewish Grandmothers*, p. 109.
50. Elizabeth Stern, *I am a Woman and a Jew* (New York: J. H. Sears, 1926), p. 16.
51. Stern, *My Mother and I*, p. 160.
52. Covello, *The Social Background*, p. 317.
53. Ibid., pp. 307–308.
54. Yezierska, *Children of Loneliness*, p. 123.
55. Yezierska, *Bread Givers*, pp. 211–213.
56. Ibid., p. 137.

13: Social Housekeeping

1. Josephine Woodward, "Woman's Clubs from a Reporter's Point of View," *Club Women*, December 1898, reprinted in William O'Neill, ed., *The Woman Movement*, (New York: Quadrangle, 1971), pp. 142–147.
2. Rhetta Childe Dorr, *A Woman of Fifty* (New York: Funk and Wagnalls, 1924), p. 119
3. Charlotte Perkins Gilman, *Women and Economics* (New York: Harper, 1966, reprint of 1898 edition), pp. 164–166.
4. William O'Neill, *Everyone Was Brave* (New York: Quadrangle, 1969), pp. 84–90, 149–152.
5. Edward H. Clarke, *Sex in Education* (Boston, 1874), pp. 33, 47–48.
6. Allen F. Davis, *American Heroine* (New York: Oxford University Press, 1973), p. 11.
7. Ibid., pp. 20, 22.
8. O'Neill, *Everyone Was Brave*, p. 79.
9. Jane Addams, "The Subjective Necessity for Social Settlements" (1892), quoted in Jane Addams, *Twenty Years at Hull House* (New York: Signet, 1960, reprint of 1910 edition), p. 93.
10. Jane Addams to Ellen Starr, June 8, 1884, quoted in Davis, *American Heroine*, p. 37.
11. Addams, "The Subjective Necessity for Social Settlements," in *Twenty Years at Hull House*, pp. 93–94.
12. Davis, *American Heroine*, p. 67.
13. William Hard, quoted in Davis, *American Heroine*, p. 96.
14. Davis, *American Heroine*, pp. 74–79.
15. Florence Kelley, "I Go To Work," *Survey*, June 1, 1927, quoted in Davis, *American Heroine*, pp. 76–77.
16. Frances Perkins, quoted in Davis, *American Heroine*, p. 77.
17. Davis, *American Heroine*, pp. 77–78.
18. Mary Kenney O'Sullivan, quoted in Andrew Sinclair, *The Emancipation of the American Women* (New York: Harper, 1965), p. 309.
19. Addams, *Twenty Years at Hull House*, p. 177.
20. See Addams, "The Problems of Poverty," in *Twenty Years at Hull House*, pp. 118–132, and Addams, *Democracy and Social Ethics* (New York: Macmillan, 1902), pp. 13–70.
21. See Jill Conway, "Jane Addams: An American Heroine," in Robert Jay Lifton, ed., *The Woman in America* (Boston: Beacon, 1965), 247–266, and Christopher Lasch, *The New Radicalism in America, 1889–1963*, pp. 3–37.
22. Davis, *American Heroine*, pp. 104, 198–211.

14: Bread and Roses

1. William I. Thomas and Florian Znaniecki, *The Polish Peasant in Europe and America* (New York: Knopf, 1927, reprint of 1897 edition), pp. 775–779.

2. Edith Abbott, *Immigration, Select Documents and Case Records* (Chicago: University of Chicago, 1924), p. 586; Thomas and Znaniecki, *The Polish Peasant*, p. 778.

3. Louise Odencrantz, *Italian Women in Industry* (New York: Russell Sage, 1919), p. 41.

4. Emma Goldman, *Living My Life*, vol. I (New York: Dover, 1970 reprint of 1931 edition), p. 16.

5. Ibid., p. 16.

6. Elizabeth Faulkner Baker, *Technology and Women's Work* (New York: Columbia University Press, 1964), p. 77.

7. Mary Ryan, *Womanhood in America* (New York: Franklin Watts, 1975), pp. 201–203. See also Elizabeth Bearsley Butler, *Women and the Trades* (Arno, 1969, reprint of 1909 edition), pp. 77–101; Dorothy Richardson, *The Long Day* (1905) in William O'Neill, ed., *Women at Work* (New York: Quadrangle, 1972), p. 43.

8. Robert W. Smuts, *Women and Work in America* (New York: Schocken, 1971, reprint of 1959 edition), p. 75.

9. Milton Meltzer, *Bread and Roses* (New York: Random House, 1967), p. 24.

10. Smuts, *Women and Work in America*, pp. 52–53, 57–58.

11. Rhetta Childe Dorr, *A Woman of Fifty* (New York: Funk & Wagnalls, 1924), pp. 188–189.

12. Marie Van Vorst, *The Woman Who Toils* (New York, 1903), pp. 283–285.

13. Smuts, *Women and Work in America*, pp. 89–91; Butler, *Women and the Trades*, pp. 44–52, 84–92.

14. Elizabeth Hasanovitz, *One of Them* (Boston: Houghton Mifflin, 1918), pp. 19, 272.

15. Ibid., p. 22.

16. Louis Levine, *The Women's Garment Workers: A History of the International Ladies' Garment Workers' Union* (Huebsch, 1924), p. 147.

17. Rose Schneiderman and Lucy Goldthwaite, *All for One* (Middlebury, Vt.: Paul S. Eriksson, 1967), p. 51.

18. Sydelle Kramer and Jenny Masur, *Jewish Grandmothers* (Boston: Beacon, 1976), p. 10.

19. Hasanovitz, *One of Them*, pp. 108–109.

20. Thomas and Znaniecki, *The Polish Peasant*, pp. 1815–1817.

21. Quoted in Levine, *The Women's Garment Workers*, pp. 221–222.

22. Schneiderman and Goldthwaite, *All for One*, pp. 86–87.

23. Charlotte Baum, Paula Hyman, and Sonya Michel, *The Jewish Woman in America* (New York: Dial, 1976), p. 136.

24. Quoted in Eleanor Flexner, *Century of Struggle* (New York: Atheneum, 1959), pp. 197–198.

25. Meltzer, *Bread and Roses*, p. 166.

26. Mary Harris Jones, *The Autobiography of Mother Jones* (Chicago: Charles H. Kerr, 1972, reprint of 1925 edition), p. 136.

27. Ibid., p. 238.

28. Kate Richards O'Hare, "Shall Women Vote?" *Social Revolution*, August, 1914, p. 5, quoted in June Sochen, *Movers and Shakers* (New York: Quadrangle, 1973), p. 55.

29. Elizabeth Gurley Flynn, *Rebel Girl* (New York: International Publishers, 1955), p. 53.

30. Ibid., pp. 57–58.

31. Sochen, *Movers and Shakers*, p. 55.

32. Flynn, *Rebel Girl*, p. 113.

33. Flexner, *Century of Struggle*, pp. 258–259.

34. Schneiderman and Goldthwaite, *All for One*, p. 58.

35. New York *World*, November 23, 1909, quoted in Levine, *The Women's Garment Workers*, p. 154.

36. Alice Henry, *The Trade Woman* (New York: Appleton, 1915), p. 93.

37. Magistrate Olmstead quoted in Levine, *The Women's Garment Workers*, p. 159.
38. Henry, *The Trade Woman*, p. 91.
39. Ibid., p. 95.
40. Levine, *The Women's Garment Workers*, pp. 166–167.
41. Henry, *The Trade Women*, p. 106.
42. See Jane Julianelli, "Bessie Hillman: Up From the Sweatshop," *Ms* Magazine, May 1973, pp. 16–20.
43. "Protocol in the Dress and Waist Industry," January 1913, reprinted in Hasanovitz, *One of Them*, pp. 329–333.
44. See Leon Stein, *The Triangle Fire* (New York: Lippincott, 1962).
45. Schneiderman, *All for One*, pp. 100–101.
46. Ray Stannard Baker, quoted in Meltzer, *Bread and Roses*, pp. 174–177.
47. Meltzer, *Bread and Roses*, pp. 174–177.
48. William O'Neill, *Everyone Was Brave* (New York: Quadrangle, 1969), p. 159.
49. Flynn, *Rebel Girl*, pp. 131–132.
50. Ibid., p. 134.
51. Ibid., pp. 132–133.
52. Ibid., p. 128.
53. Mary Heaton Vorse, quoted in Richard O. Boyer and Herbert M. Morais, *Labor's Untold Story* (United Electrical, Radio & Machine Workers, 1955), p. 175.
54. Flynn, *Rebel Girl*, p. 150.
55. Ibid., p. 151
56. Emma Goldman, "Marriage and Love," in *Anarchism and Other Essays* (1911), reprinted in Alix Kates Shulman, ed., *Red Emma Speaks* (New York: Random House, 1972), p. 163.
57. Hasanovitz, *One of Them*, p. 310.
58. Schneiderman, *All for One*, p. 248.
59. Mari Jo Buhle, "Women and the Socialist Party," *Radical America*, February 1970, pp. 36–55.
60. Flynn, *Rebel Girl*, pp. 333–334.
61. Goldman, *Living My Life*, p. 433.

15: Votes for Women

Aileen Kraditor, *The Ideas of the Woman Suffrage Movement, 1890–1920* (New York: Doubleday, 1971), is an excellent and extremely important analysis of the ideological changes that occurred in the movement at the end of the nineteenth century. Eleanor Flexner, *Century of Struggle* (New York: Atheneum, 1959), covers the woman suffrage victory in fine and precise detail. See Carrie Chapman Catt and Nettie Rogers Shuler, *Woman Suffrage and Politics* (New York: Scribner's, 1923), for an account of the NAWSA strategy for winning suffrage. For accounts of the "militant" Woman's Party see Doris Stevens, *Jailed for Freedom* (New York: Boni and Liveright, 1920), and Inez Haynes Irwin, *The Story of the Woman's Party* (New York, 1920).

1. Elizabeth Cady Stanton *et al.*, *The Woman's Bible* Part I (1895; copies in New York Public library and Radcliffe College Women's Archives). See Kraditor, *The Ideas of the Woman Suffrage Movement*, pp. 64–68, and Andrew Sinclair, *The Emancipation of the American Woman* (New York: Harper & Row 1965), pp. 199–201, for discussion of *The Woman's Bible*.
2. NAWSA *Proceedings*, 1896, quoted in Kraditor, pp. 66–67.
3. See Anna Howard Shaw, *The Story of a Pioneer* (New York, 1915).
4. Sinclair, *The Emancipation of the American Woman*, pp. 147–150.

5. See Mary Gray Peck, *Carrie Chapman Catt* (New York: H. W. Wilson, 1944).

6. NAWSA *Proceedings*, 1896, quoted in Lerner, *The Woman in American History*, pp. 162–163.

7. Kraditor, *The Ideas of the Woman Suffrage Movement*, pp. 38–57.

8. Ibid., p. 52.

9. Ibid., p. 50.

10. Quoted in Allen F. Davis, *American Heroine* (New York: Oxford University Press, 1973), p. 187.

11. Jane Addams, "Why Women Should Vote," *Ladies Home Journal*, January 1910, reprinted in Addams, *A Centennial Reader* (New York, 1960), pp. 104–107.

12. *Woman's Journal*, December 15, 1894, quoted in Kraditor, *The Ideas of the Woman Suffrage Movement*, p. 113.

13. Kraditor, *The Ideas of the Woman Suffrage Movement*, p. 107.

14. Ibid., p. 113.

15. Ibid., pp. 142–143.

16. Belle Kearney, "The South and Woman Suffrage," *Woman's Journal*, April 4, 1903, reprinted in Kraditor, *Up from the Pedestal* (New York: Quadrangle, 1970), pp. 263–265.

17. Kraditor, *The Ideas of the Woman Suffrage Movement*, p. 143.

18. See E. Sylvia Pankhurst, *The Suffragette Movement* (London, 1931) and Ray Strachey, *The Cause* (London, 1928).

19. Harriet Stanton Blatch and Alma Lutz, *Challenging Years: The Memoirs of Harriet Stanton* (New York, 1940), p. 92.

20. Flexner, *Century of Struggle*, pp. 258–259.

21. Ibid., pp. 280–281.

22. *The Suffragist*, September 30, 1916, quoted in Flexner, *Century of Struggle*, p. 277.

23. Mrs. O. H. P. Belmont to *The New York Times*, July 9, 1917, quoted in Kraditor, *The Ideas of the Woman Suffrage Movement*, p. 197.

24. Joyce Cowley, *Pioneers of Women's Liberation* (New York: Pathfinder, 1969, reprint of 1955 edition), p. 13.

25. Published by the Women's Anti-Suffrage Association of Massachusetts, quoted in Kraditor, *The Ideas of the Woman Suffrage Movement*, p. 17.

26. *Baltimore Sun*, September 5, 1920, quoted in Flexner, *Century of Struggle*, p. 323.

16: Flappers, Sex Objects, and Birth Control

1. Emma Goldman, "The Tragedy of Woman's Emancipation," *Red Emma Speaks*, edited by Alix Kates Shulman (New York: Vintage, 1961), p. 136.

2. Ibid., p. 135.

3. Ibid., p. 142.

4. Ibid., p. 140.

5. Goldman, "Marriage and Love," in *Red Emma Speaks*, p. 165.

6. Emma Goldman, *The Traffic in Women and Other Essays on Feminism*, ed. by Alix Kates Shulman (Times Change Press, 1970), p. 11.

7. Emma Goldman, *Living My Life*, vol. I (New York: Dover, 1970), p. 120.

8. Ibid., p. 153.

9. Ibid., pp. 153–154.

10. Ibid., p. 183.

11. Ibid., pp. 194–195.

12. Floyd Dell, *Love in Greenwich Village* (Bernard Tauchnitz, Leipzig, Collection of British and American Authors, Vol. 474, 1926), p. 60.

13. Marion Sanders, *Dorothy Thompson: A Legend in Her Time* (New York: Avon, 1973), pp. 61, 66.

14. Frederick Lewis Allen, *Only Yesterday* (New York: Harper, 1959), pp. 73–101.
15. Lawrence Lader, *Abortion* (Boston: Beacon Press, 1966), p. 3.
16. Margaret Sanger, *An Autobiography* (New York: Dover, 1971), p. 91.
17. Ibid., p. 229.
18. David Kennedy, *Birth Control in America* (New Haven: Yale University Press, 1970). Kennedy provides a good analysis of the birth-control movement's short-comings.
19. Ibid., pp. 124–125.
20. Oral history material gathered by the authors.
21. Helene Deutsch, *The Psychology of Women*, vol. I (New York: Bantam Books, 1973), pp. 189–331.
22. Ferdinand Lundberg and Marynia Farnham, *Modern Woman: The Lost Sex* (New York, 1942), p. 142.

17: Don't Steal a Job from a Man

Statistics in this chapter on the changing number of women in the labor force, their age, marital status, and race are drawn from Bulletins of the Women's Bureau, U. S. Department of Labor and William H. Chafe, *The American Woman: Her Changing Social, Economic and Political Roles, 1920–1930* (New York: Oxford University Press, 1972).

1. Mary Kathleen Benet, "Everybody's Gal Friday: How She Got Into Offices in the First Place," *Ms* Magazine, May 1973, p. 79.
2. Ibid., p. 81.
3. "Women in Business," August 1935, p. 50, quoted in Elizabeth Faulkner Baker, *Technology and Woman's Work* (New York: Columbia University Press, 1964), p. 217.
4. Ibid., p. 214.
5. Chafe, *The American Woman*, p. 65; see also Mary Anderson, *Women at Work* (London, 1951).
6. Women's Bureau Bulletin No. 161, "Women at Work," p. 12.
7. Ibid., No. 103, "Women Workers in the Third Year of the Depression" (A study by students of the Bryn Mawr Summer School), p. 13.
8. Mary Ryan, *Womanhood in America* (New York: Franklin Watts, 1975), p. 315.
9. Milton Meltzer, *Brother Can You Spare A Dime?* (New York: Vintage, 1973), pp. 54–57.
10. Chafe, *The American Woman*, p. 107.
11. Ibid., p. 60.
12. William O'Neill, *Everyone Was Brave* (New York: Quadrangle, 1969), p. 289.
13. Chafe, *The American Woman*, p. 87.
14. Irving Bernstein, *The Turbulent Years* (Boston: Houghton Mifflin, 1971), pp. 84–89, 616–623; Chafe, *The American Woman*, pp. 82–86.
15. Jean Tepperman, "Two Jobs: Women Who Work in Factories," in *Sisterhood Is Powerful*, edited by Robin Morgan (New York: Random House, 1970), p. 120.
16. Chafe, *The American Woman*, p. 43.
17. Joseph P. Lash, *Eleanor and Franklin* (New York: Norton, 1971), p. 457.
18. See Eleanor Roosevelt, *It's Up to the Women* (New York: Lippincott, 1933).
19. Chafe, *The American Woman*, pp. 146–148.

20. Caroline Bird, *Born Female*, rev. ed. (New York: Pocket Books, 1971), p. 32.

21. Chafe, *The American Woman*, pp. 161–171.

22. Theresa Wolfson, "Aprons and Overalls in War," *The Annals of the American Academy of Political and Social Science*, September 1943, quoted in Ryan, *Womanhood in America*, p. 318.

23. Chafe, *The American Woman*, p. 180.

24. See Robert Lynd and Helen Merrill, *Middletown: A Study in Contemporary American Culture* (New York: Harcourt, 1929, 1956), pp. 27–30.

25. Bird, *Born Female*, pp. 81–82.

26. Ryan, *Womanhood in America*, p. 325; Bird, *Born Female*, p. 63.

27. Judith Ann, "The Secretarial Proletariat," in *Sisterhood Is Powerful*, p. 87.

28. Bird, *Born Female*, p. 62.

29. Bird, *Born Female*, p. 64; Tepperman, *Not Servants, Not Machines* (Boston: Beacon Press, 1976), p. 27.

30. Tepperman, *Not Servants, Not Machines*, pp. 32–33.

31. Ibid., p. 8.

32. Tepperman, *Not Servants, Not Machines*, p. 18; Eleanor Langer, "Inside the New York Telephone Company," in *Women at Work*, edited by William O'Neill (New York: Quadrangle, 1972), pp. 311–316.

33. Tepperman, *Not Servants, Not Machines*, pp. 54–60; and Judith Ann, *Sisterhood Is Powerful*, p. 89.

34. Baker, *Technology and Woman's Work*, p. 234.

35. Studs Terkel, *Working* (New York: Avon Books, 1972), p. 59; Tepperman, *Not Servants, Not Machines*, p. 23.

36. *New York Post*, June 16, 1976.

37. Frances Donovan, *The Woman Who Waits* (Boston: Richard G. Badger, 1920), p. 211.

38. Ryan, *Womanhood in America*, pp. 320–321.

39. Terkel, *Working*, pp. 73, 79.

40. Ibid., p. 395.

41. Tepperman, "Women in Factories," *Sisterhood Is Powerful*, p. 121.

42. Langer, *Women at Work*, p. 344.

43. Terkel, *Working*, pp. 390–395.

44. Gertrude Samuels, "Why Twenty Million Women Work," *New York Times Magazine*, September 9, 1951.

45. William O'Neill, ed., *Women at Work*, (New York: Quadrangle, 1972), p. xviii.

46. Judith Ann, *Sisterhood Is Powerful*, pp. 89–90.

47. Women's Bureau, "Twenty Facts on Women Workers," February, 1973.

18: Just a Housewife

1. Leah Morton (pseudonym of Elizabeth Stern), *I Am a Woman and a Jew* (J. H. Sears, 1927), p. 218.

2. Ibid., p. 78.

3. Robert Coughlan, "Changing Roles in Modern Marriage," *Life* Magazine, December 24, 1956, p. 110.

4. Oral history material gathered by the authors.

5. Samuel Kaplan, *The Dream Deferred* (New York: Seabury, 1976), p. 2.

6. Helena Lopata, *Occupation Housewife* (New York: Oxford University Press, 1971), p. 183.

7. Coughlan, "Changing Roles," p. 109. Italics added by the authors.

8. Quoted in Betty Friedan, *The Feminine Mystique* (New York: Dell, 1963), pp. 151–152.

9. Coughlan, "Changing Roles," p. 110.
10. Ibid., p. 112. Italics added by the authors.
11. Oral history material gathered by the authors.
12. Helena Lopata, *Occupation Housewife*, p. 192.
13. Friedan, *The Feminine Mystique*, pp. 16–17.
14. Mirra Komarovsky, *Blue-Collar Marriage* (New York: Vintage, 1967), p. 156.
15. Ibid., p. 151.
16. Ibid., p. 151.
17. Ibid., p. 211.
18. Lee Rainwater, Richard Coleman, and Gerald Handel, *Workingman's Wife* (Dobbs Ferry, N. Y.: Oceana Publications, 1959), p. 27.
19. Nancy Seifer, *Absent from the Majority* (National Project on Ethnic America, The American Jewish Committee, 1973), p. 59.
20. Martha Wright, "I Want the Right to be Black and Me" *Black Women in White America* (New York: Vintage, 1973), p. 603.
21. Eleanor Holmes Norton, "For Sadie and Maude," in *Sisterhood Is Powerful*, Robin Morgan, ed., (New York: Random House, 1970), p. 355.
22. Carol Stack, *All Our Kin* (New York: Harper, 1974), p. 112.
23. Maya Angelou, *I Know Why the Caged Bird Sings* (New York: Bantam, 1971), p. 231.
24. Interview with Maya Angelou, *New York Post*, December 26, 1970.
25. Martin Luther King, *In Their Own Words: A History of the American Negro*, Milton Meltzer, ed. (New York: Crowell, 1967), pp. 176–177.

19: The New Feminism

1. Betty Friedan, *The Feminine Mystique* (Dell, 1963), p. 7.
2. Ibid., p. 17.
3. Judith Hole and Ellen Levine, *Rebirth of Feminism* (New York: Quadrangle, 1971), p. 34.
4. Betty Friedan, "N.O.W.—How It Began," *Women Speaking* (London), April 1967, p. 4.
5. Excerpts from N.O.W. Statement of Purpose, adopted at Organizational Conference, October 29, 1966.
6. Ibid.
7. Ibid.
8. Hole and Levine, *Rebirth of Feminism*, p. 95.
9. Ibid., pp. 133–134.
10. Shulamith Firestone, *The Dialectic of Sex* (New York: Bantam Books, 1971), pp. 9–11.
11. Robin Morgan, ed., *Sisterhood Is Powerful* (New York: Random House, 1970), p. xxii.
12. Meredith Tax, "Woman and Her Mind; The Story of Everyday Life," *Notes from the Second Year* (New York Radical Feminists, 1970), p. 12.
13. Ibid., p. 11.
14. Letty Cottin Pogrebin, "Rap Groups," *Ms* Magazine, March 1973, p. 80.
15. "A Guide to Consciousness Raising," *Ms* Magazine, July 1972, pp. 18–23.
16. Boston Women's Health Collective, *Our Bodies, Ourselves* (New York: Simon & Shuster, 1971), p. 19.
17. Jane O'Reilly, "The Housewife's Moment of Truth," *Ms* Magazine, Spring 1972, p. 54.
18. Sally Kempton, "Cutting Loose," *Esquire* Magazine, July 1970.
19. Susi Kaplow, "Getting Angry," *Notes from the Third Year* (New York Radical Feminists, 1971), p. 15.

20. Robin Morgan, "Rights of Passage," *Ms* Magazine, September 1975, p. 99.

21. Nora Ephron, *Crazy Salad* (New York: Bantam Books, 1976), p. 73.

22. Kempton, "Cutting Loose."

23. Phyllis Chesler, *Women and Madness* (New York: Doubleday, 1972), pp. 243–244.

24. Interview with Anne Koedt, *McCall's* Magazine, July 1970, p. 14.

25. Hole and Levine, *Rebirth of Feminism*, p. 109.

26. Vivian Gornick and Barbara K. Moran, *Woman in Sexist Society* (New York: New American Library, 1971), p. xiv.

27. Judy Syfers, "Why I Want A Wife," *Notes from the Third Year* (New York Radical Feminists, 1971), p. 13.

28. Ibid., Pat Mainardi, "Politics of Housework," p. 28.

29. Boston Women's Health Collective, pp. 83–84.

30. William H. Masters and Virginia E. Johnson, *Human Sexual Inadequacy* (Boston: Little Brown, 1970), p. 301.

31. Larry Lader, *Abortion II: Making the Revolution.*

32. Kate Millett, *Sexual Politics* (New York: Doubleday, 1970), p. 25.

33. *The New York Times,* January 25, 1976.

34. Virginia Slims Opinion Poll (Louis Harris Associates, 1972).

35. Nancy Seifer, *Absent from the Majority* (National Project on Ethnic America, American Jewish Committee, 1973), p. 15; *The New York Times,* January 25, 1976.

36. Susan Jacoby, "Feminism in the $12,000-a-Year Family: What Do I Do for the Next 20 Years?" *The New York Times Magazine,* June 17, 1973, p. 39.

37. Ibid., p. 39.

38. Eleanor Holmes Norton, "For Sadie and Maude," *Sisterhood Is Powerful,* (New York: Random House, 1970), p. 353.

39. Ibid., Frances Beale, "Double Jeopardy," p. 352.

40. Toni Cade, ed., *The Black Woman* (New York: Bantam Books, 1970), p. 88.

41. National Black Feminist Organization Statement of Purpose, 1973, quoted in Judith Papachristou, *Women Together* (New York: Knopf, 1976), p. 242.

42. Quoted in Seifer, *Absent from the Majority,* p. 36.

43. *The New York Times,* March 29, 1976.

44. Quoted in Seifer, *Absent from the Majority,* p. 40.

45. Jean Tepperman, *Not Servants, Not Machines* (Boston: Beacon Press, 1976), p. 92.

46. Ibid., p. 173.

47. Gloria Steinem, "The Verbal Karate of Florynce R. Kennedy, Esq.," *Ms* Magazine, March 1973, p. 55.

48. Morgan, ed., *Sisterhood Is Powerful,* p. xxxvi.

Index

Abbott, Edith, 231
Abbott, Grace, 231
Abolitionists, 157. *See also* Anti-slavery cause; Slavery
Abortion, 105, 169
  illegal, 293
  Medicaid funding for, 361
Abramowitz, Bessie, 248, 252, 253
Absent from the Majority (Seifer), 362
Actresses, in frontier towns, 181
Adams, Abigail Smith, 11, 28, 34–37, 69
Adams, John, 11, 28, 35–36, 69
Adams, John Quincy, 34–35
Addams, Jane, 223–33, 273, 275
Adultery, 11
  slave marriage and, 45
Against Our Will (Brownmiller), 182
Aid to Dependent Children, 338
Alawato (universal language), 166
Alcott, Bronson, 220
Alcott, William, 69, 71
Alderson, Nannie, 179, 180
All for One (Schneiderman), 260
Allen, Frederick Lewis, 292
Amalgamated Clothing Workers of America, 252, 309
  founder of, 253
American and International Red Cross, 142
American Anti-Slavery Society, 81, 82–83, 97
American Federation of Labor (AFL), 244, 260, 309
American Heroine (Davis), 229
American labor press, beginning of, 132–33
American Revolution, 23, 24, 26–34
  women and, 30–34
American Woman Suffrage Association (AWSA), 160
Anarchism, 287
Anderson, Mary, 262, 305
Andrews, Stephen Pearl, 166
Angelou, Maya, 338
Anglicans, 15
Ann, Judith, 317
Anthony, Daniel, 113
Anthony, Lucy Reed, 113
Anthony, Susan B., 88, 112–21, 149–50, 159, 160, 267–71
  and economic status of women, 115, 120, 162–64

protesting Fourteenth Amendment, 156–57
  and temperance movement, 187
  in the West, 176
  and woman suffrage movement, 159–60, 171–73, 184
Antislavery cause, 83
  women and, 79
Anti-Slavery Society of Massachusetts, 99
Antisuffrage forces, tactics of, 283
Anti-Tea Leagues, 27
Army nurses, training, 141
Arnold, Benedict, 29
Asexual, women as, 105

Bagley, Sarah, 133, 135
Baker, Ray Stannard, 255
Baltimore, Lord, 6
Baptists, 15, 188
  New Light, 21
Barry, Leonora, 244
Bartlett, Elisha, 129
Barton, Clara, 142
Bayard, Edward, 90, 91
Beecher, Catherine, 82, 129
Beecher, Henry Ward, 172
Beecher, Isabelle, 173
Beecher-Tilton affair, 172
Belmont, Mrs. O.H.P., 251, 281
Bickerdyke, Mary, 142
Bigamists, 12, 165
Bird, Caroline, 315, 372
Birth control, 199, 293–99. *See also* specific devices and techniques
  national movement, 298
Birth control pill, 297, 342, 360
  side effects of, 360
Birth rates
  American, in 1950s, 326
  declining, in 1800s, 71
"Black Maria" police vans, 251
Black women, 336–40. *See also* Slave family; Slave marriage; Slave mothers; Slavery; Slaves, female
  in postwar South, exploitation of, 155
  sexual abuse of, 51–52, 154–55
Blackstone, William, 22
Blackwell, Alice Stone, 107, 276
Blackwell, Elizabeth, 106, 141, 269
Blackwell, Henry, 105, 108, 160, 161, 163, 270

392

ABOUT THE AUTHORS

CAROL HYMOWITZ, born and raised in New York, graduated from Brandeis University and earned her master's degree in journalism from Columbia University. She is a freelance writer and also works part time for *Time* magazine.

MICHAELE WEISSMAN is a native of Belmont, Massachusetts. She studied history at Brandeis University and graduated in 1968. She lives in Manhattan and is employed as a newswriter and producer for WOR radio.

WOMEN: YESTERDAY AND TODAY

SPECIAL
MONEY SAVING
OFFER

Now you can have an up-to-date listing of Bantam's hundreds of titles plus take advantage of our unique and exciting bonus book offer. A special offer which gives you the opportunity to purchase a Bantam book for only 50¢. Here's how!

By ordering any five books at the regular price per order, you can also choose any other single book listed (up to a $4.95 value) for just 50¢. Some restrictions do apply, but for further details why not send for Bantam's listing of titles today!

Just send us your name and address plus 50¢ to defray the postage and handling costs.